Chris Castagna

True Gardens of the Gods

True Gardens of the Gods

*Californian-Australian
Environmental Reform,
1860–1930*

Ian Tyrrell

UNIVERSITY OF CALIFORNIA PRESS
Berkeley · *Los Angeles* · *London*

University of California Press
Berkeley and Los Angeles, California

University of California Press, Ltd.
London, England

© 1999 by
The Regents of the University of California

Library of Congress Cataloging-in-Publication Data

Tyrrell, Ian R.
    True gardens of the Gods : Californian–Aus-
tralian environmental reform, 1860–1930 / Ian
Tyrrell.
        p.   cm.
    Includes bibliographical references and index.
    ISBN 0-520-21346-7 (cloth : alk. paper)
    1. Plant introduction—California—History.
2. Plant introduction—Australia—History.
3. Agriculture—California—History. 4. Agricul-
ture—Australia—History. 5. Human ecology—
California—History. 6. Human ecology—
Australia—History. 7. California—
Relations—History. 8. Australia—Relations—
History. 9. Pest introduction—California—Histo-
ry. 10. Pest introduction—Australia—History.
I. Title.
SB108.U6C28 1999
630'.9794—DC21   98-5069
                                        CIP

Printed in the United States of America
9 8 7 6 5 4 3 2 1

*To my colleagues and students in the
School of History, past and present,
especially those who love a garden*

Contents

Acknowledgments

The writer of history incurs many debts, and the writer of any comparative and transnational project incurs still more. I am not sure that I can recall all of the people and institutions that have helped me over many years. But here goes:

Work from this project was presented at the American Historical Association Convention in Atlanta, January 1996; the Australian and New Zealand–American Studies Association Conference in Christchurch, New Zealand, in February 1996; and the Second International Conference on the Pacific Rim held at La Trobe University in July 1996. The participants and audiences at all three conferences deserve thanks for penetrating questions raised. In Atlanta, thanks especially go to Malcolm Rohrbough for his commentary, which set me on new lines of thinking. James Gerber of the Department of Economics at California State University at San Diego was particularly exciting to meet at the La Trobe conference because of his enthusiasm for the topic and his knowledge of Californian economic history. Equally helpful, both in Atlanta and at the La Trobe conference, was John McNeill of Georgetown University. Lionel and Warrick Frost, organizers of the La Trobe conference, gave freely of their knowledge of Australian environmental history, and this has been invaluable to me. Peter Coleman at the Christchurch conference again demonstrated his wonderful enthusiasm and knowledge of international history topics.

William Rorabaugh of the University of Washington was, as usual, generous with his comments and suggestions, though he claims to know nothing of environmental history. In 1991, Carolyn Merchant encouraged my study of comparisons between Australia and California, though I am not sure that the specific project that resulted is what she had in mind. Getting me started in environmental history even earlier, Thomas Dunlap wrote encouragingly, and he continues to be unstintingly helpful; James Kluger kindly answered my queries about Elwood Mead; David Goodman, whose own work on the Australian gold rushes and the Californian connection is a springboard into comparative environmental history, made some very useful suggestions. Shane White of Sydney University took time out from his own work to supply references beyond the call of duty. Richard Searles, Chair of Biological Sciences at Duke University, and his colleague Mark Bush, listened to my lectures on Australian environmental history as part of the Duke-in-Australia program and made invaluable comments from an interdisciplinary perspective. So too did the students in the program. Sara Maroske, from the Ferdinand Mueller Project at the University of Melbourne, supplied important leads. Ellen DuBois took an interest and tolerantly let me rave on about Californian gum and fruit trees, when we had women's history to discuss during a visit to Los Angeles. Among my own graduate students, Adele Wessell's enthusiasm and knowledge of environmental issues helped, but all in HIST 2039 have been an inspiration too. If at times I wondered how and why I came to be writing environmental history, I know they have the answer.

As usual, my colleagues in the School of History, such as Ian Bickerton and Roger Bell in American and Pacific history, and Bruce Scates and Rae Frances in Australian history, were helpful. So too were John Perkins and Barrie Dyster of the School of Economics and Graham Pont of the now closed Centre for Liberal and General Studies; Marilyn Fox of the School of Geography alerted me to materials on her own work. Beverley Kingston gave the whole manuscript a most perceptive runover with an eye to the Australian material.

The librarians and archivists at the following locations deserve thanks: National Archives, Suitland, Maryland; Stanford University Library, especially the Special Collections Department; the Water Resources Library, Forestry Library, and Biosciences Library at the University of California at Berkeley; California State Archives, Sacramento; California State Library, Sacramento; Fisher Library, Sydney University; the Public Library of Victoria (La Trobe Library), Melbourne; the National

Herbarium, Melbourne Botanic Gardens; Australian National Library, Canberra; and the John Oxley Memorial Library, Brisbane. I would especially like to thank Robert Ritchie and Peter Blodgett at the Huntington Library, and the staffs of the Bancroft Library, the David Scott Mitchell Library in Sydney, and the Library of Congress for putting up with me. At the Smithsonian Institution in Washington, the Horticultural Library needs to be singled out for its marvelous help, as does the Manuscripts Department. Pam O'Brien and staff of the University of New South Wales Social Sciences and Humanities Library have, as usual, aided my research and acquired a decent collection with which to work in American history as well as Australian history. The sources of the David Scott Mitchell Library at the State Library of New South Wales are unrivaled in Australian-Pacific history, and proved the best launching point for contacts with California. The task would also have been more difficult without the material that the General Reading Library possesses on California.

The personal generosity of two friends from California, the sociologist Ron Roizen of Berkeley and the historian Scott Haine of Foster City, in showing me great hospitality and sharing their enthusiasm for histories other than our mutual interest in alcohol and temperance history was most appreciated. The Australian Research Council and the Faculty of Arts and Social Sciences supplied me with grants to continue with my research. Thanks also go to senior editor Erika Büky, copy editor Bonita Hurd, Monica McCormick, and the anonymous readers for the University of California Press for taking an interest in this project.

My father-in-law, Kenneth Payne, a retired carpenter, has answered questions about the practical value of many American and Australian timbers and has taught me that it is possible to combine a love of wood with the love of trees. To D. C., J. T., and E. J. T., the personal bright stars of my environment: may they burn on.

NORTHERN
TERRITORY

QUEENSLAND

WESTERN
AUSTRALIA

SOUTH
AUSTRALIA

NEW SOUTH
WALES

Darling R.

Perth

Renmark

Mildura

Bathurst

Sydney

Adelaide

Murray R.

Canberra
CANBERRA

Site of early Pinus
Radiata experiments

*Goulbourn
Valley*

Bendigo

VICTORIA

Mount Gambier

Ballarat

Melbourne

 Approximate extent of Prickly Pear infestation

TASMANIA

Launceston

Hobart

Map 1.
Australia

N

Chico

Sacramento R.

Marysville

Sacramento

CENTRAL

San
Francisco

Stockton

Santa Clara
Valley

San Joaquin R.

VALLEY

Yosemite
National Park

Fresno

Santa Barbara

Pasadena

Los Angeles

San Bernardino

Colorado R.

0 20 40 60 80 100 miles

San Diego

Imperial
Valley

Map 2.
California

True Gardens of
the Gods

Environmental reform was not newly born in the modern era of conservation in the 1960s. Alarm over human influences on nature runs back well before the present crisis, and attempts to "restore" disturbed ecosystems or control damaged landscapes have a long history indeed. These waves of concern have been followed by periods of retreat or stagnation. The lessons of environmental awareness have had to be absorbed over and over again, albeit in different permutations and combinations depending on changed historical circumstances. This book details one episode in the history of this periodic and well-justified disquiet over human relationships to the natural world during the course of Europe's global outreach.

In the second half of the nineteenth century, California and Australia became involved in an innovative set of environmental reforms promoting the concept of small-scale farming settlement. Their efforts do not at first sight seem to bear the stamp of environmentalism as we understand it today, but they, too, were motivated by environmental dreams and fears. This book is a study in the *comparative* history of the ideas and actions of those who promoted forms of what would today be called environmental management, but the book does more than compare discrete geographical units. Because the study details the interactions and exchanges between these two peoples, it also constitutes a *transnational* history of an environmental sensibility shaped in a setting of colonial expansion. The myth of the garden in the American West

provided the initial source of these innovations, and especially prominent was California.

To Frances Willard, nineteenth-century temperance reformer, California was a garden. In 1883 she traveled to the West Coast of the United
States on an organizing tour for the Woman's Christian Temperance
Union, and reported: "On the Pacific Coast I felt the pulsation of the
newest America—which includes that true 'Garden of the Gods,' California, with its semi-tropical climate."[1] Willard's imagery of the Garden
of the Gods, drawn from the Colorado location of that name, was the
adaptation of a contemporary cliché of railroad tourist promotion in the
American West.[2] Yet it indicates how an influential and perceptive
arbiter of American middle-class taste classified California's landscape.
Willard visited at a turning point in the state's economic history: California was being promoted in the eastern states for its healthful climate,
its sunshine, its productive agriculture. The yoke of mining had been
thrown off, and now California's wheat industry stood challenged by the
expanding grain production of larger and more viable farms on the Great
Plains. In response, Californians began to consider the full implications
of the imagery of the garden and worked to turn the state into a horticultural paradise.

Willard's imagery raised the promise of California to become an
abundant garden, and the element of social construction that enters into
the conceptualization of any landscape. Ironically, Willard's "true garden" was not a natural environment at all, but a vision of an environment to be fashioned by social forces. Environmental historians and geographers have spoken of "cultural landscapes" shaped by the natural
world and the efforts of humans.[3] For historians, it is vital to explain the
emergence and content of these landscapes and to connect them with the
aspirations of social groups and classes. Cultural landscapes are symbols
of these aspirations located in historical time. We can think of them as
not only actually existing forms but also the product of popular dreams.

The high valuation of garden landscapes reached deep into European
history and classical antiquity, but the grand gardens European aristo-
crats and landed gentry created were far from democratic. They required
the erasure of inconvenient and untidy peasant alternatives and rested
heavily upon the labor of the lower classes. In the Jeffersonian yeoman
farmer, however, the dream acquired a new and potentially more democratic expression when linked to the garden myth in the American West.
The imagined supply of diverse, abundant resources for small-scale agriculture fed egalitarian hopes for westward expansion.[4] Everywhere, the

myth's power to inspire settlers and shape landscapes faced environ-mental constraints and pressures of land development that undermined democratic hopes. Many thought, however, that the best chance of suc-cess—of turning the myth into a social reality—lay in California, for the very reasons that impressed Frances Willard. Stimulated by rich natural resources, grand scenery, a mild climate, and Pacific position—which offered exposure to trading possibilities in the Pacific and opportunities to innovate by introducing crops and various agricultural practices used elsewhere in the Pacific region—Californians fashioned their own cul-tural landscape in the fruit garden that eventually became the purely ornamental landscape of California suburbia.

The enterprise to make California into a model garden state mani-fested itself clearly in 1883 in the practice of reformers such as John Bid-well, later to be a Prohibitionist Party candidate for president of the United States. The favorite stopping point for the temperance reformer Willard on her trip to California was Bidwell's home at Rancho Chico, in the Sacramento Valley. A wheat farmer, philanthropist, congressman, and pioneer Anglo settler, "General" Bidwell was a good friend of Willard's through the agency of his wife, Annie Kennedy Bidwell, a prominent financial supporter of the Woman's Christian Temperance Union.[5] John Bidwell later gained some personal notoriety as a man whose strong antidrink convictions led him to root out all wine-producing grapes on his vast ranch and replace them with sultanas. Annie Bidwell is best remembered for her mission and welfare work among the California Indians. But in 1883 the Bidwells' ranch was also a model of environmental philanthropy that inspired many visitors.

Just one year after Willard's tour, the ranch was visited by an Aus-tralian journalist, Thomas K. Dow, who worked for the *Australasian* (Melbourne) newspaper and was sent to observe American agricultural methods. Much impressed by Rancho Chico, Dow described it in great detail. Bidwell's ranch, he rejoiced, "must not only make dollars, but it must also teach the people how varied the productions of the state are. . . . Not even the all-powerful American dollar would be able to bring about the destruction of a favourite oak, an avenue, or a bit of charming scenery." Not only had "the natural beauties of the country been preserved," but much money had been "expended upon develop-ing and increasing the pleasing appearance of the estate." Rancho Chico's twenty-five thousand acres was "like a group of delightful parks." Dow could, with Bidwell and the "excellent lady, his wife," drive "for hours in every direction along charming avenues, past farm-houses, orchards, vineyards, grain-fields, and pastures, among browsing sheep and cattle, . . . seeing busy fruit-gatherers as well as quickly-moving harvest machinery, without ever losing the sense of rural beauty."[6] A benevolent capitalist who preached social harmony and Christian love, Bidwell had divided the ranch into twenty specialized homesteads and allocated responsibility for the overall control to paid managers. This left Bidwell free to take an interest in the "pleasure of his trees and drives" and the extension of "civilising" influences like temperance, monogamy, and thrift over the lives of his workers.[7]

THE SEEDS OF ENVIRONMENTAL EXCHANGE

This utopian garden scene, this blend of nature and contrived appearance, is common in descriptions of California agriculture in the 1880s. The idea of an abundant "natural" landscape imposed on an arid wilderness has caught the imagination of many since. It also caught the imagination of Australians like Dow who shared in the development of the ideal and created out of their trans-Pacific contacts an environmental exchange.

As Willard sensed, California's nineteenth-century search for models of the garden landscape would stimulate links with the Pacific region. California, she said, "invites not only Europe but Asia to a seat in its banqueting hall." These Pacific connections included important contacts with Australasia. In the 1860s it was still quicker to sail to Sydney than to New York. The Panama crossing reduced, by the mid-1850s, the distance to the eastern states traveled by people and gold, but bulk commodities such as wool and wheat that provided for California's prosperity continued to be subject to what Australian historian Geoffrey Blainey aptly describes as the "tyranny of distance."[8] Even after fruit began to be moved by railroad in the late 1880s, the rail freight option was dogged by monopoly practices, rate discrimination, and inadequate service.[9]

California and Australia shared not only the transportation problems linked to distance and isolation but also broad similarities of climate. Large parts of southern and western Australia have a Mediterranean climate like California's, and larger areas of Australia, as in the south and interior of California, are arid. But above all, it was people who built these distant outposts of European colonization. Climate or other geographical similarities alone do not explain the exchanges that took place. Not until English-speaking Americans took control of California in

1850, sixty-two years after the first settlement in Australia, did potential links materialize through commonalities of language, culture, and social aspirations.

Today Australia differs sharply from California in importance in the world economy. California's GNP exceeds that of most nation-states. Its population of over 30 million also easily exceeds Australia's eighteen. But these disparities are relatively recent. At the turn of the century, the population and forms of economic development of the two regions were roughly comparable. Both were exporters of staples, competing in distant markets for the sale of agricultural products.[10] Sheep and cattle grazing were also prominent in both in the second half of the century and wrought considerable damage on the native vegetation.

From the discovery of gold in 1848 in California, through the first Australian gold rushes of 1851 in Victoria and New South Wales, to the end of the 1850s, California and Australia were brought together by the common experience of the mining boom. Gold was the springboard for growth in both California and Australia. Gold also provided the first substantial links between the two as ships carried immigrants and their cargoes of supplies and possessions across the Pacific.[11] From the gold rushes came a second parallel, the common experience of a virulent form of racism arising from substantial Chinese immigration. The drive to exclude and even repatriate these unwelcome foreigners became strongly linked to anxieties over Asian invasion and strategic isolation. Anti-Chinese agitation and, later, racist fears about the "yellow peril" presented by the Japanese stirred politicians and the public deeply in both places. Australians sought to avoid duplicating the problems posed in California by the presence of a large Chinese minority. It was gold that sparked the immigration issue, however, and kept it alight as wave after wave of rushes threatened to duplicate the experience of Victoria in other colonies.[12]

The environmental degradation resulting from the mining boom also stimulated the search for more permanent and sustainable types of economic growth. In California, hydraulic mining involved spraying high-pressure jets of water at cliff faces to expose the gold for alluvial treatment. The practice swept immense quantities of mud and debris into rivers and streams, clogging the waterways that could provide life to a more diversified agricultural system. Californian miners also brought hydraulic sluicing technology to Victoria, where it especially influenced gold mining on the Ovens River in the northeast of the colony. With water supplies more limited than in California, however, and deep-shaft methods soon dominant, hydraulic mining's impact was more limited, and the reaction against gold was not so strong in later decades in that colony.[13] In Victoria, gold's impact on urban development vitally stimulated markets for small-scale agricultural produce and so encouraged hopes that a diversified agriculture could replace reliance on the pastoral and mining industries.[14] Yet other parallels in the abuse of natural resources could be observed. As in California, the demand for timber for fuel, shelter, and shafts denuded forest cover in the hinterlands and altered stream flows. Erosion and timber shortages followed. Ironically, mining stimulated efforts to establish the first native forest reserves in Victoria in the 1870s.[15]

A critical challenge facing Australians and Californians in the 1860s involved the social and environmental aftermath of the gold rush decade.[16] Concerned settlers in both places responded to the disruptive impacts of mining and pastoralism, and tried to remake their environments into what I call garden landscapes. In irrigation, forest management, and biological control, Australians and Californians swapped ideas, plants, insects, personnel, technology, and dreams, and they created in the process an environmental exchange that transcended national boundaries of American or Australian history. While comparing the discrete histories of California and Australia reveals differences in objectives and outcomes of environmental reform, important similarities cannot be denied. In part these reflected parallel domestic dynamics, but each area was also shaped by larger forces framing the actions that individuals were able to take in reshaping nature.

Several theories underlie my exploration of these larger forces. Though one region was technically a set of colonies and the other a state of the American union, both Australia and California were peripheral and colonial in the nineteenth century. They were outposts of European imperial expansion and functioned economically and socially as frontier settlement environments.[17] In terms of world systems theory, their histories were shaped, in a general way, by core-peripheral relations within the world capitalist system. Eventually California transcended its peripheral status in the twentieth century; Australia did not, and a variety of class and cultural forces help to explain those differences. Economics obviously played an important part and should not be neglected in any environmental history. Of economic explanations of the underlying forces shaping Californian and Australian history, staple theory stands out as potentially valuable. The issue of export markets for staple agricultural products and concomitant problems of transport and communication sharpen and provide more specificity to the analysis of peripheral regions in a world system. To be sure, there has been much criticism of staple theory as purely *economic* history; domestic markets and internal forces within the peripheral areas have often seemed more important, in statistical terms, than staple theory admits. Yet the complex multiplier effects of staples still impress many economic historians,[18] while both critics and supporters have missed a vital point. Californians and Australians *thought* of their economies as isolated and export dependent. They wished in many way to overcome these disadvantages by internal diversification that fueled attempts to create a garden landscape, but they also debated social and economic policy on the *assumption* that they needed export markets.

This outlook on staple economic processes introduces a third part of the analysis: the cultural perceptions of distance and isolation that were based upon realities of transport and economics. The common conception that the 1869 transcontinental railroad connection ended California's isolation is far from the truth. It did not transform Californians' mental world or bring national integration because it did not affect the core activities that sustained the state's wool, wheat, and fruit industries. California's integration into the American mainstream was protracted, allowing until after 1900 the flourishing of distinctive regional policies that were both influenced by Australian developments and part of a large process of Pacific exchange.

Perceptions of their own distance and isolation remained vital to Californians and Australians, and inevitably cultural perspectives on systemic economic forces must be integrated into the analysis of markets. But cultural history also figures in another important way. Californians and Australians shared cultural assumptions about the domination of the land and the indigenous, who did not feel similarly "isolated." Anglos' dreams about the kind of land they wanted to inhabit came from the confrontation between their Anglo inheritance and the environments they encountered. Though much has been written about race, gender, and class in American history, the role of this trinity in mediating perceptions of the environment has been not adequately explored. Here, cultural landscape theory can aid this crossover between cultural and environmental history. Environmental history must bring into its vision the history of the people who contested and controlled these landscapes. Race, gender, and class pervasively shaped the two societies, and while there were differences in emphasis between each, Californians and many in Australia shared—and exchanged—similar visions of an Anglo, middle-class "garden" landscape in which families and farms would prosper.

This book tells, therefore, of the attempt to create a landscape that was neither unique to California nor peculiarly American. The book shows how environmental contacts began with the Australian "acclimatization" society activities that emerged in the wake of the gold rushes. Although frequently condemned for their introductions of exotic animals and plants that became pests, the acclimatizers raised awareness of conservation issues, particularly regarding forests. Stimulated by the work of George Perkins Marsh, Ferdinand von Mueller campaigned against forest destruction and preached afforestation. Aided by improved trans-Pacific steamship communications in the 1870s, his advice on the adaptation of plants in Mediterranean climates soon became well-known in California. Mueller's work on behalf of the eucalyptus genus, and the intellectual inheritance of acclimatization that California and Australia soon drew upon, is explored in chapter 1. These ideas demand inclusion in Californian as well as Australian history, but Mueller's ideas would not have appealed to Californians without the necessary internal conditions created by the transition from gold to wheat as the basic staple of California's economy.

In the 1860s, many influential Californians looked to agriculture, and particularly wheat, as the solution to California's long-term economic and social viability. Raised in eastern locations and accustomed to agrarian traditions, white settlers pronounced wheat farming to be superior to gold. Wheat cultivation did not, however, solve a basic problem of political economy, that of concentrated land ownership. The population remained heavily urbanized, and land controlled by the few. Henry George, the economist who developed the Single Tax idea, analyzed these trends in the 1870s, but his work was part of a larger tradition that made horticulture central to California's social reorganization. Chapter 2 explores how aspirations for a democratic garden landscape, expressed by George, underpinned the social and cultural demands of horticulture as well as horticulture's environmental critique of gold and wheat.

Horticulture has been a neglected theme in both Californian and Australian history, probably because it lacks the drama of gold and the romance of vast pastoral runs. The critical role of the fruit industry in California's development is now being rediscovered, however, and exciting new economic and cultural studies are appearing.[19] This book seeks to integrate the new economic perspectives that show fruit as a leading sector of California agriculture, but argues that horticulture was not established for economic reasons alone, nor was it originally dominated by large-scale business interests. Existing studies emphasize the logic of entrepreneurial farming and miss the larger worldview and social relations of fruit growers. Moreover, most focus on the citrus industry and the twentieth century. We must not read the later development of California citrus into the earlier and more diverse possibilities of nineteenth-century horticulture. Extensive fruit production preceded a viable market, and smaller and middle-class operators helped shape the vision of horticulture. Fruit's expansion was driven by supply rather than demand, yet influenced by the need for resourceful farming in an arid land far from markets. Many economic and institutional forces help explain why Californians developed an industry where there was relatively little proven demand.[20] But if we bring cultural and social analysis into the picture, we can easily see that Californians sought to impose a landscape dream of fruit lands and so, at the same time, escape from remote market forces that controlled wheat, with all of its environmental, social, and economic problems.

Fruit growing prospered initially because its promoters saw horticulture as a foundation for the ideal society. This ideal was influenced by the old inheritance of an agrarian dream from European and Eastern ancestors, but it involved more than that. Californians sought to use the advantages of climate, location, and innovative farming to create a society that could overcome the disadvantages of peripheral position. Horticulturalists proposed not fruit alone but a mixture of farms, small towns, and forests that would provide California with a supposedly more balanced development than gold or wheat could. Understood as the matrix of industries surrounding fruit, flowers, and vegetables, horticulture also entailed a moral dimension. It became allied in California with middle-class ideals of temperance, health, and family values. At the center of this work was the California State Board of Horticulture and the activities of its president from 1883 to 1903, Ellwood Cooper. Through Cooper and his allies Californian horticulture provided the model of a garden landscape that the advocates of small-scale farming in Australia soon embraced as well. Colonial royal commissioners, tourists, and other visitors took advantage of the improved steamship service and traveled across the Pacific to the American West Coast to report home on advances in agriculture, particularly in irrigation and the fruit industry. Though Australian-American connections in the nineteenth century have long been recognized by historians, the special appeal of Californian models surrounding horticulture has not been appreciated.

Of course, horticultural interests did not so much supplant other economic interests as provide a new layer of activity. In this sense, horticulture never *dominated* California agriculture, precisely because of the influence of railroads controlling large land grants, and other large landholders whose interests lay more in developing an agriculture made up of "factories in the field."[21] Advocates of horticultural diversity in California (and in Australia) are perhaps best viewed, therefore, as part of an important alternative culture seeking to reform the excesses of the market economy's environmental and social impact and to resist the logic of its economies of scale—even while sharing in the larger imperial dream of conquest on the periphery of European expansionism.

Horticulture developed in tandem with the rise of environmental consciousness; both were stimulated by the dream of a garden landscape. Horticulture became crucially linked with the preservation of the forests threatened, in the 1870s and 1880s, with destruction by timber and sheep interests. Moreover, horticulturalists stood behind the movement to afforest as well as reforest vast areas of California. Everyone knows that some Californians became, through the efforts of John Muir and the Sierra Club (founded 1892), advocates of national parks and wilderness movements. Australians, too, began to establish national parks at the same time that Yosemite and others were proposed in the United States, between 1870 and 1890. Audley, south of Sydney, was in 1878 the second officially designated "national park" in the world, behind Yellowstone in Wyoming. Muir visited Australia in the southern summer of 1903–04 and admired the eucalyptus forests from Western Australia to the Blue Mountains of New South Wales, but his visit was private, unreported, and intensely personal.[22] There is no evidence to suggest a strong American *influence* on Australian national park development before at least 1910, though *parallels* in aesthetics and functions can be found. The influence came later, as part of the impact of Progressive Era conservation policies. The earlier parallels were the product of a shared garden aesthetic. Despite the later importance of park movements, national parks played a subordinate role in the story of early Californian environmentalism too. The contemporary importance of the wilderness ethic promoted by Muir has been exaggerated in retrospect.[23] Far more critical in the nineteenth century than wilderness was the concept of environmental balance between farms and forests. The horticulturalists studied in this book sought that balance, spearheading a movement to introduce Australian trees and conserve native ones in order to achieve their goals.[24]

Chapters 3 and 4 deal with the exchange of vegetation between Australia and California designed to provide the greener landscape horticulturalists deemed natural, complement fruit and farms, and repair environmental damage done by gold mining and sheep. Horticulturalists imported fruit trees, including citrus from Australia, but these were not the most important and distinctive antipodean contributions.[25] Eucalyptus, acacia, and other Australian trees found favor in California as early as 1870. Simultaneously, Australians imported Californian plants. Monterey (radiata) pine developed into Australia's leading plantation timber. Though the Australian plantings would take until the 1960s to reach their economic potential, the groundwork was laid in the early acclimatization process. After 1900, the noted American private plant-hybridizer Luther Burbank of Santa Rosa, California, became known in Australia as a result of his attempts to breed a spineless cactus. He kept in close touch with officials of the New South Wales Department of Agriculture, and from seed merchants and collectors in Australia he imported many plants that he thought suitable for California, such as the popular flannelflower (*Actinotus helianthi*, called by Burbank the Australian star-flower) and bunya pine, or bunya-bunya (*Araucaria bidwilli*), that he grew at his Santa Rosa property.[26] Yet major exchanges occurred in forestry and began much earlier, as a result of Mueller's work.

Innovations in the use of Australian vegetation did not fully succeed in transforming California into a garden. As a result, Californians in the 1880s turned to irrigation to solve their economic problems and create a more aesthetically pleasing landscape. In chapters 5 through 8, I examine the underlying reasons for the popularity of irrigation, how that popular concept crossed the Pacific as part of the Californian model of horticulture, and how Australian experiments in irrigation in turn influenced those in California. Why was irrigation so popular, particularly since other land uses such as cattle and sheep grazing were often more rational from an economic viewpoint? I find the explanations not in economics or technology, but in the desire to create white, Anglo societies and specific cultural landscapes defined in gender, class, and racial terms.

The fruit industry in California is usually identified with irrigation. Yet this is an oversimplification. The horticulturalists did not entirely agree on the subject of irrigation, which would potentially move California's agriculture toward a more manipulative environmental ethic and a more speculative and corporate base. Land developers saw chances for immense private gain that disturbed many horticulturalists. Advocates of the garden landscape were thus both attracted to irrigation's potential for greening the landscape and for social engineering, but also repelled by the possibility that large landowners stood to benefit with windfall profits. No solution to this contradiction could be found within the limits of capitalist marketplace thinking, though some of the horticulturalists studied in this book did struggle against the economic logic the market imposed.[27]

Australians, too, were impressed with irrigation's potential to turn deserts into gardens. Faced with great shortages of water and the domination of the land by pastoralists, they turned to government intervention to aid small-scale agriculture through irrigation. This happened simultaneously with Californian irrigation projects and was greatly influenced by Californian examples and expertise, despite the greater Australian reliance on government. Irrigation met early failure in Victoria in the 1890s and would always struggle against greater odds to succeed, yet in neither Australia nor California did economic and environmental conditions allow small-scale farming to prosper through irrigation. The dream of closer settlement faltered, but irrigation continued to expand on both sides of the Pacific. While Australia had initially been the receiver of information and aid in the form of personnel from the United States, after 1915 Elwood Mead, later Bureau of Reclamation commissioner in Washington, tried to implement Australian-style, government-directed irrigation in the United States.

At the same time that irrigation schemes appeared, a pioneering modern program of biological control developed as part of the Pacific exchange. The struggle to combat the *Icerya* scale that threatened California's citrus industry saw the State Board of Horticulture championing a locally directed biological control program, against Washington's wishes. Australians and Californians cooperated in this program (see chapter 9). California's success against the scale with the Australian vedalia beetle, imported in 1888, led ultimately to a campaign in Queensland and New South Wales to use biological control to stamp out the pest prickly pear, which prevented development of small-scale farming (see chapter 10).

These promising initiatives in horticulture, forestry, irrigation, and biological control were together underpinned by a form of environmental reform that has been neglected by historians. Neither the idea of wilderness nor the modern idea of conservation for rational economic use encompasses the full range of nineteenth-century environmental thought, and it is an important aim of this study to recover the lost sensibilities of this movement. I argue that the movement aimed at an early form of "sustainability," though the term was never used. What "sustainable" means today is a matter of contention.[28] What is economically sustainable is not necessarily ecologically sustainable, yet a version of this same contest raged in the nineteenth century. Much garden-landscape thought concerned the creation of an environment that would last because it would not overwhelm nature, yet would at the same time serve the needs of humankind through a contrived diversity and abundance. The garden was, therefore, often informed by social and economic objectives rather than strictly ecological ones.

I label this movement environmental "renovation." Critics of nineteenth-century environmental damage did not try to reconstruct nature as it was before European contact. They sought an "equilibrium" in which they tried to "resuscitate" the land or "reclaim" its natural abundance.[29] But they sought these goals by introducing new plants, insects, and agricultural practices that added layers of cultural landscape to the already altered "natural" environment. In this sense they were closer to being, in the Australian historian Alan Gilbert's term, "rectificationists" in their impact on the land, rather than restorationists.[30] They espoused forms of sustained yield, but their nonutilitarian, holistic views blended economic and moral arguments. Their work was strongly linked to nineteenth-century social reform. They evinced religious, even perfectionist, motives in the search for an abundant lifestyle that drew upon Edenic inspiration and the spiritual springs of romanticism. Above all, they viewed forests not as farms or wilderness but as gardens to be tended.

Why did this mixture of environmental themes develop? I argue that it did so as a response to peripheral position and the synergy of the exchange of ideas that this position set up with Australia. There are precedents for this in human history. Europeans certainly transformed areas of the globe through their "ecological imperialism" and damaged them severely in the process, as Alfred Crosby has shown. This "biological expansion of Europe" could be very much a one-way street of European domination and destruction, but other more subtle environmental exchanges were possible. As Richard Grove argues in *Green Imperialism,* Europeans sought long before the mid-nineteenth century to overcome damage done by colonialism. To control the havoc of Europe's impact, the neo-Europeans sought out comparable environments.[31] The rapid transformation of "tropical Edens" such as the French territory of Mauritius led some European colonial officials to embrace an early form of environmentalism and attempt to stem deforestation and extinction of species. Yet California and Australia were not small islands conceptualized as tropical Edens. Shortage of labor; distance from markets; large, sparsely settled areas; and novel environmental conditions of aridity encouraged different models. This was one reason why horticulturalists like Ellwood Cooper looked to contemporary developments in Australia for guidance rather than to older examples of environmental management.

Why did this movement fade in California after 1910? Transport increasingly integrated California into national markets, and technical expertise tended to impose policies through a national conservation elite. The national became more important than the regional. The 1902 National Reclamation Act, which delivered irrigation, and the triumph of federal biological control in 1907 marked the beginning of an end in California's participation in the Pacific exchange. But the effects continued to be felt in Australia, and these themes were worked out in the 1920s in renewed efforts in irrigation and biological control there.

Nor did the garden dream entirely die. Rather, it became marshaled to the extension of agribusiness, and to wider economic development and the growth of urban conglomerations. Within this setting, the idea mutated to form the suburban garden landscape—manifest in cities like Los Angeles and Sydney in the 1920s—that is the subject of the epilogue of the book. In a sense, the effects of the garden dream and the aspirations that accompanied it still influence us. Yet the end point of the suburban garden existing amid vast and ecologically unsustainable cities is a long way from the objectives of the 1860s and 1870s. To the attempt to renovate the landscape changed by gold we must turn.

But first, two caveats about topics this book does not treat. The exchanges with California were much more about plants and insects than about animals. Horticulturalists encouraged complementary small-scale farming occupations such as dairying and poultry-keeping which could provide produce for farmers' families and manure for fertilizer. Animals that could keep pests in check—such as the turkeys used to pick grubs in some fruit fields—were also accepted. Both self-sufficiency and aesthetic considerations lay behind the keeping of fishponds and the stocking of dams and streams with imported fish.[32] But generally, the acclimatization mania for animal introductions found in mid-nineteenth-century Australia did not extend to the later horticultural exchange with California.

Horticulturalists represented their activities in opposition to the leading industries based on animals—sheep and cattle—and rejected the pastoral economy as a damaging competitor for space and resources. Moreover, circumstances did not favor the transfer of animals between Australia and California. Though Australians imported many animal species that became pests, such as rabbits, foxes, and camels, none of the "successful" importations discussed in the chapter on acclimatization were of American origin (Californian salmon and quail were tried but did not thrive). Californians displayed even less interest in Australian animals than Australians did in California's native fauna. Unlike the Australian colonists, Californians had no need of new animals for hunting, given the abundance of bears, eagles, cats, and other wild creatures considered vermin. Australian wildlife was discussed in the California press, but only to acknowledge how relatively "poor in quadrupeds" the southern continent was.[33]

The second caveat concerns the need to acknowledge other Pacific exchanges. The California-Australia exchange was only one part, albeit an important one, of larger and more complicated patterns of environmental contact in the Pacific. This story, therefore, can be viewed as a case study in a particular type of environmental exchange neglected by historians. After European settlement of California, links developed with East Asia as well as Australia. California imported large quantities of East Asian fruit stock and ornamentals, such as roses from Japan in the 1880s and 1890s, but these imports were not distinctive to the American Southwest, never stood out against similar fruit trees imported from the eastern states, never roused the kind of passion that surrounded the more obviously exotic Australian species, and were not crucial in the greening of large areas of the southwestern landscape.

The California-Australia exchange was also complemented by links with New Zealand and Hawaii, which deserve further study. Ships bound for the antipodes stopped at Honolulu, and the islands also traded with semitropical and tropical Queensland and Fiji. Yet the climate as well as the scale of environmental change and range of economic interests differed between these exchanges and those of California and temperate regions of Australia. For this reason, the Hawaiian case will only be discussed as part of the link between California and Australia. I adopt a similar approach to New Zealand, treating those islands only where they contributed to the contacts between the Australian colonies and the West Coast of the United States. True, New Zealand's ecological connection with Australia involved intercolonial migration, and exchanges of flora and fauna occurred extensively. All this awaits its historian.

Yet Australians, more than New Zealanders, had grandiose hopes of building "another America."[34] Only Australia in the South Pacific could conceivably rival the United States in its quasi-imperial ambitions to dominate an entire continent and an environment previously managed successfully by indigenous peoples. Boosters recognized the immense potential of the "nation for a continent" for planned environmental transformation that would turn the Australian colonies into a grand dominion of its own, one that would rival older empires.[35] Such a quest for control was roughly comparable to the aspirations of an "imperial" transformation of the American West.[36] This theme of an empire that mastered Nature mixed uneasily with environmental concern in the topics that are discussed in this book. Nowhere was this unstable mixture more apparent than in acclimatization and the work of Ferdinand von Mueller.

CHAPTER I

Renovating Nature

Marsh, Mueller, and Acclimatization

This chapter is a tale of two of the greatest of nineteenth-century environmental thinkers. One, George Perkins Marsh, author of *Man and Nature* (1864), is so well-known that it is almost obligatory in a work on American environmental history to begin with his achievement. The other, Baron Ferdinand von Mueller, is today almost unknown in the United States, though in his native Germany, in Britain, and in his adopted Australia he is recognized as a major figure in world botanical history. But in the nineteenth century, his work was a powerful influence in remaking nature in the American Southwest.

As far as we know, Marsh and Mueller did not correspond, but each was aware of and influenced by the work of the other. On the subject of the "acclimatization movement" their lives were drawn together. Looking at the two in comparative perspective provides a setting for the story that follows, but it also throws new light on Marsh. Despite his wide recognition, Marsh is a much misunderstood character; his role, and that of the nineteenth-century conservation movement he helped stimulate, is often misinterpreted. Looking at Marsh as an acclimatizer, in parallel with Mueller, will reveal Marsh's influence upon the Pacific exchange.

United States historians depict Marsh principally as a product of American conditions, a pioneer environmental thinker who addressed American forest depletion. The international context and impact of his thought, however, has been neglected.[1] Marsh is also interpreted as part of an ineffectual, elitist form of conservation that concentrated on preserving existing forests. These two points are linked—the international implications of and influences in Marsh's work help show that he was not quite the preservationist he is depicted to be.

Indisputably, Marsh expressed American concern for the destruction of forests, but his work involved more than that. The international reception of his work, so favorably reviewed in such places as the Australian colonies, New Zealand, Europe, and British India, revealed a global concern with the diminution of tree cover that long preceded the 1864 publication.[2] This forest scare cannot be explained in terms of American western expansion, a regional shortage of wood, or the reaction of European-Americans to wilderness. Marsh drew many of his examples from Europe, where he spent most of his time from the mid-1850s to his death in 1882. Above all, Marsh was documenting widespread concern with the destruction of old-growth forests in Europe and its empires, while also taking account of developments in reforestation in such countries as Germany and France.[3]

Modern views of Marsh are also tied to our broader view of nineteenth-century environmentalism. Marsh was a member of the old New England elite, privileged and yet out of step with the pace and scope of economic change in postbellum America. A social conservative, a Republican "mugwump" at odds with the corruption and crassness of the American Gilded Age, Marsh wrung his hands in despair at the excesses of American politics. He much preferred his trees, his garden walks, his botanical research. He was in a practical sense ineffectual even though his research was underwritten by his diplomatic appointment as American minister to Italy by a succession of Republican presidential administrations after 1862.

Historians' views of nineteenth-century "conservation" are similar to the received wisdom on Marsh. They are shaped by the hindsight provided by the Progressive Era. The conservation movement became centered, according to Samuel Hays, in the work of an administrative state in which scientific expertise helped shape policy. Less attention has been devoted to the movements that preceded this nationalizing process. Earlier environmental reform has been seen as an ineffectual prologue to the Progressive Era's ferment. Most authorities have agreed with Hays that until the 1890s, conservation was dominated by amateurs and conservatives—preservationists all, people who wanted to stop deforestation. The American Forestry Association, established in 1875, was "composed primarily of botanists, landscape gardeners, and estate owners" emphasizing "arboriculture, an aesthetic appreciation of forests, and the study of individual trees."[4] As a result of more recent research, we now know much more than this about the worldview of Marsh and his followers, though the most successful attempt to reconstruct this mentality concurs that nineteenth-century conservationists were a defensive, hesitant elite. Yet nineteenth-century conservation appealed to far more than just eastern mugwumps like Marsh—demonstrated by the enthusiastic way promoters on the Great Plains and the Pacific Coast took up his urgent plea to consider the forests—and this appeal had a strong, practical grassroots content reflected in the extensive tree-planting campaigns of the 1880s. Preservation was indeed a theme, but nineteenth-century conservationists were as much concerned with planting trees as with saving existing ones.[5] Marsh was an enthusiastic advocate of afforestation who closely monitored tree-planting schemes in California.

Any implication that nineteenth-century conservationists ought to have chosen between preservation and sustained management would also be misleading. These were pragmatic thinkers who leaned toward afforestation rather than preservation when the opportunity presented itself. Early conservationists were, at bottom, advocates of a constructed landscape that would improve nature, not preserve it. In short, they were advocates of the garden concept. The real difference between these conservationists and their Progressive Era successors is that the former conceived of the forest as a garden of mixed plantings rather than a form of broad-acre agriculture, or farming devoted to monoculture on an extensive rather than an intensive basis. Marsh's friend and confidante Charles Sprague Sargent, director of Harvard's Arnold Arboretum, edited an influential periodical aptly named *Garden and Forest* that hinted at the older aesthetic and melded the interests of horticulture and forestry.[6]

The mentality of nineteenth-century conservation must be understood before we can proceed. There is no better place to start than with a close analysis of the themes in Marsh's work, particularly those in *Man and Nature,* a work with a deserved reputation as one of the most important in the history of environmental thought. In many instances, Marsh's concern for the "woods" involved a process of restoration rather than preservation, and here he was keen to adapt new flora to American conditions rather than seek the reconstruction of a primeval wilderness. And when he did urge preservation in the areas of the American West not yet extensively deforested, Marsh depicted these areas as arboretums and gardens rather than recreational parks or reserves. Marsh's metaphors for the primeval forest were those of civilization's constructed and ordered landscape. He especially made clear the mixed character of his planting preference. He referred to forest preservation specifically by the metaphor of the garden. "It is desirable," he urged, "that some large and easily accessible region of American soil should remain, as far as possible, in its primitive condition." But this would not mean the preservation of wilderness. Such a preservation would be "at once a museum for the instruction of the student, a garden for the recreation of the lover of nature, and an asylum where indigenous tree, and humble plant that loves the shade, and fish and fowl and four-footed beast, may dwell and perpetuate their kind."[7]

For reclaimed forests, or afforested areas, the idea was not to plant an arboreal equivalent of broad-acre agriculture. Marsh spoke of the need to restore the mixture of woodland and farmland space in the eastern parts of the United States, for example, where the "life of incessant flitting" deterred "permanent improvements." Of this region, Marsh lamented: "We have now felled forest enough everywhere, in many districts far too much." Here Marsh used the language of restoration. "Let us restore this one element of material life to its normal proportions, and devise means for maintaining the permanence of its relations to the fields, the meadows, and the pastures, to the rain and the dews of heaven, to the springs and rivulets with which it waters the earth."[8]

Yet Marsh's proposal involved nothing like a restoration of "wilderness" areas. Rather, he made clear his strong aesthetic appreciation for European systems of balanced cultivation. From his European experience, he saw that farmers who remained attached to the soil would conserve the natural world better. Social mobility in America was "unfavourable for the execution of permanent improvements. . . . It requires a very generous spirit in a landholder to plant a wood on a farm he expects to sell," Marsh lamented.[9] His hope, for the long term, was for a substitution of a European style of agriculture based on intensive rather than extensive cultivation. Marsh found extremely distasteful the system of political economy common in his homeland which discouraged the long-term view. Nonetheless, the planting of trees on farms would "attach the proprietor more strongly to the soil for which he has made such a sacrifice." Plantations thus sown would be "paternal acres" akin to the peasant inheritance of Italy or France, which would provide a "moral check against a too frequent change of owners" and tie the proprietor and his heirs more firmly to the land and to the state itself. In this way, Marsh's concern with forests derived in part from European peasant models of the garden landscape.

If Marsh could not decide between preservation and afforestation, this was for good practical reasons. He accepted the authoritative arguments of European foresters that density of population and patterns of land use determined the mixture of extensive and intensive forestry practices. Jules Clavé, the noted French authority, argued in *Études sur l'économie forestière* that Americans could never adopt the French *intensive* forestry management practices while the area of available land remained so *extensive* in relation to the population. Marsh accepted this judgment, but he did so reluctantly and with severe qualifications. Marsh was, for example, convinced of the "superiority of the artificial forest, both in quantity and quality, as compared with that of the natural and spontaneous growth."[10] Despite differences between the "aboriginal and the trained forest," the "sooner a natural wood is brought into the state of an artificially regulated one, the better it is," he argued.[11]

Because of his acceptance of Clavé's economic logic, Marsh proclaimed in his original 1864 edition that the preservation of the existing woods was of greater importance in America. He noted "the terrible evils necessarily resulting from the destruction of the forest" and "the far more costly extension of them where they have been unduly reduced." But as soon as afforestation promised viability in the 1870s, Marsh was eager to endorse it. In later editions of *Man and Nature,* he "took a more sanguine view of the economic practicability of private afforestation" in the United States.[12] Artificial forests would reap earlier and greater rewards than in Europe because of the milder climate and longer growing season, he now concluded. Under irrigation, he predicted, plantings of fast-growing Australian eucalypts and casuarina would soon pay their way.[13]

MARSH AND ACCLIMATIZATION

Marsh's endorsement of afforestation, particularly the adaptation of trees from Australia to the arid lands of the southwestern United States, was one aspect of his deep interest in the subject of "acclimatization." Strangely, this important theme has been neglected in the tendency to see Marsh's other writings in isolation from his work on forestry and to downgrade the importance of the chapters of *Man and Nature* that do not deal with forests. True, forests made up the bulk of the manuscript, but Marsh was always interested in more than trees.

One of the most striking absences in scholarship on Marsh is the failure to connect his work to international concerns about the adaptation of plants and animals. Marsh's work has parallels in and connections with the work on acclimatization in Europe and the British Empire. The afforestation movement that he endorsed was principally concerned with matters of adapting suitable flora from other climes to that of the American West. This acclimatization issue is important because it distances his ideas on forestry from the preservationist stereotype. Marsh was deeply concerned with introducing new species to enrich the environment.

Acclimatization, institutionally speaking, was preeminently a European and British Empire phenomenon. Acclimatization societies concerned with the systematic adaptation of the products of the New World to the Old, and the Old World to the New, came into vogue in the 1850s. The French Société zoologique d'acclimatation, established in 1854, was followed by a number of similar societies in the British Empire.[14] These groups of botanical enthusiasts were concerned with making the most out of the ecological transformation of the New World. In France, the movement was concerned with settlement in Algeria and French Polynesia. In the British Empire, the new colonies in Australia and New Zealand were prime sites for botanical and zoological experimentation.[15] The concern everywhere was not only economic but aesthetic as well. Acclimatizers believed that the beauty of the newly invaded colonial landscape could be improved with the aid of science, but these visionaries expressed little or no concern about the possible damaging effects of introduced species. The native fauna and flora in the New Worlds were regarded by these Eurocentric botanists as inferior.

The United States lacked the strong, self-conscious acclimatization movement noticeable after 1850 in many other of the white settlement societies derived from British rule. The much longer period of European settlement, over 250 years compared to just 70 in Australia, partly accounts for this, since many significant domestic introductions had already been made to the Americas before the explosion of explicitly imperialistic botany. Unlike nineteenth-century Australasia, the United States was not a set of colonies deeply influenced by imperial schemes. The Americans' break with Europe, and their intellectual declaration of independence, came much earlier and made deference toward European fauna and flora rarer. Also, the humid northeastern zone had similarities to northern European climates from which the vast majority of the white population had originated. Most Americans had little incentive, therefore, to think laterally about the introduction of species from unfamiliar climatic zones. North America's eastern and central regions were too cold to be hospitable to many of the tropical plants and animals that concerned the imperial societies.

Some Americans were, nonetheless, interested in acclimatization. That great agrarian Thomas Jefferson stated that the "greatest service which can be rendered any country is, to add an [sic] useful plant to its culture," and he personally encouraged the acclimatization of olives and African upland rice in the American South.[16] The American government had tried in the 1850s to introduce camels into the southwest for military service, alpacas had been taken there for grazing, and large-scale propagation of German carp occurred with the founding of the United States Fish Commission in 1871.[17] Under the commission's encouragement, many species of fish were soon introduced into California's rivers and lakes. But this acclimatization did not include a Pacific exchange. In fact, most of the fish involved were indigenous American fish from back East.

Whether eastern American, European, or Australasian introductions were involved, acclimatization principles became more relevant to Americans from the 1840s onward as the population moved west into new and largely unfamiliar environments on the Great Plains and in the arid Southwest. On the plains they tried to recreate the woodlands of the east by planting trees, but those adapted were still within a temperate climatic aesthetic. The Southwest was very different and circumstances encouraged more radical experimentation. In California, because of distance and climate, a de facto acclimatization aesthetic did emerge, and ideas compatible with those found in Australia became common. In a curious way, California became, ecologically, a colony, just as Australia was. Both were pioneer areas with environments very different from those experienced previously by northern Europeans.

Marsh's links with acclimatization reflect both his exposure to European acclimatizers and the impact of American frontier expansion. Marsh's responses can be seen in his letters to Charles Sprague Sargent. Over three years of correspondence, from 1879–82, the two discussed such matters as the acclimatization of olives in Massachusetts, the grafting of figs and pomegranates, "and the supposed sanitary effects of eucalyptus in California."[18] This came near the end of Marsh's life, but strong hints of his natural sympathy for the acclimatization principle were evident much earlier. On occasion Marsh displayed the aesthetic consideration for improvement of the environment that underlay acclimatization ideas elsewhere in the Anglo-Saxon world. Marsh believed, for example, that the American landscape could be improved with exotics weeds that flowered profusely. The European scarlet poppy, he reported, was competing with economically valuable crops in some American wheat fields. No matter: "With our abundant harvests of wheat, we can well afford to pay now and then a loaf of bread for the cheerful radiance of this brilliant flower," Marsh concluded.[19]

Still more important and obvious evidence of his acclimatization sympathies can be found. In his report on the spread of the camel, Marsh noted its importation into many places, including Australia, and into Texas and New Mexico, "where it finds the climate and the vegetable products best suited to its wants, and promises to become a very useful agent in the promotion of the special civilization for which those regions are adapted."[20] In 1857, in a report on the fisheries of Vermont commissioned by the state legislature, Marsh had further opportunity to explore his interest in acclimatization. He concluded that the "introduction of fish from distant waters, and their naturalization in their new homes is also practicable to an indefinite extent." Like the early acclimatizers in Victoria and New Zealand who sought to spread salmon culture, he recommended not public investment in fish stocks, but action by private citizens to develop artificial breeding.[21]

On the other hand, Marsh's support of acclimatization programs was tempered in ways that help to distinguish his contribution from that of counterparts in Australia. The whole text of *Man and Nature* was designed to show how extensive the impact of humans on their environment had been, and how that impact ought to be controlled. Marsh was particularly aware, since his residence in Italy, of the role of quadrupeds like sheep and cattle in destroying grasses and tree cover in the Mediterranean. Even in camels he found a source of environmental damage, according to the 1864 edition of his book, published after his extensive research and tours of the Mediterranean region: "I am convinced that forests would soon cover many parts of the Arabian and African deserts, if man and domestic animals, especially the goat and the camel, were banished from them."[22] Moreover, Marsh had a preference for the native flora and fauna of his home country that survived his long residence in Europe. "It is an observation familiar to everyone acquainted with both continents, that the American trout and other fresh-water fishes are superior in sapidity to the most nearly corresponding European species," Marsh confidently asserted in the tone of an American nationalist. This he believed resulted from the fact that humans had less effect on fish species in America, not from inherent differences in the types of fish. In the New World, "wild nature is not yet tamed down to the character it has assumed in the Old."[23]

On the subject of trees, too, Marsh tended to favor the native species where forest already existed. In his 1864 edition he noted proudly that

American forests were superior: "The multitude of species, intermixed as they are, in their spontaneous growth, gives the American forest landscape a variety of aspect not often seen in the woods of Europe," and "the gorgeous tints" of "the American maples, oaks, and ash trees" were "unsurpassed."[24] In this judgment he was joined by others who might have served, in other circumstances, the same function for acclimatization in America that Mueller would serve in Australia. Sargent, for example, criticized excessive reliance on imported plants. The "first qualification of a beautiful plant" was "health and vigor," he argued. When natives plants were selected, "we are sure, to begin with, that they are adapted to the climate."[25]

This recommendation did not extend to California, however. Both Marsh and Sargent believed acclimatization was more appropriate there. As Sargent put it, "California will doubtless always be obliged to depend somewhat upon other parts of the world for her materials for ornamental planting." It was "to Australia" above all, that "California planters must look."[26] Marsh reinforced this opinion. He reported extensively, just three days before he died, on the forestry station at Vallombrosa, Italy, where eucalyptus plantings were prominently displayed.[27] In the last edition of his book, published posthumously in 1885, Marsh noted the prodigious growth of the eucalypts and predicted that they would make artificial forestry a success in the American Southwest. The largest of the eucalypts, he reported with astonishment, "would prove good investments even in an economic aspect."[28] Marsh's pronouncements on eucalypts attracted attention from other members of the eastern elite influential in the development of American forestry. In 1882, the United States government forester Franklin Hough, relying partly on information supplied by Marsh, declared the growing of eucalyptus as exotics to be "a philanthropic enterprise for the benefit of mankind."[29]

Despite Marsh's prominence, his influence on this debate over the potential of the eucalypts as an item of adaptation in the United States had limits. First, he was merely responding to innovations already made by practical foresters and "nurserymen" in the American West. "If we may credit late reports," he noted, "the growth of the eucalyptus is so rapid in California, that the child is perhaps now born who will see the tallest sequoia overlapped by the new vegetable emigrant from Australia."[30] Second, his own knowledge of the eucalypts was entirely derived from his European sojourn, and this experience made him sceptical of the wider application of the genus in North America. Eucalypts did not thrive in colder climates, he noted. Marsh was on the side of those who cautioned against excessive reliance on this exotic, arguing that the genus "can not be expected to flourish in any part of the United States except the extreme South and California."[31]

A third qualification of Marsh's influence on acclimatization must be made. In his statements on the prodigious growth and potential of the eucalypts, his work was entirely derivative of that of Ferdinand Mueller, the driving intellectual force in the wider dissemination of the genus in Europe and the Americas.[32] It was Mueller who boosted the belief in the giant eucalyptus as a rival to the sequoias, and who most inspired the plantings of Australian natives in California. To his work we must turn to understand the effect of acclimatization on California.

THE BARON BOTANIST

Marsh's interest in acclimatization and the transformation of nature had echoes in Melbourne, Australia. Mueller was an enthusiastic reader of *Man and Nature,* and he described Marsh as the best authority on climate change and the value of trees to the environment.[33] Mueller cited the usual arguments derived from Marsh about the value of trees for rainfall, erosion control, and evaporation, but he emphasized acclimatization more than Marsh did. Born in Germany and trained as a botanist, with a Ph.D. from the University of Kiel, Mueller came to Australia as a young man in 1847 for the clean air doctors prescribed as vital to the restoration of his health. Mueller traveled widely in the country of his adoption but never returned to Europe. This isolation might have bred a parochial vision. Yet Mueller was a man with worldwide connections. His realm of activity was not just Australia and the United States. In fact, his links with the Americans were incidental and cursory until the 1870s. In Australia, he became Government Botanist in 1853, and director of Melbourne's Royal Botanic Gardens four years later. As a result of his international promotion of the eucalypts, Mueller was appointed a hereditary baron by the King of Württemberg in 1861 and a Knight of the British Empire in 1869.[34]

Mueller became associated with the acclimatization movement in Melbourne, serving as vice-president of the Victorian Acclimatisation Society established in 1861. He also exchanged specimens with the directors of many botanical gardens; but few Americans figure in his early letters. The "initial impetus" for the Acclimatisation Society's formation in the colony "was homesickness for Britain. British animals and birds were to be imported and bred so that the sights and sounds of 'home' might be comfortingly heard and seen again."[35] Many European hunting animals were introduced for the benefit of the colonial elite that stacked the membership of the Society. But economic motives also became important, and Mueller was deeply involved in these. As director of the Botanic Gardens he claimed "the path of predominant utility," and his writings are studded with attempts to "improve" the colonial environment.[36]

The mixture of motives among the acclimatizers is clearly conveyed in the 1864 Victorian Acclimatisation Society report. These mostly amateur scientific enthusiasts and environmental improvers sought to "stock this country with new, useful, and beautiful things, to add to our national wealth, to suggest new forms for our colonial industries, . . . and to add new elements to the food of the entire people." Behind all this was the garden metaphor and its connotations of fertility, fructification, and diversity. Acclimatizers were "diligently seeking to sow" the new colonies of Australasia with the seeds of abundance that would ultimately "fructify in a complete harvest."[37] The Victorian society was particularly concerned to establish, in the wake of the gold rushes, new economic activities in "intensive farming" to replace gold's waning force in the colony.[38]

Acclimatizers dreamed not simply of an abundant environment but one conducive to the moral virtues of the yeomanry. The Acclimatisation Society believed that importations of fish, birds, and animals would provide at the same time such "manly sports" as trout fishing that would "lead the Australian youth to seek their recreation on the river's bank and mountain side rather than in the cafe and casino." Morality would wax still stronger through the aesthetically pleasing landscape of introduced plants and the impact this would have in encouraging domesticity. This is why acclimatizers promised to "surround every homestead" with "new forms of interest and beauty."[39]

The early acclimatization movement in Australia showed little interest in a Pacific exchange, however. This is simple to explain. Acclimatization at first concerned itself primarily with animals, reflecting the desire to enlarge the sporting opportunities of rich colonials and English visitors. Hence the introduction of such traditional European hunting quarry as the trout, rabbit, deer, and fox. Economic introductions like camels, water buffalo, and alpacas came from more diverse sources, but North America provided no candidates for this category either. Only on the subject of fishing did the Pacific exchange excite interest, and attempts were made in the 1860s and 1870s in Australia and New Zealand to introduce Californian rainbow trout and salmon ova, introductions that acclimatizers hoped would profit both sports lovers and fish eaters.[40]

Another reason for the initial failure to consider North American introductions was the imperial framework of the acclimatization societies and scientists. The leading Australian botanists and zoologists had trained in Britain or Europe, and they steadfastly maintained scientific and cultural allegiances to them in the 1860s. The imperial preference was revealed in the case of plant exchanges, which in the 1840s and 1850s occurred predominantly through the Royal Botanic Gardens at Kew, which had assumed worldwide leadership in plant distribution.[41]

MUELLER AND ACCLIMATIZATION

Mueller too was at first mainly interested in the imperial framework. He stressed his European connections, which was to be expected, given his upbringing. Mueller looms large indeed in nineteenth-century Australian science, and his name has been linked, as Marsh's has in America, with the origins of Australian environmental thinking. This recognition is only faintly embarrassed by the acclimatization connection. One biographer portrays Mueller as avoiding the worst excesses of the acclimatization movement and argues that he was "never directly involved in their sillier carryings on."[42] Mueller was, it is true, lucky enough to avoid responsibility for most of the serious ecological blunders, such as the disastrous introduction of the European wild rabbit. But if Mueller was innocent, it was only by accident, since he did not eschew zany acclimatization schemes. His publications advocated the introduction of so many exotic species that, if successful, he would have created an environmental potpourri.

Mueller's apparently contradictory attitudes are stark enough to unsettle anyone seeking the origins of modern environmental consciousness. In his "Forest Culture in Its Relation to Industrial Pursuits" (1871), the German gushed over "the silent grandeur and solitude of a virgin forest" that "inspires us almost with awe." But alongside such hymns of praise to pristine nature he argued that "the truffle, though not an article of necessity, might be naturalized in many of our forests." Such wilderness could also be improved, he believed, by the introduction of blackberry, a plant that has assumed alarming pest proportions in Australia in the twentieth century. Blackberry he disseminated himself with the imprimatur of the Botanic Gardens. Spending many days scattering seeds along the headwaters of the Yarra River at Mount Baw Baw, Mueller rejoiced that "this delicious fruit is now established on the rivulets of that mountain."[43]

Mueller's hymns of praise to rainforests matched the outpourings of California's preeminent wilderness advocate, John Muir. In "our innumerable forest glens," Mueller acknowledged "the deep, rich detritus of soils and fallen leaves, accumulated in past centuries," and he found in the tall eucalyptus trees some "of the grandest features of the world's vegetation." Mueller self-consciously developed parallels with the California redwoods to put the value of the *Eucalyptus regnans* forest into proper perspective. "Mammoth-eucalypts" rivaled the *Sequoia* of the California forests in height, stately grandeur, and longevity, he claimed. But just at the point that Mueller threatens to assume the modern mantle of wilderness advocate, he presents us with a strange juxtaposition. "Can this grand picture of nature not be further embellished?" he asks.[44]

Underlying Mueller's advocacy of the forests was a deep spirituality derived from German romanticism. Quoting his compatriot Schiller, he reminded his audience that "it was in the forests where [Schiller's] poetic mind . . . first of all awoke to its deep love for nature." The virgin forest also conveyed "involuntarily to our mind a feeling as if we were brought more closely before the Divine Power by whom the worlds without end were created, and before whom the proudest human work must sink into utter insignificance."[45] The terminology was as European as the romantic movement itself. His accounts are replete with references to "glens," "cathedrals," and "monuments."[46]

In practical terms, too, Mueller sought to reshape the Australian forests in ways that would make them more familiar to European nature lovers. Mueller wanted to establish in native forests and pasturelands exotic tree species that could be valuable for either utilitarian or aesthetic purposes. He advocated as part of his grand scheme the introduction of walnuts and hickories from North America for their fruits and quality wood. Alongside his advocacy of the spread of the eucalypt abroad, Mueller sought the introduction of four hundred or so types of coniferous trees around the world that would prove adaptable. Three hundred species of oak he also recommended adding to the glory of the rainforests and bush. For Mueller, *Eucalyptus regnans* and similar grand species he admired did not amount to nature's perfection. Alongside such stately trees as these, exotic conifers would "live through centuries," even millennia, "as great historical monuments."[47]

Mueller had utilitarian reasons for promoting the improvement of pristine forests. The timber "famine" predicted in the United States by Marsh's disciples meant that Australia could "not indifferently look forward for soft-wood from these places." To supplement the native hardwoods he so loved, he pushed the planting of softwoods, including Californian pines. He distributed these through the Botanic Gardens seed program and predicted many of the exotic pines would in "our winterless zone" soon "advance with more quickness to maturity" than in their native habitats.[48]

IMPERIAL AMBITIONS

Though German by birth, Mueller was staunchly loyal to the land of his adoption and the British imperial connection. He envisaged, as did other advocates of acclimatization, that scientific experimentation would provide a platform for the development of Australia as a great power: "Judicious forest culture, appropriate to each zone," would "vastly ameliorate the clime, and provide for the dense location of our race." But Mueller never considered forest culture in isolation. He linked it to the concept of an abundant and improved environment. Mueller sought to acclimatize the world's produce and provide "for transplanting of almost every commodity, both of the vegetable and animal empire, we possess." The image he had was of a densely settled, sustainable agrarian civilization: his ideal Australia would be a garden continent.

Mueller joined this vision of the future to an Australian version of national exceptionalism. Australia had a priceless advantage over Europe because it could experiment in biological and agricultural improvement "by ancient usages unretarded." But this alone did not distinguish Australia from other New Worlds. Australia was a continent with a unique geographical heritage. "Our continent, surrounded . . . by the natural boundaries of three oceans, free and unconnected, must advance by extraneous influences undisturbed," he rejoiced. The Australian colonists' possession of a single continent made Australian development unique. This geographic fact laid the basis for experimentation in colonization and plant introductions. To environmental good fortune was added political good fortune; the presence of "British sovereignty" would "ever give a firm stability" to Australian development along a path to "greatness."[49]

Mueller's abundant garden, shielded by British naval power and the rule of law, was for whites only. Unlike those colonial experiments of the British and others in Africa and Asia, settlement in Australia did not have the immense ill fortune, he opined, of having "to encounter extensive hordes of savages to dispute the possession of the soil." Acclimatization meant "civilization"; preservation of the wilderness meant savagery; and savagery meant in turn the obstruction of "the progress of civilization."[50] Domination of nature, including domination of the hunter-gatherer peoples known as "aboriginals," was at the forefront of Mueller's dreams, despite the German's reverence for pristine wilderness.[51]

But Mueller's vision was to be a domination scientifically controlled. "Steam power and the increased ingenuity of machinery applied to cultivation" would "render the virgin soil extensively productive with far less toil than in older countries." This use of science would solve one of Australia's problems, the labor shortage. Mueller was aware that the arrival of Western-style capitalist agriculture brought environmental problems galore. But these could be controlled because Australian development coincided with the application of modern technology to agriculture and forestry. Remembering the great contributions that such German scientists as Justus von Leibig made to soil science, Mueller proclaimed that the "teachings of science" would guard the colonists "against the rapacious systems of culture and the waste of fertilizers which well-nigh involved ruin to many a land."[52]

All in all, Mueller's plan entailed a grand ecological transformation, not respect for the wild. He sought as a classic acclimatizer to "improve" the environment. Underlying this aim was the assumption that Australia must hold a denser population if it were to survive and prosper in a world of empires. A larger population for the sparsely settled continent was possible, he believed, without environmental degradation. This hope rested in turn on the forests, and it explains why forests were considered so vital in nineteenth-century environmental thought. He noted that Belgium was able to sustain a far greater population while retaining a proportion of forest cover in excess of that available in Australia. The more forests, he reasoned, the larger the population that the land could comfortably carry. Yet Belgium was so small. If Australia could be clothed in belts of green, the prospects for national advancement would be bright indeed, since the size of the continent almost matched that of the mainland United States. To turn green such a vast brown land made afforestation as well as preservation essential. These ambitions for the new land were every bit as expansive as those that Americans held for their own dominion of the trans-Mississippi West.[53]

THE DECLINE OF ACCLIMATIZATION

The fantastic dreams of acclimatizers were backed up by the state. The game laws promulgated in the colonies prevented killing of certain animals during the breeding season. Disastrously, these provisions were often more restrictive for introduced animals like deer than they were for native fauna.[54] By the early 1880s, the damage that acclimatization was doing to environments in the antipodes was clear enough. The beginning of a shift in sentiment is illustrated in the work of Richard Schomburgk, second director of the Adelaide Botanic Garden. In 1868, Schomburgk released sparrows imported from England, stating that "the great utility of the sparrows is now a settled question in Europe, and the injury they do to a few fruits must be overlooked." Acclimatizers hoped that the sparrow would help in "destroying many of the worms and insects destructive to growing corn." But Schomburgk soon changed his mind. In 1881 he told the local Chamber of Manufacturers that "these destructive birds are reaping [sic] havoc with the crops near neighbouring mountains. It is hoped that the Acclimatisation society will look well into their interests[, so] that they sanction into the colony only those known to be not pests to an adopted country."[55]

Acclimatization came under attack for two quite opposite reasons. Some of the introductions were too successful, as in the case of rabbits and sparrows. Others, like llamas and the experimental herds of alpacas, were miserable failures, and the latter's purchase and maintenance in the early 1860s cost the colonial government of New South Wales dearly. Fifteen thousand pounds initially and a thousand a year in upkeep for a species "that died quicker than it reproduced" was too much for even the staunchest parliamentary supporter of these environmental visionaries.[56] Their funds limited by parsimonious legislatures, the acclimatization societies could not afford such costly ventures. As a result, the societies' ambitious programs of transplanting were heavily cut back in the 1870s.

Acclimatization did not die, however. For instance, its reach extended to the aesthetic of the first Australian national parks. Far from being preserves of wilderness, the earliest of these, such as Audley in New South Wales (established in 1878) and Belair in South Australia (established in 1891), included exotic flora and fauna introductions designed to "improve" the parks and establish recreational facilities for urban populations.[57] Acclimatization also developed in closer connection with governments through botanic gardens and colonial forestry programs that began in the 1870s and 1880s in response to warnings about the destruction of indigenous forests in Australasia and the United States. Within this changed context, plants became more important and displaced the original focus on animals. In part this change reflected the obvious fact that the embarrassments of early acclimatization had been most apparent in—though by no means exclusively limited to—animal life. Also influential was the rise of the specialized zoological movement that catered to this aspect of the work. Some of the acclimatization societies, like the Victorian, shifted their focus to become essentially zoological societies concerned with the exhibition rather than release of imported animals. In other cases, as in Queensland and New Zealand, the acclimatization movement remained strong into the 1890s and served as a conduit for the introduction of some American flora and fauna.[58]

Animal transfers had never been central to the interests of the botanist Mueller, but with the focus on exotic plants, public attention increasingly shifted to his own efforts at acclimatization.[59] Between 1885 and 1890, the Victorian government conducted an elaborate study by the Royal Commission on Vegetable Products, stimulated by Mueller's tireless propagandizing. Luminaries of irrigation and the fruit industry appeared, and the commissioners sent copies of the entire report to every horticultural body in the state. The massive, nine-part report included brief testimony from Mueller but copious evidence from others illustrating the continued faith in acclimatization, and it linked introductions to the ideal of the garden landscape as presented in the model of California.[60]

Acclimatization in Australia began by trying to replicate the Old World, but gradually it became clear that the western coasts of North and South America also offered promising candidates for adaptations. Early examples of this perception led to the introduction of Californian fish, but the growing interest in the environmental impact of forest destruction, described in Marsh's 1864 book, put the focus on the possibility of using American trees in Australia. The introduction of the Timber Culture Act in the United States in 1873, though in practice a failure, demonstrated to colonials that Americans were trying to address the problem of tree deficiency through a practical measure of acclimatization. As many areas of Australia resembled the conditions envisaged by the 1873 legislation, this measure stimulated special concern with introducing American softwoods in the colonies.[61]

Just as Australians began to look to the United States for the refashioning of their own environment, some Californians began to look to Australia. Both places had inherited environmental problems associated with gold mining and the already apparent removal of much native vegetation, as well as economic-development problems posed by distance from markets, lack of labor, and arid climate. In this context, innovative acclimatization ideas pioneered in Australia began to be noticed. California had become, in effect, a peripheral region shaped by the powerful forces exerted by land settlement, markets, and Anglo-Saxon culture derived from the metropolitan eastern United States, and from Europe. As a peripheral region, California had interests not identical with those of the metropolitan center. The state had strong affinities with the "settler societies" developing in parts of the British Empire across the Pacific, particularly those in southeastern Australia. Since Americans were never interested in the introduction of Australian animals, the shift of focus toward acclimatization of plants enhanced Mueller's influence, because the introduction of exotic flora was, in the case of the American Southwest, of great importance.

Improved trans-Pacific transport in the 1870s helped foster awareness of these links in environmental circumstances. Especially important in the framing and channeling of common aspirations and blueprints for environmental change was the introduction of a regular steamship route. A temporary steamship connection made in 1871 became permanent in 1875 through the efforts of the American entrepreneur H. H. Hall.[62] Trade with California leapt fivefold between 1871 and 1890 on the strength of the improved communications. This new link had an environmental impact.[63] Sailing ships that had irregularly plied the waters between Sydney and San Francisco from the time of the gold rushes continued to carry important bulk cargoes, but the faster steamships introduced in the 1870s enhanced contacts by carrying mail and tourists on a regular basis. This facilitated the quicker exchange of ideas about forestry and agriculture, and the route served as an efficient conduit for seeds, tree stock, farm technology, and insects. Mueller rejoiced at the "regular and quick communication with California." The steamship service was "giving now easy opportunity for importing" trees and fulfilled the acclimatization societies' plans for seed exchanges. American nurserymen waxed enthusiastic over the "monthly communication with Melbourne" and were able to obtain from Mueller a "variety of Australian eucalypti and other seeds not normally imported."[64]

Yet a more vital force than improved communications brought Australia and California together in a Pacific exchange. In each society, similar patterns of social development had emerged. Both possessed similar social aspirations to transform the gold- and pastoral-based economies into something more egalitarian, as the promise of gold vanished from capital-intensive hydraulic and deep-shaft mining. Above all, it was not similar environments or coincidental transport links, but similar class aspirations and political economies that brought the two societies together. California became the driving force in this exchange because, there, the challenge to the dominant political economy of mining, pastoral industries, and broad-acre agriculture was first and most clearly fashioned in the shape of an alternative model of a horticultural "garden of the world."

CHAPTER 2

Wheat, Fruit, and Henry George

The Political Economy of California Horticulture

The cross-national influences that linked California and Australia through improved communications after 1870 were part of global shifts in political economy. Ecological transformation in one corner of the world now resulted, as George Perkins Marsh explained, from changes in markets thousands of miles away.[1] The capitalist economy, Marx and Engels also concluded at about the same time, was contributing to environmental transformation where, "in place of the old wants, satisfied by the production of the country, we find new wants, requiring for their satisfaction the products of distant lands and climes."[2]

The distant and impersonal forces of global political economy were, however, deployed by and for real human beings. In areas newly touched by the commodification of nature, some people noticed that these environmental changes often benefited the few at the expense of the many. Social critics strove to take account of these changes and put them to the service of humanity. Even some political economists who emphasized the role of capital in nature's transformation showed an awareness of the critical contribution of land as a resource. What is most striking about the critiques emanating from the "dismal science" of the nineteenth century is the role played by controversies over land utilization. From Adam Smith to Thomas Malthus to the American protectionist Henry Carey of Philadelphia, land was firmly on the agenda. The work of Henry George, California's most prominent exponent of political economy, lies squarely within this early tradition that made land use and ownership crucial in class struggle.

LAND AND LABOR: HENRY GEORGE

The creation of American California as a divided, class society characterized by vast discrepancies of wealth proceeded very rapidly in the 1850s and 1860s. The promise of California's natural resources to provide an abundant livelihood for emigrants was not evenly shared in its realization, and the hoax seemed more vicious in the brighter California sunshine.[3] Many plans arose to analyze the apparent fall from an expected state of grace and to explain how the situation could be rectified. The most prominent of these was George's Single Tax. A Philadelphian by birth, George grew to manhood in California and worked as a compositor in San Francisco in the 1860s, hoping to become an editor. Quickly he became involved in Democratic politics and the land question.

George argued persuasively that special interests and loose land laws had wrought a cruel disappointment for the laboring classes, and that the greater part of California's resources had been taken by well-connected and often unscrupulous entrepreneurs. Already by 1870 these constituted a "landed aristocracy."[4] The price of land was being forced up not by improvements upon the land but by the pressure of California's increased population, which created a vast imbalance of supply and demand. George argued that the unearned increment from increased demographic pressure on monopolized land should be taxed.

George has been typecast as an urban political economist with an urban vision.[5] Yet his thought had a strong agrarian streak, and the issue of humankind's relations with nature lay close to the center of his thinking. George charged that faulty political economy was undermining the natural world and leading to the rape of its bountiful resources. Though he learned much about rent and value from the English political economist Ricardo, George articulated his own agrarian vision of happy yeoman farmers complementing the trades of small towns. This was the California of his dreams.

George revealed his image of environmental declension as early as 1871, in a long section on "The Lands of California" in *Our Land and Land Policy*.[6] The essay is distinguished by a strong aesthetic appreciation of small-scale, diversified agriculture. According to George,

California's landscape suffered from a "blight" that had offset "the rich-
ness of her soil and the beneficence of her climate"—too many renters,
too few owner-occupiers, and farms that were far too large either to provide for the aspirations of the masses or to improve the landscape. At
the heart of the problem was land monopoly, but this was manifest in a
particularly displeasing form of agricultural specialization. What stands
out is the link George draws between monoculture and land degradation. Despite the fact that "nature has so lavishly endowed this Empire
State of ours," George argued, ranching and wheat farming had
bequeathed the aesthetically displeasing landscape he criticized.[7] The
typical wheat farmer, he charged, had "too much land" for diversified
cropping "or for beautifying his home." These farmhouses, "as a class,
are unpainted frame shanties, without garden or flower or tree." The
rich farmers' land was often "covered by scraggy cattle, which need to
look after them only a few half-civilised *vaqueros*." The counterparts of
the sometimes millionaire absentee landlords were "the labourers of the
California farmer"—the "tramps, with blankets on back" who "plod"
over "our ill-kept, shadeless, dusty roads, where a house is an unwonted
landmark, and which run frequently for miles through the same man's
land." George dwells heavily on the shiftlessness and impermanence of
the landscape and links the patterns of broad-acre land use to its negative environmental effects. He quotes a "Californian gentleman" who
testified that "I have seen farms cropped for eighteen years with wheat,
and not a vine, tree, shrub or flower on the place. The roads are too wide,
and are unworked, and a nest for noxious weeds."[8] This was an image
of environmental degradation driven by land monopoly.

George widened his observations to a general theory in his later writings, but he never abandoned this vision based on the creation of a mixed
agricultural economy that would be environmentally sustainable. In
Social Problems, George reminded readers that by abolishing the land
monopoly, "agriculture would cease to be destructive and would become
more intense, obtaining more from the soil and returning what it borrowed."[9] The historian John L. Thomas comments, "In proceeding from
rent and monopoly to the theme of land and the fecundity of nature,
George was invoking an agrarian mystique that the great majority of
Americans understood." But he was doing more than sustaining an older
vision of yeoman farmers. He was also charging landed monopolies with
the responsibility for the rape of nature, and invoking an image of an
alternative and sustainable society characterized by broad distribution
of land ownership and recycling of resources.[10] "We do not return to the

earth what we take from it," he charged: "Each crop that is harvested leaves the soil the poorer. We are cutting down forests which we do not replant; we are shipping abroad, in wheat and cotton and tobacco and meat, or flushing into the sea through the sewers of great cities the elements of fertility that have been embodied in the soil by the slow processes of nature, acting for long ages."[11] The absence of a garden landscape of small farms linked with towns in agrarian harmony had further divisive consequences. Land monopoly and environmental decay accompanied racial strife. "The division of our land into these vast estates," he wrote in *Our Land and Land Policy*, "derives additional significance from the threatening wave of Asiatic immigration whose first ripples are already breaking upon our shores." What "the blacks of the African coast were to the great landlords of the southern States, the Chinese coolies may be, in fact are already beginning to be, to the great landlords of our Pacific slope." This was the concluding and clinching argument of his California prophecies.[12]

The linking of the small farm aesthetic with the preservation of racial homogeneity created a powerful image in the aftermath of the Civil War and the death of slavery. The idea spread quickly that intensive agriculture would save California from racial and class conflict. George's environmental critique would be repeatedly used by advocates of the garden as they sought to create an ideal environment for the middle classes. Despite its attempted appropriation as part of a working-class ideology in turn-of-the-century Australia and Britain, George's was fundamentally a middle-class vision in which the proletariat became small-scale property holders and social harmony prevailed.

This middle-class ideology had immense social appeal, and the appeal was at the foundation of California's environmental consciousness as well. From the 1870s to 1900, advocates of the shift to horticulture from wheat appropriated George's message, perhaps subconsciously but just as surely as if they had read every word of the *Collected Works*. The challenge to the dominance of wheat farming contained the same messages as George's text. The challenge began in the 1870s when wheat farmers themselves began to realize the drawbacks that their very specialized agriculture entailed in a world capitalist market, and hence for their own welfare. The farmers attacked the way shipping rates and the railroad monopoly undermined their welfare by obstructing competitive access to distant consumers. While many called for controls upon the railroads, others advocated a shift of products which would, through diversity, relieve the farmer's misery.

Ezra Carr, of the University of Wisconsin, appointed in 1869 as first professor of agriculture at the University of California at Berkeley, took up the challenge. He embraced the organizations representing the embattled wheat farmers, the California Farmers' Union and its successor, the Order of Patrons of Husbandry (the Grange). Carr's propagandizing on behalf of the Grange invoked George's "land monopoly" and the stranglehold of the railroads on transportation of the farmers' products. But Carr's message to the farmers involved something more than control of railroad rates. He dared to suggest to the Farmers' Union Convention in 1873 that they should abandon their monoculture entirely in favor of "other agricultural products suitable to our climate" and "a more diversified, and consequently a more independent[,] system of industry."[13] Carr recognized, however, that the climate and geography of California was so "altogether different" from that of other sections of the country that special measures would be required to break the vicious cycle of dependence on a single-crop system. In his history of *The Patrons of Husbandry on the Pacific Coast* (1875), Carr advised farmers to establish small-scale cooperative settlements. More than irrigation, he advocated the importance of forests, utilizing the theories of Marsh as he did so: "The most magnificent schemes of irrigation will prove but temporary measures of relief, unless our existing forests are spared, or an equivalent of their value as condensers and equalizers of moisture obtained by artificial planting." To obtain improved water supplies and timber for farming tasks, farmers should plant Australian eucalyptus trees. "Happily for us, Australia has given us trees, of marvellous strength, size, durability, and rapidity of growth, in the eucalyptus or sweet gum family, of which not less than thirty-five useful and ornamental species are now acclimated."[14]

Horticulturalists built upon these interrelated themes of landscape change and egalitarian social reform during the next twenty-five years. They fostered a range of self-help institutions to further their own sense of direction and cohesion, and to exert political and economic clout in the state. Largely this involved the spreading of information on high-value horticultural crops through the medium of trade- and farm-oriented newspapers such as the *California Fruit Grower* and the *Pacific Rural Press*. The growers established fruit exchanges and developed canneries and dried fruit technology to diversify their product. Fruit growers first met within the confines of the California State Agricultural Society, but, dissatisfied with that body's emphasis on sheep, cattle, and wheat and concerned about the need to combat pests and diseases specific to the fruit industry, they broke away to form their own organizations after 1880.[15] In 1881, the first California State Fruit Growers' Convention met and an Advisory Board of Horticulture was established within the State Board of Viticultural Commissioners. This became the basis in 1883 of an independent State Board of Horticulture, which gave the growers the imprimatur of the state of California. The fruit growers' conventions were soon held in conjunction with the state board meetings and were printed in the same annual reports.[16]

The fruit growers' efforts were by no means limited to the economic. They took up the "business" of fruit growing in the "broadest spirit" possible. A sympathetic observer claimed, "They not only discuss prices and markets, stocks, varieties, and the constantly multiplying details of horticulture, but they appeal to the higher intelligence of their class, and point out the larger relations of the problems involved."[17] President of the state board from 1883 to 1903, Ellwood Cooper believed that if the fruit growers continued to maintain an "unselfish interest in the general welfare," they would "eventually become a controlling interest in state affairs."[18] The journalist Charles Shinn claimed that "politicians of the cheaper sort" were "beginning to be afraid of the fruit growers, who come straight from their orchards twice a year, often with their wives to help, and sit in council with members from every other district in the state."[19] Shinn had a point. The state board, as the visible expression of horticultural power, would survive drastic state economies in the 1890s, including an attempt to abolish the board itself. In contrast, the state viticultural board was axed, and other state authorities had their activities severely curtailed under Governor James Budd in 1895.[20]

This is not to say that these horticulturalists were united. The State Fruit Growers' Convention never spoke in one voice for all of California horticulture. Divisions occurred between the supporters of Ellwood Cooper and his opponents; between northern and southern California interests; between irrigating and nonirrigating farmers; between richer and poorer farmers; and between the advocates of the different types of fruit, particularly citrus versus other fruits. In the 1870s and 1880s, however, fruit growers and other horticulturalists were united by the need to combat their common enemies in broad-acre agriculture, pastoral activities, and mining. The aggressive promotion of fruit and its appeal for new settlers never ceased to amaze the advocates of other and older industries such as wool. Sheepherding, ranchers admitted in alarm, had "greatly declined under the influence of the popular mania for fruit culture."[21]

Who were these horticulturalists? It is perhaps imprecise to call them middle class, but they were neither the poorest nor the richest in California society. They *were* "capitalists" and "entrepreneurs" in the sense that they employed labor, invested in land, pioneered new industries, and expected to make a profit, but they did not represent extremes of wealth and power. In the main they were well-educated, propertied people, often of urban and professional origins, and they frequently had been born elsewhere, in the Midwest or East. They were overwhelmingly Anglo and Protestant in origin. F. H. Babb called the horticulturalists "a most enterprising class, the pick of the land beyond the Rockies. They have come from all other occupations, have been lawyers, doctors, business men, with broad and varied experiences."[22] To call them middle class is not to deny the presence of wealthy people, however. An example was Abbot C. Kinney, a New Jersey–born citrus grower, land developer, prodigious writer of moral tracts and political and economic homilies, and owner of the agricultural paper, the *Los Angeles Saturday Post.* Kinney was the fifth-largest property holder in Los Angeles County in 1880, with $98,785 in taxable wealth.[23]

Kinney is best remembered today as the entrepreneur who built Venice, California, where "buildings were designed with Italian motifs, artificial waterways served as streets, carrying gondolas poled by singing boatmen." Kinney sponsored "improving lectures, Chautauqua meetings, and art exhibits, and provided free transportation from Los Angeles." But the masses preferred Venice beach to high culture, and in 1906 Kinney was forced to turn his Venice into a Coney Island to make it profitable. By 1930, ten years after Kinney's death in 1920, the stench from the stagnant canals had caused all but three of the sixteen miles to be filled in.[24]

Another prominent horticulturalist was John Bidwell, whose ambitious project to create a garden landscape in the midst of the wheat fields of the Sacramento Valley has already been described; still another was Norton P. Chipman, who called himself "an orchardist."[25] *Out West* identified him more with "efforts aiming to conserve the public welfare than with the money-mad race for personal aggrandisement. He particularly represents Northern and Central California, where he has been for many years a leader and a prophet of progress." In reality, Chipman was better known as a capitalist with interests in wheat farming, lumber, and the law.[26]

Few of the horticulturalists were such prominent landholders. They did not appear in John Hittell's *Resources of California,* nor among the rich mentioned in George's *Our Land and Land Policy,* nor in Ezra Carr's "landed peerage."[27] More representative were middle-range entrepreneurs or retired professionals such as Dr. O. H. Congar and Jeanne Carr, prominent residents of Pasadena. Jeanne Carr, the wife of Ezra, had been a schoolteacher, and, after her husband retired, the two moved permanently to Southern California in 1880, where they had bought land and planted a citrus grove of forty-two acres in 1877. Congar was a doctor, a University of Wisconsin graduate who arrived in 1874 and whose thirty acres "were all set to oranges, grapes, and a variety of deciduous fruits."[28] Contemporary descriptions of southern California horticulture emphasized the mixture of holdings and the relatively small sizes. A few larger holdings of five hundred acres there were, but the Australian John L. Dow described the village of San Gabriel in 1884 as surrounded by a diverse fruit production "studded at frequent intervals" with "the cosy cottage of the 10, 20, 40 or 80 acre man."[29]

Statistically, of course, California as a whole remained dominated by the large landholdings of the railroad, the cattle ranchers, and other leading capitalists. One modern estimate gives the average size of a fruit farm in 1900 as ninety-six acres, compared to four hundred acres for California farms as a whole. The "average" was "skewed by a relatively small number of huge livestock and wheat ranches." Even the "average" fruit farm size was distorted by the truly large holdings of five hundred acres or more. A well-to-do but still middle class of rural settlers had appeared as an alternative to such "factories in the field." The size of their landholdings was small because of the escalating price of land under irrigation for fruit production. Irrigation "colonies" of smaller growers, such as at Riverside and the settlement of Pasadena, were well represented in the fruit growers' conventions and raised hopes that horticulture could combat the vast imbalances Henry George had denounced.[30]

These middle-class property owners fashioned a class ideology based on the construction of an ideal garden landscape. Through this they sought to speak for the wider interests of the fruit growers and claimed to represent the larger social and moral interests of the state of California. Their annual conventions broached all aspects of social life. A vital element in the horticulturalists' drive was to develop an aesthetic concern for California's built environment; they frequently discussed how the beautification of California could be achieved with the aid of garden plantings. Women, mostly from orchardist families, took a prominent part in this work, though the promoters of floriculture, the seed merchants and nursery proprietors, were also involved. Among these women

was Sarah Cooper, whose husband was State Board of Horticulture president. She spoke and wrote regularly on the cultivation of farm and suburban gardens and advocated planting trees and flowers as part of an
aesthetic improvement of California's natural environment.

This interest in gardens rested on a moral philosophy that depicted
the business of fruit as a superior way of life. The growers presented their
work as a moral reform with its roots in a quasi-utopian worldview.
Even the crops that growers produced served moral purposes in their
view. Citrus was declared "healthy" for both mind and body, and olive
growers depicted their product as "a moral agent." The use of olive oil
as a skin treatment would remove toxic elements from the body and stem
"moral, mental and physical deterioration."[31] Temperance reform was
integral to this moral scheme. Because of the strength of this sentiment,
wine growing did not occupy a central place in the imagined landscape
of California horticulture. Not only did John Bidwell root out his
grapevines in a fit of prohibitionist pique, George Chaffey, the irrigator
of Ontario, California, was another prohibitionist, and Cooper
denounced links between the liquor interests and California politicians.[32] Grape growing and wine making did not figure much in the discussions of the fruit growers' conventions, though some leading
vignerons such as George Hussmann and L. J. Rose attended. A separate viticultural board catered to the interests of vignerons, but little discussion occurred within that board similar to the sweeping plans for
environmental renovation posed by the fruit growers. Instead, the winegrowers concentrated on "self-defense against erratic and impractical
reformers" who demanded prohibition, and on reducing the American
public's ignorance of wine.[33]

The viticulturists may have meant to include the fruit growers among
the "impractical" and "erratic." Never did the fruit growers' conventions become captured by a temperance agenda, let alone prohibition,
but temperance themes surfaced in the debates whenever these could be
linked to the advancement of health through fruit promotion. In her welcoming address to the Eleventh State Fruit Growers' Convention,
orchardist Flora Kimball of National City quoted reformers who argued
that "an unlimited use of fresh fruits as food will ultimately satisfy the
craving for intoxicating stimulants." Kimball endorsed these views and
received strong support from the audience. The "asylum for the inebri-
ate" was one of the welfare institutions "that ought to be established in
a fruit orchard, and the advancement of the temperance cause" should
be added to "your moral missions," she told the convention.[34] The gar-

den landscape would, according to Kimball, create an ideal environment in which moral thought and action could flourish.

Through an emphasis on the floral adornment of the landscape, the horticultural movement of California would stimulate home life and safeguard the raising of the next generation. "The love of the beautiful is one of the finest emotions of our nature," argued Sarah Cooper in another prominent address to the fruit growers: "It arouses within us activities that lead on to high and grand ideals, and nothing awakens and increases this love more than watching and studying the beautiful forms and colors in trees and flowers. Our homes should be surrounded by them. Our children should be trained to notice them and to study them." A knowledge "of vegetable life" in the impressionable years of youth was "one of the essentials to our intelligence," she concluded. Sarah Cooper's address was enthusiastically discussed by male as well as female garden lovers in the audience.[35]

This moral reform had a class basis, however. The growers were, after all, employers of labor who were determined to extract value and make their businesses pay. They opposed labor unions and distrusted "laboring men of all classes, men far below the level of intelligence" of themselves.[36] Attitudes toward the nonworking poor were strongly negative too. Ellwood Cooper believed the state spent too much money, and hence taxes, "upon the vicious and unfortunate"; he championed instead "the virtuous, industrious and self-supporting." Alternatives to expensive prisons should be sought in other reform initiatives, he argued. Horticulturalists believed a greener and more pleasant environment would help overcome misery caused "by drunkenness, by idleness, and . . . the extravagances of modern society." Plants could even be the antidote to crime. "No matter how degrading may have been the surroundings of little children," Cooper claimed, "as soon as their notice and attention, their responsibility, are turned towards the care of plants, their watchfulness and guardianship are manifested." Contact with plants could therefore be "a bar against surrounding evils."[37]

The moral preference for fruit also had gender dimensions. Nineteenth-century reform and turn-of-the-century feminists both identified the horticultural landscape as one that allowed the uplift, and even the liberation, of women. Charlotte Perkins Gilman's utopian tract of 1915, *Herland,* depicted a feminist colony thriving without men, all centered on the raising of fruit in "a system of intensive agriculture." Here, in "the mighty garden" constructed by the women horticulturalists, was "Mother Earth, bearing fruit."[38] California was the area of the United

States upon which Gilman projected these dreams. The valley of Herland had a climate "like that of California, and citrus fruits, figs, and olives grew abundantly." These primordial images drawn from Arcadian legends and biblical references were reinforced by the reality of California horticulture. Gilman had lived in Pasadena for several years around 1890, and she gushed as freely over the beauty and utility of the landscape as did Frances Willard. These utopian possibilities were acted out by some who saw California as the hope of single and independent women. A Woman's Floral Colony established in San Mateo in 1890, backed by Leland Stanford, involved one hundred women, all former schoolteachers, who bought small blocks of land under contracts to produce seeds, flowers, and bulbs.[39]

As the example of Sarah Cooper indicated, women took an active role in the state horticultural board, and the image the board projected was one centered on the value of the family farm, where women could prosper as growers. Harriet Strong's successful walnut and pampas grass business in Whittier stood out nationally,[40] but the State Fruit Growers' Conventions revealed many other successful female growers, such as Flora Kimball and Mrs. L. U. McCann, as examples of the way horticulture would be a civilizing influence on the California landscape. Said McCann, "I belong to the vanguard of the great army of women whom the evolution of the age has freed from many a cumbersome care, and who look up to the wide open doors of horticulture for possibilities undreamed of by their mothers."[41] Women's "progress" and civilization already formed a familiar alliance in traditional eighteenth- and nineteenth-century agrarian rhetoric and political economy. Here in California, the material progress of small-scale horticulture not only cemented this strong cultural identification but extended it.[42] The State Fruit Growers' Convention formed the Women's Agricultural and Horticultural Union of California in 1900 and sought to publicize and thereby encourage the employment of women in landscape gardening, arboriculture, and forestry, as well as promote the activities "of working amateurs" in suburban gardens. It was a Californian delegate who had proposed at the 1899 meeting of the International Council of Women in London that an international union of agricultural and horticultural women be formed.[43]

Race and ethnicity also connected with the civilization theme. Horticulture's champions affirmed Anglo-Saxon superiority as part of their rejection of the labor and ethnic concomitants of the wheat and pastoral economies. The initial targets were Hispanic. Native Americans were too marginal a presence to evoke anything other than regret at their ill-treatment by miners and ranchers. Indeed, prominent horticulturalists like Abbot Kinney and John and Annie Bidwell crusaded on behalf of Native Americans in California.[44] Later, the alleged disorder of Chinese and Japanese market gardens would come under attack, but in the 1880s the specter of the Japanese and Chinese as competitors in farm ownership and production, rather than as a problematic workforce likely to raise prejudices among white workers, still lay largely in the future. It was the Hispanic vaqueros and Basque shepherds who first encountered the horticulturalists' distaste. In her welcoming address to the 1889 convention, Flora Kimball rejoiced that the "Yankee's ploughshare" had taken over from "the retreating herds of Mexican cattle."[45] So contemptuous of the shepherds was she that they were not even singled out from the animals they tended. In affirming the garden, the middle class staked out its preferences against these ethnic groups.[46]

Horticulturalists linked their attack on labor and ethnic diversity to their environmental agenda, and this in turn meant they took aim at the rich as much as at the poor. They mounted a sustained attack on wheat and cattle barons and on mining and other industries regarded as extractive rather than environmentally sustainable. It is ironic that the horticulturalists should indict wheat, since apologists for the wheat industry had earlier seen mining as the extractive and environmentally insensitive villain. Grain farmers of the Sacramento Valley spearheaded the fight against mining in the battles of the 1870s and early 1880s to control erosion and stop flooding in order to prevent mine debris from ruining agriculture.[47] For John Bidwell, it was not a "pleasing scene to see havoc made of hills, and mountains, and stately forests, and a once lovely prospect changed to a desolation" by "hydraulic mining." Agriculture, Bidwell concluded, "is the only enduring interest."[48] But by the 1880s, strong opposition had already developed toward the domination of California's new prosperity in agriculture by wheat. These animosities were deeply informed by the Georgian critique of land monopoly.

Horticulturalists asserted that wheat should give way to fruit and the complementary forest cover. One issue was the likely future unprofitability of wheat under competition from Canada, Russia, and Australia. John Bidwell personally testified to the feeling of helplessness of farmers at the mercy of distant wheat markets and the low profits these markets returned.[49] Yet the critics of wheat specialization also emphasized, as George had done, the environmental drawbacks of broad-acre agriculture and linked the triumph of horticulture with the creation of a more sustainable form of farming. "That wheat culture exhausts fertility," Bidwell told the State Agricultural Society, "does not admit of argument. . . . We must make restoration."[50] Norton P. Chipman addressed the State Fruit Growers' Convention in November 1888 and focused on declining yields that resulted from reliance on a single crop. "An inflexible law of nature is not to be ignored. The soil cannot be made to give up its properties without exhaustion, unless we return in some form an equivalent." Chipman urged wheat farmers and fruit growers to cooperate and live in peaceful coexistence, but the nub of his message was that wheat should in many instances give way.[51]

Perhaps the most remarkable statement was that of one ideologue of the garden paradise, B. M. Lelong, small-scale orchardist and secretary of the State Board of Horticulture between 1887 and 1901. Lelong contrasted in 1892 the condition of the state under the impact of fruit with that "even a few years ago." Virtually plagiarizing Henry George's *Our Land and Land Policy*, Lelong reported: "Then, for many months of the year, the country seemed a barren waste, with here and there great bands of sheep and cattle, eating grass, flower, and shrub, until the picture was one of sheer desolation. A few uncouth vaqueros with their wild mustangs and wilder ways, were about the only human beings to be seen. Houses were separated by leagues of distance, and when one was found it stood in some bleak place, where the desolation was seemingly greater than in the open fields. . . . No garden, no vineyard, not even a tree or shrub to keep off the fierce rays of the summer sun."[52] The horticultural journalist Charles Shinn made the point even plainer. Drawing on the ideas of Edward Bellamy as well as Henry George, he declared that "at the very root of the social order lies the land tenure question."[53] "Twenty years ago," he wrote, "the tendency of things in California was to destroy the small farmer, the fruit-grower, the ten-acre colonist, the gardener, and the garden. Vast empires were being conquered by capitalists, stolen from the government, seized from the herdsman and miner, watered by riverlike canals, and sown to wheat and alfalfa." But, under the impact of "the disintegrating influences that oppose a landed aristocracy," Californians had begun to "to destroy the fabric" of wheat culture. By 1890, "the small homestead set in the midst of a garden is becoming the California ideal."[54]

Middle-class radicalism derived from the attack on the land monopoly affected more than the evaluation of environmental impacts resulting from farming, mining, and ranching. Georgian ideas also influenced these Californian horticulturalists' attacks on the despoliation of the state's natural treasures. George had condemned the "monopolisation" of such natural resources as timber and water as well as land.[55] Later, Abbot Kinney, influenced by both Henry George and Edward Bellamy's nationalist philosophy, told the state horticultural board that "we are all socialists or nationalists to the extent of admitting that certain things are of the nature of monopoly. These things we confess can only be properly administered for the whole people by the people's representatives." Among these things was forestry.[56] As a southern Californian citrus grower, Kinney's main concern was to employ George for the benefit of the fruit industry. Without adequate watershed protection, he argued, the flow of streams would be curtailed, the supply of water diminished, and flooding and erosion maximized.[57]

George's ideas could be made to serve more radical environmental causes—and were by some Californians. John Muir is famous as the preeminent advocate of wilderness preservation in the late nineteenth century. But his occupation from the 1880s till his death was not simply that of a journalist. He became, through marriage, a horticulturalist and successfully managed his family's Martinez orchard. Like more economically motivated fruit growers, Muir attacked the rich landed interests that sought to destroy the natural wilderness. Muir made good use of George's attack on the principle of private ownership of land in fighting the alienation of part of Yosemite National Park for the Hetch Hetchy Reservoir.[58] Muir condemned "this grossly destructive commercial scheme" as dominated by the "Almighty Dollar" and bent on destroying the "people's parks."[59]

HORTICULTURE, THE GARDEN, AND PRESERVATION OF THE FORESTS

Modern wilderness preservation is almost the antithesis of the manicured landscape of farms and fields that horticulturalists desired. Yet paradoxically, it was the aspirations of fruit growers to turn California into a garden that stimulated, more than anything else, the appreciation of the state's natural beauty and great resources. The desire to protect the native flora, particularly the forests, had obvious links with the economic interests of agriculture in the West. This is a commonplace of historiography, and the argument is based on sound evidence. As Abbot Kinney put it bluntly in his denunciation of the timber interests: "No forests, no farms."[60] Those who sought to create a garden landscape in the interests of horticulture soon discovered the practical importance of trees to the conservation of moisture, especially in the mountainous catchment regions of California.[61]

If the new enthusiasm for native flora was partly pragmatic, there was more to the horticulturalists' growing love of the natural California environment than economic interest. Economics cannot explain the growing preference for preservation of Californian flora, unless horticulturalist thought is considered an elaborate hoax, since it was the middle-class women gardeners who, above all, waxed eloquent on the ethical dimensions of preservation in the 1880s. Not only did these women praise native trees as essential to the watersheds, they simultaneously hailed native flowers and grasses for their beauty as well as their utility. Nowhere was appreciation of the natural environment stronger than in these ideologues of the garden landscape who spoke at the horticulturalists' conventions. Their debates in the 1880s and 1890s reflected a growing regard for California's natural scenery and treasures. So much so that the key farmers' organ, the *Pacific Rural Press*, could observe in 1891 the change in middle-class sensibility: "Some time or other the thought that the proper plants to grow in any given place are those native to it, may perhaps spread until it finally reaches popular acceptances." That time had not quite been reached, but a fashionable slogan announced that "the proper plants for California gardens are California plants."[62]

An important part of Sarah Cooper's agenda was an enthusiasm for native plants. She proclaimed a "desire to have our native plants looked after." This concern was stimulated by personal experience of European settlement's impact. Cooper noted the rapid decline of the wildflowers, from the time of her emigration to California in 1870, the result of the "watchful farming at my home," which had substituted other vegetation and eliminated the competing natives. She lamented that "one *now* can scarcely get enough for a bouquet." Cooper also noted that demand elsewhere for California's wildflowers had its impact. Native flowers were, because of their novelty and beauty, increasingly sought by florists in the East, and this demand for the unusual had reverberations in California itself. "Those of us who have rural homes," she counseled, should be making "efforts to preserve in nooks and corners about our ranches the native flora of our respective localities."[63]

Their love of the natural beauty of flowers and trees in the garden setting led horticulturalists to find sources of beauty elsewhere in the existing landscape. One male fruit grower urged gardeners to "beautify our homes in proportion to our climate" in conformity with "the paradise of nature painted on almost every mountain side."[64] From cultivation of native flowers, it was but a short step toward a higher valuation of California's native trees in their natural habitats. The Pasadena garden expert Jeanne Carr rejoiced at the spread of arboriculture and landscape gardening and the fact that it raised sensibilities concerning forest preservation. In horticulture she found a sign that "man" was bringing under control "his own selfish and destructive instincts, which have hitherto allowed one generation to impoverish many succeeding ones, by the reckless destruction of forests."[65] State Board of Horticulture reports that in the early 1880s had focused on fruit trees alone included within five years extensive discussion of the beauties of native trees. The "mighty" sequoias won praise from many fruit growers, and the Monterey pines and cypresses were declared to be as good as any imported tree for citrus windbreaks or the decoration of farms.[66]

Ideas of preservation flourished among the horticulturalists based on "sentiment" and notions of moral and spiritual uplift. F. H. Clark of Yountville approached the redwoods with "reverence" and called for a section of the "noble" forest to be "set aside" in perpetuity.[67] To wander among them recalled the "grandeur" of antiquity and the perfection of symmetry, he argued. Horticulturalists backed, through the fruit growers' conventions, the campaigns of John Muir and others to stop the destruction of the Sierra and preserve it as part of the national forests and parks. Many, like John H. Fowler of Santa Rosa, urged that "the redwood must be regarded as a special endowment by the Almighty to this, our more than favored State."[68]

As early as 1888, the horticulturalists urged Congress to pass a Forestry Bill proposed by the California State Board of Forestry under Kinney. This bill would withdraw all federal timber lands for sale until surveyed for watershed purposes. The State Fruit Growers' Convention also urged the state to withhold all unsold school lands from sale and put them under the control of the State Board of Forestry for "sale, renewal, and preservation of the timber."[69] Neither of these measures succeeded, but the fruit growers did back the successful reservation of sections of the San Bernardino Mountains as national forest under action of President Benjamin Harrison in 1892, and the creation of Yosemite and Sequoia National Parks.[70]

The links between horticulture and valuation of the natural environment were revealed in John Muir's friendship with the Carrs and Bidwells. Ezra had taught Muir at the University of Wisconsin, and in California they renewed the acquaintance, but the deeper and more interesting friendship was that between Jeanne Carr and Muir. The two engaged in a long correspondence between the late 1860s and 1879. Sometimes Muir seemed tempted by Carr's descriptions of the constructed southern California landscape. "Your description of the orange lands makes me more than ever eager to see them," Muir wrote in January 1877; and, from Los Angeles later that year: "I've seen your sunny Pasadena and the patch called yours. Everything about here pleases me, and I feel sorely tempted to take Dr. [O. H.] Congar's advice and invest in an orange-patch myself." In 1880, Muir made good this aspiration, by marriage, and became "an expert orchardist."[71]

For his part, Muir employed the garden imagery in a way designed to play upon the aesthetic of the horticultural paradise. He called the doomed valley of Hetch Hetchy "a grand landscape garden" second in value only to Yosemite, and his image of it was not of a "meadow" but of "groves" and parks and stone monuments; in "its flowery park-like floor," he could almost be describing Frederick Olmstead's Central Park. Reflecting his profound Protestant heritage, Muir also likened Hetch Hetchy to the Garden of Eden and accused the utilitarian arguments behind the decision to flood the valley for a dam of being "curiously like those of the devil, devised for the destruction of the first garden."[72]

The formation of the Sierra Club in 1892, the first major organization devoted to preservation of the forests, did not mark a break between the horticulturalists and the preservationists. The club's membership in 1900 was over 90 percent urban and suburban,[73] but the fruit growers were among those "lovers of nature" who had prepared the way for the new organization. The Sierra Club initiative won strong support from the older-style arboriculture group centered on the journal edited by Charles Sargent, *Garden and Forest*. This journal had prominent Californian horticultural contributors like Charles Shinn in its ranks, and Shinn campaigned through the journal's pages on behalf of the preservation of old-growth forests and the creation of forest reserves and national parks.[74]

Horticulturalists in the Central Valley and elsewhere also valued the high country of the Sierra as a recreational zone that complemented their economic activity. The valley was, despite the claims that it could be turned into a garden paradise, unpleasantly hot in summer, and families would take their leave of the searing temperatures there and in the southland for vacations in the cooler mountain air. John and Annie Bidwell, for example, were lovers of Mount Shasta and the forests that surrounded it in the north. Other Californian horticulturalists like Jeanne and Ezra

Carr shared this enthusiasm for camping in the Sierra and the coastal ranges, while mountaineering also fostered an appreciation for the high country.[75] This recreational impulse may have underpinned, as much as the desire for tree cover, the growing appreciation of Californians for the wild Sierra in the 1880s, but the phenomenon also illustrated the way the feelings that Californians had for the plains and the mountains, the wild and the tamed of nature, developed in a symbiotic relationship as part of the projected garden paradise. The historian Kevin Starr has commented that Yosemite epitomized the essence of this relationship: "Its configuration of mountain and valley was a grand paradigm of California's geography as a whole. . . . Its soaring cliffs seemed to hold safe from violation the fabled Garden of the West so that it might be there when Californians needed a reminder of what the land offered."[76]

Though Muir courted the support of the horticulturalists, tensions existed between the two views. Muir's letters reveal a divergence of aesthetic sensibility—between the idea of a contrived beauty of human creation, and the idea of a transcendent natural beauty—that presaged the division between the preservationist and the utilitarian conservationists after 1900. Of Carr's ambitious Pasadena garden, Carmelita, Muir jibed, "You know how little real sympathy I can give in such play-garden schemes."[77] Muir thought that "those lemon and orange groves would do, perhaps, to make a living, but for a garden I should not have anything less than a piece of pure nature."[78] With Dr. Congar, his former classmate at the University of Wisconsin, Muir toured Pasadena in 1877 and "drove down through the settlements eastward, and saw the best orange groves and vineyards." But he seemed, as he reflected, to be gently parting company with his friends from Wisconsin, though the break was not clearly made. "The mountains," Muir added, "I as usual met alone. Although so gray and silent and unpromising they are full of wild gardens and ferneries, and lilyries."[79]

Most California horticulturalists did not see the issue of preservation of nature in such all-or-nothing terms. Sarah Cooper's love of native flowers, for example, did not mean that wild areas should be untouched. Like most other horticulturalists, she was an environmental improver rather than a preservationist. She urged the cultivation rather than the simple preservation of these plants. The native flora should be indirectly preserved through the hands of (wo)man as part of the development of a colorful and pleasant garden environment to surround Californian homes. Since the object was the creation of diversity and beauty, not purity of the native stock, she also advocated an eclectic adoption of flowers and shrubs from all over the world, but especially from compatible climates like Australia's. Echoing the acclimatizing sentiments of her husband and Mueller, she argued that "California ought to take the lead in the activity that is now going on in collecting the rare and beautiful things of other countries." Speaking of the E. ficifolia, the red-flowering gum, Cooper exclaimed, "The eucalypti in California make a much finer appearance than those growing in their native home." Jeanne Carr shared this idea of improvement, despite all of her sympathies for Muir, and for Yosemite's natural wonders. Carr saw the garden concept not only as a means of appreciating and preserving the natural environment but also "as indicating the final triumph of man over wild nature."[80]

A parallel attitude was taken by the architects of State Board of Forestry policy. The board's chairman, Abbot Kinney, argued for creation of a balanced landscape in which both imported and native trees would be appreciated. In the north of the state, he argued, "we find the forest covering a larger proportion of land than is considered necessary for the best interests of agriculture and climate." Moreover, these forests were able to regenerate naturally, "so that the duties of a forester would largely consist in protecting and thinning out the new growths so as to make them commercially valuable." In contrast, Kinney claimed, in "the south the proportion of forest is far less than it should be."[81] Board policy pointed toward a balance—an ideal amount of tree cover that did not always occur in nature but must be contrived by human hand. The Sierra Club, too, desired such a "balance between the two sides of conservation—aesthetic and economic"—in these early years of its existence. In Garden and Forest, Mark B. Kerr noted that the club had influential San Francisco backers who, though "lovers of nature," were driven by "a conviction that the future agricultural development of the Pacific coast is at stake."[82] A State Board of Forestry official agreed that the "necessity of organizing and perfecting a system of irrigation" through forest preservation was a matter of great importance to the club, because it was a matter vital to California's economy. Water would "make gardens of her deserts," and guarantee "future prosperity and greatness."[83]

From a viewpoint more aesthetic than utilitarian, Charles Shinn also urged a balance between natural beauty and created natural beauty. In the course of deploring the destruction of timber and arguing for a controlled cut he declared: "An ideal California is yet possible, but a few more years of neglect will forever destroy that ideal. California should be a state with one-third of its surface one vast garden and orchard, one-third occupied by great and permanent forests, yielding a revenue almost as large as that of the lowlands, and one-third snow peaks, wild Alps of rocks, high, open pastures and level tule islands reclaimed and changed into such Grass-fields as those of Holland."[84] Shinn took this stand despite his championing of the redwoods and his vocal role in supporting the Sierra Club.

The afforestation crusade fitted this concept of balance. After 1890, the concern with preservation of the existing forests of coastal redwoods and giant sequoias became more urgent, but was always combined with appreciation for imported trees that would complement this natural landscape. Before 1890 horticulturalists and their allies in urban and suburban areas had already accumulated much experience in trying to make the landscape greener by introducing new trees, particularly to the San Francisco Bay Area, the burgeoning fruit lands, and other arid lands in the southern part of the state and the Central Valley. In many parts of California, adequate tree cover was lacking, and this was where the horticulturalists attempted to establish their garden paradise first. The garden aesthetic was of great importance to the tree importation craze. To fulfill their ideal, horticulturalists looked toward Australia, a land where similar climate and land/human ratios existed; the trees that succeeded there would do equally well, they hoped, in California.

CHAPTER 3

Trees in the Garden

The Australian Invasion

A German authority, Dr. Heinrich Mayr, surveyed the state of American forestry for *Garden and Forest* in 1890. He was most impressed by what he saw in California. "In fifty years," Mayr reported enthusiastically, "it will be inconceivable that California, the beautiful fruit-garden of the Union, was once treeless. Amid magnificent forests of Australian Eucalyptus and Acacia" a foreign visitor would "be inclined to doubt that he is really in America. The hard, sun-baked plains have been transformed into a sub-tropical garden under the influence of this delightful climate."[1]

Eucalypts appealed to Californians for a variety of reasons, but Mayr's linking of the garden with the forest illuminated the campaign's core. The Pacific plant exchange was spearheaded by horticulturalists who first and foremost imported fruit trees. Many of these trees came from Asia and Europe, but they included lemon and orange stock from Australia. The Australian navel orange was almost as widely sought in the 1880s as other varieties but was supplanted by the superior Washington navel adopted at Riverside.[2] Australian native trees also served the horticultural landscape. In part, the attraction was pragmatic. Without trees there would be no water; without water there would be no horticulture. The horticulturalists' simple equation gained force through the forest famine debate that Marsh had stimulated. In some parts of California, conserving the tree cover and hence water supplies meant preserving primeval forests, but in others it meant the fashioning humanmade landscapes of forests to complement the fruit gardens then being promoted. Concern for tree cover was, however, more than simple utilitarian conservation of water and soil. The demand for eucalyptus and other Australian trees reflected the horticulturalists' aesthetic considerations: the craze was integral to creating a garden landscape that would signal the transformation of California from its mining base and make the land more suitable for middle-class civilization.

Despite the dramatic impact of eucalyptus on California, its history remains largely untold. Even those who have written perceptively about the invasion have tended to divorce the importation from its Pacific and global contexts. Historians have only been interested in what the eucalyptus has meant for California's identity, not the part the plants played in a now forgotten transnational story. The few accounts that have dealt with the eucalypt in California treated it in isolation from such themes. For Kevin Starr, the most recent and distinguished contributor to the debate, transplanting the eucalypts helped the "materializing" of the "California dream" through landscape design.[3] Starr analyzes the way Americans have imposed their dream on the land and, in the process, materially altered California. For others, like Viola Warren, writing in 1962, "the mere outline of a eucalyptus tree against the horizon serves to identify California to the rest of America, because our state alone has the tree, and we have it in fantastic abundance."[4]

This gloss of Californian distinctiveness must be qualified. The spread of eucalypts was more than a local story. It was a widespread, almost global, phenomenon. The eucalyptus was already extensively planted in southern Italy and Spain in the 1860s, and in Algeria. Subsequently its reach extended to many other countries, such as South Africa, Palestine, Chile, India, and Brazil. Few countries in the warmer climate zones escaped significant impact from "emigrant eucalypts" in the nineteenth century, and the invasion continues.[5] California's experience was part of a pattern of adaptation in areas with "tree deficiency" and climates similar to those in Australia. Even within the United States, the use of eucalyptus trees was not completely confined to California, since the genus flourished in Hawaii. Relatively small parts of southern Texas, New Mexico, Arizona, and Florida proved somewhat hospitable on the mainland: in all of these places developers tried the genus, but cold winter temperatures prevented eucalypts from taking over.[6] What is unusual about the Californian plantings today is the relative importance of aesthetics. In parts of the third world, eucalyptus trees continue to provide wood for the fires of the poor, and sturdy but rough hardwood building materials. Fuel and shelter figured prominently in American plantings, too, but aesthetic considerations loomed larger than in many other places in the adaptation of this Australian genus.

The most important conduit was not originally across the Pacific. The story of eucalyptus transfers to California had its origins in Mueller's European contacts. In the German-born botanist's work can be found not only the idea of mass transplanting of eucalypts but also the complex aesthetic of planting that comprised both cultural and economic considerations. Mueller was already corresponding with European botanists on the export of the eucalyptus when a member of the French Acclimatisation Society, Prosper Ramel, visited him in 1854. Ramel noted the rapid growth of blue gum (*Eucalyptus globulus*) in the Melbourne Botanic Gardens and sent seeds home to France, whence he assisted in the tree's extensive planting in Algeria.[7] From France, *E. globulus* was introduced to Italy in 1868, where it was planted in the region of the Roman campagna known as the Pontine Marshes.[8] Ramel's ideas were soon widely known in many countries, including the United States, and were used to justify the planting of eucalypts in California. But the introduction of the genus into California had already begun.

The exact date of introduction of the eucalyptus to California is unknown, but it seems to have accompanied the gold rush. Hans Hermann Behr initiated cultivation in San Francisco sometime before 1853. A student of the famed geographer Alexander von Humboldt, Behr was a German immigrant who had spent the years from 1844 to 1847 in Australia studying the native flora, and there he had met Mueller. Behr returned to Germany and then went to California in 1851, where "as a result of his friendship with Mueller" he received "a large number of Australian species" for introduction.[9] In 1881, Behr prepared a report for the California State Horticultural Society on "Mueller's Select Extra-Tropical Plants," and Mueller was made an honorary corresponding member of the society.[10] Behr remained an important figure in Californian science until after the turn of the century, and through his Australian connections the claims for Australian plants were advanced.[11] But the influence of Mueller and Behr could not have been achieved without a pattern of wider Pacific contacts. Australians in search of the big gold strike brought seed with them to California in the 1850s, and by the end of that decade a number of nurseries advertised eucalyptus seed and seedlings for sale.[12] Another contributor was Bishop William H. Taylor, who visited Australia in 1863 on an evangelistic tour for the Methodist cause and sent seeds home to his wife. She planted them in her Alameda garden and dis-

tributed thousands. According to one source, at least one million eucalyptus trees had been planted by 1874, at the beginning of the main invasion.[13]

This early enthusiasm rested largely on ornamental planting to create
a garden aesthetic. Charles Nordoff, who wrote the most famous and
influential of the early travel descriptions of American California, enthusiastically reported the success of these plantings as part of his efforts to
promote California as a bountiful garden and traveler's paradise. "The
eucalyptus, or Australian gum, is deservedly a favorite tree in all parts
of California," he wrote in 1872. Nordoff was impressed by the tree's
prodigious growth: "It has made, in favorable places, a growth of
twenty-five feet in a single season." The advantages of the tree for the
creation of a green, abundant environment did not rest merely on the
tree's growing power, however. Nordoff dwelt also upon its beauty and
its place in the creation of a contrived landscape, when he emphasized
that its "bluish-green foliage contrasts finely with such trees as the lively
Monterey Cypress."[14] In subsequent years, many horticulturalists were
to make similar enthusiastic comments on the beauty of the eucalypts.
Byron Clark of Pasadena urged the use of eucalypts as well as the *Grevillea robusta* because of their colors and shapes. Eucalypts, Clark told
the State Fruit Growers' Convention, were "tall and majestic." They
"have the additional charm of handsome flowers," and should be used
not to reflect an existing aesthetic but "to *create* a landscape that will be
a constant delight to the beholder, be it December or June." He urged
gardeners to give preference to these evergreen trees in "this semi-
tropical climate."[15]

ELLWOOD COOPER AND THE BOOM OF THE 1870S

Mass eucalyptus planting accelerated in the early 1870s. There followed "so avid" an enthusiasm that at times the planting "became
almost a mania."[16] Whether the motives for the mania were ornamental
or not, no one did more to popularize the eucalyptus than Ellwood
Cooper. Born of Quaker stock in Lancaster County, Pennsylvania, in
1829, Cooper worked in the import-export trade in Philadelphia in the
1850s and then lived in Port-au-Prince, Haiti, where he worked as an
agent in the shipping business. In 1868, he toured the West Coast of
the United States after traveling to Central America, and, liking especially the coastal region of southern California, settled permanently just
northwest of the town of Santa Barbara at Goleta in 1870. From

William W. Hollister, Santa Barbara's leading capitalist, Cooper pur-
chased a property that he named "Ellwood." Cooper would live there
for the next forty-two years, cultivating fruit as one of the state's most
prominent horticulturalists. Soon he introduced walnuts and olives,
becoming the pioneer in the development of these industries in California. Cooper also began to plant, almost immediately, row upon row
of Australian eucalypts.[17]

In 1876 Cooper published *Forest Culture and Eucalyptus Trees*. This
work of more than two hundred pages is a curious compendium. It opens
with a lecture he gave in 1875 at the short-lived Santa Barbara College,
of which Cooper was then president. This lecture contained much about
Cooper's own horticultural and moral philosophy. Cooper also drew on
a variety of authorities on eucalypts. Among his sources were the catalogue of Anderson and Hall, the Sydney seed merchants, and the writings of Franklin Hough, George Perkins Marsh, Prosper Ramel, and others. But the most important of his citations came from Mueller. In fact,
Cooper published two versions of Mueller's works with, confusingly
enough, the same name and identical publication details assigned to
each. The second and longer *Forest Culture and Eucalyptus Trees*, a
work of more than four hundred pages, was little more than a compila-
tion of Mueller's writings with a brief preface. Cooper had corresponded
with Thomas Adamson Jr., the United States consul general in Melbourne. Adamson had sent Cooper copies of Mueller's pamphlets and
speeches and had received from Mueller permission to republish them
in the United States. The other, somewhat shorter, version of *Forest Culture and Eucalyptus Trees* contained heavy quotations from other
forestry experts, as well as much of Cooper's own material, in addition
to Mueller's major texts.[18] That Cooper borrowed so heavily from
Mueller should not be surprising, since Mueller was by 1876 the world's
leading authority on eucalypts.[19] But Mueller's larger attempt to create
an abundant garden of resources for human beautification and suste-
nance was congenial to Cooper's own emerging worldview. Through
Cooper's efforts, Mueller's impact on the Californian environment
would be considerable.

Cooper's own arguments in *Forest Culture and Eucalyptus Trees* also
drew environmental parallels between Australia and California using the
evidence of an American, T. W. Herkimer. Herkimer had worked for ten
years in Victoria and Tasmania, the home of the blue gum. As superin-
tendent of the construction gang building the telegraph line from the
north of Tasmania to the colonial capital of Hobart, Herkimer had spent

a great deal of time in the Australian bush. "I have seen Blue Gums larger and taller than I have seen redwoods," he reported. Reassuringly, Herkimer concluded that southern Australia was in climate "very similar to the Redwood districts of California," and hence suitable for acclimatization projects.[20]

As with the earlier plantings, Cooper's advocacy did not neglect the ornamental aspect. Eucalyptus trees Cooper constantly depicted as stately giants that would bring a "general increase" of "beauty" to California.[21] To these ornamental considerations Cooper joined other more practical questions. Trees could stabilize erosion, increase rainfall, produce lush vegetation, and control other climatic factors as discussed by Marsh and the Vermonter's more extravagant disciples. Of these considerations raised by Marsh, the most important was the argument of shelter. Much of California was, for Cooper, as alien and unclothed a land as the Australian landscape was to British colonists. He therefore advocated "belts of trees" in a passage stimulated by the example of shelterbelts in the Prairie states, where the settlers were said to be planting "one hundred and fifty million trees annually."[22] Belts 100 to 150 feet wide at each quarter mile should be planted at right angles with the prevailing winds, and lining all the highways as well. This plan included unproductive land as well as farms. Cooper asserted that one-quarter of all farmland should be covered with trees. This would not reduce agricultural productiveness, he believed. Drawing on Marsh's suggestion for the whole country, Cooper insisted "that the three fourths of the surface will produce more, if protected by trees planted on the other fourth, than the whole would without the trees." Consequently the farmer lost "nothing in the productiveness of his farm." Rather, he increased "the certainty of his crops" and eliminated "one fourth of his labor."[23]

Cooper also claimed eucalypts would solve pressing economic problems of erosion that California's farmers suffered with special severity from hydraulic gold mining, grazing, and forest fires. In dry, desolate spaces and on land affected by erosion and flooding, argued Cooper, farmers could plant the gulches with blue gum "to prevent further washing" and halt farm deterioration. Indeed, Cooper called for cover on "all steep side-hills inconvenient to cultivate, or any waste lands that are non-productive."[24]

Eucalypts were, moreover, a staple timber in Australia, Cooper noted, and could surely be so used in California. In this way, Cooper was one of the first to stress the economic potential of eucalypts for his state. Californians needed hardwood for their expanding economy, for fences, piles, wharves, railway sleepers, shipbuilding, and firewood. Fortunately, these were some of the most common uses of the hardwood eucalypts. Not just any hardwood tree could be an economic success, however. Eucalypts satisfied the problem of the labor shortage. They required little effort in planting and no care afterward while they shot toward the sky. Eucalypts were hardy plants, he reported, and ideally suited to dry Mediterranean climates. They did not require irrigation and could thrive in poor soils. A related economic advantage lay in the character of eucalyptus seed. Mueller had stressed "the extraordinary facility and quickness with which the seeds are raised, scarcely any care being requisite in nursery works."[25] Eucalyptus seeds were also abundant, light and easy to transport. One ounce of blue gum seeds contained 10,112 seeds, while *Pinus pinaster,* a common exotic considered for plantation use, yielded 730 seeds to the ounce.[26] But what impressed Cooper most of all as a potential economic asset was the extraordinary growth of eucalypts outside their native environment. Superior soil and the absence of predators in the form of native birds and insects that ate up to one-third of the leaf production of gum trees in Australia favored rapid growth in suitable exotic locations.[27]

Cooper's text involved another innovation. Drawing again on Mueller, Cooper went beyond the common fixation with blue gum to advocate the potential of other eucalypts. He was already aware of reports that blue gum thrived best in moist, coastal areas with fair rainfall, mist and fog, and moderate temperatures. Although the tree was not suited to the desert locations of the south or the dry interior valleys, other eucalyptus trees could be adapted to this purpose. Cooper advocated for the hotter and drier locations *E. rostrata,* or river red gum (today known as *E. camaldulensis*), claiming that the profits on the sale of hardwood would outstrip that of any American wood.[28]

The appeal to economic interest rested on the assumption that planting must pay if the scheme was to work in a frontier society based on private ownership of land and other resources. Cooper invoked the spirit of American republicanism, in contrast to the theme of governmental direction found in European and British imperial conservation thought of the period.[29] Self-interest, Cooper believed, was a necessary wellspring of action under an "independent, free Republic," in which "the State is powerless in the execution of any [such] measure." Realistically Cooper argued that his and similar efforts could only succeed "by convincing owners of land that financially it will be a great success. Individual effort alone must accomplish the work."[30] Cooper's own instincts and those of many late-nineteenth-century American conservationists meshed here with Marsh's distrust of big government.

Despite the prominence of economic arguments, Cooper's pro-eucalyptus stance revealed a much broader philosophy. Behind the utilitarian arguments, Cooper displayed a persistent aesthetic preference for a green and tree-covered landscape and the belief that California's well-endowed environment could still be improved by the introduction of tall trees. Cooper invited his readers to "contemplate the beauty, the grandeur, the productiveness of the great valleys . . . and of every strip of arable land in the state, with belts of Eucalyptus-trees planted as I have recommended. With such shelter California would become the paradise of the world."[31] Only the "prevailing high wind, and an uncertain, as well as an insufficient quantity of rain-fall" stood between much of the state and "perfection." Trees would "moderate the wind, increase the rain" and bring about that perfect condition. Whereas in the East, earlier settlers found what they regarded as an abundant and luxurious Eden, in the West, Americans sought to manufacture their Edenic landscape with the help of trees.[32]

This aspect of Cooper's work had a strong moral and religious foundation, which went back to his Quaker upbringing. As principal of Santa Barbara College he emphasized its Christian but nondenominational character. The "pure morality and piety of the scriptures, excluding everything sectarian and denominational" underlay his educational system. Morality was strongly allied with religion in the college prospectus, pupils were denied access to such amusements as the theater, and tobacco was strictly forbidden on the campus grounds. The college would inculcate the American work ethic and a strict discipline. Work, Cooper argued, "refines the mind and strengthens the body. Nothing is so dangerous as idleness."[33] This work ethic he carried into his environmentalism, and he linked it to the notion of environmental improvement through practical action. "A blessing" was due, in Jonathan Swift's aphorism, to the "man who would make two blades of grass grow in place of one," but, Cooper insisted, even more to the man who "plants a tree where nothing grew before."[34]

Cooper practiced what he preached by planting some fifty thousand eucalypts on his 2,000-acre Ellwood Ranch in the early 1870s.[35] Ultimately he would plant over two hundred thousand. But he did not plant them as a single species, as was common later. Cooper's ranch was a classic example of the attempt to create a diverse garden-style agriculture, aesthetically pleasing, morally uplifting, and economically profitable, all at the same time. Despite his enthusiasm for blue gum in coastal locations such as his own, Cooper constantly experimented with different varieties. Nor did he plant them in massed forest formations, but rather in diverse clumps, groves, and windbreaks as set out in *Forest Culture*.

Of great importance to the story of the garden landscape is the fact that Cooper combined his interest in eucalypts with extensive horticultural pursuits tied to his aesthetic. His 250-acre olive orchard was the first in the state; he also devoted 1,000 acres to deciduous fruits. An exemplar of "Yankee" ingenuity, he invented machinery for hulling and pitting almonds and washing walnuts, and ran Jersey cows as well.[36] As Kevin Starr has remarked, "Superbly sited on a foothill, the Cooper residence commanded a georgic vista of olive and walnut groves, drying ovens, oil presses, packing sheds, and subsidiary orchards of orange, lemon, peach, and pear trees."[37] Ellwood Ranch represented an attempt to live and work with the environment of California in a way that Cooper would champion over the next forty years. His choice of walnuts and olives was astute. These fruits did not depend upon irrigation, would not suffer in the long journey to eastern markets, and could be preserved much better and more easily than deciduous fruits.

Innovative though he clearly was, Cooper would hardly warrant extensive attention were it not for his role over thirty years in the development of the Californian fruit industry. As president of the State Board of Horticulture from 1883 and a respected industry leader, Cooper became an influential figure in the development of this crucial industry until his political downfall in 1907. This position he used to push ideas of environmental management that proved persuasive among fruit growers. The reports of the board and the annual state conventions of the fruit growers that Cooper orchestrated frequently contained references to the forests, resolutions on the need for their preservation, and ubiquitous papers on the issue of afforestation in which the value of Australian trees stood out.

Cooper's crusade quickly bore results. Charles R. Orcutt, a nurseryman of San Diego, told *Garden and Forest* in 1890 that "many a hillside and plain—a few years ago treeless, parched and brown—has been transformed into a mass of living green, furnishing the refreshment of shade and filling the air with a health-giving, grateful fragrance." Orcutt saw the transformation as part of the conversion of arid California into a garden through eucalyptus trees. "Thanks to this friendly genus" it was only a question of time "before the now desert-like plains of southern California can be covered with a growth of gigantic trees."[38]

The gardenlike emplacement of gums especially impressed Australian visitors, accustomed as they were to the higher valuation of exotics down under. Early in the 1880s, Australians could already see the effects of their native flora on the American Southwest, and they reported the phenomenon with pride. It gave them confidence in their own efforts to emphasize parallels between economic development in Australia and California. In 1883–84, Thomas K. and John L. Dow both noticed the prevalence of the gums. John Dow spoke of Mission San Gabriel and its tree-lined streets: "The poplar, the cedar, and the oak alternate with our gums, and mixing with all are the luxurious oleanders." There, and in similar village settlements, "you drive among avenues of trees, among which the Australian blue gum takes so important a position as to quite flatter you."[39]

These plantings went ahead precisely because the gums seemed to serve the variety of purposes Cooper had stressed. They could also counter the environmental degradation European settlement had brought and restore the environment to what Europeans believed it ought to be. Clearly, this desire was based on a perception of environmental normality and "balance"—the latter was a key term in Cooper's vocabulary. Southern and much of interior California seemed unclothed in terms intelligible to settlers used to green eastern forests and farms, and eucalypts quickly filled the void. But more than the dream of an idealized eastern or Edenic landscape was at issue. The early European settlement, both Spanish and American, had already considerably altered the land and contributed to the "browning" of California that Cooper observed. Clearing for mining and settlement, forest fires, and the trampling of exotic animals had destroyed the native vegetation of grasses, chaparral, and river oaks.[40] The herds of the Basque shepherds ate everything, said one Chino farmer, while John Muir commented on the sheep as "hooved locusts" as he trailed behind them in the Sierra in the late 1860s, on arriving in California.[41] Ellwood Cooper himself had contributed to the environmental degradation when he first arrived, running thousands of sheep in partnership with William Hollister that ate the native grasses on the Santa Ynez Mountains.[42] In *Forest Culture and Eucalyptus Trees,* Cooper made his effort to redress the balance of nature that settlement had disturbed. But the restoration of grasses and chaparral did not satisfy these European invaders. They liked eucalyptus trees because the gums promised to do more than restore "nature"; eucalypts would renovate California and create Cooper's green paradise.[43]

KINNEY, THE REAL ESTATE BOOM, AND
EUCALYPTUS TREES

While many of these plantings stemmed from Cooper's early proselytiz-
ing, the eucalypts won other determined champions. Of these, none
would be more important than Abbot Kinney.[44] After an extended world
tour in the 1870s, Kinney settled in Los Angeles permanently, bringing
with him money to spare from the family tobacco fortunes in New Jersey to boost the southern Californian region. Kinney first pushed the Australian genus while roadmaster of Santa Monica, and he stressed the gum
trees in roadside plantings and in his property developments in Los
Angles County.[45] Kinney wrote widely on a variety of subjects from the
"race suicide" of abortion, to the virtues of the secret, or "Australian,"
ballot and denunciations of the evils of machine politics, to the prospects
of the eucalyptus trees. His 1895 book, simply titled *Eucalyptus,* summed
up his environmental passion. A meandering compendium of information that reflected Kinney's undisciplined but curious mind, *Eucalyptus*
was nevertheless the first book-length American guide to the Australian
genus. Like Cooper, Kinney stressed the multiple uses of the gums.[46]

How Kinney acquired his obsession for the Australian trees is unclear.
He had visited the Blue Mountains of New South Wales during the early
1870s, where he was not impressed by the condition of the trees in the
wild. "In Australia," he wrote, "the general effect of the Eucalyptus
'bush' and forests is monotonous and depressing. Ashey hues predomi-
nate and the growth is often scattered and scrawny. I recollect one
tract . . . where a Eucalyptus that shed its bark in long bands predomi-
nated. The foliage was scant and the trees contorted. . . . There was
something weirdly human about it, as though an army of ill fed beggars
had taken root in the soil with tattered covering still hanging about
them."[47] This none too flattering statement came from a man who
orchestrated the planting of hundreds of thousands of eucalypts in California alongside roads and on farmland, and who personally subsidized
plantings. Clearly Kinney was not concerned with foisting an "Australian" aesthetic on the California landscape.

How can enthusiasm for a genus perceived as scruffy and ill-formed
be explained? The ornamental crusade undoubtedly stemmed from a
variety of motives. Real estate development was one. The presence of a
prominent land developer like Kinney, as well as railroad executives,
among the apostles of the eucalypt draws attention to the role played by
Australian trees in transforming the look of the land and so giving it new

value.[48] The Southern Pacific Railroad encouraged the planting of eucalypts and acacias on its land grants, hoping the wood could be used for
fuel and railroad ties, but land promotion was also involved. In 1877,
railroad land east of Tulare Lake in the Central Valley was "an unoccu-
pied waste, used only sparingly for pasture." One half-section of 320
acres was planted with blue gum and acacias, "with a view to demon-
strating that this treeless waste could be made fit for homes." The experiment succeeded and "soon presented the appearance of a grove," thus
providing an example that "was followed by settlers who bought
land."[49] As Professor Alfred J. McClatchie observed in 1904, "Were
some agency to destroy all the Eucalypts now growing in California, the
price of real estate would fall at once."[50]

Nevertheless, Kinney's real estate development was motivated by a
complex aesthetic that sought to make California gardenlike. Like
Cooper, Kinney had strong aesthetic impulses that he expressed in the
planting of the genus. He displayed a purist's commitment to the uniformity of street plantings, recalling that Nevada Avenue in Santa Monica, which he had planted, "had a beauty due to the large size of the trees
and the dignity of its harmonious planting." Subsequently, this effect had
been lost, much to Kinney's distress. Some home owners had chopped
down the *E. globulus* and replaced them with peppers or grevilleas to
leave "a broken medley of little and big, old and young trees of inhar-
monious character without force or effect." Kinney proclaimed the owners and the authorities "aesthetically blind."[51]

Kinney's aesthetic of mass and uniform plantings found extensive
favor across California. Streets, highways, farms, and orchards were
lined with blue gum, and forest groves dotted the landscape. A prominent example was the University of California's new home in Berkeley
in the early 1870s, which was covered with eucalypts supplied at low
cost by a wealthy nurseryman. Professor Ezra Carr, an early champion
of the blue gum, supervised the planting, but the campaign had the support of the board of regents and influential local residents.[52] A similar
drive at Golden Gate Park in San Francisco was under way in 1876, with
mass "forest tree plantations" of eucalyptus prominent.[53]

THE REACTION AGAINST BLUE GUM

These plantings had detractors. Not aesthetically blind, critics simply
had a different sense of what constituted an appropriate blend of trees
and shrubs to transform the land. John Ellis, landscape gardener at the

state capitol, noted of Berkeley that "large groves of trees have sprung
into existence" in an "unstudied system of planting."[54] Charles Shinn,
who later worked for the University of California Agricultural Experiment Station, was a trenchant critic of the philosophy underlying the
early Berkeley plantings. "Instead of the garden art that every Californian wanted to see," complained Shinn, "Berkeley became for years a
wilderness of tall, crowded Eucalypti, and all its natural beauties were
obscured. . . . Even the town yielded," Shinn lamented, "to the prevailing Eucalyptus craze, and soon rivalled the University in its stiffness."
Shinn carried his attack beyond the example of garden landscaping to
include the program of agricultural planting. Shinn caricatured "monotonous people" who "would like to plane down all the mountains, divide
the soil into regular squares of 160 acres, . . . surround each square with
the same number of the same kind of trees, and put a square house, with
a railing on top, exactly in the middle of each farm." Shinn demanded
instead a larger role for wild nature in the farmland plantings. Californians "love wild places," he asserted, with "woodland, and belts of forest, and wind-breaks that wind along the horizon."[55] The eucalyptus
craze seemed incompatible with this aesthetic.

These attacks attest to the depth of feeling against blue gums, even
among apostles of the garden landscape. However, the vitriol was never
more clearly spelled out than by the *San Francisco Argonaut* in 1877,
when that conservative paper attacked the "craze" over the blue gum: "Its
odor is so immatchably unpleasant that nothing but man can endure it. In
point of beauty it is about as desirable as the scaffolding of a factory chim-
ney. This absurd vegetable is now growing all over this state. . . . It
defaces every landscape with blotches of blue, and embitters every breeze
with suggestions of an old woman's medicine chest."[56] From another van-
tage point, claims that eucalyptus could be a cornerstone of a sustainable
garden environment met criticism. Jeanne Carr denounced "robber eucalyptus" trees that sucked the nutrients out of the soil. Giant gums planted
in groves did not fit Carr's desire for a sustainable agriculture, and she
abandoned these in favor of more diverse plantings from many countries.
Carr went so far as to suggest that even in grove plantings, the eucalyptus
was inferior to the native pines and cypresses.[57] Influenced by this "robber" stereotype, many citrus growers pulled out their windbreaks in the
1880s and replaced them with natives. The propensity of gums to remove
moisture and nutrients required by the citrus was the reason given.[58]

Under the impact of such attacks, the blue gum crusade threatened to
stall.[59] Yet all the criticism failed to stop a renewal of enthusiasm for

Australian trees. The attack on eucalyptus remained limited to the excessive planting of blue gum, and interest in the Australian genus revived. The use of eucalyptus types other than *globulus* expanded; Kinney experimented with Karri and Jarrah (*E. diversicolor* and *E. marginata*), and ornamental gardeners like Jeanne Carr shifted attention to the small and showy *E. ficifolia*. Carr gushed over the latter as "by far the most gorgeous of its large family" after seeing the description of it in "Baron von Muller's [*sic*] great work on eucalypti."[60] Soon critics had to eat their words, even on shelterbelt plantings. The blue gum's removal was premature, horticulturalist Professor Edward Wickson proclaimed, since severe weather in 1888 in southern California left unprotected crops devastated. E. W. Holman of Riverside observed the widespread replanting "of rows of eucalyptus on the very line where four or five years ago such trees were removed."[61]

HEALTH: THE FEVER TREE

At about the same time, ornamental and economic rationales received reinforcement from an entirely different argument. Southern European plantings known to George Perkins Marsh had been principally designed to help combat malaria, and the gum became known as the "Australian fever tree." In 1876, Cooper documented blue gum's supposed disinfectant properties in malaria control to justify extensive planting. The eucalypts were expected thereby to contribute to the health as well as the wealth of Californians. According to Australian seed catalogues that Cooper cited, the medicinal "qualities" of *E. globulus* placed it "transcendently above any other plants . . . in hygienic importance."[62]

According to nineteenth-century medical theory, "miasmatic vapours" caused many infectious diseases. Health authorities regarded stagnant water as a source of these vapors, but polluted soil could also contribute. From these sources the air could spread malaria, cholera, and other deadly diseases. Prophylactic measures concentrated on improving the flow of waterways, but also included use of eucalyptus trees to drain swamps. According to H. N. Draper, "The putrescible constituents of the stagnant water are absorbed by the roots, and become part of the vegetable tissue of the tree." But the gum trees had an additional and direct sanitizing effect upon the vapors. The leaves of eucalyptus trees secreted "large quantities of an aromatic essential oil." Under the combined action of air and moisture, these oils were "rapidly oxidized" to release "large quantities of peroxide of hydrogen," which was a "very active disinfectant." Such claims that eucalyptus could disinfect the air were widely publicized in the California press and commended to farmers.[63]

No matter that some authorities were skeptical. According to enthusiasts, the eucalyptus had health-giving properties that far exceeded its role in malaria control. It was "antiseptic for wounds—its essential oil being a stimulant." Moreover, the tannin on the leaves allegedly acted as an "astringent" that hastened healing.[64] "Steeping the leaves" in boiling water made "an excellent remedy for coughs," claimed A. C. Sullivan, while "tainted meat wrapped in the leaves a few hours" was "said to become fresh again."[65] As early as 1879, a German doctor testing a Victorian Eucalypti Extract made by Sander and Sons asserted that "the Eucalypti Extract proved magnificently successful in very severe contusions, bruises, sprains, wounds, scaldings, broken ribs and limbs." Other authorities claimed the extract cured cancer of the tongue, breast cancer, diphtheria, and a host of minor maladies.[66]

The concern with public health meshed well with the problem of agricultural development. Eucalyptus trees gained extra value in California because irrigation exacerbated natural drainage problems, particularly in the Central Valley.[67] Malaria was widespread in central California in the second half of the nineteenth century, and for this reason Cooper's claims to make "uninhabitable districts healthy" had some purchase.[68] Yet health arguments were not the major cause of the revival of the eucalypt, delightful and eccentric though the debate over malaria control could be. Malaria control proved a highly controversial topic, and many eucalyptus advocates distanced themselves from extravagant claims.[69] Southern California did not suffer from malaria infestations and yet was a stronghold of the next phase of the crusade. Arguments other than health came into play.

KINNEY AND THE STATE BOARD OF FORESTRY

Just as the health argument began to wane, the destruction of the redwoods and other old-growth forests became impossible to ignore. The formation of the California State Board of Forestry in 1885, with Kinney as chairman, provided the impetus for a new campaign. In part, the new lease of life reflected Kinney's own energetic promotion.[70] The state board under Kinney fully embraced Marsh's idea that destruction of forests spelled ecological disaster, but the board's first efforts to right the situation involved not preservation of redwoods, but the planting of arid and cutover landscapes with imported trees. To do this, the board established experimental stations, notably one at Santa Monica, and another in northern California, at Chico, on land donated by John Bidwell. Since Kinney lacked any forestry lands to administer, these all being under federal control, the board was limited to moral exhortations to loggers and sheepherders to reduce their destruction of California's natural heritage. But what Kinney could do was to engage in tree propagation, distribution, and roadside and park planting, aims he enthusiastically embraced. He encouraged broad participation, praising, for example, philanthropist Adolph Sutro's Arbor Day endeavors in San Francisco, where civic-minded citizens and schoolchildren planted thousands of seedlings in the city and on islands in the bay in 1886.[71] The forestry board's program included native *Pinus insignis* and cypress, but stressed newly imported and promising varieties of gum trees. The board also gave away huge quantities of seed, sold many eucalyptus trees at cheap prices, and advised farmers and gardeners on their planting and care. Board publications quoted Australian botanical works such as Mueller's "Select Extra-Tropical Plants," and Kinney corresponded with several influential antipodean botanists and foresters—not only Mueller but also Frederick Bailey of Queensland and Joseph H. Maiden of Sydney, the government botanist of New South Wales and later director of the Botanic Gardens, 1896–1924.[72]

In this broad-ranging campaign, the focus shifted from blue gum to new favorites like the sugar gum, *E. cladocalyx,* which seemed better mannered for street situations than blue gum and stood dry conditions well. Acting on the advice of South Australia's state conservator of forests, John Ednie Brown, the forestry board distributed sugar gum seed throughout California.[73] This species and *E. viminalis* (manna gum) spread more successfully into quite cold locations such as Butte County in the north, as well as hot dry areas in the south of the state. Sugar gum, *E. rostrata,* and *E. viminalis* were the ones most widely planted in the Central Valley, with strong concentrations around Fresno in the heart of the irrigation belt. More than half of the board's seventy-five thousand seedlings raised in 1888–89 came from these three species, of which twenty-three thousand were red gum.[74] Eucalyptus now dotted large areas of California's landscapes.

The popularity of eucalyptus trees—a result of their successful adaptation and prodigious growth—also brushed off on other Australian species. Eugene W. Hilgard corresponded with his fellow German, Mueller, and helped popularize the publication "Select Extra-Tropical Plants" in California. Hilgard speculated that the "adaptation" that saw eucalypts grow more rapidly than in Australia would hold true of other Australian vegetation.[75] He hoped that the problem of salty or so-called alkali lands associated with irrigation might be overcome by the planting of Australian saltbush as recommended by Mueller. When Mueller had sent seeds of *Atriplex nummularium* and other Australian saltbush species to California in 1881, these proved easy to propagate and became widely used in the dry inland regions, especially around Tulare where cattle devoured saltbush avidly when used as a fodder. "At last there is a downright 'boom' over here on the subject of your salt bushes," Hilgard told Mueller in 1895. "Thousands of them have been and are being planted in the alkali district," he announced in the course of distributing seeds of *Atriplex semibaccatum* sent by Mueller. As a result, sales of alkali lands had surged. The agricultural experiment station at Tulare joined the venture between 1890 and 1896, producing much seed for distribution.[76]

The state board also propagated and spread throughout California a huge variety of Australian trees. Some were for salty inland conditions, others for coastal positions. The state forester William S. Lyon tested *Casuarina* species (she-oaks) in lands often rendered uninhabitable by excessive irrigation and found that in the less badly affected alkali soils, she-oaks "made records for hardiness and rapidity of growth."[77] *Grevillea robusta*, known in California as "the Australian fern tree," was employed as an avenue planting in real estate subdivisions in the 1880s because its fernlike quality softened the bare outlines of roads and buildings and imparted a semitropical air that complemented Canary Island palms and sugar gums. The *Melaleuca*, or paperbark, genus also won favor for soggy and flood prone areas. Other trees that Lyon encouraged were principally ornamental, including "the famous and beautiful" bunya pine of Queensland, *Araucaria bidwillii*; and the Moreton Bay fig, *Ficus macrophylla*, which grew well in the Santa Barbara area.[78] The ornamental aspect was also emphasized by the importation of Australian ferns and tree ferns, again as recommended by Mueller.[79]

Yet the single most important genus after the eucalyptus, and the only other one to attain economic and ornamental importance over a wide range of California's landscapes, was the acacia, or wattle. In 1888–89, one acacia was planted for every five gums. The state board produced a special report by Lyon on "Wattles, and Wattle Planting in California." This drew heavily on Maiden's "Wattles and Wattle Bark," published in Sydney in 1890,[80] but Kinney and Lyon also followed earlier recommendations by Hilgard, who in turn drew upon Mueller. According to the reports of the state board, "in some parts of our state" the golden wattle (*A. pycnantha*) had "found a more congenial home than in its native habitat of South Australia" and reached "its fullest size and maturity at an earlier age than there."[81]

Just as promotion of eucalyptus trees suffered from the poor identification of species, the advance of the acacias was limited by confusion with the economically useless *Albizia julibrissin* from Asia and by problems with propagation from seed.[82] Nevertheless, many varieties continued to be extensively planted, principally for their potential as sources of tanbark, but also because of their ornamental and shelter value. The *A. melanoxylon,* or blackwood, served widely for street planting prior to 1914.[83] Abbot Kinney himself was one of the acacias' greatest defenders, and he sternly resisted the attempts of farmers to root them out when the genus stood accused in 1888 of harboring the cottony cushion scale when planted alongside southern California's fruit groves. Of all of the trees in Berkeley, Kinney claimed that the acacias were most beautiful, especially *A. decurrens,* whose "feathery foliage in dense masses" was "both charming and effective."[84]

Kinney's focus was as comprehensive as Cooper's and reflected ideas of creating a sustainable environment through forest planting. Not only did ornamental considerations influence him, he sought out multifarious uses of the eucalyptus, such as honey production. The denuding of native tree cover by pastoral activities and the consequent erosion had played havoc with the bee-keeping industry, Kinney believed, and he noted how widely used and prized the eucalyptus was for the production of honey in Australia.[85] But, a citrus grower himself, Kinney's prime concern was with the prosperity of fruit. He dwelt not so much on profits from timber as on the role of gum trees in restoring tree cover to aid irrigation and prevent soil erosion. Kinney preached and wrote tirelessly on the subject of environmental restoration and frequently addressed the State Fruit Growers' Conventions, drawing heavily upon the work of Marsh and Mueller, whom he regarded as important figures in world forestry.[86]

Again the dreams were not quite fulfilled. The Board of Forestry found powerful enemies in sheepherders, ranchers, and renegade lumbering interests that wished to preserve the open-slather approach to forest exploitation. Yet it took the state legislature's economy drive of the depression in 1893 to bring about the abolition of the board, and hence the chief platform for the afforestation interests backed by the horticulturalists. Subsequently, the experimental stations came under the control of the University of California, and the state-sponsored afforestation program ceased. The political attacks also threatened the State Board of Horticulture, which was criticized for straying too far from the promotion of fruit.[87]

Even before this happened, Kinney had conceded in 1891 that eucalyptus trees could not do the job of controlling floodwaters: "Large numbers of trees have been planted in Southern California, but these are all in the valleys, and while helping the climate cannot control the floodwaters coming from the denuded mountains." Kinney concluded that these floods "must be controlled in the mountains and foothills." Forestry debates in California now focused more on preventing "forest destruction" than on afforestation, and covered such important issues as forest fire control. Kinney took a prominent part in the development of the Southern California Forest and Water Association after 1895, and the defunct forestry board's nascent preservation activities shifted to lobbying at the federal level.[88] Simultaneously, the aesthetic appreciation of trees began to shift in favor of natives.

THE TIMBER FAMINE

Just as the second phase of the eucalyptus promotion led by Kinney stalled, a new enthusiasm began to arise. This third phase, however, departed somewhat from the landscaping and horticultural concerns of the earlier impulses. Economic arguments related to the timber shortage, though never absent from earlier promotions, now came to the fore. The development of timber farms on a broad-acre agriculture model threatened to substitute the concept of sustained yield for that of sustainable development based on the garden ideal.

Practical reasons helped shape this transformation. Because in the 1860s the eucalypts were expensive, few growers touted their possible economic uses above the obvious ornamental ones; but with the arrival of regular and reliable quantities of seed via steamship services pioneered in the 1870s, the price came down by the mid-1870s and cultivation of eucalypts increased. An expanding number of nurseries familiar with eucalyptus varieties aided dissemination. Most important, economic arguments were stimulated by a 1904 Forest Service survey announcement "that the supply of eastern hardwood would be exhausted in about sixteen years."[89]

A prodigious source of demand for wood, and a commonly cited cause of the approaching timber famine, was the expansion of the railroads. Softwood ties (known in Australia as sleepers) were commonly used because of the shortage of hardwoods in the West, and these soft-woods, often white pine, had an extremely short life of four to six years. In sharp contrast, the New South Wales government got more than twenty years from its eucalyptus-based sleepers. Ironbark (*E. sideroxy-lon*) had an especially long life span.[90] Impressed by the evidence from New South Wales, the Santa Fe Railroad sent an expert there in 1907 to evaluate the position. He noted that his own railroad had three times the track of the New South Wales system but used eight times the number of sleepers. At seventy cents a sleeper, Santa Fe Railroad executives con-cluded that American railroads could save $35 million a year by grow-ing eucalyptus and cutting sleeper use.[91] Complementing the use by rail-roads, some mining companies in California planted eucalypts to ensure a steady supply of hardwood timber for mine shafts.[92]

Yet another economic use was soon found. Until 1900, eucalyptus timber had been little used for furniture and household construction in California. The shortage of eastern hardwoods and softwoods changed that, just as Australian authorities like Joseph Maiden and Richard T. Baker began to extol the virtues of eucalyptus species as a high-grade timber. Californian timber millers, worried about the decline of the red-woods, oaks, and pines, sought to offset the high cost of importing suit-able timbers from the East or Pacific Northwest.[93]

The ambition to use eucalyptus for high-grade joinery in California had few precedents and little scientific backing. Ellwood Cooper and Mueller had not stressed the furniture and joinery applications of most eucalypts, and nineteenth-century references usually concerned the util-ity of the species for rough work. True, Cooper left open along with Mueller the possibility of other uses; they did mention *E. obliqua,* a species that today serves along with *E. regnans* as a major furniture and joinery timber under the names Tasmanian oak and mountain ash, respectively, but these species were not used widely for joinery in Aus-tralia until the 1920s, when problems of seasoning them were addressed. This was beyond the time frame when use could conceivably have been made of them in the United States. The state forester William S. Lyon had experimented with propagation and growth of these species in 1889–90 and was aware of English reports that credited *obliqua* with "great strength, toughness, and durability." But tests on this species failed in California.[94]

The new economic uses proposed after 1900 went far beyond what Cooper and other early enthusiasts had envisioned. Cooper and Ezra

Carr, in particular, had advocated economic benefits as a part of the diverse garden landscape and did not propose broad-acre "farming" of gums. In fact, such an approach was quite foreign to the moral and aesthetic foundations of the original schemes. In 1873, Ezra Carr noted in his "Forest-Planting a Source of Wealth" that "nature never plants a field or forest with a single species; she loves an infinite diversity. A plantation of Blue Gum would be an abomination in her sight, and, we may be sure, she has some chosen parasite in reserve with which to destroy it."[95] This concept of balance was fundamental to the "environmental" vision of the garden but, in the work of the early twentieth-century conservationists, the demands of economic profitability and rationalized production modeled on industrial systems took precedence.

Yet the shift after 1900 to eucalyptus as a farm product rather than a garden component was more complicated still. Planting for economic purposes threatened to engulf rationality with speculative land deals. Given the limited amount of information available concerning the uses of most eucalypts, the fact that Californians planted them for profit in the first decade of the twentieth century became highly dubious. Growers often planted first and thought later. Dwight Whiting put in over nine hundred thousand eucalypts at his ten thousand–acre southern California ranch near Del Mar between 1903 and 1905, but admitted that "little" seemed to be known of the eucalypts' "technical values for manufacturing into useful articles, or when they should be felled, or how to cure the timber when sawn."[96] After he had made the decision to convert valuable barley and wheat land and embarked on a large-scale planting program, Whiting wrote for seeds to Richard T. Baker, who had succeeded Maiden as curator and economic botanist at the Sydney Technological Museum in 1901.[97] Whiting had seen Baker's major publication on the use of eucalypts in medical preparations, *A Research on the Eucalypts, Especially in Regard to Their Essential Oils* (1902), and sought more information, explaining that he did not have any particular strategy for the utilization of his new crop.[98] Gushing with enthusiasm, Whiting simply concluded that "at the rate that our native forests are being devastated by axes and fires it won't be long before each and every tree I have will be worth ten shillings a piece or more."[99]

Whiting did draw, however, on the scientific advice of Professor Alfred J. McClatchie (1861–1906), who wrote *Eucalypts Cultivated in the United States,* based upon his work at the U.S. Department of Agriculture's Arizona Experiment Station in Phoenix between 1899 and 1902. McClatchie was the closest equivalent to Cooper and Kinney as an intellectual leader of the new movement, but his work was technically superior to that of the two earlier apostles. His concern was more scientific and systematic than theirs. McClatchie had lived in Pasadena in the 1890s, where, as a professor of biology at the Throop Polytechnic (now Cal Tech) he had known the work of Abbot Kinney and the Carrs. McClatchie quoted copiously from both Mueller and Cooper in developing his own pro-eucalyptus arguments. The United States forester and conservationist Gifford Pinchot wrote the foreword to *Eucalypts Cultivated in the United States* and praised the genus for its "phenomenally rapid growth" and "the special adaptation of many species" which "render these trees of peculiar economic importance to the Southwest."[100] Yet no one person stood out in this last phase of eucalyptus expansion, which reflected a congruence of conservation, private capitalist, and government assessments that the day of the eucalyptus as an economic proposition had finally arrived.

With scientific support, and backed by both California and federal government research, the economic push for eucalyptus came to a head between 1908 and 1914. Many thousands of acres of prime agricultural land were given over from grains to the supposedly superior crop of eucalyptus hardwood. United States government officials repeatedly gave their blessing to the speculation. The National Conservation Commission (NCC) called by President Theodore Roosevelt in 1908 found the economic possibilities of the eucalyptus in the Southwest impressive enough—in an age of timber shortage—for special comment. Its report acclaimed the *Eucalyptus globulus* that grew an inch in diameter and five feet or more in height per year from seed. "As a wood producer in favorable localities free from frost," the NCC noted, "it has no equal."[101] Because of its heavy eucalyptus plantings, California received high praise in terms of efforts at reforestation. The development of planting there and its "remarkable cases of profitable returns from a quick-growing species," showed "the value of further experiments with exotic species in the United States."[102]

THE DECLINE OF THE EUCALYPTUS CRAZE

Embarrassingly, the greatest interest in the Australian trees immediately preceded their demise as a viable commercial timber. A U.S. government survey in 1910 showed that growth rates did not meet expectations.[103] Yet typical explanations for the fact that the eucalyptus timber industry failed to flourish after such high hopes center on the inferior quality of the California-grown wood, not the rates of growth. As one commentator has asserted, "By 1912 the sad truth was discovered that the eucalyptus is not a good lumber tree. Australia's timber species must be several hundred years old before cutting."[104] Eucalypts in California certainly suffered from the side effects of rapid growth. They were frequently spongy and they seasoned poorly. Trials run by the Santa Fe Railroad, which had been prepared to invest heavily in eucalyptus ties, damaged the reputation of the genus. The ties warped and cracked, and could not be made to hold bolts, so badly did they split. As far as furniture was concerned, none of the eucalypts acclimatized in California served this purpose satisfactorily.

"Green"—or poorly seasoned and easily split—eucalyptus timber was indeed a difficulty. But ironically, this problem often applied in Australia as well. There, little eucalyptus timber was used in furniture and precious little more in houses after the mid-nineteenth century. The wood was seen, to be sure, in some joinery where great durability was required, such as timber sills, but after 1889 the hardwood market succumbed to competition from "Oregon pine" imported from the West Coast of America for use as the basic timber in household construction.[105] Because of its inferior seasoning properties, eucalypt timber was rarely used for flooring: builders preferred the outstanding New Zealand Kauri pine and "Baltic pine" softwoods from Europe. Eucalyptus flooring was subject to severe shrinkage; not until kiln-drying of timber was tentatively introduced in Australia around 1912 and generally after World War II did Australian hardwoods come into wider use for floors, except in industrial and commercial construction.[106]

The problem of seasoning was exacerbated by the trees' conditions of faster growth in California. Hilgard recognized that the eucalyptus was a "fast-growing tree" but "a miserable failure" as timber precisely for this reason. "It is fit for firewood only," Hilgard complained, "and that when cut green. . . . The rapid-growing tree is necessarily a tree that has that spongy wood."[107] As a result, some American experts doubted whether they would "get quite as strong or lasting trees as in Australia."[108] One Victorian forest commissioner concurred, confident that inferior American gums would never squeeze out the local product.[109]

Blue gum was not the sole source of inferior wood. The alternatives chosen involved equally faulty planting. American timber merchants sometimes disastrously recommended river red gum (*E. rostrata*) as a furniture timber, apparently having confused it with *E. resinifera* (red mahogany). Red gum was, as one American expert stated, "impossible as a furniture timber."[110] Yet this tree was what many California timber merchants and land developers planted after 1900.

The deficiencies of the chosen eucalyptus species provide only the superficial cause of the demise of the timber drive, however. The problem in California did not lie in supply, as commonly assumed, but in demand.[111] The same faults found in American eucalyptus trees did not stop the utilization of those forests on an ever-increasing scale in Australia as wood technologies improved. Even in California, the faults revealed in the 1910 study did not stem the enthusiasm.[112]

Some of the largest Californian plantings occurred between 1910 and 1914. The formation of a Eucalyptus Hardwood Association in 1913 evidenced the determination of growers and manufacturers to widen the use of the timber by furnishing "authentic information regarding eucalyptus" and protecting the association's "members and the public from dishonest dealers."[113] Timber merchants, sawmillers, and investors scoured California for suitable sites for planting, particularly in the San Joaquin and Sacramento Valleys. The promoters argued that the 1910 study covered groves not explicitly planted for forestry purposes, but instead—because they had been planted much earlier—ones planted for windbreaks and fuel supply on poor quality land. Ventures after 1910, like the six thousand–acre endeavor of Grant Wallace's American Eucalyptus Timber Corporation of Chicago, stressed the importance of giving the trees priority on good soils. Wallace also drew upon the garden concept; he planted in "the great Eucalyptus and orange producing region" where "oranges, lemons and pomelos" ripen "several weeks earlier" than farther south and the valley had "a twelve months of roses." Such luxuriant and clichéd horticultural images embellished the company's expensive prospectus.[114]

The new promoters also played upon the Progressive Era conservation ethic, arguing that eucalypts would spare the redwoods. Wallace's corporation condemned the "timber buccaneers" for their destruction of old-growth forests. By arguing that the "looters" of timber threatened to put the United States in the position of "the Chinese, the Egyptians and the people of the deserts, whose wastes once were water and rich of soil because protected by forests," he also repeated the old conviction that linked the forest issue with the garden concept.[115]

Wallace, like W. Graves's Eucalyptus Timber Company of St. Louis, got strong support from Midwestern capitalists to invest in California plantations, but locals, prominent citizens among them, also embraced this latest enthusiasm. Jack London planted 100,000 trees on the slopes of the Sonoma Mountains. The writer was persuaded to convert a three-hundred-acre vineyard to this purpose by his friend, Grant Wallace.[116] Even serious students of the American forests and lovers of the native trees joined in enthusiastically. A notable feature was the involvement of U.S. Forestry Service officials in promoting ventures in the private sector. A respected authority on the native trees of southern California and former U.S. Forest Service agent, Theodore Lukens of Pasadena took up with the help of United States forestry officials thousands of acres of Los Berros Ranch real estate near San Luis Obispo from 1907 to 1917; by 1909 he had planted 305,000 trees.[117]

Since the craze did not abate in spite of unfavorable reports of poor timber, what did end the plantings so abruptly during World War I? One crucial defect in the new enthusiasm was the speculation that accompanied the timber famine. Brokerage firms entered the market to trade in what amounted to futures in eucalyptus.[118] The movement of eastern capital and neophyte tree-planters into the eucalyptus enterprise gave cultivation of the trees a bad name, and the market collapsed after 1914. A great many companies had been organized ostensibly for planting but actually to disguise and dispose of inferior quality land. This was often salty land and, said *Sunset Magazine,* even "land submerged and land bone dry, all manner of waste land was palmed off on the public." Though Theodore Lukens understood tree planting, genuinely admired the eucalyptus, and believed it to be a part of the timber future of the West, as proprietor of a Pasadena real estate firm specializing in "Fruit & Eucalyptus Lands" he too was caught up in the equation of tree planting with land sale. Part of the enterprise involved purchasing land, planting eucalyptus trees, and then selling off lots to investors from the Midwest. Land development rather than timber culture became the driving force. Most of the promoters went to the wall because they could not sell their investments. Lukens, too, could not sell his and abandoned the enterprise after 1917.[119]

A second nail in the coffin of the eucalyptus boom had little to do with the disrepute such speculation brought. The predictions of a timber famine did not vanish after 1914, but the detail of the predicted famine shifted to reflect actual changes in the patterns of production and consumption of timber in the United States. Timber usage declined after the first decade of the twentieth century—in both lumber and fuel the usage was down after 1907. Gross production of lumber rose to a maximum of 9.555 million cubic feet in 1907, and fell to a minimum of 3.4 million in 1932. The cut did not again exceed 1907 levels until 1956, and then not in per capita terms. These figures are compelling, but they nonetheless obscure the true decline. For lumber alone, hardwoods constituted 24.1 percent of total domestic cut at the year of peak production in 1907, compared to 20 percent in 1932. The figures are more striking still when imports are taken into account. A more rapid decline in imports of hardwoods took place over the years from 1908 to 1932, indicating a steady downward trend in demand.[120] Forestry officials continued in the 1920s to talk about a timber famine, but this was now overwhelmingly a softwood famine that they feared.

Patterns of demand for lumber explain the decline in hardwoods. The reasons for the change in eucalyptus demand are obvious in the trade publications of the timber industry before 1914. These reasons have little to do with speculation and everything to do with the changing technology of building and construction. The trade papers expressed alarm at the shifting emphasis in construction toward nonwood materials claimed to be more durable and less hazardous for use. Most important, wooden construction was liable to be fire-prone; concrete was not.[121]

After 1914 concrete and steel were used more widely in construction, illustrated by the building of sporting facilities. Formerly, sporting stadiums had been constructed entirely from wood, but this material was dangerous and the buildings did not last. The development of concrete—and better steel products as a result of the Bessemer production process—allowed increasing numbers of universities and municipal authorities to erect large and durable stadiums that made only limited use of wood. Gone too was the need for the great quantities of hardwood for bridges, offices, and factory buildings. These were, in Australia, major users of eucalypts, and the market in the United States was also potentially large. But at precisely the time Californians began to invest in Australian hardwoods, the market began to collapse. As the economic historian Peter Shergold concludes, "Steel beams and girders, combined with reinforced concrete floors, transformed construction techniques."[122] The use of cement increased by four and a half times to 90 million barrels between 1901 and 1913.[123] But resort to substitute materials was only part of the story.

Wood preserving extended the life of the softwoods and so aided conservation. Creosoting had been practiced by some companies in the railroad business as early as the 1880s. Indeed, the process was known even earlier, but it became generally used when better techniques emerged for preserving existing timbers; this development was particularly important for railroad ties, a potential market for Californian eucalypts. Trade

papers revealed an increased use of creosote "to tremendous proportions" around 1912 that made softwoods such as white pine more competitive with hardwoods.[124]

As Michael Williams has shown, in the 1920s American forests themselves began to recover, confounding expectations of decline. Underlying
the demise of the market for Australian hardwoods was the renewed productivity of American softwood forests under sustained yield management, including fire prevention and control, more accurate measurement
of the wood supply, reduction of wastage, regrowth of cut areas, and similar "conservation" developments that allowed natural regeneration with
minimum human labor.[125] In comparison, eucalyptus species suffered
because they did not reproduce well without human intervention in California. The economic advantages of the gums in growth and cost of seed
were partly lost where continual replanting and thinning were required.
According to reports, self-seeding occurred only on rich soils in river flats.
As early as 1882, in his *Report on . . . the Arid Regions of the Pacific
Slope,* Hilgard noted reservations about the capacity of the species to turn
the desert into a garden. The eucalypts bore "seeds abundantly, but apparently the latter does not find, as a rule, the proper conditions for ger-
mination. . . . Except with the aid of the hand of man, therefore, the eucalyptus will not sensibly encroach upon the treeless area."[126] Promoters
argued that the ability of the gums to sprout after cutting was a com-
pensation, but the labor costs in planting still had be to be faced.[127] This
deficiency spelled long-term decline in popularity of the eucalyptus in
California, when weighed against the natural regeneration possible with
many native trees, especially quick-growing softwoods. This, together
with the promotion of substitutes for hardwoods, eliminated the serious
economic demand for eucalyptus trees in North America and buried the
dreams of the promoters. But that is not quite the end of the story.

THE RETURN OF THE ORNAMENTAL

The eucalyptus survived and even enjoyed a modest revival by the 1920s.
The latter-day plantings focused on highways, parks, and gardens, as the
ornamental functions of the genus took precedence once more and returned the eucalyptus crusade to something closer to its original aesthetic
foundation. A volume published by the state forester Merritt Pratt in
1922, *Shade and Ornamental Trees of California,* and John McLaren's
widely circulated *Gardening in California: Landscape and Flowers* highlighted these sentiments. McLaren called *E. piperita* "as graceful as the

Birch" and claimed that no willow could have "a finer drooping effect" than *Eucalyptus saligna*. Pasadena's Charles Saunders also favored continued ornamental plantings in private gardens as indispensable alongside the acacia, noted in his 1926 volume, *Trees and Shrubs of California Gardens*.[128]

By this time, Californians had come to accept what Heinrich Mayr had predicted—the legitimate and "natural" place of the gums in the Californian environment. "Of California's cultivated trees," one authority claimed in 1928, "the most striking" were "the towering, serried ranks" of eucalyptus that "dominate the landscape and lend it an unique, exotic flavor totally lacking in other parts of the United States."[129] Eucalyptus had become assimilated as something distinctively Californian. In 1935, another authority urged renewed planting, and justified this in terms of the cultural heritage already established: "The eucalyptus is now one of the outstanding trees over almost any California landscape where trees have been planted. Many people fail to realize that the tree is not a native."[130] Because of public acceptance of the genus' ornamental functions, the number of eucalypts cultivated in California has continued to grow.[131]

THE MODERN ECOLOGICAL CRITIQUE

Today, a further challenge confronts the eucalyptus in North America, this time from the rise of contemporary ecological consciousness. Fear over its fire potential and perceived ecological impact on native vegetation threatens the place of the genus even as an ornamental.[132] The modern attack was dramatically illustrated in the wake of prolonged frosts in the Oakland hills in the winter of 1972, which killed large sections of the blue gum forests. More than a million dead eucalyptus trees were logged out, and environmentalists proposed native vegetation as an alternative to gum trees, which they denounced as "a dirty species." Ignoring the prior impact of grazing, the California Native Plant Society deplored the survival of both *Pinus radiata* and eucalyptus as "man-planted forests" that "have a great deal to do with disappearance of fields of wildflowers from the local scene."[133]

The ecological critique is sound in the observation that gum trees have replaced natives, but unlike some other ecological invasions the eucalyptus has never been out of human control. Its presence in California reflected earlier human activity that had removed a variety of forms of native vegetation, including redwoods. Its survival depends now, as always, on cultural landscape preference because of the poor record of eucalyptus regeneration in the new environment.[134] This means that the gums did not present the ecological catastrophe that other, more invasive plant species threatened, including Central American prickly pears in twentieth-century Australia. The long-term survival of the eucalypts in California remains dependent on landscape fashions of human beings.

The perception of eucalypts prior to 1920 was, generally speaking, different from ours today. In the long history of the eucalypts in California, rarely did critics demand in a purist fashion a return to the native vegetation of each area of California, though they frequently sought alternative native trees from other areas of the state. It is precisely this more subtle form of ecological imperialism, importing species from one region of California to another, that the California Native Plant Society opposed in the early 1970s. But in the 1920s and earlier, the demand for the restoration of ecologically authentic vegetation lay well in the future. Renovation still ruled over restoration. Californians still preferred their garden ideal of an "improved" landscape of forests, farms, trees, and gardens to the authentic beauty of the (still-imagined) natural environment.

COMPARATIVE PERSPECTIVES

The fate of the eucalyptus in California has many points of comparison with its fate elsewhere, but important differences also emerge. The Food and Agricultural Organization (FAO) of the United Nations reported that at the end of the 1970s there were about 272,000 acres of eucalypts planted in the United States—up substantially from the 1950s—of which some 198,000 were in California and 30,000 in Hawaii, but that the trees now existed mainly in ornamental settings and shelterbelts. Eucalypts were rarely planted for commercial purposes. The economic failure of the eucalypts was so striking as early as the 1950s that the FAO declared the case "exceptional enough to be worth stressing" in a global survey of eucalyptus planting. This failure certainly contrasted with the success in some other parts of the Americas, such as in Brazil, where more than 2 billion trees now grow.[135] The long-run economic insignificance of eucalyptus in California reflects the different patterns of forestry and of wood use in the United States compared to that of many third world countries. There, eucalypts remain an important source of fuel for poor people. In first-world California, cheap fuel-timber lacked the same strong demand, except before 1900, when pioneering conditions applied and alternative sources of fuel remained deficient.

This experience can also be usefully compared with that in Australia. The Californian eucalyptus crusade had an influence in the trees' original home. It heightened Australians' awareness of the value of their timbers and the folly of cutting them down in the profligate way so common in the nineteenth century. American timber merchants, scientists, and entrepreneurs visited Australia or sent for seeds and information. They extolled the virtues of the eucalypt and so raised its reputation in Australia. As Richard Baker testified to New South Wales's Royal Commission of Inquiry on Forestry, such enthusiasm presented "an object lesson in 'gum-tree' planting!" This contrasted with the "typical Australian attitude that could be easily ridiculed were it not so sad: 'Is it a gum tree? Then cut it down.'"[136] Queensland's director of forests Philip MacMahon warned that "it is not beyond the bounds of possibility that we shall have to import eucalypts from California in the same way that we are importing Australian black wattle bark from South Africa . . . for tanning purposes." MacMahon used this tactic to emphasize the need to conserve existing hardwood stocks.[137]

American visitors to Australia carried the message of conservation too. In late 1907, Edwin D. Faulkner, the manager of the ties (sleepers) division of the Santa Fe Railroad had visited Australia to investigate the most suitable eucalypts for his business. He had already planted at the company's ranch in Del Mar, California, a large number of river red gum. Faulkner reminded Australians, "We are buying really good agricultural land to plant in trees. . . while your people are destroying the best hardwood timber in the world." Australians did not practice conservation, according to Faulkner, and he suggested some practical reforms.[138] He urged Australian authorities to measure timber royalties by cubic content rather than by the number of trees cut or acres cleared, so that timber cutters paid for waste. Ironbark bridge girders, he was appalled to find, were hewn instead of sawn, with the result that only one-third of the timber was useable. He recommended the reservation of timberlands, strongly decried the preference given to agricultural clearing in good timber country in Australia, called on state governments to pay attention to the problem of forest fires that caused major wood loss in both countries, and recommended the purchase of private land for reforestation. In short, he advocated the type of scientific forestry being introduced in the United States.

In this way, the story of the eucalypts in California had a reciprocal conservation impact on Australia. Much testimony in the Royal Commission hearings in 1907–08 urged Australia to follow the American example. American documents were tabled at the Royal Commission and references made to American conservation policy by important witnesses. A. W. Stillwell, principal assistant engineer of the Roads and Bridges Branch of the Public Works Department of New South Wales, stated that "there is much to be learnt . . . from the American publications . . . respecting the regulation of forest growth." Drawing on the writings and speeches of Pinchot, Stillwell claimed that "while lumbering or cutting to excess is destructive, within limits lumbering is beneficial."[139]

The experience with gums in California helped reinforce in Australia the message of environmental renovation articulated by Mueller. It is ironic that Mueller's schemes for a sustainable society based on both the planting and the preservation of forest cover first flourished abroad. Only after 1900 did the destruction of Australian forests lead to wider political interest in this question. The creation of national parks in all states, mostly after 1900, the formation of the Australian Forest League, activities of bushwalkers' clubs, and establishment of the Australian Forestry Conference in 1911, all testified to the growing (though still a minority) concern with the rape of the bush in Australia between 1900 and 1930.[140] The harbinger of these protracted changes was the New South Wales Royal Commission. There, Richard Baker proposed a scheme that presaged later debates in Australia and reflected Californian influence. Baker endorsed witnesses who spoke of the need to plant *Pinus radiata* on a large scale to prepare for the same timber famine that had stimulated thinking on conservation on the other side of the Pacific. He also reflected new theories in botany, commenting favorably on biological succession. Baker joined this evolutionary theory to the example of environmental renovation practiced in California. He speculated that humans could intervene to promote a more advanced and contrived succession process by rehabilitating lands with forest cover.[141]

This was the more general message from the export of eucalypts. The example suggested not only the need to conserve native trees but also to plant exotic pines such as those that complemented gums in shelter plantings in California.[142] Baker was not the first to urge a reciprocal exchange, however. When gum seed was being exported to California, forest enthusiasts in Australia were already advocating the importation of trees to "improve" the appearance and productivity of the Australian bush. One principal target was the lowly Monterey pine of California, and one of its strongest advocates was Ferdinand von Mueller.

The Remarkable Pines
of Monterey

Californian Softwoods in Australasia

In Australia and New Zealand at the turn of the century, reports circulated of an American pine with a remarkable growth rate. Sir Arthur Douglas, surveying contemporary New Zealand in 1909, pointed out the "astonishing rapidity of the growth of imported trees" and used as his example a *Pinus insignis* planted on the North Island in 1883. Cut down in 1899, it measured one hundred feet in height, with a trunk nine feet in circumference.[1] At Australian forestry conferences, foresters heard such favorable reports of this exotic that they gave it the name "Remarkable Pine." Known at the time by the botanical name of *insignis*, today it is recognized as *Pinus radiata* and known by the common names of Monterey or radiata pine.[2] A native of central coastal California, the pine was far from prominent in its home, but in Australasia it served as the reciprocal exchange for the extensive planting of eucalypts in California.

Monterey pine was not totally unappreciated in California. Edward Wickson, one-time editor of the *Pacific Rural Press* and later a professor of agriculture at the University of California, spoke in glowing terms of *Pinus insignis*. It was "a rapid, high-growing tree, and, though a native of the coast, has proved itself well adapted to the interior valleys of the central portion of the State. Its foliage is dense for a pine, and its shelter, therefore, the more complete."[3] Similarly, Charles Shinn felt that Monterey pine was underutilized for shelterbelt planting, despite the advantage of being "the easiest to transplant of all our modern evergreens."

Ironically, one of the reasons Californian authorities recommended the pine was its success in Australasia, "where it makes a remarkable growth."[4] The purely economic insignificance of the Remarkable Pine in its native environment cannot be doubted, however. *Pinus insignis* was not commercially exploited for timber, nor was it introduced in plantations, because it compared poorly with other American softwoods.[5] Theodore Lukens acknowledged in 1902 that Monterey pines were "short-lived." With few reaching the age of twenty-five years in southern California, their application in shelterbelt positions was limited, and in 1910 the state forester recommended against their planting for this purpose.[6] The tree was valued, therefore, chiefly for its shade and ornamental potential. A San Jose woman, Mrs. M. H. Field, wrote so movingly about the beauty of these pines in their natural setting that her praise was printed in the State Board of Forestry reports and quoted by other authorities: "In storm or sunshine, by day or by night, no tree was ever more individual, or more alluring than the Monterey pine, and no grove ever had greater charm than that which fringes the beautiful bay."[7] In Australia, such glowing recommendations were read, and may have encouraged the conviction that pines could add a new dimension of beauty to the bush.

Though used for ornament and shade in the United States, the contrast with Australia and New Zealand in commercial application could not be plainer. This pine proved one of the most successful of Pacific transplants from an economic standpoint, though the economic value was not originally anticipated. The initial hope of using *insignis* as part of a garden landscape with complex aesthetic and utilitarian uses was not be to realized. The story of how and why the pine spread best begins, as with the eucalypts, with Mueller and the aftermath of the gold rushes of the 1850s, as Australians sought to rebuild the environment already damaged by Europeans. Gold miners may have brought seeds of this and other pines, but the first documented case was its importation by the Sydney Botanic Gardens in 1857. Mueller also listed it as planted in the Melbourne gardens by 1858.[8] Specimens of *radiata* had already been established in a number of European sites prior to this, but the first mass acclimatization program began in New Zealand with seed imported from Australia and California. The officers of the Colonial Botanic Garden in Wellington were prominent in the spread of this plant in New Zealand from 1870 to 1878, just as Mueller was in Australia.[9]

Mueller had urged the widespread introduction of *insignis* in the 1860s as part of his acclimatization work.[10] In his lectures, reprinted by

Cooper, Mueller defended his distribution of half a million imported trees while head of the Melbourne Botanic Gardens. These were spread across Victoria in the late 1860s, and they included "many of the magnificent or quick-growing Himalayan and California Pines."[11] Mueller also mentioned *insignis* in 1871 in his lecture "Forest Culture in Its Relation to Industrial Pursuits," but he never stressed it over other pines.[12] Mueller's aim was not to create plantations of Monterey pine but to see a variety of pines mixed with Australian hardwoods, European oaks, and food-bearing trees like North American walnuts, so that timber and food needs could be fulfilled in an aesthetically pleasing and sustainable forest economy.[13]

Mueller's advocacy drew its first major results not in his own Victoria but in South Australia. South Australians gave the Remarkable Pine a chance in forestry practice for a mixture of reasons. In a practical sense, South Australia was the colony with the least adequate forest cover, and the one most comparable to California in climate. Only in the southeastern corner was rainfall sufficient to promote significant forest reserves and, by the 1870s, much of this had already been cut for timber destined for the urban markets of Adelaide or had been cleared for agriculture. As for the rest of the colony, much was covered by low-spreading acacia scrub and mallee varieties of dwarf eucalypts unsuitable for timber. South Australia had little choice but to seek afforestation, rather than rely, as the other colonies could, on native forests.[14]

The first plantings of *insignis* were made in 1876, and they reflected the influence of Marsh, Mueller, and George Goyder, the surveyor-general of South Australia. Although American ideas about the link between trees and rainfall had been debated in the South Australian and Victorian parliaments in the 1860s and 1870s, Goyder's main concern was the timber supply. It was Goyder who in an 1873 report drew attention to the alarming shortage of timber and recommended forest reserves on which both native and exotic species such as pines could be planted. In the first plantings, however, the worldwide reputation of *Eucalyptus globulus* was at work. Nearly 60 percent of the trees planted in 1876 were of Tasmanian blue gum, and only eight thousand *Pinus insignis* (7.6 percent of all seedlings) were planted. Also planted were other pines, but North American trees comprised only one-tenth of the total number of trees planted.[15]

These pines were planted because of a practical necessity, but one reinforced by political and ideological circumstances. The decision to plant was influenced by economic pressures and underlying conceptions about what the South Australian landscape ought to resemble. *Pinus insignis* plantings were part of the widespread attempt to acclimatize plants and create a garden landscape. The peculiarly regional impact requires us, however, to understand the political economy of colonial South Australia.

The early attempts at afforestation in South Australia strongly resembled the tree-planting phenomenon on the Great Plains of the American West. Alongside the notable natural aridity of the South Australian landscape went social aspirations for the settlement of the region that exacerbated the shortages of wooded land and created novel demands for more trees. As the urban population built up in the 1860s and the gold boom in nearby Victoria subsided, Goyder mapped the area suitable for agricultural settlement and specified limits beyond which agriculture could not be sustained because of low rainfall. This—roughly one hundred miles from Adelaide—became known as Goyder's Line. His predictions were uncannily similar to those of American John Wesley Powell concerning limits of small-scale agriculture's potential west of the hundredth meridian. As head of the American Geological Survey, Powell wrote a famous *Report on the Lands of the Arid Region* in 1878 that Donald Worster has called "a model of ecological realism in an unsympathetic age of unbounded expectations."[16] Goyder's Line exhibited similar ecological realism, but the area of South Australia beyond it was opened for agriculture after 1874, despite Goyder's dire warnings. Along with the extension of settlement went the idea, frequently expressed by settlers and promoters, that "rain follows the plough."[17]

This rain-making mania paralleled an American idea too. Nebraskan Samuel Aughey claimed that after plowing broke virgin soil, rain would be absorbed "like a huge sponge." The soil would then give "this absorbed moisture slowly back to the atmosphere by evaporation." Accordingly, it was "the great increase in absorptive power of the soil, wrought by cultivation, that has caused, and continues to cause, an increasing rainfall in the State."[18] Such crackpot forecasts about the adaptability of dry landscapes to agricultural settlement were quoted in South Australia to counteract Goyder, who, farmers claimed, was in league with pastoralists to prevent more intensive settlement. "Goyder's Line of Rainfall was all nonsense," proclaimed would-be settlers. Parliament caved in to such pressure. The land act amendments of 1874 opened up the northern lands and abolished Goyder's "imaginary line," as the farmers called it. In the new colonization areas, yields of up to thirty bushels of wheat per acre were recorded and the average across

the plains was more than ten bushels. These yields seemed quickly to vin-
dicate the breaching of Goyder's Line.[19]

The plow theory developed alongside the idea—again the parallel with
the Great Plains is striking—that the removal of trees in other parts of
the world had reduced rainfall and that the planting of trees would therefore increase it. The introduction of Arbor Day in the western American
states rested partly on this belief, and the idea was soon adopted in South
Australia and other colonies.[20] Mueller had already stated in his "Forest
Culture in Its Relations to Industrial Pursuits" (1871) that as a result of
"the American method" of planting shelterbelts, there were "one million
and four hundred thousand miles of treeless plains . . . which, in due
course of time, will necessarily be converted, to a great extent, into agricultural areas."[21] John Ednie Brown drew on these ideas and gave the
theory great importance in South Australia. Brown was a young Scot who
had visited the United States and Canada in 1871–72 and had written
two reports delivered to the Highland and Agricultural Society of Scot-
land entitled "Report upon Trees Found in California" and "Forests of
the Eastern States of America." His essay "The Trees of America" won
him the prize of the Scottish Arboricultural Society. As a result of his
North American experience, Brown was offered the job, at the age of
thirty, as conservator of forests in South Australia.[22] There, he elevated
trees from a mere influence to a means of almost complete control over
climate "and explained the aridity of interior Australia simply by the
absence of trees."[23] Brown differed from the farmers in his assessment
that the plains lacked adequate water prospects at the time of first settlement, but the effect of his argument was similar to the plow theory,
since trees would almost effortlessly make up the moisture deficit.

The first significant plantings of Remarkable Pine, between 1878 and
1880, resulted from Brown's influence. It was he who was really responsible for the introduction of this exotic. His *Practical Treatise on Tree
Culture* declared *insignis* "an excellent pine for planting on the sea-coast,
even within the influence of the salt water." Like contemporary commentators in California, Brown distinguished between characteristics of
radiata and *insignis,* which later botanists identified as minor variations
of the same species.[24]

Brown's plantings were designed to replicate in South Australia the
"garden of the world." The Scot aimed to create a framework for small-
scale agricultural settlement and to promote a diversity of vegetation.
He experimented with a wide range of species and encouraged plantings
in many different areas by his recommendations to farmers and home

gardeners on the value of trees for shade, shelterbelts, the adornment of buildings, and such functions as fuel wood and construction.

Utilitarian arguments figured in his brief but aesthetic arguments were equally common. Planted in masses, pine trees could, said Brown, "give such a clothed look to the farm as to enhance its value very much in the estimation of persons of refined taste." He recommended planting "to give each and every subject that pleasing and ornamental aspect which at the present time is so much wanted and sought after."[25] This aesthetic was strikingly similar to Ellwood Cooper's. The Californian argued that the planter of trees not only increases "the productiveness of his farm" but also "beautifies his home, improves the climate, doubles the value of his land, receives inspiration from this work of his own hands, elevates his own condition, and adds to the refinement of himself, his family, and all his surroundings."[26] Like Cooper, Brown even saw a spiritual purpose in tree planting: "As our surroundings become physically more perfect, so in the same ratio do we become morally better." This moral and spiritual improvement Brown linked to the progress of civilization. Where tree cover was removed, as in the formerly lush and gardenlike but now desolate Middle East, "the civilization which once regulated their affairs has fallen with them [the trees] and left them [the people] in the condition of semi-barbarism."[27] This catastrophe occurred because without trees, agriculture suffered, and farming was the basis of civilized prosperity. "Denuded land," said a Brown protégé, George Perrin, "slowly but surely loses its fertility year by year." True, "artificial treatment" by manures could supply some wants, but tree planting more completely and effectively "renovated" worn soils and enriched the land for agriculture.[28]

EARLY SUCCESSES

Brown's predictions brought him into conflict with Goyder, whose views on the connection between climate and tree cover were more circumspect. That Goyder had the better of the intellectual argument became clear as drought across the newly settled region north of Goyder's Line after 1880 dashed the hopes of agriculturalists—and Brown—that a garden of the world might be easily created. By 1890, the experimentation in farming unsuitable land north of Goyder's Line had been checked, but Brown's experimental pine plantations farther south were a runaway success. Quite accidentally, he had discovered quickly how remarkable the Remarkable Pine really was. Brown noted in 1881, just a few years after its introduction, that "this is one of the few introductions of pines to the colony which have succeeded to the best of expectations."[29] Because it grew well on poor South Australian soils and in salty winds, *insignis* was suitable for coastal rehabilitation planting. But most of all, it could be harvested in just twenty years, far earlier than any other pine. It was successful in the southeastern part of the state, where "the strong growth of *insignis*" began "partly suppressing the eucalypts," which seemed to suffer more from disease than did the import. Although forest planting had partly been conceived as a means of extending the tree cover to areas previously covered only with scrub, in practice it served to replace old-growth native forests and so transform parts of the South Australian landscape to resemble the more symmetrical and cultivated appearance of Northern Hemisphere forests.[30] The difference in land use was starkly visible in the contrast between radiata pine forests and dominant euca-lyptus and grazing land that met immediately at the Victorian–South Australian border.[31]

Brown left South Australia in 1890 to take up a similar post in New South Wales and subsequently moved to Western Australia in 1893, where he continued to push his ideas on tree cover until his death in 1899. He also influenced the planting of the pine in Tasmania, where George Perrin had gone from South Australia to be conservator of forests.[32] But Brown's successor in South Australia, Walter Gill (1851–1929), proved even more successful with the pine during a thirty-three-year tenure as conservator of forests that ended in 1923. From 1897, *insignis* became the dominant species in forest planting in South Australia, eclipsing the earlier complementary experimentation with acacias and eucalypts.[33]

The success of *insignis* was such that by the first decade of the twentieth century the South Australian Woods and Forests Department had to look around desperately for outlets for the timber windfall. A government timber mill was established in 1903 to utilize the product. The wood was used, in an appropriately symmetrical expression of the garden concept, in packing cases for Renmark's irrigation district fruit. Thus the pine would neatly complement the garden landscape established through irrigation schemes.[34]

Throughout Australia the Remarkable Pine was, according to proud foresters, easy to plant, required little maintenance, and suffered few pests or diseases. A dieback caused by zinc deficiency set back the cause during World War I,[35] but the species regenerated naturally from this malady. The other potential problem foresters identified was the susceptibility of the seedlings to rabbits, and they soon concluded that meshing was required for the young plants. But the rapid growth and economic returns outweighed the costs imposed by these conditions.

From South Australia, use of *Pinus insignis* spread in forestry management to Tasmania, to Victoria—where forty-three thousand acres had been planted by the mid-1930s—and to New South Wales after 1914 through Gill's tireless advocacy.[36] Its tasks included rehabilitation of badly degraded areas where seemingly nothing else would grow. In a successful effort to renovate the landscape in 1916, the Victorian Forestry Commission planted *insignis* in areas of "tailing" left by dredges on the Ovens River goldfields.[37] At about the same time, landscape gardeners used exotic conifers, including *insignis*, to achieve a clothed and verdant look in more domestic settings. Their use signified, as in the case of some domestic, highway, and plantation uses in the Blue Mountains and to the west toward Bathurst in New South Wales, a statement about the planting of European civilization in the bush, not just an economic proposition. Pines were planted around homesteads to mark symbolically the boundaries of civilization and human control and were clearly visible on the crests of hills and ridges where farmhouses had been established or roads and paths hacked out of the wilderness.[38] The garden city of Canberra, planned by the American architect Walter Burley Griffin, also included among its early exotic plantings of pine trees the transformation of the bare, "rabbit-infested hillside" of Mount Stromlo "into a well-forested slope." From that small beginning in 1915, the area under pines in the Australian Capital Territory grew to fifteen thousand acres in 1950 and twenty-four thousand acres in 1961, over 90 percent of them radiata pines.[39]

Plantations of this type had important visual effects. Because the trees were often visible from roads and planted in blocks, their presence, especially when planted commercially, involved an aesthetic transformation that could not be missed.[40] More so than the eucalyptus in California, the Monterey pine planted in these locations had the capacity to become an invasive "weed" in Australian conditions, where it successfully competed with open eucalyptus forests and sometimes spilled beyond plantation areas.[41] Nowhere, however, did the pine become a serious pest as prickly pear did.

As with California's eucalypts, the major thrust behind planting after 1900 became economic rather than aesthetic. The N.S.W. Royal Commission of Inquiry on Forestry recommended in 1908 the introduction of *insignis* because of "its hardy qualities and vigorous habits of growth." It was still known as the Remarkable Pine, and in the Royal Commission report no reference was made to its place of origin.[42] The New South Wales government began its first plantings in 1914 in poor coastal locations but soon added several more-successful ones in moist tableland regions west and south of Sydney.[43]

New South Wales and Victoria had become interested in the pine because of the forecast worldwide shortage of timber that spurred the boom plantings of eucalyptus in California. This panic was accentuated in Australia. The country already imported much of its softwood because of the destruction of the limited supplies of indigenous alternatives in many areas by 1900, and because of the dominance of hardwoods in the original forest stock. New South Wales Royal Commission witnesses noted with relief that eucalypts regenerated naturally in the state and did not constitute such a severe problem as the softwood deficiency did.[44] The commission displayed ample evidence that attitudes toward forests in Australia were changing under the impact of both foreign ideas and the practice of scientific forestry in South Australia. Here, the pine played an important role in showing what could be done by way of managed plantations under Australian labor and climatic conditions.

FROM FORESTRY AS A GARDEN TO FORESTRY AS A FARM

John Ednie Brown had seen forests as a complement to the farm and advocated *insignis* as part of an abundant gardenlike environment that trees would help create and preserve. After 1900 this sentiment occasionally persisted. Joseph Maiden, director of the Sydney Botanic Gardens and a specialist on the eucalyptus, mentioned to the 1908 Royal Commission the moral and aesthetic value of forests: "I cannot conceive of a race of human beings whose minds are not elevated by contemplation of forests." Clearly, this was important to him as an arboriculturalist,[45] but the ethic had already shifted toward getting the most growth, which usually involved planting in each particular area just one species chosen on the basis of its role in timber production. This meant that forestry services would plant only a small range of trees found to be suitable in particular locations. These trees would be planted at specific intervals and harvested at specified times. Profits and efficiency had begun to transform the garden ideal in Australian forestry, as was paralleled in California in the same period.

The clearest indication of the change came at the Australian Forestry Conference in 1922, when Walter Gill of South Australia documented the success of *insignis*. Queensland's Edward Swain praised Gill's achievement. Gill had "demonstrated for all to see that forestry is timber-farming, and that timber is a profitable crop to grow." Continuing the metaphor of a farm to replace the older concept of a cultivated garden, Swain referred to Gill's paper in glowing terms: "We have unrolled before us the whole history of a forest from the time of its sowing upon newly-ploughed ground, through thirty years' of growth, until the final reaping of the timber crop."[46]

The focus on cultivation of forests as a resource had roots in the depression of the 1890s, as a response to the increased emphasis on economy in government. No longer could timber resources in Crown lands be virtually or even literally given away. This financial imperative meshed with growing international fears of a wood shortage. In turn, the rise of conservationist sentiment and the prominence of ideas of efficient resource use imported from the United States and Europe drew attention to deficiencies in governments' haphazard forestry practice in Australia.[47] Added to this, the sheer success of *insignis* in South Australia reinforced the foresters' message that the country need no longer rely on nature to provide all the timbers required for economic development.

Impelled by the cumulative force of economics and rational conservation sentiment, a shift occurred in forestry philosophy by the 1920s. Sentiment moved closer to broad-acre principles. Radiata pine served here as an exemplar of the potential of the new approach and demonstrated how forests in Australia could be more efficiently managed to make them into tree farms. Yet a wide gap persisted between the foresters' acknowledgment of the need for policy change, and broad acceptance by politicians and the timber trade of the value of the new softwood timber.

COMBATING RESISTANCE

Extensive planting required success in marketing the crop produced. Royal commissions could advocate Monterey pine as a softwood savior, but the toughest battle was to get the timber accepted for building purposes. Here California gave no cause for optimism. As the state forester Merritt Pratt pointed out in 1922, "Monterey Pine is not cut into lumber these days because of the knottiness of the wood."[48] How could Australians be persuaded to use this poor quality timber?[49] The timber met with outright resistance from potential users. The Master Builders Association of New South Wales was unwilling to pronounce radiata pine suitable for first-class joinery or other work requiring either strength or good finish.[50] Builders also expressed concern that radiata pine could not be used externally, though such use was common in New Zealand. Witnesses to the 1908 New South Wales Royal Commission even cast doubt on its sturdiness for use in the manufacture of packing cases. The knots made working the wood difficult, and forestry experts rated it poorer than imported North American timbers. Tests carried out at Adelaide University after World War I showed that Monterey pine was not as strong as competing softwoods such as *Pinus canariensis* and Oregon (*Pseudotsuga menziesii*), although it grew 15 percent quicker.[51] Even the *insignis* name tag was a liability, according to some foresters. Said Chief Commissioner of Forests R. Dalrymple Hay of New South Wales, in 1922: "Its name is not one likely to make it popular in commerce; it is too cumbersome and does not rest easily on the tongue."[52]

In their response to such criticisms, the pine's champions emphasized the importance of scientific investigation and improved forestry management and argued that the first plantings could not be used to judge the suitability of the wood. Walter Gill deflected concern about the "somewhat coarse" quality of the timber by arguing that labor conditions had made European silviculture methods inappropriate. He pointed out that in the original plantings then coming to maturity, the ground had not been cultivated and the trees had not been planted close enough together because of the high labor costs involved. A distance of eight feet by eight feet had been standard before 1900; this gave the trees room to bend, twist, and sway, which put stress upon the wood and produced more knots. Now the South Australian Woods and Forests Department promised it would produce "the better quality of timber" that the building trade desired—the "grand, massive, regular body of trees" that closer planting promoted.[53]

This advocacy had some result. At this time Australian foresters began to adopt silvicultural techniques in a serious fashion, and experimentation with *insignis* was at the forefront of moves to specialize in pine production under intensive cultivation. The Victorian School of Forestry's Demonstration Forest indicated the trend. It opened in 1923 and included a yearly conversion of 62 acres of eucalyptus forest to a variety of pines under silvicultural methods. By 1949 the trees began to reap a financial reward for the School, which became a valuable forestry property.[54]

In a striking parallel with the eucalypts in North America, Monterey pine's appeal was decidedly regional in Australia. Alongside its impressive achievements in South Australia, it had also succeeded by 1922 in several districts of New South Wales. Yet suitable land was limited there and in other states. In Queensland the pine had been well established around Stanthorpe in southeastern Queensland—a cooler, tableland region with good rainfall—but had failed to flourish in comparison with the cypress and other native pines on trial farther north. Monterey pine required much labor to combat sun blister, rat-tailing, and other diseases, and its mortality in Queensland was "very much greater" than that of native hoop-pine where left unattended, reported Edward Swain, chief forester of Queensland. Failure of the pine to flourish in Western Australia was a cause of some concern, too; it had been planted in areas where the water table was too high.[55]

Professional foresters' "misgivings" over the pine plantings around Australia diminished in the 1920s, however. Monterey pine was endorsed in 1923 by the British Empire Forestry Conference.[56] British capital was sanctioned by the conference to undertake large-scale plantings in suitable areas through the Commonwealth Development and Migration Commission. Loan money was provided at very low interest to promote the afforestation of 50,000 acres and bring out British forestry workers to help.[57] J. J. Rodger, Gill's successor, made larger plantings that underlay South Australia's "prominent position as a supplier of softwood timber" for the remainder of the twentieth century.[58] By 1954, South Australia was supplying more than 50 percent of Australia's domestic production of softwoods, despite its unpromising environment for forest development. A minor crisis occurred in the 1930s and 1940s over declining yields,[59] but the issue of yields did not become serious until the 1960s, when the South Australian Woods and Forests Department began for the first time to get quantitative evidence of decline in second-growth plantations.[60] By the late 1940s there were 200,000 acres of such plantations—now universally called radiata pine—throughout Australia, and by 1955, plantation softwoods, mainly radiata, supplied 300 million board feet of timber per year. Yet the softwood industry was still dwarfed by the hardwood industry, which produced a total of 6.4 billion board feet of timber; the small quantity of softwoods produced was the result of the fact that only relatively small areas outside South Australia had reached maturity.[61]

THE NEW ZEALAND COMPARISON

Despite Gill's efforts, plantations of Monterey pine were much more successful in New Zealand than anywhere in Australia. New Zealand had 279,000 acres in 1940, more than the whole of Australia had in the late

1940s.[62] Partly this trend reflected the fact that private capital in the form of timber investment went into radiata in New Zealand to a greater extent than in Australia, where logging of the native forests remained the prime objective.[63] According to the New Zealand Government Timber Trade Commissioner in Australia, New Zealand by the mid-1950s had 900,000 acres of exotic conifers, over 700,000 of them being *radiata,* while the total for Australia was only one-quarter of this.[64] By the 1970s, New Zealand had the largest commercial plantings in the world, and the pine constituted a major export. Australia was a major destination of those pine products.

This greater effect related in some measure to climate. The moist, temperate climate of New Zealand was even better suited to the pine than was southeastern South Australia, and as a result the rates of growth were more astonishing in New Zealand. Planting these pines took advantage of this coincidence. Cultural heritage may also have played a part. The American geographer Andrew Hill Clark surmised in the 1940s that acceptance of the conifers had been a product of the cultural baggage of Europeans in the Southern Hemisphere. But this does not explain why the resistance of similar British peoples to conifers in Australia was greater after 1920, when support for the native eucalyptus timbers and trees began to develop. The key may lie in the original character of the forests. New Zealand forests were predominantly softwoods, including the magnificent Kauri "pine" (*Agathis australis*). When these were essentially logged out commercially in the first decade of the twentieth century, replacement of a "pine" with a pine was a logical, almost unremarkable substitution of softwoods in commercial operations, since Kauri did not quickly regenerate.[65] Aesthetically New Zealanders may have found it easier, too, to substitute, because their native trees reminded them enough of Europe to call them "pines" and "beech" (*Nothofagus*). Eucalyptus seemed radically different. New Zealanders had already become used to pine-dotted landscapes, whereas Australians had begun to see eucalypt forests as the normal condition of their own country. Far more than in Australia, New Zealand botanical descriptions rejoiced over the beauty of the pine, and still do.[66]

This aesthetic explanation of New Zealand's success is strengthened by the way the lovers of eucalyptus in Australia resisted radiata. The turn of the century saw new appreciation of the Australian gum trees. The Australian Forest League decried the loss of native timbers and argued that part of this permanent degradation was "undoubtedly due . . . to ignorance of the value of our native trees." Reforestation in Australia was, the league argued, "chiefly applicable to hardwoods."[67] The Victorian forestry conservator Owen Jones reported in 1922 that members of the Victorian Forest League, "as good Australians, are all in favour of gum trees and . . . consider any man who suggests introducing exotic species as an absolute vandal."[68] A developing nationalist identity here influenced forestry practice in subtle ways.

This shift in sensibility enhanced the long-term welfare of the natural environment of Australian forests and the wildlife they sustained, but it should not be believed that this federation-era nationalist sentiment in Australia focused on appreciation of the value of primeval forests qua forests. These sentiments were, in theory, acknowledged in the "national parks" founded at the turn of the century in most states, but national parks were not inviolable in Australia.[69] The nationalist sentiment was directed as much toward seeing Australian *wood* as equal in value to imported woods as it was toward appreciating the scenic value of native forests. This change involved the aesthetic appreciation of those woods. Richard Baker was a great booster of the value of Australian hardwoods, which, "differing in colour and figure from any imported timber, particularly lend themselves to every branch of architecture." He noted Australians' heightened appreciation of the great beauty of the wood of Australian trees like the "once despised stringy barks [*E. obliqua*]."[70] The Australian Forest League championed Australian hardwoods as much for their timber value as for their contribution to "other aspects" of the forest question.[71]

This activity of the nature lovers underlined the economic advantages of natives for parsimonious legislatures. One Tasmanian parliamentarian said just after World War I that "it was of no use putting in groves of pine trees; hardwood was our timber and this would grow without reafforestation."[72] Even Victoria, the only state other than South Australia with plantings to serve its own requirements by 1935, had considerable quantities of mountain ash (*E. regnans*), which Edward Swain reported could be used "for many purposes for which softwoods are normally used."[73] In Swain, both the aesthetic appreciation of Australian native forests and economic considerations merged to resist the triumph of the pine outside the southeastern states. As Queensland's forestry commissioner in the 1920s, Swain championed natives over the American conifers. An acute observer of national and regional differences in forestry practice, Swain drew a sharp distinction between Australia and New Zealand in the matter of afforestation. He slammed New Zealand, which had "nailed her forestry flag to the method of planting, and has abandoned almost irrevocably her fine natural forests, because their growth is alleged to be slower." The costs of planting per acre in New Zealand were uneconomical, Swain claimed, at seven to thirteen pounds per acre compared to the costs of American forestry of one pound five shillings. Swain's critique made economic sense at the time for most Australian states, given the preponderance of self-renewing hardwood forests.[74] The debate over exotics was further complicated by the discovery that Australian timbers could be adapted to different regions within the country and thereby, it was hoped, would overcome the problem of softwood shortage. Cypress "pine" (*Callitris columellaris*) did poorly in what Swain described as its "native lair" in western Queensland, but on "waste lands" like Fraser Island—today listed under a United Nations convention as a World Heritage area noted for its unique conservation values—it thrived much better than exotic pines.[75]

Ironically, American forestry practice influenced Swain in defending these native plantings. In 1918, after undertaking a 1916 study tour of Montana, he published *An Australian Study of American Forestry*, which praised the American conservation movement. He believed that planting was too "laborious and costly" and the Australian "forest flora too valuable to be jettisoned." With "its powers of reproduction too great to be overlooked," Australia, like America, had to "pin its faith" on "natural regeneration." As a result, Swain indicated that *radiata* was not preferred in Queensland.[76]

Swain was, however, criticized by other Australian foresters, and during the remainder of his stormy career he engaged in a running battle with those who staffed the new Commonwealth Forestry School in Canberra. C. E. Lane-Poole, the principal, emphasized intensive silviculture, and this included use of radiata pine.[77] More than legislators and nature lovers, the silviculturists appreciated the softwood shortage, and the next forty years saw a war of attrition between the forces of silviculture and natural regeneration which was never clearly won by either side. In the long term, champions of natural regeneration stimulated concern with native forests and their ecology, but simultaneously deprived Australia of the possibility of substituting domestic softwoods for the imported variety on a systematic basis. The third alternative of cultivating eucalyptus and other native forests grown in plantations was a course of action that received very little consideration.[78] The Melbourne industrialist and forest enthusiast Russell Grimwade did plant experimental plots of eucalyptus in Victoria between 1912 and 1925. Undoubtedly he was inspired in part by the example of eucalyptus plantations abroad, because he made specific references to those in California. However, his farm was planned for the production of essential oils rather than timber, and, in any case, the scheme did not prove commercially viable.[79]

Cost also featured in the timber industry's opposition to plantation hardwood development. The rotation time for eucalyptus in natural forest conditions of eighty years or more compared unfavorably with that of plantation pines, which required twenty-five to forty-seven years. Yet the example of California's eucalypt plantations did not attract proponents either, because the shorter rotation was off-set by the poor quality of wood produced under those different growing conditions.[80] As a result, almost all of the (limited) interest in plantations centered on softwoods. Examples of success with eucalypts, such as that of Penders Plantation on the South Coast of New South Wales near Bega, failed to shake the conventional wisdom.[81]

The long-term result of the failure to establish sustainable forestry through plantations of either pine or eucalyptus on a national scale has been, in the 1970s to 1990s, the plundering of the last of the old-growth forests outside national parks. At the very time Swain wrote his most severe criticisms of New Zealand's policy in the 1920s, Oregon pine was challenging Australian hardwoods in the building industry;[82] radiata is imported from New Zealand today because local supplies are still inadequate despite further significant and successful plantings across southern Australia. In the end, Australian forests remained based on native hardwoods, as they had been at the time of first settlement. The attempt to create a garden landscape of mixed European and Californian tree plantings and farms had not succeeded, but neither had North American pines come to dominate national forests. Australians now face, in the conflict over old-growth forests, an ominous legacy of continued timber shortage and damage to native habitats.

CHAPTER 5

Irrigation and the Garden in California

Popular Thought

For the historian of popular environmental thought, irrigation is not about drains, pumps, pipes, and dams, but about dreams. Central to the meaning of irrigation were the dreams of transforming nature into a garden—and the harsher realities that the garden ideal had to confront in the experience of irrigation. The fundamental facts of aridity drew together the history of California and Australia in the late nineteenth century. But aridity meant little in the absence of the aspiration to fashion a garden out of desert, and Australia and the arid regions of California shared this aspiration too. True, civilizations have for millennia pursued this dream. In California and Australia, however, the idea developed that a democracy of small-scale farmers should take charge of this process, and that small urban communities should develop in balance with more intensely occupied rural landscapes.

Underlying popular irrigation rhetoric for a gardenlike environment was the preference for a broader and more equitable distribution of wealth, for the shoring up of rural communities against the attractions of the city, and the defense of the Anglo-Saxon race against the threats of Asian and other "servile" labor. Irrigation quickly attained the dimensions of a popular crusade to create a middle-class utopia. Fashioned first and most clearly in California, stimulated by ideas of California's exceptional status and favored prospects, this cultural definition of the landscape quickly gained considerable appeal on the other side of the Pacific in the British colonial settlements in Australia.

The attempt to link the irrigation crusade with the aspirations of a cooperative white democracy was an ironic development. In the late twentieth century, agribusiness and the economic interests associated with the development of urban conglomerations gained most from the precious supplies of water in the American West. Irrigation ultimately served as a source of wealth concentration too. This possible outcome was obvious enough to some early critics. George Perkins Marsh feared that irrigation's requirement for large capital outlays and skillful management promoted "the accumulation of large tracts of land in the hands of single proprietors" and consequently dispossessed "the smaller landholders." In a report to Congress in 1879, Marsh warned that irrigating the West would strengthen the power of the wealthy, just as he believed irrigation had done in Europe. The tactical need in irrigation activism was for a democratic form of water distribution. Marsh himself saw a way out. He called on the federal government to limit the size of irrigated landholdings. The government should "promote the division of the soil" into "farms of relatively narrow extent" by giving small farmers "a larger proportion of water and at lower rates."[1]

Irrigation promoters built upon Marsh's argument in the formative debates of the 1890s that led to the National Reclamation Act of 1902. The National Irrigation Congresses after 1891 and William Ellsworth Smythe's *Irrigation Age* editorials did not seek to foist large-scale capitalist "industrialism" upon the American West, but rather to shore up the role of the petty bourgeois proprietor through the aid of the state. This chapter and the one that follows it study those aims and show how and why that vision appealed to Californians and Australians.

To make irrigation a weapon of democratization, irrigation propagandists stressed a moral and aesthetic vision to complement the economic one. Their appeal was at the same time egalitarian and middle class. The gardenlike and abundant landscapes they envisioned would allow more people to live on the land. Through the production of high-value goods such as fruit, the standard of living could be raised, the health of the masses enhanced, and the dangers of a pauperized farm labor force avoided.

The garden paradise depicted in irrigation propaganda resembled the society that middle-class horticultural interests projected. The two interests developed in tandem from the 1870s to the 1890s, thus raising a key question: To what degree was the social aspiration of horticulturalists to create a society of independent producers living in agrarian harmony the driving force in irrigation in California? At first glance, it seems axiomatic that the two interests were identical. Some very prominent California horticulturalists were strong supporters of irrigation. As early as 1865, during a term as a U.S. congressman, that apostle of the garden John Bidwell advocated planned irrigation to replace the piecemeal development of California agriculture.[2]

The involvement of the horticultural interest in irrigation was a logical development. For many areas of the state, particularly in the south, no irrigation meant no fruit. The USDA irrigation official Richard Hinton spoke of the area west of Pasadena to Redlands as "almost worthless even for grazing purposes, and as incapable of sustaining a population as the great Mojave Desert itself." But now this land was "the most valuable in all California," thanks to the life-giving properties of water. In Los Angeles and San Bernardino Counties, Eugene Hilgard reported in 1882, there were already eighty-five thousand irrigated acres, much of it in fruit and "but little land being cultivated" without artificial water schemes.[3]

Yet the fruit growers were not united on the subject of irrigation. As late as 1900, only 40 percent of orchard fruit was irrigated.[4] Because of the diversity of the state, some fruit growers needed no irrigation at all. Fruit growers in the highly productive and well-watered Santa Clara Valley generally avoided artificial watering; rainfall in the ocean belt meant that irrigation was not required in coastal areas, advised the secretary of the State Board of Horticulture, B. M. Lelong, "except in the southern portion."[5] Even in the Los Angeles area there were some who disagreed with the idea that irrigation was essential to fruit culture. Ezra and Jeanne Carr of Pasadena had planted forty-two acres after 1877, and of this not more than half was irrigated in 1882. With Ezra opposed at first to artificial watering, the Carrs experimented assiduously with varieties of fruit trees that did not require irrigation.[6]

Individuals' interest in irrigation varied with the type of fruit planted and its requirements. Ellwood Cooper pointed out that for his olive groves "in Santa Barbara, near the coast, no irrigation is necessary." He found sufficient the "very frequent stirring of the soil" in the growing season.[7] Olives could also be cultivated without irrigation as far west as Pomona, though some growers were skeptical about the quality of the product.[8] Some viticulturists were especially suspicious of irrigation because it was thought to affect the quality of the fruit, rendering it unfit to make fine wine. Henry Brainard, speaking of central California, claimed that "wine grapes should never be planted where irrigation is required."[9]

Where irrigation was not essential, farmers often avoided it because of expense or because of the perception that stagnant water brought malaria.[10] Academic authorities, too, were not convinced of the panacea of irrigation. Eugene Hilgard, usually quoted as an advocate of water schemes, was much more circumspect about the chances for irrigation than were promoters like the land developer James De Barth Shorb. Irrigation was expensive, Hilgard cautioned, and could leave behind soluble salts. Its desirability needed to be carefully studied in particular cases.[11]

Because of these reservations, irrigation failed to emerge as a serious issue at most fruit growers' meetings in the 1880s.[12] The Wright Act's introduction in 1887 and the creation of irrigation districts occurred without discussion at the growers' conventions or in the reports of officials of the State Board of Horticulture. Ellwood Cooper highlighted the ambitious case for irrigation made by Shorb, that "only water is required" for boundless fertility in the San Gabriel orchards, but warned his horticulturalist followers that these claims were "contrary to every theory as laid down in all the agricultural journals in the country."[13]

Horticultural caution soon diminished in the 1890s, however, and the rise of irrigation consciousness tracked closely the demise of the early phases of the eucalyptus craze. Droughts in the American West in 1889, 1890, and especially in 1893 dashed the hopes of farmers that rain would follow either the plow or the planting of shelter. The transformation of climate did not occur simply by supplying tree cover.[14] By 1893, practical experience had considerably modified thinking about the role of trees as an environmental transformer. In response to these failures, attention shifted to attempts to control water supplies directly through irrigation.

The shift in the American debate was driven, too, by the worldwide depression of the 1890s and by changes occurring in California agriculture. It was not just the idea of irrigation that won increasing support in that decade, but the idea of using governmental intervention. Private irrigation projects had existed for several decades in the American West. Now the meetings of the National Irrigation Convention began to demand that "government must assume a greater responsibility." Economic conditions "had radicalized the irrigation movement." Before the 1890s, the demand in the United States had been for ceding of public lands for irrigation purposes, but most of these had been acquired already by big companies. The depression dried up investment, and business interests backing irrigation pulled out, thus prompting demands for greater public involvement.[15] At the same time, the changing composition of California agriculture created the pressure for more irrigation. The gradual shift away from wheat—where irrigation was not usually employed—to fruit, and especially to thirsty citrus in southern California, undermined opposition to water schemes.[16]

As the fruit industry expanded and yet also faced the prospect of depression and drought, the demands for irrigation grew shriller. This pressure coincided with the drive across several western states for federal assistance, and culminated in the Reclamation Act of 1902. Indications of the changing attitude were many. "Experience has shown," argued one observer, "that cultivation [alone], even if it be the most careful and thorough, will not produce fruit." A correspondent to the *Rural Californian* in 1895 described Ezra Carr as a skilled and dedicated horticulturalist who had "succeeded in producing as fine and healthy a growth on his trees as we ever saw." Yet the same writer gloated that Carr's "crops were never profitable until several years' experience broke down his stubbornness, and he supplied water freely, with the result of more than quadrupling his yield."[17] By 1900, Cooper, too, had abandoned his earlier skepticism about the claims for irrigation made by Shorb. In fact, Cooper quoted Shorb again—this time approvingly—that "agriculture in California" could "be made as certain" as in the Nile Valley. Dry conditions dictated a change in horticulturalist attitudes to a pro-irrigation stance.[18]

This shift reflected horticulturalists' search for more efficiently and carefully controlled products. Some growers spoke of "the fruit tree" as "a most wonderful manufactory."[19] They were keen to bend nature to their advantage in many ways, from biological control to artificially created forest cover. Yet the irrigation promoters pushed the idea of environmental manipulation much farther. They increasingly argued that water could be turned on and off at will and could transform totally arid lands into flourishing farms. Local farmers, said one trade paper in 1893, preferred irrigation because it "imparts that certainty to crops which is wanting in rainy climates."[20] In humid regions, the growing season was retarded by the presence of clouds, and the rains did not necessarily arrive at optimum times. Irrigation could be cheaper in the long run, promoters claimed, since yields would be higher.

The result was potentially a mechanistic attitude toward farming in tension with the desire to reestablish an environmental balance. At the same time, American irrigators settled on the language of "reclamation." The idea of "reclaiming" desert "wastes" entered American usage in the

1890s, but it connoted something more than restoration of natural abundance. Rather, it asserted human *claims* to primacy and possession that fitted the theme of imperial domination of nature.[21] The idea of balance remained in all of this, but increasingly it was a social and economic balance rooted in small towns and farms that irrigation promoters emphasized. In this search for a sustainable society rather than a sustainable ecology, irrigation enthusiasts lauded the role of science. At the International Irrigation Congress in Los Angeles in October 1893, the stage was decorated with a banner that read "Irrigation—Science, not Chance."[22] This viewpoint did not yet dominate horticulture at the expense of ideas of natural equilibrium. Indeed, irrigation would serve, apologists believed, to enhance older notions of the garden landscape that all saw as more natural than deserts. Still, the demand for greater environmental manipulation through science did become more insistent in the 1890s as rainfall failed to satisfy the ever-expanding demands of the fruit lands and their urban markets.

The horticulturalists' concern with water policy was both stimulated by—and expressed in—the many irrigation congresses of the 1890s. The International Congress of 1893, especially, provoked wide discussion and praise in the trade papers and conventions.[23] At the 1893 State Fruit Growers' Convention, a session on irrigation was held for the first time, and irrigation endorsed in enthusiastic terms. "But for irrigation," the Riverside delegate James Boyd argued, "much of our best fruit lands necessarily would be still a desert waste, and some of the special productions of the irrigated regions would be almost unknown in the great markets of the East."[24]

Although many California horticulturalists were involved in private irrigation works, it did not necessarily follow that they wanted federal government intervention. The widespread use of private irrigation and the local irrigation districts under the Wright Act of 1887 meant that irrigation demands in California tended to lag behind those elsewhere. There was little call among fruit growers for the extensive federal government involvement that came with the National Reclamation Act. Demands for federal action came more from other states and from the national sphere, though the voice of a Californian resident, William Ellsworth Smythe, was prominent. Smythe, editor of *Irrigation Age* and convenor of the National Irrigation Congress, addressed the State Fruit Growers' Convention on behalf of the California Water and Forests Association in 1900 to try to stir support for new legislative reform, but no resolution of the conference followed.[25]

Horticulturalists were, however, susceptible to one vital message from the promoters of national legislation. Smythe's address appealed "for the support of the fruit-growers of California" in "storing the waste waters" and "saving the forests," as part of "the national irrigation cause."[26] For the southern Californian growers, whose support for irrigation was strongest, irrigation was tightly connected to the preservation of mountain forests. Rather than support expensive federal government involvement in building dams and drainage systems, Southern Californians emphasized the importance of forest cover for the control of stream flow.[27] Abbot Kinney noted in 1894 that "every city, village, home, orchard, and field in Southern California is subject to damage and destruction by unwise forest denudation" through "diminished summer water supply" or "by excessive flood delivery of water, or the creation of new torrents," a pattern of natural disaster he claimed was increasing with the exploitation of southern California's natural resources.[28] Fruit growers stressed that forest preservation would, by enhancing water conservation, reduce the size of required dams and save them from damage caused by flood debris. Kinney joined the Southern California Forest and Water Association to lobby the federal government for action, and he linked the two causes, trading wider political support in Washington for forest preservation in return for Californian support for "judicious irrigation works."[29]

IRRIGATION ARGUMENTS AND THE GARDEN CONCEPT

Horticulturalists' expectations about the virtues of an irrigated landscape converged with the arguments of irrigation promoters at many points, but subtle differences persisted. One dispute was over the role of irrigation for land development and urbanization. Horticulturalists were often troubled by the way their hopes for the creation of a garden paradise might be compromised by such schemes. Ironically—and fatally—horticulturalists were at the same time tempted by the attractions of a suburban environment that would bring modern improvements and technology to their farms and raise the value of their land.

One driving force behind the extravagant rhetoric of irrigation was, critics charged in hindsight, land speculation by wealthy entrepreneurs.[30] Because water could turn arid land into profitable farms, powerful pressures to accumulate capital lay behind irrigation. As far back as the 1870s, developers such as William Chapman sought quick profits by subdividing key holdings along the San Joaquin River.[31] This and other early irrigation settlements partook of the spirit of speculation that motivated land transactions in the American West. Some large landowners tried to use the rhetoric of the garden paradise to further their own battles over water access with other, more deeply entrenched riparian proprietors. Such was the case of James Ben Ali Haggin, famed contestant in the *Lux v. Haggin* case of 1881, in which Haggin challenged Henry Miller and Charles Lux, rich riparian landowners in Kern County. Haggin employed the language of "community builders" who, instead of running sheep and cattle, sought to use irrigation to turn an "absolutely uninhabited and uninhabitable desert waste" into a "garden spot" where "thousands of families would one day live."[32] Haggin lost the case over water rights, but he was not alone among the economically powerful in the battle to use irrigation to develop land.

Some spokesmen within the state horticultural board were influential landowners, and land buying and selling was never-ending in the fruit-growing districts. This trade at times also benefited smaller-scale buyers like those in Riverside, whose allotments grew in value under irrigation.[33] In the boom of the 1880s when irrigation first took hold of the popular imagination, one spin-off of the development of the citrus industry was the sale of rural land for town lots to service the intensive agricultural districts that many predicted would prosper under irrigation. According to Professor Henry Norton of the California State Normal School, "No other state in America was so much for sale from end to end and side to side."[34] As the railroad executive James H. Benedict confided to Shorb in 1890: "Land by the acre in the San Gabriel Valley, located as yours is, should not be judged by its productive capacity." There was "no money at all in orange or grape culture, for a series of years on a large scale," but "a great deal of money, in my judgment, in holding land within a reasonable distance of Los Angeles, for the rise that is sure to come, for homes."[35]

Benedict had his eye firmly on the main chance, but many California horticulturalists remained uneasy that their land was simply an item of speculation. Jeanne Carr lamented the way the introduction of the railroad in the 1890s had destroyed the rural tranquillity of the San Gabriel Valley. Pasadena was no longer the "Crown of the Valley," she confided in 1896. "Satan entered this paradise, finding his opportunity in a branch Railroad, and congenial occupation in the creation of a boom. . . . The ideals of a community of fruit growers, were not those of numbers who came later . . . to build 'palatial homes.'"[36] The State Board of Horticulture also maintained its distance from developers on this subject. Board employees condemned "unscrupulous real estate dealers,"[37] while other publicists for fruit attacked speculative land development for directing investment away from the long-term promotion of the industry. In the dizzy land boom of the late 1880s, argued Charles Shinn, "thousands of promising young Orange-groves were neglected; progressive horticulture received a check; the weeds often grew waist-high in orchards where the land-boomer had driven his town-lot stakes." Promoters of the garden landscape like Shinn deplored this tendency and grabbed at any evidence that California farmers practiced "old-fashioned" values.[38] This hostility to speculation may have stemmed from experience in dealing with the economic pressures presented by larger, predatory neighbors. Many of the critics were middling to smaller irrigators who had bought their land from large developers or had labored, as in Riverside, on alternative small-scale or cooperative schemes.[39]

Perhaps in response to the unease of potential buyers, but more likely because they believed their own dreams, many irrigation promoters discounted the centrality of the profit motive and stressed the aesthetic appeal of their enterprise. Smythe deplored speculation such as that which accompanied the development of the Imperial Valley, and denied that irrigation was in any way reducible to economic motives: "No consideration of the subject can be appreciative when it starts with the narrow view that irrigation is merely an adjunct to agriculture." The positive preference for the garden reflected a high valuation of lush and profuse types of vegetation—a green environment for people whose intellectual heritage was in the humid lands of Europe, where small-scale farming based on centuries of careful husbandry was thought to be common. "The Anglo-Saxon race is dealing with new conditions in California," Smythe concluded. "Coming from dense forests, from a land of heavy rainfall, and from a temperate climate where winters are long and stern," Anglos had settled in unfamiliar "treeless deserts."[40]

Yet the humid eastern landscape of the United States or northern Europe could not be reproduced. What was the alternative? Should California be envisioned as some version of the antipodean wilderness of Australia? Some contemplated this when they imported Australian gum trees. Nonetheless, it is clear that the kind of landscape identified by the irrigation promoters differed from the Australian. Partly that difference denoted the immaturity of irrigation in Australia, which meant that useful models did not exist in those Anglo-Saxon outposts, but the absence reflected more than that. The Australian bush was too raw, too much a product of pure Nature. Kinney had found the landscape in Australia weird, rugged, and grand, but never beautiful. It was no garden.[41] Instead, Californians sought in irrigation greater degrees of human manipulation. The models were Mediterranean. The prominent journalist Charles Dudley Warner referred to southern California as "Our Italy."[42] But the Italian landscapes were ambiguous, even disturbing in their implications. Irrigated Italian lands involved peasant proprietorship rather than the sturdy and democratic yeomanry of American myth. Moreover, the moral implications of Italy's Catholicism and its relaxed atmosphere did not sit well with anxious Protestant promoters. Smythe therefore invoked alternative visions in the form of Egypt and the Holy Land to describe the Imperial Valley, truly a desert far removed from the peasant- and landlord-made landscape of the Italian countryside. Smythe began his account of "the miracle of irrigation" with a description of "the beauty of Damascus" and the "glories of the Garden of Eden."[43] By peopling the desert, Americans would be carrying on a Biblical tradition. However, in both cases, the Italian and the Biblical, the aim was to make the allegedly sterile landscape bloom.

The mostly Protestant settlers brought with them to California powerful cultural traditions to back Smythe's claims. Religious motivations and utopian overtones appeared in the creation of such communities as the Mormon ventures in Utah and San Bernardino. Other utopian schemes, some religious in origin and linked mostly to horticulture and irrigation, flourished in late nineteenth-century California.[44] Though derived in part from the image of the Garden of Eden, the ethic was also linked to an agrarian ideology that had flourished in the American East, with its vision of yeoman communities. The Arcadian ideal, rooted in classical mythology and reinforced by pastoral scenes in eighteenth-century painting and poetry, contributed, too.[45] The eastern and midwestern settlers who encountered California's distinctive, varied, and usually more arid landscape carried this heritage with them. It is not surprising that they still desired a luxuriant, well-wooded, mixed farming and forestry economy that would promote the social virtues of Old World villages in a new setting.

The propaganda of the garden posed an almost antinomian contrast of waste and plenty; the garden landscape was productive, certainly, even bountiful, and contrasted starkly with desert in its natural state. Warner referred to "a continuous fruit garden, the green areas only emphasized by wastes yet unreclaimed."[46] Smythe plausibly dismissed the Imperial Valley without irrigation as an "empire of hopeless sterility." But the argument did not claim arid lands to be inherently barren. They simply lacked water. Irrigation alone was required to bring them to life. But the argument became more audacious still. Irrigators asserted that arid lands were actually superior in nutrients to others: they constituted an unexploited treasure trove of resources. Such arguments won the backing of science. Professor Eugene Hilgard claimed that arid lands were naturally fertile because their nutrients had not been washed out by centuries of rain: "These soils have for ages been subject to a most thorough system of summer fallowing, unaccompanied by the leeching process, which is inseparable from an abundant rainfall." "Water alone," Hilgard concluded, "is wanting to render these deserts productive of whatever crops their climatic position will permit."[47] This argument was similar to that of the promoter Shorb. So fertile were the citrus lands of San Gabriel, Shorb claimed, that they could continue their heavy cropping of fruits indefinitely without additional fertilization. Smythe, however, remained the most expansive dreamer of all. He quoted Hilgard extensively to concoct the argument that soils of the waste desert lands "lie there now like an inexhaustible bank account on which the plant-life of the future may draw at will without danger of protest."[48] To this assertion, irrigation experts issued a note of caution, since they knew from the Indian Empire experience that irrigation could introduce some soil problems and exacerbate others.[49] These caveats were lost on Smythe, who seized upon the utopian possibilities underlying the potential of unlimited irrigation.

Since nature contained the elements from which the garden landscapes could be fashioned, nature itself was not the chief enemy. The irrigators' revulsion was not directed against aridity as such, for, if it had been so directed, then any greenery should have sufficed, whether reproductions of Northern Hemisphere forests of pine or oak, or farmland replete with livestock and waving fields of wheat. Rather, the preference for the garden was a positive one, chosen over other constructed landscapes. Pandering to the image of the abundant garden as a horticultural paradise, the advocates of irrigation professed a marked revulsion against broad-acre farming and pastoral activities and against the social and economic inequalities these produced. This preference was rooted in the same struggle of the horticulturalists to defeat the land barons excoriated by Henry George.

Smythe denounced the "land monopoly" inherent in wheat growing, which had "kept labor servile and gave the most fruitful of countries to four-footed beasts rather than to men." Echoing the ideas of George, he predicted that the decline of wheat would follow the fall of prices as

California grain lost out to Great Plains competitors able to apply even greater economies of scale than present on the Pacific Coast.[50] In Smythe's eyes, "the great farmer of California" did not contribute to the store of wealth that could underpin a broad-based democracy. Rather, he was "the successor of the gold-hunter. Both were speculators of the thoroughbred type." Of homes and institutions "they were neither architects nor builders, for they sought only to take the wealth from the soil and spend it elsewhere."[51]

The wish to transcend, through irrigation, the impermanence of broad-acre agriculture was as strong among expert engineers as among barefaced promoters and publicists. The influential Elwood Mead, for one, added a moral as well as an environmental dimension to the social critique when he argued in 1901, in the course of his *Report of Irrigation Investigations in California,* that California wheat farmers were soil miners because they planted cereals in "unremitting production." The language of Mead's report drew upon the Georgian legacy in California: "Each season the crop has been harvested, the grain shipped away, and the straw burned, and nothing done to replace the plant food withdrawn. A more exhaustive form of agriculture could not be imagined."[52] Such broad-acre agriculture was "sinful," in Mead's view. In contrast, irrigation encouraged intensive agriculture of high yield and value, with a "rotation of crops which" was "one of the most effective means of preserving the fertility of the soil."[53] Mead merely echoed statements already made ad nauseam in the fruit growers' conventions and used these to justify the further development of irrigation schemes.

Smythe joined horticulturalists who railed against the social consequences of large-scale farm production too. The application of factory-style conditions in the fields would reduce farmers, said James Boyd of Riverside, to "mere machines or automatons" and so destroy the farmer's independence and status in society.[54] Conditions that normally applied in agriculture—and were typical of California wheat farms— were "reversed" in irrigation, promised Smythe. The "large farms, hired labor, [and] a strong tendency to the single crop" would give way to the "diversified production" and "intensive cultivation" that were "inseparably related to irrigation." The result would be the creation of a class of "small landed proprietors resting upon a foundation of economic independence." This social organization of yeomanry, he concluded, was "the miracle of irrigation on its industrial side."[55]

Despite this preference for small-scale agriculture, irrigation promoters subtly altered the message of the garden: they linked its ideal landscape to a suburban civilization and all its modern conveniences, to the beautification of towns, and to development of an alternative to urban slums through the planned-community images of garden cities and garden suburbs. This revision of the horticulturalist argument may simply have reflected the greater need to house growing urban populations and thus respond to the social crisis of 1890s America. Yet the argument also involved perceived technological change and modernization through mechanical and electrical power. The shift was congenial to development of an urban mentality that subordinated nature ever more securely. California's "Ontario" settlement begun in 1882 was the first in the American West to harness hydroelectric power in the aid of lighting and irrigation pumping.[56] By 1893, one prominent fruit trade paper could say that "irrigation and electricity are to be the great agents of salutary reform in American rural life." Soon hydroelectric power would not only warm the farmer's "parlors, cook his food, transport his produce to market, and light his dwelling" but would also "eventually drag the plow[,] . . . harvest the grain," and "propel the farmer's pleasure carriage."[57]

From this utopian vision of the improvement of rural life through technology, it was but a short step to using that power to develop urban communities. When they undertook the latter task, irrigation promoters had the precedent of Henry George's ideal landscape of villages and farms linked in a communications and power grid. George had wanted to see the masses liberated from the "festering" conditions "in the tenement-houses of our cities" and dispersed in small towns, each family with "its healthful home, set in its garden."[58] George envisaged, like Smythe, a network of "closer settlement." The land monopoly broken, rural life would return to the village type "surrounded by cultivated fields, with its common pasturage and woodlands." George's work anticipated the garden city solution of the British reformer Ebenezer Howard, whose influential book *Tomorrow: A Peaceful Path to Real Reform* was published in 1898.[59] Howard had lived for a time in the Midwest, and he may have been influenced by knowledge about American utopian communities.[60]

Whether this international connection be valid or not, Smythe invoked the image of suburban gardens and showed how the garden farm idea was closely related to the garden suburb.[61] What irrigation did, Smythe believed, was make the garden suburb democratic. In the East, only the "business or professional men who have risen above the general level of society" could afford the luxury. But in Riverside, 90 percent of the people lived "in homes which front on beautiful boulevards, presenting to the passer an almost unbroken view of well-kept lawns, opulent flower-beds, and delicate shrubbery."[62]

This imagined civilization would be a mixture of the best of urban and rural values. In phraseology that echoed George, Smythe conjured up the image of the future farmland of the West studded with cities. These would not be "cities in the old sense, but a long series of beautiful villages, connected by lines of electric motors, which will move their products and people from place to place. In this scene of intensely cultivated land, rich with its bloom and fruitage, with its spires and roofs, and with its carpets of green and gold stretching away to the mountains, it will be difficult for the beholder to say where the town ends and the country begins."[63] This typical view championed a "rural-urban" environment rather than agriculture in isolation. Jeanne Carr, who saw herself as an egalitarian opponent of developers as well as a lover of the wild, wrote a series of revealing articles, each titled "The Rural Homes of California," which praised the semirural houses and gardens of the well-to-do. Carr pressed the point that "the best furnished soul knows both town and country at its best," and showed "how to combine most happily the advantages of both."[64]

Despite democratic connotations, the garden idea revealed conservative social implications in irrigation thinking. Alongside the reformist rhetoric aimed at breaking up the big estates and giving workers the chance of self-sufficiency, irrigation promised to entrench the smaller producers. Though Smythe and others like him were trying to establish a cooperative commonwealth, with a mild form of state socialism to back it up, their aspirations were profoundly petit bourgeois. The irrigation movement's ideologues hoped that social discontent would find its safety valve in the artificially constructed safety valve of the irrigation frontier. "Irrigated farms of small acreage" would, said the *California Fruit Grower and Fruit Trade Review,* be "the ultimate solution of several of the most vexing questions of political and social economy." They would "relieve the congested and over-populated cities, by a more rational and equitable distribution of population, and enable a far greater number of people to gain a high-class livelihood directly from the soil than is possible under present conditions."[65]

The reality of American life involved movement from country to city, and for horticulturalists the social appeal of irrigation propaganda lay in its claim to stem that flow.[66] Even in the 1920s this theme persisted. Despite mounting evidence that many detested the hard rural life, the panacea of irrigation was still trotted out as the answer to the nation's rural problems, when Elwood Mead reasserted irrigation's destiny. "It is not simply a question of making irrigation enterprise pay," he wrote in 1922, "but of maintaining a more attractive rural life, and checking the present exodus from farms."[67]

This antiurban bias was linked to class fears. Horticulturalists accepted the conventional Jeffersonian agrarian equation that the cities were sources of social unrest. "Our cities, under modern conditions, are not so favorable to the growth of what is best in intelligence and morality as is the modern [irrigation] colony," lamented James Boyd.[68] The message also involved the labor strife inherent in the transient class arrangements of broad-acre agriculture. As a result of his very large acreage and his attempts to make such production compatible with Christian values, John Bidwell was particularly concerned with workplace inefficiencies. He emphasized that wheat entailed much waste of time, damage to machinery, accidents, and lack of thorough cultivation. In regard to the labor force, methods "elsewhere practiced upon small farms would give the most profitable results here also."[69] The irrigation expert Professor Eugene Hilgard agreed. In the case of the small farmer, he reported, "the work is done in large measure by himself and family," and "the men and women that may be hired are brought into intimate relations with the proprietor, and not regarded as inferiors." In such a community, "distinct classes of proprietors and laborers" would not exist.[70]

Gender underpinned irrigation's conservative message too. The language of the irrigators was masculinist, in which male householders subdued the harsh environment. The ideology stressed *men* opening up the land. *Women* are noticeable in their virtual absence in the promotional material, but families are omnipresent. When Smythe said that in the California irrigation colonies "the main part of the population" is "independent and self-employing," he referred to the household economic unit in which women participated as subordinates. His ideal of "the small-farm unit" that "one family can cultivate" required unpaid women's labor.[71]

Another side to the gender construction of the irrigated garden revealed still further its conservatism and its links to urban industrial life. If women could be construed in popular discourse as part of the "natural," to be suppressed in a male social order, contemporary social thought also powerfully associated women with nature's nemesis, "civilization."[72] Their status rose as nature itself was tamed by irrigation. Smythe believed that women suffered more in the pioneering stage of agricultural development. He acknowledged that a woman's response to the irrigation frontier would not be the same as a man's because she got "the heavier end of the burdens peculiar to the pioneer." The "household duties falling to the woman's lot" in town, city, or frontier "are lightened as civilization increases," Smythe observed. The West did not lack "natural resources" but "artificial refinements." The absence of modern technology and conveniences women "keenly felt." How telling then that the whole scope of his book was to explain that the West could be civilized effortlessly through the application of water to desert. The civilized form of landscape would not be farmland as such, rather the closeness of settlement would encourage urban social amenities equal to "most of the social and educational advantages within the reach of the best eastern town." Settlers would have "kindergartens as well as schools" for their children, and houses would possess "domestic water through pipes" and be connected to public facilities by electric street cars. This was the gendered image of irrigation propaganda, even if the reality differed.[73]

Finally, irrigation proposed to end racial tensions by fostering the white family farm. The larger orchards utilized Chinese labor extensively in the 1890s, despite community criticism. Many horticulturalists were anxious about using such labor, which they claimed was a practical necessity rather than a desirable state.[74] Like Mrs. Georgie McBride of San Jose, they wished to be "independent of the unskilled Chinaman."[75] This unease about Chinese labor included the aesthetic of a racial landscape. In the opinion of speakers at the fruit growers' conventions, foreigners did not tend their farms neatly. Asian gardeners showed, said one county horticultural commissioner, "a reckless disregard of the requirements of successful culture. . . . They almost invariably grow cabbages, potatoes, onions, strawberries, etc., between the trees, and the necessity for irrigating a succession of these green crops—for they never allow the ground to lie idle—ruins the trees and injures the quality of the fruit."[76] State board commissioner-at-large Edwin Kimball, a prominent olive grower, favored complete repatriation of the Chinese as the only answer. Chinese laborers brought vice and ill health, charged Kimball, and should be removed: "Send with him all the swine, from which his manhood and religion springs, and with it the whole foul product—scrofula and physical evils—that curse the race." With quasi-Biblical rhetoric, Kimball dreamt of a future in which "our orchards shall smile under the hands of intelligent labor" and where "we and our children shall dwell together in the land forever."[77] Water propagandists built upon such virulent fears and utopian desires to assure the wider community that irrigated fruit culture would resolve, not exacerbate, racial tension. Irrigation would allow whites to cultivate smaller areas profitably and efficiently without recourse to hired, "inferior" labor.[78]

This complex of desires expressed in irrigation propaganda has been neglected. Propagandists such as Smythe have been ignored or alternatively described as impractical idealists. The gap between stated intention and long-term results, namely the creation of a vast agribusiness interest, is certainly striking, and it is tempting to be cynical about the dynamics of irrigation promotion itself.[79] But we must not confuse the results of irrigation policy with the social climate—and all of its class, gender, and racial elements—that made irrigation a powerful image of how to reorder California's environment. Otherwise, we cannot fully understand the persistent appeal of irrigation to legislators, an appeal that transcended the ability of irrigation laws to deliver on the promise. The survival of the yeoman farm underlay, especially, California's Wright Act in 1887, which created local irrigation districts, with waterworks funded by bond issues. As Norris Hundley explains, "The new law represented an effort to foster community values, promote small family farms, and curb the monopolistic excesses produced by the rampant individualism of California's pioneer capitalists."[80]

Implementation of the values of the garden was a different matter. The laws did not work out the way that irrigation propaganda suggested. The Wright Act's reliance on a local district irrigation administrative system rather than a statewide administrative framework proved crucially defective, but added to this were the droughts of the 1890s and court challenges from monopolist water interests anxious to further their own domination of the vital and scarce resource. Neither did the Act creating the Bureau of Reclamation at the federal level in 1902 succeed in implementing the yeoman ideal professed by its promoters and enshrined in sections of its legislation.[81] Elwood Mead felt deeply frustrated at the way special interests stymied the 1902 law. The National Reclamation Act, he argued in 1915, should "have made the west the land of opportunity" but it had "not done so because the forces in control" were "so narrowly selfish."[82] Private landowners had reaped windfall profits in reclamation projects when the federal irrigation water was turned on. Rather than farm the land, landowners had simply speculated and then sold out.[83]

When popular commitment to the irrigated version of the garden landscape took shape in the 1880s, the demise of the dream lay well in the future. Far away in Australia, California's mix of a racial democracy and innovative water technology attracted popular support. While the antipodean decision to irrigate was framed by internal influences—patterns of land development, state power, and class relations—external influences did help shape the content of policy.

Among these linkages, the American connection has been striking. True, the Pacific exchange of irrigation technology and personnel was hardly unique. Irrigation had been especially important in India and Egypt, and prominent in Italy and other Mediterranean countries. Americans and Australians were aware of this history. Yet the development of irrigation in California and Australia was closely related in time and context. The Wright Act almost coincided with the Victorian government's pioneering 1886 legislation under the leadership of the minister for water supply, Alfred Deakin. Both arose from the same milieu. Similarly, the National Reclamation Act was followed shortly by further Victorian legislation in 1905. At first the American experience ran much in advance of the Australian and served as a model—but not just a technical model of irrigation. The popular ideology of a garden environment was influential as well. In Australia, pro-irrigation groups found appealing the same kind of social arrangements projected in California under the impact of horticultural expansion. Australian irrigation advocates favored the intensive agricultural exploitation, breaking up of large estates, and substitution of a "manufactured" garden landscape. All this would "renovate" nature and undo the environmental damage that pastoral and broad-acre land use had bequeathed.

Dreams and Ditches

Deakin, Australian Irrigation, and the Californian Model

Australian irrigation plans have always drawn heavily on overseas expertise, but not until after 1880 did the American West became an important model of what could be achieved. As late as 1880, a Victorian booster canvassed the irrigation issue with reference only to European and British imperial projects.[1] The Reverend James Ballantyne's *Our Colony in 1880: Pictorial and Descriptive* invoked the idea of the garden, yet made no reference to the United States. This absence reminds us that the garden image did not derive from American experience alone, since Britons shared a heritage of humid lands and fertile farms. The relevance of British experience proved limited, however, when the social aspirations of Australian colonials to shape an irrigated landscape became clear. Traffic in irrigation ideas and technology became a critical part of the Pacific exchange.

Before that exchange developed, India provided the premier irrigation model in the British Empire. Some of the colonial engineering experts had served in India, and others knew of the achievements there. The use of this example continued in the debates of the 1880s. Even though irrigation in India often involved considerable use of government power, in Victoria this experience was first employed to justify very limited state intervention. Paradoxically, the United States, and California in particular, better served the exponents of wider use of government. The paradox is closely related to the whole enterprise of the garden landscape. To justify the expenditure of large sums of money, promoters of irrigation needed to mobilize popular support, and this could not be done by emulating India, where irrigation was closely identified with imperial despotism and the native people were deemed by British settlers to be inferior and uncivilized.[2]

The turning point in attitudes toward irrigation came at the end of the 1870s. Two decades of attempts to "unlock the land" from squatter control in Victoria and New South Wales had largely failed, just as the comparable Homestead Act of 1862, the Timber Culture Act of 1873, and the Desert Lands Act of 1877 of the United States Congress had not ensured widespread land distribution and agricultural prosperity in the American West. In Victoria and New South Wales, much of the squabbling between farmers and squatters—large pastoral landholders whose occupation had been validated by Crown land leases—concerned scarce water supplies. As farmers tried to stake their claims to land under the "Free Selection" acts, their moves were frequently stymied by pastoralist possession of the watercourses that alone made agriculture possible.[3] Colonial officials and other irrigation promoters now began to look to the United States for examples of irrigation's value in promoting the closer settlement that land acts had failed to achieve. American irrigation schemes became relevant precisely because Americans in the western states dealt with problems similar to those that Australian legislators faced.

Early Californian efforts had already attracted the attention of the Scots-Australian apostle of water development Hugh McColl, in the 1870s. McColl noted that Americans were in advance of Australia in this matter though they, too, were pioneering a new land. He preached the need for large-scale works, urging the establishment of surface canals that could carry water by gravity over long distances and irrigate large areas of the Victorian pastoral country. He invoked the garden imagery and pointed to the bounty of California's new agricultural yields to illustrate his point. Finally, McColl recommended a commission of inquiry that would call on expert American opinion and utilize American canal construction techniques. McColl corresponded with William Hammond Hall, a state irrigation engineer in California, in the preparation of his case.[4]

DEAKIN'S IMPRINT ON IRRIGATION LEGISLATION

Colonial officials treated McColl's lobbying skeptically, believing that his simultaneous promotion of a private irrigation scheme—the North-

Western Canal Company—tainted his arguments. More important, detractors were only too aware of the parlous state of the colony's finances at the beginning of the 1880s. Financial probity required officials to proceed slowly, and for this reason the government initially resisted state involvement in irrigation works. Two reports on irrigation authored for the Victorian government in 1882 and 1884 by the engineer George Gordon championed realistic engineering rather than social criteria in the planning of works, and scoffed at the suggestion of vast schemes on McColl's model.[5]

Drought changed political and popular opinion, however. Dry seasons continued in the mid-1880s, pushing the colonial government into more radical and definite action than Gordon wanted and ensuring that McColl's plea would be heard. The American example became of vital importance to the young minister for water supply in the Victorian Government, Alfred Deakin, who steered through the parliament a Water Conservation Act of 1883 that implemented, "almost entirely," a proposal for the creation of irrigation districts in California then pending before the state legislature in Sacramento. The bill did not pass in 1884 in California, though a similar initiative resulted in the Act establishing irrigation districts in 1887.[6] The Victorian legislation created similar institutions but called them irrigation trusts. They were licensed to borrow money but without any state backing. Then Deakin persuaded the cabinet to appoint a royal commission in 1884 to travel to the United States, accompanied by, among others, John Dow. Published in 1885 as *Irrigation in Western America,* Deakin's *First Progress Report* of the Royal Commission became the basis for subsequent legislation.

Deakin's document reads as a hymn of praise to the California model. It buzzed with enthusiasm for Californian achievements, particularly in horticultural development, but also expressed a more general admiration for American institutions and proclaimed that, socially and politically, a marked affinity existed between the American republic and the young colonies. This affinity did not end with democratic political institutions, but included private enterprise and organizational and technological achievement. "The most potent factor in the achievement of American successes is the untiring energy and self-reliance of the people, many of whom, unfettered by tradition, independent of professional men, and original in idea, have conquered difficulty after difficulty," Deakin claimed.[7]

Deakin, to be sure, was mindful of the drawbacks of American examples. Because most irrigation works in the American West were under

private control, irrigation American style required speculative investment. More important in Deakin's view, it also led to duplication of
essential services such as canals and reservoirs.[8] Above all, Deakin
attacked the system of confusing and paralyzing riparian rights operating in California, but he also pointed out that many Americans agreed
with him.[9] Deakin's assessment of the role of private enterprise in Californian irrigation was never truly hostile, however. He firmly believed
that "the basis of successful irrigation must be that individual energy and
that joint action on the part of the farmers themselves which no State
can possibly supply." It was Deakin's aim to unleash the dynamic forces
of individualism that he saw operating in the United States; this he
described as the "natural impetus which leads men to invest their capital and put forth their labour, in order that they may obtain a better
return."[10]

While acknowledging differences between Australia and the western
United States, Deakin emphasized that American irrigation showed the
"lines upon which to develop the political side of our irrigation law, so
as to encourage small proprietors and discourage great estates." In this
model of intensive development, of greatest importance were the projects
where "fruit growing" was "the interest to which all others, whether
stock, poultry, cereals, or lucerne" were "subordinated."[11] Deakin included as part of the fruit enterprise the potential of the wine industry,
which he noted would be "remunerative" even though in the United
States it suffered "in the face of a prejudice quite as unreasoning as that
which has till lately faced colonial vintages." Nevertheless, winegrowers
relied much less on irrigation in California than did fruit growers, and
fresh and dried fruits demanded much more attention from those like
Deakin who wished to emulate the American example.[12]

In his arguments he combined social and racial affinities with economic circumstance. Deakin told a group of Victorian irrigators in 1890
that the "mainstay of our confidence" must be the experience in "Western America—a new country like our own, with labour as dear as it is
here, and markets in many places nearly as difficult to reach." He tried
to sting the racial pride of Australians by reference to their Anglo-Saxon
cousins. "If we are to confess that we are unable to make irrigation a
success in Australia, we must first confess that our colonists are altogether inferior to their relatives who left the mother country at the same
time as they did, and started under the same conditions."[13]

Deakin broke with the Californian model, however, on the role of the
state in building the infrastructure necessary to irrigation development.

Deakin quoted William Hammond Hall's public view that the state should stay out of such works because of the waste and inefficiency that would be involved.[14] Deakin ignored this aspect of the published American evidence, but private correspondence between Hall and Deakin reveals that Hall enticed him to consider a greater degree of government intervention. Hall, a man of large ego eager to dispense advice, criticized Deakin for his timidity in the issue, and for following California's precedents too closely.[15]

Deakin proposed a central role for the state in the raising of money and construction of large-scale dams and reservoirs, though his arguments had nothing to do with the alleged technical superiority of state-run irrigation in India. Rather, Deakin advocated eclectic use of state power. In California and most other places in the American West, he argued, irrigation investment had been successfully made by private capitalists. In Australia, circumstances of environment, financial markets, and demography meant that different mixes of private and public finances had to be chosen. By 1886 Deakin could advocate a bolder intervention than originally envisaged in the 1883 Water Conservation Act. The irrigation trusts sanctioned under that Act had not been a success, with only one organized in the first two years of operation. Moreover, the continuing drought swept away earlier inhibitions against activism.[16]

Also by 1886, government finances had improved and technical assessments of the available land had given hope of increased potential for irrigated areas.[17] The latter point was particularly important. Deakin feared that the 1883 legislation would stimulate local projects that might obstruct later and necessarily larger ones when the technical problems of irrigation were overcome. Fragmented action would create duplication. This concern that "small isolated schemes are productive of the greatest danger" was heightened by the differences in available water. With "sources of water supply being fewer than in America, it becomes imperative," he stressed, "that those sources should be utilized to the fullest possible extent." Only state action to obtain watershed control would achieve the desired result of maximum utilization of a scarce resource. Deakin therefore provided for the government to undertake the capital works—the dams, weirs, and reservoirs—required for entire watersheds and not leave development entirely to the irrigation trusts.[18]

Interestingly, Deakin discounted the alternative of artesian bore irrigation (or, in American phrasing, well irrigation) even though he had reported on the use of groundwater in his *Irrigation in Western America*.

Well water was already used in outback Australia, particularly in Queensland, pioneered by the engineer J. B. Henderson.[19] For well-digging machinery, Deakin later noted, Australians were "indebted to our American and Canadian cousins." Yet in Victoria the government had spent "thousands of pounds upon deep bores, which have proved of little or no value." The lack of mining equipment similar to that common in the American West, and the lack of understanding of the "geological strata," hindered the advancement of artesian well development.[20] Even where such water was discovered, it suffered from the reputation of excessive salinity in comparison with American supplies and was often assumed suitable only for stock.[21] For this reason, artesian well water became identified in Australia as the ally of pastoralism. This association may have made Deakin pause, convinced as he was of the need to direct development away from the large-scale sheep economy. The Californian experience and knowledge of the local environment emphasized the need for surface-level projects.

Deakin's Royal Commission and his subsequent legislation were vociferously criticized as too visionary, too radical, too ambitious. George Gordon responded negatively in a major and widely circulated attack. No unbiased observer, Gordon was enamored of Indian achievements that included his own work on the Madras irrigation system, and he adopted a dismissive attitude toward American precedents. "The irrigation works of one country cannot be taken as models to be copied or reproduced in another," Gordon warned. He argued that Deakin had pressed political and economic similarities at the expense of close and hard-headed acknowledgment of the engineering difficulties in Australia. Irrigation would not be as easy to achieve in Victoria as in California, Gordon predicted. The rivers of California were shallow, calling only for light structures capable of elevating the water a few feet. The rivers of northern Victoria cut deep into the surrounding countryside, making it difficult to utilize them for irrigation. The heavy snowpack of the Sierra Nevada supplied the California system, while many of the Australian rivers periodically ran dry. The California rivers ran along ridges, making them easier to divert through inexpensive channels to irrigate a wide area. Nor were they, he asserted, subject to flooding to the alarming extent true of most Australian rivers. Engineering difficulties and damage to irrigation works from flooding were likely to be far greater in Victoria.[22] Yet these strictures fell on deaf ears. Deakin's critics in the parliament were in a distinct minority, and though they used Gordon's arguments and pointed to the success of some types of fruit culture in

California without irrigation, they were unable to muster even a quarter of the members of the Assembly against the Water Supply and Irrigation Bill of 1886. Deakin had his way.[23]

Why did Deakin succeed against these quite rational arguments? Given that the colony depended on taxes, land sales, and freight rail revenue, Deakin could argue that the infusion of public funds for large-scale irrigation works would in the end be justified financially by the stimulus to agricultural prosperity. At another level, Deakin succeeded because Victorian politicians were desperate to do something to stem the drought. The 1886 Act was a leap in the dark, but for many members the only leap that could be taken. As one hostile member put it, "There seemed to be a general feeling in the House" that, despite the uncertainty, "the experiment of irrigation should be tried."[24]

Behind the immediate financial motives were social influences similar to those operating in California in the transition from mining and sheep to wheat and then to fruit. Without irrigation, said Deakin, the population of the northern plains would "be swept away, and the land must go back simply to sheep-farming." Deakin fundamentally defended the measure as a means of relief to agricultural experimentation. The clinching metaphors in this argument involved the creation of the garden landscape. Deakin's speech on the bill ended powerfully with the plea that instead of the "barren wilderness" of the northern plains, irrigation would make "this small Victoria" in "many senses a greater garden than it is now." Here Californian ideology and experience of the garden were crucial. Irrigation there had brought fruit as a viable alternative to wheat. "Intense culture" in California had "increased the value of lands enormously," Deakin claimed, and "under irrigation, the produce of one acre of vines" brought more freight revenues and general community prosperity "than nine acres of wheat."[25]

Deakin was articulate and personable, but he could not have succeeded without the supporting presence of a larger flow of influence and information. His viewpoint on the irrigation issue was representative of popular culture in southeastern Australia, particularly Victoria. His accounts of American irrigation were broadly consistent with the observations of John Dow and others who visited the West Coast in the same period. Deakin's tour in 1884 was neither the beginning nor the end of the journalistic pilgrimages. In 1890 the government sent John West (1856–1926), a Victorian journalist, nurseryman, and one-time publisher of the *Goulbourn Valley Yeoman,* to further study American irrigation methods. He was styled an irrigation expert but is better described as an avid irrigation promoter and horticulturalist. West was hardly impartial, since his nursery supplied vine cuttings to irrigation projects and he imported peach stock from California as part of his business. West returned to lecture widely not only on irrigation but also on the development of dried-fruit technology.[26] New South Wales, where pastoralism and broad-acre agriculture were more influential, proved more circumspect on the subject of irrigation but received a report from its representative to the World's Columbian Exhibition of 1893 that included an assessment of irrigation and horticulture in California.[27] Yet another visitor was Frederick C. Smith of Angaston, South Australia, who studied California's fruit industry and irrigation in 1893. Smith's family owned one of Australia's most successful wineries, Yalumba, but Frederick Smith was also an "an expert horticulturalist" with extensive interests in deciduous fruits.[28] Later, the South Australian parliamentarian, pastoralist, and vigneron George Riddoch went on a similar fact-finding tour for his government in 1903, to be followed by other observers such as the Victorian journalist Henry Somer Gullett and the parliamentarian Frank Clarke.[29]

These contacts were supplemented by other information networks. The journals of the fledgling agriculture departments of Australia reprinted American irrigation information, pertaining both to the general advantages of irrigation and the techniques that could be used to maximize the benefits.[30] Also complementing the visitors going east was a small number of American visitors who sought to develop irrigation. Most notable among them were George, Charles, and W. B. Chaffey and their associates, but another was Bailey Brown, who moved to Queensland from the American West Coast in 1885.[31] Yet of all these contacts, the Australian visitors to California were the most important. They embodied in many cases the opinion of government and elicited a favorable popular response that makes their contributions worth studying.

The visitors swept widely and yet selectively across the American West. They certainly drew many insights, when it suited them, from places other than California. West, the Dows, Deakin, and Gullett went to Utah, Colorado, and other places where irrigation was practiced, and they reported favorably on those experiments, such as the well-known Greeley colony in Colorado. The Australians found that irrigation could be put to many uses in the production of common farm products, such as potatoes, whose cultivation could be duplicated in Australia. American winegrowing also encouraged those who saw sanguine prospects for

Australian vineyards. Yet fruit growing attracted the most comment, and particularly that in California.

SIMILARITIES BETWEEN CALIFORNIA AND VICTORIA

Irrigation propagandists depicted California as the area of the United States most like southeastern Australia in population size, climate, political culture, and stages of development associated with a succession of staple exports.[32] When Deakin was accused of exaggerating the similarities, he replied that he had drawn evidence from across the American West, not just California.[33] This tactic of using the Californian example when suitable, yet drawing on irrigation experience elsewhere when necessary, exposed a lack of consistency in the thinking of Australian irrigation promoters, but it was a tactic that deflected criticism. Riparian water rights—so complicated in California—rather than perceived differences in the natural environment, were the source of many of the Australian observers' reservations. John West, like Deakin before him, acknowledged the problem of riparian rights and argued that in this matter Colorado provided the best example for Victoria.[34]

Irrigation's negative environmental effects barely registered on Australian observers, so keen were they to promote the use of the technology. When objectors pointed to the drawbacks, partisan supporters suddenly switched course to emphasize the dissimilarities between California and Australia. This enabled promoters to discount less desirable consequences of irrigation already evident in parts of California. John West noticed that "the soils . . . are in places largely impregnated with 'alkalis'" that "rise to the surface" and "kill off vegetation," but this circumstance, he asserted, stemmed from an inherent inferiority of California's natural environment. Victorian soils were superior, West argued, and would yield better results than those evident in California. So arid was much of irrigated America that it approximated the great sandy deserts of central Australia, far beyond northern Victoria where irrigation was contemplated.[35]

The Victorians' representations of California abundantly illustrate that the irrigation debate did not revolve around technology transfer alone. The Californian settlers, West told enthusiastic audiences, "are thriving and prosperous, and their home surroundings exceedingly beautiful."[36] The response indicated that the irrigation craze gave vent to important desires in popular culture concerning environmental renovation. West's talks at the Working Men's College in Melbourne were illustrated by limelight views, and reports of them are punctuated with the stenographers' register of applause. Nowhere was this popularity clearer than when he stressed the yeoman farmer imagery, but a second appealing theme was the need to employ government to implement the agrarian dream.

The American example was valuable not only for irrigation but also for the wider model of a public-private mix. The Australian travelers noted that in the 1880s American government aid to agriculture far exceeded that in Australia, where the pastoral model still dominated political economy. John Dow stressed the "admirable system by which the head Agricultural department at Washington keeps itself in communication with every State in the Union." The United States commissioner of agriculture provided vital agricultural statistics, while state agriculture departments gave practical local advice. Both John and Thomas K. Dow applauded, too, the involvement of the University of California in the dissemination of scientific information.[37] The system of American agricultural education they admired had been inaugurated through the college land grant system under the Morrill Act of 1862, and would soon be augmented by the Hatch Act of 1887, which established agricultural experiment stations attached to the great public universities in such states as California.[38] As minister of agriculture in the Gillies-Deakin government in Victoria from 1886 to 1890, John Dow sponsored the extension of agricultural education on the American model. Similar acts were also introduced in a number of other Australian colonies at the same time.[39] In several colonies, the departments of agriculture supplemented this influence with American-born administrators. In Queensland E. M. Shelton was particularly active in the 1890s in transferring American know-how as "Instructor in Agriculture" to the government. His reports were full of references to the state of agriculture in "those Western States of America" that "have made such enormous strides."[40] John Dow also praised the practice of the state horticultural and viticultural boards in California in supplying agricultural advice. These impressed him, as a small "l" liberal, with their mix of state intervention on the one hand and local control and voluntaristic endeavor on the other.[41]

It was not inconsistent, therefore, that the Australian commentators also stressed the role of private capital when stimulated by government grants, legal frameworks, or expert advice. John Dow noted the great importance attached to private enterprise in the United States, even in an issue like irrigation promotion where governments did have a role. For "a 'big thing'" like irrigation, "you can always depend upon the private competition entering into it in the liveliest manner."[42] This ethic also won support in the conservative press at home. In 1891, the *Sydney Mail* regarded it a "matter of congratulation" that the first irrigation project in New South Wales would use "private enterprise, instead of State aid."[43] Such hopes for a strong private input would not be fulfilled, however. Because of environmental difficulties and shortages of capital, Australian irrigation development would often be forced to rely more on the government than did such development in the American West. Nonetheless, in view of the extensive role attributed always to the state in Australian colonial development, the praise in irrigation discourse for the infusion of private resources is striking.[44]

Australian observers also hailed the development of irrigation-related technology and organization in California. Fruit canning, railroad freezer cars, packing techniques, and grower cooperatives all attracted attention. Here, the wider model of horticulture always had importance greater than that of irrigation alone.[45] The *Register* (Adelaide) said that Frederick Smith's inquiry into the marketing, canning, and drying of fruits "should have a fullness which no mere specialist on 'irrigation of orchards,' . . . could give."[46] At a meeting of the California State Horticultural Society, Smith presented samples of South Australian canned fruit and Yalumba wines.[47] He then traveled on to Europe, all the while sending home reports to the press. Despite the attractions of many locations Smith visited, he stressed the Californian example in "pruning, packing, shipping, and spraying fruit," and in "the selection of the varieties best suited for export." Australia could match these advantages with its own, but local growers nevertheless needed, in Smith's view, "to follow California very closely" in order "to compete with her in the English and other markets."[48] American experts coming to Australia similarly stressed the organization of the fruit industry in such areas as canning and packing, rather than irrigation techniques alone.[49]

HENRY GEORGE AND THE GARDEN IN AUSTRALIA

Supporters of agriculture in Australia and New Zealand tied Henry George's ideas to these economic and technological aspirations. Ideas on the evils of land monopoly had considerable appeal in Australia. Just as plants, animals, insects, and technologies crossed the Pacific with improved communications, so too did ideas about the social consequences of the land's transformation. George was popular in many countries—he was something of an international celebrity for a time— but his following in Australasia was particularly strong. George toured Australia in 1890, coming from San Francisco by the new Pacific route.[50]

George's work was taken up by Australians with similar visions of society's future. Not only did they latch onto the Single Tax panacea, they also sought to create another version of the horticultural paradise favored by George's middle-class disciples in California. In 1877, just six years after publication of George's *Our Land and Land Policy,* John Dow wrote a pamphlet with a remarkably similar title. In *Our Land Acts and a Land Tax,* Dow attacked the "sheep owners" of Australia "who do nothing but graze their stock upon unimproved lands," just as George had attacked cattle ranchers and broad-acre agriculture in America.[51] For Dow, even the gold miners had contributed to Victoria's development through an export duty. The case of the squatters "was the one exception who had never yet been got at by any tax at all." To get this powerful landed class to contribute to society's welfare, Dow adopted George's tax on the unimproved value of land.[52] Within just a few years, Dow would join Georgian ideas to irrigation development.

Colonials did not wish to use the Single Tax simply to raise revenues more justly, and they certainly did not favor the Georgian system for economic efficiency alone. They used George's ideas to advocate opening up the land to closer settlement by yeoman farmers. The idea first took legislative expression in New Zealand, where Edward Gibbon Wakefield's ideas of a property-holding middle class were strong. Sir George Grey introduced a tax on unimproved land into New Zealand in 1878, and South Australia, another Wakefieldian colony, followed in 1884.[53] In 1886, the link between the garden concept and George's attack on large-scale farming was strengthened by Deakin's irrigation policy. In the Irrigation Act in Victoria, as historical geographer J. M. Powell notes, "a kinship with Henry George's 'single tax' notion . . . was . . . declared; the intention was to discourage private speculation and to protect the wider community's claims to a share in the increased land values."[54]

In Australia, this penchant for the Single Tax could be a way station to socialism for some, but it was the middle-class and petit-bourgeois character of the Single Taxers in both Australia and California that was most impressive.[55] The Single Tax movement had a strong moral dimension that included such reforms as temperance, as well as a commitment to the creation of a more aesthetically pleasing landscape.[56] Because of their middle-class roots, the Georgian ideas failed in both California and

Australia to appeal to the growing trade union movement. In Australia, trade unionism quickly spread to electoral politics through the emerging Labor Party in the 1890s and eclipsed the Georgian strain, though land tax arrangements remained an important part of Labor Party policy in several states, such as, for example, in New South Wales.

California was different. There the labor movement remained more marginal politically, and the currents of middle-class socialism had to work through vaguer and less effectual progressive reform institutions. While this situation weakened the Georgians' possible influence on labor, it meant that middle-class radicalism could survive better in its own right than in colonial Australia. Through such organizations as William Ellsworth Smythe's short-lived California Constructive League, the discontented middle class still deployed George, as late as 1902, in their unsuccessful efforts to unlock the land from the grip of the large landowners who controlled antiprogressive state government policies for most of the 1880s and 1890s.[57]

Like Californians, Australian irrigation promoters envisaged irrigation as part of a wholesale environmental transformation that would produce a superior, gardenlike land. Merely by supplying water in ditches, great changes in Nature could be wrought. James Ballantyne hoped in 1880 that Victoria would be transformed by irrigation into "one of the gardens of the world." He predicted that the "scorching effects of the hot wind would be largely neutralized. Vast plains now completely worthless would soon be transformed into luxuriant pastures. Treeless wastes would become valuable water meadows. Thriving farms and richly-producing market gardens would abound, where now we see bare soil or stunted scrub."[58]

Irrigated tracts would be superior to arid "waste lands." As a pamphleteer put it, "One has but to imagine the sombre profitless bush supplanted by orchards and vineyards, dotted with homesteads, to call into existence a picture of quiet and restful beauty."[59] This was a theme shared by Californians, but the transformation was conditioned by reactions to the unfamiliar antipodean vegetation. This idea that irrigation would replace the bush gelled with the strong revulsion early settlers and visitors felt toward the Australian landscape. The somber tones of grass, scrub, and desert struck Europeans as even more foreign than California's landscape, and thus the irrigation panacea was particularly appealing. At least California had numerous pines, mountains covered with snow, and forests that approximated eastern American ideals of flora. Australian nationalist that he was, Deakin conceded California's fir and pine forests to be "richer, more varied, & more majestic" than the gums of his homeland. The environmental transformation expected in the Australian landscape under irrigation would, in a sense, restore the "bush" to something like European ideals of balanced and pleasant vegetation. "Artificial" irrigation would achieve this end by introducing the "dark green" foliage of the citrus that, in Deakin's opinion, had made the dusty southern Californian desert so "very beautiful."[60] True, the beginnings of a new appreciation of the eucalypts can be found in the work of Mueller in the 1870s. As the colonial writer Marcus Clarke put it at about the same time, "The dweller in the wilderness. . . becomes familiar with the beauty of loneliness" and learns to read "the hieroglyphs of haggard gum-trees."[61] Rainforests of ferns and tall trees already had their enthusiastic supporters, Deakin among them.[62] But even after the taller varieties of eucalypts came to be appreciated, dismissive attitudes continued to prevail toward what Australians called "scrub." Colonists could see value in stately gums but could not extend this empathy to arid vegetation. Such were the areas of dwarf mallee eucalyptus common in dry country. Frank Myers in the *Argus* (Melbourne) described the Mallee district of Victoria, seat of the projected Mildura irrigation "colony," as "a wilderness of dull green leaves, of ragged brown stalks, seeming to afford nothing more nutritious or useful than the arid soil which produces them."[63] A. R. E. Burton, a Christian evangelist and irrigation booster, told how the region had been nothing but "wild-dog and scrubby country." In its place the irrigators were fashioning "an oasis."[64]

The ideal gardenlike landscape was productive, certainly, even bountiful, as the Reverend Ballantyne's account suggested, in contrast to "unproductive bush" or desert in its natural state. Yet the argument that arid lands were genuinely barren, and not just lacking in water, was one that irrigation promoters had to combat in Australia as in the United States. They needed to portray scrub land as providing the raw materials from which an "improved nature" could be produced by human intervention, along the lines of acclimatization society activity. A New South Wales irrigation colony prospectus stated, "Nature has provided the elements of loveliness," which could be realized with "human power."[65] The Mallee, even more, was depicted as an environmental cornucopia, despite its scruffy condition. "The Soil Teems with Gold," the

Reverend Burton rejoiced, and the nearby Murray River "contains a large quantity of fertilising matter."[66] But this wealth was not available without technological manipulation.[67]

Of all the parallels in the ideology of transformation, the most striking is the aesthetic. The imagined landscape of Mildura and other Australian irrigation centers came from American blueprints, but these were blueprints in which Australian flora figured as points of reference in the landscape design. The aesthetic appeal of irrigation appeared in the response of John West, who emphasized the popular rhetoric of the garden as the source of California's beautification. It was important to him that irrigated California was the "richest part" of the state, but equally important that under irrigation's impact, it had "been made a beauty spot besides."[68] This aesthetic revolution involved an appreciation of agricultural diversity as a means of relieving the monotony associated with the Australian bush, wheat farms, or pastoral runs. A later Australian correspondent, Henry Gullett, argued in defense of irrigation and closer settlement that "the town of the wheat districts—that unlovely, dusty, sparsely-planted town that you meet from one end of the wheat-belt to the other—should not be repeated on the country of irrigation."[69] Irrigation towns in California and elsewhere in the American West were different, Gullett said. They sported pleasant gardens and tree-lined streets in which Australian natives figured prominently.

Yet it was not just towns that irrigation improved aesthetically. Deakin's group, noted the *Argus,* found attractive "the enchanting design" of farms and towns that made up the horticultural lands in southern California. John Dow delighted at the role of eucalyptus trees in making the horticultural districts over into a distinctive built landscape, but his account involved more than wonder at the blue gum's success. He also focused on the diversity of vegetation, "surrounded by orange groves, wine vineyards, [and] orchards," where peaches, grapes, plums, apricots, grew "in greatest profusion." His work, in short, is a testimony to the garden image and its partial implementation in California. Though a diverse landscape, it appealed to Dow as a constructed environment with an underlying sense of harmony. Dow loved the sense of order associated with the straight lines of the vineyard and orchard, with fruit trees and vines "all set out under a perfect system," so as "to combine the highest productive capabilities of the soil with the keeping of a due proportion of high graded stock."[70]

It is tempting to agree with cultural geographers that irrigation ditches themselves connoted order, with their long straight lines in marked preference to the supposed disorder of the desert or the Australian landscape of pastoral confusion. Once expert engineering criteria were adopted in Australia and California after 1900, this appeal became manifest, though Deakin noted how patchwork the Californian canals and ditches of the 1880s really were. They were roughly constructed and often in competition with one another. The social and aesthetic transformation that water could bring appealed more.[71]

In Australia, parallel social problems of broad-acre farming and land concentration powered enthusiasm for irrigation, California style. Underlying the garden's appeal was the complaint that land ownership was too concentrated,[72] but the economic attack on large-scale agriculture as environmentally extortionist was not antithetical to the pleasing image of the garden. Rather, the aesthetic and the economic were part of the same cluster of sensibilities. The wheat and wool industries impoverished not only the landscape, leaving it barren and empty in irrigators' eyes, but impoverished society as well. These putatively extractive industries provided wealth for only a few, while others were condemned to be part of a rural proletariat. The fruit industry would give more people a chance to become proprietors in their own right; its diversely productive agriculture would lay the foundations for a more egalitarian society.[73]

Of equal appeal was the promise of American irrigation to reconcile town and country, a particularly important issue in Australia in view of the already high level of urbanization by world standards.[74] While nationalists eulogized the bush as the country's distinctive feature, most people lived in cities and appreciated their amenities. Decentralization in small-town environments created by irrigation seemed an appealing compromise to the middle class. The garden suburb ideal was displayed in the Mulgoa scheme, near Penrith in New South Wales. Because of its proximity to Sydney, developers marketed this privately financed land settlement as town lots and villas, as much as "horticultural lots." Advertising "Country Homes for City People," the company claimed that "a few acres" in "so delightful a locality" would enable "city families . . . to surround themselves with moderate luxury." The pitch to the urban resident's desire to escape inner-city grime was as unmistakable as in the garden city idea. Stated the Mulgoa company prospectus, "A home in one's own garden, a garden covering acres, and realizing one's own preferences in tree, flower, and vegetable growth, is incomparably superior to renting a section of somebody else's terrace in a region where streets and backyards are almost the only open spaces."[75] The Mulgoa company went farther to make quite explicit the link between irrigation as an idea of environmental change and the home garden. "Almost every home plot in the world, whether devoted to fruit or flowers, or vegetables, is an illustration of and argument for irrigation. The irrigation channel is but the economic extension of the watering pot or the hose."[76]

This suburban image had an especially strong ability to assuage social conflict arising from the great depression of the 1890s. For a commodity-dependent set of colonies, the economic downturn was severe and disillusioning, and marked by labor unrest centered on the Maritime Strike. The impetus in the 1890s toward "closer settlement" was intimately related to the depression and the desire of legislators to get the poor out of the growing cities. Bailey Brown, a champion of irrigation in Queensland, stated that such schemes would "decrease the temptation to town settlement, which is a curse to this Colony . . . and has largely contributed to the production of a new class called 'The Unemployed,' which, in the Old Country and America degenerate into TRAMPS."[77]

In response to widespread fears of a floating proletariat, social reformers made an effort to promote back-to-the-land movements through village settlements and other cooperative land schemes. These, backed by government legislation in Victoria, embodied the same "Arcadian" vision that advocates of the garden landscape endorsed, and they showed how widespread was the enthusiasm for change toward a more balanced landscape of farms and small towns. Horace Tucker's successful utopian novel *The New Arcadia: An Australian Story* tied the development of small-scale cooperative agriculture to the theme of the garden and to prudent water conservation in a dry land. Tucker contrasted the "oasis" of the well-watered settlement of the fictional Vale of Mimosa with "the howling, poverty-stricken wilderness" inhabited by the wheat farmers just "twelve miles away, with soil as good as this, but parched for lack of water." Irrigation was incidental to Tucker's main theme of cooperation, but the village settlements erected along the Murray and Goulburn in the 1890s made use of those rivers for irrigation.[78]

Australian irrigation promoters tapped these sources of public concern. They preached the importance of irrigation for the realization of the ideals of closer settlement that were behind the cooperation movement. John West told a group of "workingmen" that it was the irrigation colony system in America that allowed people to live and work "closely together" and so provided an opportunity for "great numbers of the younger men" to settle down "in these areas to the cultivation of the soil, instead of crowding the avenues of labour in the cities." In such statements, promoters ensured that the message of irrigation as a panacea for class conflict functioned as prominently in Australia as in California.[79]

It is tempting to say that Australians also harbored racial fears similar to those in California, but the racial purity theme waxed more strongly in the Australian case. There, irrigation propaganda was more likely to demand exclusion of all nonwhites, and fruit was the key to this policy. The racial aspect of small-scale horticulture was vital to Deakin. Against the racial and aesthetic order of the fruit colonies of Riverside and Ontario, Deakin noted the ethnic hodgepodge of the pastoral landscape. He singled out for adverse comment a Bakersfield ranch with "a queer jumble of races & nationalities," including Chinese, Negroes, Mexicans, and "half-breeds." At San Bernardino, he found "a Mexican settlement turned Yankee," though there were still "plenty of Mexicans with their dark skins & strange dress" to remind him of the cultural and racial transformation under way.[80] Yet even the horticultural landscape in California was more racially diverse than Australians desired.

The racial ambivalence and conflict found in California's horticulture, which were almost unknown in Australia, reflected differences in labor market realities. Dependent on Chinese for fruit-picking, Californian growers found themselves unable to give full vent to racial animosities that pervaded sections of the wider community. Furthermore, the Chinese and other nonwhite populations remained larger in California, since fewer Chinese returned home after the gold rushes and many Asians continued to arrive despite attempts to restrict their entry and land ownership. In Australia, conditions were different, and rather than deal with a racial problem, legislators claimed to preempt it.[81] In introducing the Chinese Influx Restriction Bill in Victoria in 1881, the Honorable S. F. Dobson reported that "the Chinese difficulty has arisen elsewhere besides in this colony. It is a very serious question, especially in the state of California. . . . We should legislate here in time against them, before we find ourselves flooded with Chinamen."[82]

Irrigation would help in a different but complementary way. With water alone could Australia populate the outback intensively and thus stake a claim to a land grossly underoccupied by European standards. If British Australians did not settle their vast lands, Asians would, said irrigation promoters. John West noted the necessity of "filling this empty continent with people of the white race."[83] All nonwhite races were excluded from the dream, including aboriginals and even some European peoples not considered Caucasian. As a promotional magazine noted in 1905, irrigation in Australia could be based as nowhere else on racial and national homogeneity: "There are no racial differences, no alien or inferior population, . . . and no warlike nations to disturb settlement." Aborigines were "always harmless" and were now confined to reservations, the document claimed.[84] When "Julian Thomas," the noted Melbourne journalist, toured the Renmark scheme in South Australia in 1894, he was pleased to discover that, "wonderful to relate, there are no Chinese or Hebrews in the settlement." Equally important, this transformation of arid Nature had occurred upon a dull plain "where blackfellows not so long ago camped and beat their gins [aboriginal women]."[85]

This last remark serves as a reminder that democracy in Australia underpinned by irrigation was to be a democracy of white men. Alfred Deakin did not directly refer to women but depicted Victorian irrigation as an aid to the achievement of the "manliness and independence of its citizens."[86] When irrigation promoters in Australia did mention women, it was to explain their place on the farm. With "frugality and industry" the new (male) settler could "rear his family and make a home for himself," utilizing the unpaid labor of women and children within this household economy.[87] "The cultivation of an orchard is, of course, man's work," announced John West.[88] But, West continued, women's dexterous hands and sense of detail made them most useful for fruit-picking, and everywhere poultry raising, a part of the mixed farm economy, could also supplement diet and income "as the special province of the housewife."[89]

More positively, irrigation promoters also tried to encourage women to settle in irrigation districts by pointing out the virtues of small-scale horticulture for unmarried women. West hailed "women's opportunities in Australia" that garden industries could provide to English immigrants. "Harvesting apples" was "congenial employment" for such women, as was tending raspberry bushes. Modern technology and science had removed much of the drudgery in horticulture, which now demanded "skill and patience rather than physical strength."[90] Julian Thomas agreed, and hoped that the movement of respectable males into horticulture would prove a stimulus to women's influx. Young women would easily find domestic bliss in such a healthy rural environment. "We are not far behind the time," he rejoiced, when young middle-class women would "take their share of the work that. . . [is the] nearest approach to perfection in the life of a wise man, that is, gardening."[91]

Unlike Californians, these Australians could not point to much evidence that women actually farmed irrigation plots or worked for wage-labor on them. Thomas wondered why women did not settle in Mildura in such numbers as in California, where he reported more than twenty-six thousand working in the fruit-picking industry alone.[92] If Thomas remained perplexed, contemporary feminists were not as impressed by the conditions of women's labor in the Australian outback as male promoters of irrigation were. Jessie Ackermann, the American temperance advocate, wrote *Australia: From a Woman's Point of View*, arguing that women were unequally treated, and that life for them in frontier areas was harsh and their farmwork unappreciated.[93] Factory life had greater appeal, as some irrigation promoters implicitly conceded. Thomas admitted that women did not like the social isolation of the bush frontier, while West agreed that a "certain amount" of "roughing it" was unavoidable in the outback.[94]

Yet irrigation propaganda was not about such harsh realities, whether of environment or social circumstance. Irrigation had its place in any modern agricultural system, but the promoters promised more than this. Using irrigation as a panacea for a variety of social ills, they touched a utopian strain in the aspirations of middle-class Australians. Irrigationists aimed to triumph over human and natural obstacles using ingenuity, technology, and law to master their environment. Backed by the powerful complex of social forces made up of racial exclusion, gender relations, and social class, these irrigators persisted in their dreams of a closely settled, egalitarian white man's paradise to be realized through a landscape of farms, gardens, and suburbs. This dream of watering the outback continued to touch the Australian imagination deeply for decades to come.[95] The social forces that underlay the triumph of Deakin's policy in the 1880s over the critics of intensive irrigation explain why irrigation was tried before other agricultural possibilities were exhausted. The strength of these social forces also explains why Australian social thinkers and policymakers maintained faith in irrigation's garden ideal despite repeated rebuffs. They were determined to use the American model, appropriately modified for Australian conditions, to renovate the Australian environment.

CHAPTER 7

Transplanting Garden Landscapes

*The Chaffey Ventures and
Their Aftermath*

In the 1960s, Alfred Deakin's great biographer, John A. La Nauze, reflected on the 1886 Victorian Irrigation Act and Deakin's part in its creation. The Act "was a landmark because it was the first to lay down a policy for irrigation in the world's most arid continent."[1] La Nauze's judgment upon Deakin's work reflected the confident developmentalism of the 1950s. Few Australians resented the costs of irrigation; in fact, they dreamed of more and more such schemes. Attitudes toward irrigation in Australia have changed dramatically since then. Because the negative effects of such enterprises on alternative developmental paths and natural environments are now well-known, it is easy to tax the failures of those older dreams.[2] The point, however, is to understand the implementation of those dreams in Australia. In this endeavor, American personnel assisted vitally in the transfer of irrigation organization, law, and technology.

Deakin's innovations were less startling than legend has it,[3] and the road to "success" was a tougher one than either the promoters or opponents of irrigation realized at the time. The 1886 Act was in the short term a failure. Many of the irrigation trusts became insolvent in the depression that followed a few years later. They had to be bailed out with government aid, after a Royal Commission of Inquiry in 1896 condemned lax government controls and financially imprudent management.[4] In hindsight, critics such as Elwood Mead could see that the legislation fell between two stools. The state lacked the controls over the recruitment of types of farmers necessary to make irrigation work, but furnished money "and took all the risks." The government had simply assumed that providing the financial backing for loans was enough. No technical advice was given to farmers.[5] Existing farmers on the northern plains, in any case, preferred to use the broad-acre methods of wheat, which they understood, rather than try something different. If irrigated horticulture were to pay, new farmers willing to cultivate intensely would have to be imported, and these, from the cities and overseas, were often ignorant of Australian environmental conditions and markets that favored large-scale holdings. Pockets of irrigation resembling Californian conditions developed, such as that pioneered by John West at Ardmona, near Shepparton, but these failed to make a dent in the grain and mixed farming that drew on irrigation only as a supplement in years of drought and for the fattening of stock for market.[6]

This misuse of irrigation was encouraged by poor planning of some of the construction works. Dams were small and slow to be built, and channels were simply run through the existing freehold land with no obligation on the farmers to use the water. Even then, "engineering blunders" often left farmers without water when it was most needed.[7] Holdings remained too large, with farms in the irrigated area ranging from three to six hundred acres; the state made no attempt to subdivide them to make the more intensive agriculture work in practice. The irrigation usage tended to be primitive flooding, which could not produce the returns that might make the high cost of irrigation pay. The government had, in effect, grafted the irrigation system onto the existing patterns of pastoral and agricultural land use in northern Victoria.

Given Deakin's expressed preference for garden landscapes, this timidity is curious. One need not go too far for an explanation, however. Deakin was a liberal in Australian terms. He favored government intervention to right wrongs that the market created—he was, for example, the author of important early factory legislation—but wished for only limited state control. The heavy hand of government typical in many irrigation schemes in India he feared, and he was also mindful of criticism that the schemes proposed would be too costly. Thus the compromise as introduced in 1886 gave a large measure of local control to the irrigation trusts.[8]

The criticism of Deakin for failing to follow his garden rhetoric was only partly valid, however. The second arm of Deakin's policy, the provision of land to the Chaffey brothers at Mildura, was designed to establish a model of small-scale horticultural development that would entice others to follow. The Act under which the Chaffey indenture was granted became law on the same day as the General Irrigation Act and must be seen as part of the same policy. Irrigation at Mildura was, in contrast to a good deal of the other irrigation of the time, a genuinely intensive scheme aimed at creating a garden landscape, and one of real magnitude, though it too became mired in controversy.[9]

TRANSPLANTING ONTARIO, CALIFORNIA, TO AUSTRALIA

The Australian visitors to California in 1884–85 were particularly attracted to the Ontario settlement in San Bernardino County, founded in 1882. John Dow wrote a glowing article for the *Age* (Melbourne) in 1885, describing Ontario as a "model irrigation colony" indicative of what Australia could accomplish.[10] By the time Dow made this visit, Ontario had already become an exemplar of "permanence, utility, and beauty" for the fashioning of the California landscape into a human-made environment based on the garden ideal.[11] According to historian Kevin Starr, Ontario was intended to "demonstrate the full possibilities of a Southern California life-style based on irrigation, technology, and middle-class cultural values." The four principles intrinsic to the concept were "water rights, urban planning, an agricultural college, and the prohibition of alcohol." To emphasize its utopian dimension, Ontario was laid out in geometric form. Euclid Avenue, the broad central thoroughfare, impressed the Australian visitors as a "magnificent tangent" in the grid pattern of streets. Planted out in the center with palms and peppers, and on the sides with Australian *Grevillea robusta* and "thriving eucalyptus trees," it stretched seven miles in a straight line from the railway to the mountains, a scene that, according to the correspondent from the *Argus* (Melbourne), "almost took one's breath away contemplating the vista."[12]

The colony's inspiration and design came from George Chaffey. A Canadian by birth, he began his working life as a marine engineer in southern Ontario, Canada. His father was an American, and the young Chaffey worked for a time in Cincinnati, Ohio, before moving to British Columbia in 1879. He then followed his father to Riverside, California, in 1880 to make his fortune in irrigation. As historian Frederick D. Kershner correctly points out, Chaffey's was "not merely an American story—it belongs to the Pacific World."[13]

According to some accounts, Deakin encouraged Chaffey and his brothers to come to Australia, but it was Chaffey's Ontario associate, Stephen Cureton, who returned from a trip to Victoria to paint an optimistic picture of the colony's prospects.[14] Clearly impressed with what he heard, Chaffey proceeded to Melbourne in February 1886, hoping for large grants of land. The "Indenture Agreement" signed initially with the Victorian government in October 1886 was complicated. Set aside for development were 50,000 acres available as a grant of land to the licensees at 1 acre for each five pounds' worth of improvements; a further 200,000 acres were available under a twenty-year license to be effected within three years, at one pound an acre for matching improvements. The Chaffeys could not retain more than 5,000 acres of cultivated and irrigated land in their own names at any time, and they had to sell land for fruit-growing in blocks of less than 80 acres and for general agricultural purposes at 160 acres or less; a water diversion license for the Murray River gave their enterprise enormous horticultural potential. "If fully utilized," said Chaffey's biographer, "it would have been equal to a rainfall of twenty-four inches at Mildura, double the average fall in this portion of the Mallee." Fixed sums totaling three hundred thousand pounds were to be expended over twenty years at prescribed rates to retain the development rights. But there was opposition in the legislature to this unusual treatment, and the agreement was ratified in May 1887 only after the South Australian government upstaged Victoria by signing a matching offer for the development of Renmark, also on the Murray River.[15]

These agreements with the Victorian and South Australian governments marked the grand opening of Chaffey's Australian promotions. The scale of operations had vastly increased, since Mildura was many times the size of the Ontario colony. The Chaffey "system" involved subdividing large estates into small ones suitable for intensive agriculture; the extension of the time-payment system to enable potential horticulturalists to make the estates their own; and application of the firm's capital to engineering works to bring the best irrigation yields.[16] Yet, as historian Morris Wills points out, probably the most important innovation introduced from Ontario "was the Holt-Chaffey Mutual Water Company, which provided for each land title and its water right to be legally inseparable."[17] The whole enterprise, too, depended on the banks that underwrote the scheme and its strategy.

The engineering difficulties Chaffey attacked with innovative brilliance. He solved the problem that baffled his contemporaries, who could not see how irrigation could work on the Murray, whose waters flowed well below the surrounding countryside. Chaffey knew that the water would have to be pumped up, but because of his own engineering experience—he had used electric power to pump water in California[18]—he expected to overcome the difficulties. The direct-drive, shaft-driven pumps Chaffey designed and used at Mildura were named in his honor and won him election to the Institute of Mechanical Engineers of London. Said one publicist, "The most powerful pumping engines in the world" had been erected to lift water up eighty feet so it could flow down to a channel for distribution over 25,000 acres.[19] Chaffey played on these engineering feats in the marketing of the other, more questionable, speculative aspects of his land development schemes such as Mulgoa in New South Wales, where the machines proposed were "considered to be triumphs of mechanical economy."[20]

Yet there was more to Chaffey than engineering. He got support from the Victorian government not for his technical expertise but because of his inspiring vision of environmental "transformation." The mentality of the Mildura scheme revolved around a "wilderness won." After clearing the Mallee with its low timber value and poor reputation, Chaffey would create a landscape far more productive and aesthetically pleasing. Stretched before the approaching traveler in Mildura was "an undulating plain of fertile land, studded thickly with well-kept orchards and snug homesteads."[21] Nathaniel B. McKay, editor of the *Mildura Cultivator*, explained how mass destruction of Mallee scrub by steam traction engines and steel cables had opened the land to the introduction of "hundreds" of "vegetable products" as advocated by "leading authorities, at the head of whom stands Baron von Mueller." In this description, Mildura allied the garden landscape with acclimatization's message of environmental improvement.[22] At the same time, the indenture agreements that the Chaffeys signed with the Victorian and South Australian governments specifically provided for the removal of rabbits that had infested the land. This underlined the element of environmental renovation or rectification, since it was always made explicit that the country was not pristine but degraded pastoral land.[23]

The garden landscape of the proposed irrigation settlement carried heavy moral freight too.[24] Chaffey would create a utopian "Temperance Paradise." The Reverend A. R. E. Burton, the organizing secretary of the Australian Scripture Education League, served as a moral booster of the project.[25] As in Ontario, the Chaffeys set aside land for an agricultural college and, in the same spirit of improvement, duplicated their temperance ethic. "There is no publichouse [sic] or drinking saloon" for the "impoverishment or demoralisation" of upwardly mobile farmers on the Mildura tract, announced Burton approvingly.[26]

The socially conservative nature of the irrigation impulse was also congenial to Burton, a good evangelical. Chaffey's paternalistic capitalism shone through not only in his prohibition edict but also in his attempts to quell potential sources of labor unrest by making workers part of the cooperative venture. The publicist Burton opposed "the frenzied struggle of the labouring classes for special legislation" but admitted that "labour troubles" were "chiefly the result of fear of the consequences of overcrowding" in the cities. Burton was writing in 1892, at the height of the bitter strikes of the early 1890s depression, and he was especially concerned to inform prospective settlers that they would experience no such troubles in Mildura. The skilled workers such as those in the engineering plant and carpentry and joinery works would not strike to interrupt irrigation work or the construction of shops and houses, because the employee was in almost every case "a landowner on the estate, while every apprentice is the son of a settler."[27]

As in other Chaffey enterprises, the landscape served to reinforce through aesthetic statement the social objectives of the reformers. At both Mildura and Renmark as in Ontario, tree-lined streets were laid out in an ordered grid pattern with wide boulevards, and similar trees were planted: the landscape of fruit trees and gums that the Chaffeys used in California was repeated in the Australian colonies. Of the twin colony at Renmark, Julian Thomas remarked that Charles Chaffey's "ranch" had "groves of sugar gums, planted as windbreaks," which "relieve the monotony of straight rows of orchards and wire fences."[28]

The Chaffeys did not succeed in reproducing Ontario, however. The temperance policy was abandoned within a few years because of popular resistance. In Renmark the Chaffeys built a municipally owned hotel on the Swedish Gothenburg plan, one that would return its profits to the community. The agricultural college remained nothing but a foundation stone, and many building lots stood empty, with only three thousand in the Mildura colony and one thousand in Renmark before the Canadian brothers filed for bankruptcy in the middle of the depression, in 1894. Two years later, a Royal Commission of Inquiry investigated the debacle.

George Chaffey blamed changed political circumstances in Victoria for the collapse of his scheme. Deakin was now in opposition. Having himself lost money in the land boom, he sat gloomily on the backbench while Royal Commissions attacked Mildura and probed his policies, though Deakin appeared before the Mildura inquiry to give a spirited defense.[29] The commission damned many financial and technical aspects of the Chaffey venture, but remained supportive of the attempt to create a horticultural industry there and recommended closer government control and more financial aid than Deakin (or his successors) had provided.

Chaffey later claimed that this desire for state control was a critical obstacle to his success. As Kevin Starr summarizes the argument, "the incipiently socialist attitude towards resource development in Australia, the belief that irrigation should be carried on by government as a public interest venture, thwarted Chaffey's entrepreneurial instincts." Chaffey was bankrupted as a result.[30] This interpretation relies too heavily on Chaffey's own self-justifications, however. It confuses results with causes. To be brutally honest, the faults lay largely with the Chaffeys' own risk assessment. Economic conditions were different from the Ontario case as a result of timing: starting new schemes at the end of the 1880s land boom in Australia proved disastrous. Colonial Victoria in 1893 suffered a financial collapse from which government and business took several years to recover. Still, not just the timing was at fault: the strikingly speculative methods of the Chaffeys brought them down. Not only did they have the major Renmark and Mildura ventures, they also negotiated unsuccessfully for land grants in Queensland and gambled on schemes for suburban and market-garden land development through irrigation at Werribee near Melbourne and at Mulgoa. These boom-era developments all soon collapsed as banks failed and mortgages were recalled.[31]

The Mildura site was about as risky as the speculative economics. It lay far from the nearest rail transport, with the railhead over 150 miles away. In contrast, Ontario was built directly on the railway line, thus assuring access to markets. The river Murray was navigable for some months of the year to ship produce, but in summer the flow slowed. Other local environmental problems of salinization and erosion also plagued the settlement, and failure to line the channels was a critical error. Chaffey essentially took a gamble on this engineering problem because the lining of channels with concrete would have made the scheme uneconomical. The gamble did not pay off. The Murray River yabbies, a freshwater crayfish, unknown in California, burrowed holes in the channels and caused drastic diversions of water. Even more damaging, the Mildura colony was far bigger in its grandiose plans than any Californian irrigation scheme up to that time. This might not have mattered, but the Chaffeys had not paid attention to differences in the market potential. The populations of California and Victoria were similar, but California had larger markets elsewhere in the United States that began to be developed extensively, precisely at the time when the Canadian brothers gambled on the Australian venture.[32]

The importance of markets is underlined by the fates of the two major partners. Though George Chaffey failed to solve his marketing problems, one of his brothers, W. B. (Ben) Chaffey, weathered the economic storm in Australia, founded the Australian Dried Fruits Association, and eventually became mayor of Mildura. After his death in 1926 Ben Chaffey's home, Rio Vista, was made a cultural center, and statues were unveiled in both Mildura and Renmark. Ben Chaffey adapted to the conditions and morals of the local community and abandoned his temperance stance, pioneering the development of the Merbein, later named Mildara, winery. In the late 1930s, the winery he founded was sending one hundred thousand gallons of port and muscat to Britain every year.[33] But more fundamental was his role in the shift from lexia grapes to sultanas, as the latter were well adapted to the climate and could be used in the dried fruit industry. Chaffey imported American technology to dry his fruit, though the Dried Fruits Association was a more critical part of the adaptation of the Chaffeys' utopian ideal into a business success.[34] Yet all this lay in the future, after 1900.

Ben Chaffey probably could not have succeeded in the long run if the Victorian government had not come to Mildura's aid in the short run. In quite the opposite of George Chaffey's own interpretation, government had to bail out the scheme after 1895. The Victorian government turned the Chaffey enterprise into one of Deakin's irrigation trusts, gave it government subsidies, and built a branch railway line (completed in 1903) for the express purpose of providing Mildura with the market link it required. Large sums of money were also provided to line channels with concrete and thus find a solution to the difficulties of erosion and water diversion.

Despite their dramatic failure, the Chaffeys retained a good reputation in Australian history.[35] Deakin maintained his praise for Mildura as "the best object lesson we have received in irrigation for intense culture."[36] Another sterling endorsement came with the perspective of 1928, when the settlements had attained a better economic footing. Prime Minister Stanley Melbourne Bruce praised the Chaffeys for teaching that "the problem of Australia's unsettled interior is not one of unproductive land, but that water conservation and supply can make the land 'yield forth its increase.'" Through George Chaffey's "genius and enterprise," Australia had been, Bruce claimed, "permanently benefited, and we and future generations of Australians will remember him and his work with gratitude."[37] George Chaffey lived to hear this praise, but a question mark remained over his Australian activities, and this episode dogged him upon his return to the United States.

THE IMPERIAL VALLEY SCHEME

George Chaffey set sail for the United States in August 1897 to become involved in further suburban land development, and then in the Imperial Valley scheme to divert the waters of the Colorado River to irrigate sections of the southern California desert. From 1900 to 1902, he served as president of the California Development Company (CDC) to further this project. If the Australia experience had turned Chaffey against involvement with government, this reluctance was reflected in the entrepreneurial ethos of the Imperial Valley scheme.[38]

Not that the Australian experience was entirely negative for Chaffey. H. T. Cory, an associate, noted that the Canadian returned from Australia with a more expansive view of irrigation's possibilities. The climate of the Imperial Valley, far hotter and tougher than that in Ontario, approximated conditions in the outback of Australia. Chaffey's "experience in successfully establishing an irrigation enterprise in the interior of Australia . . . led him to undertake the work here in 1900," Cory insisted.[39] It was from Chaffey that the name "Imperial Valley," with all of its connotations of environmental domination, derived in 1901 to replace that of the Salton Sink. Ever the audacious engineer, Chaffey showed the entrepreneurs how to reroute water from the Colorado to their land by diverting the river just north of the Mexican border and building a canal through Mexican territory and then back into the United States. In this way the company was able to obtain a satisfactory water flow and bypass the troublesome sand dunes that stood in the way of a direct route through U.S. territory.[40] The lands developed in the Imperial Valley had been or were being acquired by the developers under the extremely favorable conditions of the Homestead Act of 1862 and Desert Lands Act of 1877, and now the CDC gleefully faced the prospect of windfall profits from public land as the desert was made, in the terms of the promotional literature, to bloom.

At first, as in Mildura, settlers streamed in. But the CDC became embroiled in disputes with the United States Reclamation Service, which believed that the potential of the great Colorado River ought to be developed under federal control. Its proposed Yuma Dam and irrigation scheme, located upstream from the CDC's diversion, would effectively bypass the private venture. The Reclamation Service also argued that because the Colorado was potentially navigable, its control remained legally in the hands of the U.S. government.[41] To legal problems and the opposition of the Reclamation Service was added a fundamental engineering blunder. Chaffey's channel, cut at minimal expense, utilized an old canal for part of the way. Heavy silting in the original channel, together with the conflict with the Reclamation Service, enticed the CDC to cut a second diversion in the Colorado River, this time within Mexican territory, out of United States government jurisdiction. The company did not reckon, however, on the immense power of the Colorado. Heavy floods in 1905 and the inadequacy of the engineering of the second cut caused a dramatic break in the river's banks, and 360 million cubic feet of water began to pour through the ever-widening breach into the Salton Sink depression, transforming it into the Salton Sea. Chaffey was, through the financial maneuvering of other businessmen, no longer part of the CDC operation, but his reputation was nevertheless tarnished by the disaster. In 1907, President Theodore Roosevelt sent a message to Congress denouncing the California Development Company and its officers.[42]

After this debacle, Chaffey retired from the public limelight with a poor record and a poorer reputation than he deserved. But from the perspective of the Pacific exchange, the result was to discourage emulation of Australian precedents for irrigation law reform, already overshadowed as they were by the financial imbroglio of the 1890s. The bad reputation of Australian irrigation was documented in the work of William Hammond Hall. Hall was engaged in 1896 to survey irrigation round the world for the Cape Colony government, and his wide-ranging report makes clear why the Deakin era reforms were not regarded favorably in international irrigation circles. Hall was intensely critical of inadequate government supervision of district irrigation developments in Australia, though he lumped together the Californian and Australian examples on this point. Hall also had contact with Alfred Deakin at the time of the Royal Commission visit in 1884–85, and from the beginning he was critical of Deakin's actions.[43]

The Mildura scheme fulfilled his worst fears of antipodean irrigation. Hall wrote his South African report in the wake of the financial collapse dramatically revealed in the Royal Commission report that delved into the Mildura Colony. So convinced of the errors was Hall that he refused to speak of the Chaffeys as Americans, referring to them as "the Canadian gentlemen." He flatly indicated that "neither American precedents nor American advice were in any way responsible for the projecting or the failure of Mildura Settlement in Victoria." To "well-informed" Californians, Hall asserted, the enterprise appeared "from its inception, a bubble of the lightest description. There was no little speculation, at the time, in California on the seeming fact that American experiences, which had been officially studied in the interest of Victoria, could not be availed of to better purpose than it was for the benefit of that Australian Colony."[44] Hall also tarred Deakin's larger irrigation policy with the same brush; it had given away Crown lands carelessly to the Chaffeys and committed public funds to irrigation development without assuming financial and technical supervision to ensure that the expenditures were justified. The half-measures adopted by Deakin represented the worst of all possible worlds, in Hall's view, and Australian irrigation was an example to be avoided.[45]

The Royal Commission report of 1896 continued to be used in the United States to discredit both Chaffey and Australian irrigation. In 1906 Chaffey filed water claims on a number of streams in the Owens River Valley, with the intention of developing irrigation and hydroelectric projects there. This move brought him into conflict with the city of Los Angeles, which had its eye on the same water. The project concerned a right-of-way over federal lands, and the city stymied Chaffey's efforts to develop the land, eventually buying out his interests. In the argument submitted to the secretary of the interior, Los Angeles relied heavily on the history of the discredited Mildura sojourn, citing the 1896 Royal Commission in its arguments.[46]

Not only were such disparaging comments made about Australian irrigation policy: awareness of Australian irrigation policies declined in the 1890s, possibly as part of a reaction against the perceived failures of that decade, but also because financial cutbacks held back further Australian initiatives during the depression. Deakin's *Irrigation in Western America* and his volumes on Egypt, Italy, and India made him a highly respected figure in western American irrigation circles, and his achievements of the 1880s were well publicized in the United States.[47] Yet at the so-called International Irrigation Congress held in Los Angeles in 1893, only one Australian delegate attended, as a result of the stringent financial situation, and he was simply a colonial official passing through to the 1893 World's Columbian Exhibition.[48] Other delegates made little reference to Australia, with the exception of the Canadian expert, J. S. Dennis.[49]

The leadership in irrigation reform, moreover, had temporarily passed to other places. When Elwood Mead published his *Report of Irrigation Investigations in California* in 1901, he drew to only a limited extent on "what Deakin has done in part for Australia" in forging an "enlightened" irrigation code. Mead was much more impressed with Canada's Northwest Irrigation Act.[50]

Not until after 1905 would interest in Australian irrigation policy revive.[51] When state intervention to promote the garden concept through large-scale works of irrigation became more fashionable in the United States, the Australian example emerged again as a relevant model of government financial action, of legal reform in water rights, and of scientific planning. In the antipodes, government loomed larger in turn-of-the-century economic development than in the United States. For example, in Australia the railways were all government owned, whereas the American federal government concentrated on giving land grants to private railroad companies. Given the place of the state in the Australian economy, and the fact that Australia's government-sponsored achievements in irrigation have figured strongly in national myth, it seems reasonable to suppose that Australian precedents should become important internationally.

Reality, however, was more complicated. A key problem that Victoria attempted to surmount was ancient riparian law. The old English doctrine that the owner of land adjacent to a flowing stream had priority of use made sense in humid England, but in the American West, and in much of Australia, such a doctrine prevented the development of the land along those lines of farming considered appropriate by Europeans. The Victorian innovation in doing away with riparian rights, begun with the 1886 Act, remained incomplete until the Water Act of 1905, and for this reason the Victorian action had limited appeal as a model for revision of water rights elsewhere. The Victorian Act of 1886 had abolished riparian rights "unless a contrary right could be proved."[52] No new riparian land could be acquired after 1886, which would have limited riparian rights to pre-1886 diversions, but legal opinions had thrown this position into confusion. Some lawyers argued that those who had acquired Crown grants before 1886 could make new diversions after 1886, and that the Act only applied to new grants of land made after 1886. The 1905 Act aimed to clear the confusion. It abolished all private water rights acquired after proclamation of the 1886 Act by Crown grantees dating back to before the 1886 Act, gave the state total control over water use, and established ownership of the beds and banks of water frontages and watercourses except where already alienated.[53]

This radical shift came too late to influence policy in the United States. Of far more significance than legislation on riparian rights were the efforts of governments, especially in Victoria, to improve the delivery and efficient use of water through stricter and more expert supervision. After the initial irrigation experiments of the 1880s and 1890s proved unsuccessful, the government intervened further to promote closer settlement. The effect of these Australian precedents upon American irrigation came well after Deakin's initial reforms.

This delay did not occur because of American rejection of Australian enthusiasm for state socialism. Rather, the neglect of Australian examples reflected the very timid and unsatisfactory governmental irrigation development in Australia up to 1900. Colonial experiments, informed by a liberalism still hesitant in the use of state authority, had made only limited use of potential government power, compared to what would happen after 1900. By 1920, some administrative and policy developments in irrigation in Australia ran ahead of those in the United States. Yet, ironically, many of the innovations were implemented by an American, Elwood Mead, and it was also Mead who did more than anybody else to bring publicity about Australian irrigation institutions back to the United States.

CHAPTER 8

To Australia and Back

Elwood Mead and the Vision of
Closer Settlement

Victoria leapfrogged over the United States in the decade after 1904 in several key aspects of irrigation policy. The federation of the Commonwealth of Australia in 1901 had brought a new confidence in national development. Deakin was now out of Victorian politics and had embarked on his distinguished career as Australian prime minister, but the dream of irrigation development still flourished at the state level, where water and land policy remained under the new constitution. The second phase of Victorian irrigation development began with the Closer Settlement Act of 1904. Like the first, American experience and personnel contributed. Closer settlement moved now beyond a generalized program to specific initiatives in financing, credit, farming practices, and immigration, as well as to tighter supervision of, and a more technical approach to, irrigation itself. The specific initiatives of closer settlement drew on the example of New Zealand government aid to small-scale farming, but the Australian version had to be much more closely tied to artificial water supplies. The Victorian water supply minister George Swinburne explained that "it will be impossible to go on with any great scheme of closer settlement unless we work in conjunction with irrigation." Areas with good rainfall had risen to such a value that it was "imprudent for the government to buy them at their present prices." Only through irrigation could the government develop cheap agricultural blocks for prospective farmers with little capital.[1] When the 1905 Water Act replaced the 1886 Act, the locally controlled irrigation trusts established by Deakin were abolished, and the Victorian State Rivers and Water Supply Commission took complete control. Two years later, the government drew upon American expertise to fill the state's top water job. At the age of forty-nine, Elwood Mead, professor of the institutions and practice of irrigation at the University of California, succeeded inaugural Chairman Stuart Murray as head of the State Rivers and Water Supply Commission.[2]

Mead's motives in coming to Australia after the shift to federal control of American water reclamation remain murky. Careerism was certainly involved, as he had become caught up in conflicts over the implementation of the National Reclamation Act of 1902. These disagreements were partly personal and involved infighting with Frederick Newell and George Maxwell, who had influenced the framing of the Act. Mead was motivated not only by this personal feud, but also by concern about the competence of federal irrigation appropriations to make irrigation work. He remained a champion of state control, and believed the water system he had devised in Wyoming in the 1890s was better than the federal alternative. Mead expressed extreme concern at the way Congress had mandated that irrigation works should proceed in proportion to the contribution of the sale of public lands in particular states. The relationship between the availability of public lands for disposal under the Act and the genuine economic need for and benefits of irrigation was not directly proportional, Mead felt. Yet only under such a coincidence could corruption, mismanagement, and waste be avoided.[3]

Though Mead was an engineer, his principal interest lay not with the technology of irrigation but with the same set of aesthetic and social values that had shaped California's horticulture in the 1880s. Mead came from a farm background in Indiana, and he sought a greener landscape in the American West.[4] Throughout his career, he attached great importance to the preservation of rural values. His ideal society involved small-scale settlement, cooperation, attractive orchards, and cosy farmhouses shaded by leafy trees. But like the Chaffeys and other irrigation promoters, he saw the necessity of small towns as well as farms, and he praised irrigation as productive of an ideal environment that invoked the garden suburb as much as it did Mead's rural boyhood. Prominent in Mead's 1901 report on irrigation in California were illustrations of "typical homes, gardens, and orange groves of southern California" designed to "show the beautiful landscapes which irrigation . . . is destined to create."[5] The "rise in land values" and the value of the crops were not "the chief benefits" of irrigation for California, he argued. "A far larger gain" had come from the "landscapes created in these deserts by the oases of fruit and foliage." These garden landscapes meant that a farmer there could not only grow a diverse selection of crops but also "beautify his surroundings with the perpetual green of a lawn" and create "rural homes" whose "average of human comfort" was "hardly to be equalled elsewhere."[6] This outlook was congenial to thinking in Victoria, where the government was trying to promote its image as "the garden state" of Australia.[7] Mead was needed in Australia for his organizational competence and technical knowledge, but his pitch to help the little man was a powerful one that fitted democratic aspirations.[8]

Economically, the idea behind the hiring of Mead was similar to that which had encouraged Chaffey's schemes: to turn southeastern Australia into a competitor for California's horticultural industry, yet one modeled on that successful example. According to the State Rivers and Water Supply Commission, California had "no advantages over Victoria." With equal skill, organization, and industry, "equal returns" could be expected.[9] Journalist Thomas Dow tied this competitive possibility to developments in "scientific invention and the process of refrigeration." Pointing out "how Australia corners the Summer" in "the World's Christmas Climate," he argued that Australia had advantages over California because the new Commonwealth produced fresh products in the northern winter season.[10]

Mead was sharply critical of Deakin's legislation but agreed with the ideals that had driven it. A sound and prosperous society peopled by yeoman farmers remained the motivation for developing irrigation systems. According to Mead, Deakin had thought that the government's only task was to make the water available, "instead of first educating and converting land owners" in order to implement the California ideal of "the improvement of small farms, gardens, and orchards by their owners." Everything turned around economics. In the United States good results had been achieved "mainly from investments of private capital," but Deakin had not succeeded in creating a similar economic incentive in Australia. In a break with Deakin's nineteenth-century liberalism, Mead and his political overseer Swinburne realized that the state must be used more forcefully and directly to implement the garden concept.[11]

Irrigation policy was seldom made by one individual alone, of course. Mead arrived at a time when politicians such as Swinburne and Water Supply Commission bureaucrats such as A. S. Kenyon were already convinced of the need to finish Deakin's work and achieve the "nationalisation" of water resources.[12] Alarmed by the squabbles over the river Murray leading up to federation, and also by the rise of private and unauthorized water diversions in the 1890s, Kenyon noted that "the total available waters are less than the prospective demand[,] and strict economy in their use will become imperative." He saw this case as "a strong argument in favour of the law relating to water rights being defined,"[13] but the issue of allocation was equally important. Swinburne sent another politician, James H. McColl, son of Hugh McColl, to the United States in 1905 to report on the very matters of water allocation, measurement, irrigation techniques such as night watering, education on water wastage, and other assistance that would distinguish Mead's tenure.[14] Ideas of economic efficiency in conservation had already penetrated the water bureaucracy and influenced the Act under which Mead would work.

Mead himself was an example of the new professional expert versed in the technical detail necessary to make the system work, and he fitted in well. During Mead's stay in Victoria, cheap financing and expert technical assistance in farm problems became cornerstones of policy. More vigorous bureaucratic supervision resulted in the marked rise in the number of irrigated farms and areas under irrigation. In line with his Wyoming experience, Mead also developed the most stringent water rights policy in Australasia. His most important innovation in Victoria entailed a compulsory charge for water rights apportioned to every holding according to its size, irrespective of whether the water was used. Farmers in irrigation areas were virtually compelled to take proper advantage of the resource or make way for others who were prepared to do so.[15]

Mead's interests encompassed larger issues of water control. Nowhere was this clearer than in his advocacy of the efficient allocation of water in the Murray River that flowed through three squabbling states. The Murray Basin is the largest of Australia's river systems and, because of its proximity to the markets of Melbourne and Sydney, was the one most in demand for agriculture. But in Australia, federation had left water and forests in the hands of the states, and these continued to argue with one another over water, just as the colonies that preceded them had done before 1900. South Australia feared the loss of river flow it believed essential to navigation, while New South Wales and Victoria differed over the uses and division of irrigated water. An interstate conference in 1902 proved to be only the start of a protracted process of obtaining agreement on dividing the waters. Mead entered the controversy midstream, as it were, but characteristically favored horticulture and efficient resource control on a watershed basis. To the 1911 Australasian Association for the Advancement of Science Congress in Sydney, he urged completion of an agreement for the Murray so that "development may be systematic and continuous." In Mead's view, "the solution of these questions should not be influenced by . . . the selfish interests of a particular State." The emphasis must rather be on how and where water could be used with "the least waste and made available at the least expense, and where land is the most productive, so that the least irrigated acreage will support a family in comfort." Such a policy, drawn upon American Progressive Era ideals of efficiency in conservation, would promote "the wellbeing [sic] of the largest number of people."[16] Mead knew that the lack of control of "the head-waters of our rivers" held back provision of "irrigation at a reasonable cost." The absence of intercolonial agreement had been a powerful stumbling block in the way of efficient development of water resources and had weakened Deakin's reforms.[17]

Recognizing that the Murray was also used for navigation and to supply town drinking water, Mead nevertheless sided with the irrigation interests. He favored "immediate and large storage provision on the main stream to safeguard the settlements . . . already inaugurated, as well as to make safe provision for further expansion."[18] Mead helped create the River Murray Commission established in 1915 after the interstate agreement of 1914 had been signed by Victoria, South Australia, and New South Wales. Mead's persuasiveness happily coincided with a drought that saw the Murray fall to historically low levels. Interstate rivalry became modified in the light of this harsh reality, and with the agreement in force, the commission built weirs and dams on the river in the 1920s and divided the water supply.[19]

As the Murray dispute indicated, Mead's involvement in conservation policy was not confined to Victoria, though that state held the vast majority of irrigated lands at the time of his residence. Mead achieved many honors in his years in Australia, among them presidency of the Engineering Section of the Australasian Association for the Advancement of Science. He was able to use such positions to further his social and economic agenda as well as to gain consultancy work in other states. Thus, in 1909–10, Mead advised Queensland on its water policy.[20] There he emphasized the limitations of irrigation for the northern state, given the conditions of agricultural markets and available land. Irrigation investment would be premature because of the extensive availability of "amply watered lands," he argued, but he counseled also that irrigation would have "great value in the future." In the meantime it would be mostly useful on a small scale for special crops like sugarcane. Mead also argued for legislation to achieve state control of water, and urged the Queensland government to implement this before irrigation commenced. The Rights in Water Conservation and Utilisation Act of 1910 followed this recommendation, though loopholes remained in the Act.[21]

Of larger significance were irrigation's beginnings in New South Wales. In 1911 Mead was employed by the New South Wales government to help plan the Murrumbidgee Irrigation Area (MIA).[22] Most authorities agree that the MIA development, begun in 1912–13, took a path broadly similar to that pursued by Mead in Victoria and was influenced in its early stages by Mead's advice. But World War I temporarily delayed ambitious developments there and other smaller ones in South Australia.[23] It was not until the 1920s that irrigation promotion resumed in Victoria and only then did extensive development begin in the other states. This trend owed much to the stimulus of government repatriation policies, which gave the garden ideal a new lease on life.

In the 1920s, the garden dream received a sharp boost from soldier settlement schemes. Wartime legislation in the Australian states, passed in response to the terrible sacrifices of the troops on the western front, offered free land to repatriated soldiers. Federally backed schemes to settle these men became closely linked to the further development of the Murrumbidgee in New South Wales, and to the Murray irrigation areas in Victoria and South Australia as well. A group of ninety-seven Australian soldiers was chosen in 1919 by the federal government to study irrigation and agriculture in California at the State Agricultural College in Davis, under the supervision of Mead, who had returned to California. Most of these soldiers came back to Australia after a year to put their experience to work in horticultural settlements that became a prominent form of repatriation development, especially in New South Wales.[24] In two new Murrumbidgee Irrigation Area settlements, a total of 622 farmers had taken up land in the two years to 1922, and of these "the greater proportion" were former soldiers "devoting their attention to horticulture."[25] Of an additional 355 farms established in the MIA during the following year, 223 were taken up by returned soldiers.

In 1923, Mead returned as a consultant to participate in the further development of the Murrumbidgee scheme. He envied the idea of soldier settlement—though he could not find support for implementing it in the United States—but noted in a confidential memo that two-thirds of the MIA farmers were "incompetents" and that the scheme in New

South Wales was financially unsustainable.[26] Certainly the dreams of soldier settlement could not be realized, and many farmers faced backbreaking labor for little return as fruit and other agricultural prices turned downward.

Mead not only found himself at odds with the New South Wales government over the soldiers' prospects during the 1920s, but he also argued unsuccessfully that fruit should no longer be the staple export sought in any further expansion; he wanted to enlarge the acreage devoted to fodder crops.[27] Ironically, Mead had come to realize the danger of overproduction in horticulture, but his pre–World War I message that fruit offered the best prospects returned to defeat his new realism.[28] "Our total horticultural area," boasted the MIA irrigators, "will eventually be equal to about 8 or 9 Milduras."[29] Only the depression, not Mead's sober advice, put a brake upon the boosters.

Tropical parts of Queensland, with far more rainfall than the southern states, could not avoid the irrigation mania in the 1920s either. Water was not evenly distributed in the North either by area or season, and irrigation promoters argued that the irregularly flowing but impressive rivers of Queensland could be harnessed through dams and channels to provide year-round water in drier areas. Irrigation could thereby aid intensive and decentralized settlement in the northern and central coastal regions. In the nineteenth century, development of sugarcane in the tropics had relied on large-scale use of Pacific Island labor. The memory and embarrassment of this quasi-slavery made the goal of small-scale farming through fruit and tobacco, as well as sugar, all the more vital to popular aspirations for rural development. Despite Mead's earlier warnings that the time was not ripe, planned irrigation for the promotion of white dominance in the tropics was appealing, facilitated by the policy of state economic intervention adopted by the ruling Labor Party under E. G. Theodore. Development began in 1922–23 with the Dawson River valley scheme in central Queensland, which sought to turn broad-acre grazing country into cotton, dairy farming, and sugar country. Queensland Irrigation Commissioner A. F. Partridge told Mead that "the works will reach among the largest in the world in point of storage and land served." The example of California and its Mildura offshoot was apparent in the design of the main town in the Dawson scheme. The settlement, appropriately named "Theodore," would be a pleasant "model garden township" with a palm-lined central "boulevard" and tree-lined side avenues, similar to the famous schemes of southern California.[30] These grand plans soon faced financial cutbacks and the large dam remained unbuilt, though smaller weirs served the Theodore Irrigation Area of thirty-five hundred acres, rather than the potential seventy thousand acres.

THE AUSTRALIAN IMPACT ON MEAD

By 1915, Mead had believed that the changed American political environment would allow him to return home and implement ideas he had pioneered in Australia. As a by-product of his return, he gave impetus to the Australian example in Californian irrigation policy and ensured some reciprocity in irrigation thought and practice. Mead was anxious to join in the Progressive movement and was heartened by electoral victories in California by Governor Hiram Johnson and Senator John D. Works. Though Mead stated that Australian governmental intervention had moved in advance of the American, he did not believe this would be true for long. "It hurts my patriotism to have to do my best work away from home," he told Works. Convinced that a "moral awakening" and a "new sense of social responsibility" would sweep through government, he snared a job back at the University of California, where he believed he would be able under the new conditions to advance the claims of the Victorian legislation.[31]

Mead's social philosophy had broadened during his Australian sojourn. Especially between 1915 and 1924, Mead used the Australian experience to push his schemes for greater use of state power to control special interests and enhance the prosperity of small-scale farmers against larger landholders. Australia became for him an example of Progressivism in action.[32] This theme he outlined in *Helping Men Own Farms* in 1920. Mead knew that many Americans were hostile to big government, and he tried because of wartime hostilities to distinguish between the kind of "socialism" he had witnessed in Australia, and that in Germany. "The best feature of the Australian state activity," he argued "is that it has not been handed down from above . . . ; it has been created and is maintained by the free vote of the people."[33] He praised government ownership of railroads and other utilities, but especially commended the fact that, after 1905, Australia avoided California's costly water rights battles by means of state control and ownership of water. "The publicly owned strips of land along the margins make rivers and brooks forever accessible to all the people," he rejoiced.[34]

The extension of financial help through rural credits, however, was the heart of his program. He called this "the Australian plan" and pushed it as a model for irrigation development on the federal level as well.[35] But his first success in translating the Australian experience came in California. The land settlement ideas he had brought from Australia involved the creation of planned communities. These would, he claimed, ultimately result in the investment of $300 million in, and the addition of 250,000 farmers to, California. From 1915 to 1924 he served, while a professor at Berkeley, as head of California's Commission on Colonization and Rural Credits, and he was the force behind the Durham and Delhi irrigation projects. These Central Valley community projects involved small-scale farm settlement with government help in the form of cooperative marketing arrangements similar to those already developed in Australia. Underlining the influence of his Australian experience, Mead continued to use, as one of his right-hand men, George Kreutzer, a Colorado-trained engineer who had served as an assistant in Victoria, and Kreutzer continued to work with him after Mead moved into the Washington bureaucracy.[36]

The Australian experience informed Mead's later irrigation policy in ways other than technique or personnel. Mead had left America as an advocate of the Wyoming scheme in opposition to the National Reclamation Act. He returned a defender of federal rather than state power. In Australia, Mead spoke out against the control of land policies by the states, controls which meant that Australian forestry policy, with all of its implications for watersheds and irrigation, was handicapped in comparison to developments in the United States during his absence.[37] This prepared the way for him to take control of federal irrigation policy when he became head of the Bureau of Reclamation. Ensconced in that office after 1924, Mead argued that the development of closer-settlement plans was "a national problem not a state one." He now sought to apply the Australian ideas well beyond the irrigation zone of the arid West.[38]

Possibly Mead had his racial prejudices reinforced in Australia, too. After his return he voiced fears of Japanese penetration of California similar to fears expressed by Australian politicians about the "yellow peril." Mead's ideal yeoman was of white stock; in contrast to the "Oriental farmer," California's first white settlers were "the finest type of American citizen this nation has produced." In 1929, in his article "Making the American Desert Bloom," he announced triumphantly that federal irrigation project settlers were 96 percent old stock Americans or European immigrants.[39] It is unlikely that Mead derived his racism from Australian sources entirely, however. An academic symposium on the Japanese land "problem" published in 1921 illustrated how pervasive these fears were in California.[40] Nonetheless, Mead did find in Australian experience an alternative to the use of "servile aliens." Instead of a farm proletariat of "men from the Orient," Australia provided reinforcement for the old idea that whites settled as families could be the source of their own farm labor force.[41]

This alternative involved a plan similar to that adopted in "the progressive nations" to create a class of quasi-peasant laborers. It was necessary to "give the man who works for wages a comfortable and respected place in the country neighborhood." Government aid could help such people to own small plots of land with their own garden environment in which to raise children in a healthy rural atmosphere and with a stake in the local community. These allotments invariably went to whites. Victoria's Closer Settlement Act of 1904 influenced Mead's choice of schemes profoundly. Mead quoted from the "Land Settlement Act" of that state showing the workers' allotments, which were "in time . . . nearly all made two acres in area." This gave "land enough to keep a cow and chickens and to grow a home garden."[42] Thus, from Australia he also drew support for his view of the importance of contriving a supply of farm labor. This could be achieved, Mead argued, by creating in irrigation settlements a hierarchy of owners and laborers. The latter would be apprentice landowners and would replenish the native-born stock as older farmers died or moved.

MEAD'S IDEAS IN THE UNITED STATES

These ideas on race, labor, and government intervention were strikingly in accord with Mead's Australian experience, but he was not as successful with them in the United States as he had been in Australia. Controversy dogged the two model irrigation colonies created under the Commission on Colonization and Rural Credits program after 1915. The schemes raised the ire of conservative politicians and private real estate interests, but politicians were able to point to practical shortcomings in the choice of settlements as well. Durham was the more successful of the two, but the Delhi settlement had been particularly poorly chosen. With its sandy soils, it was not even the modest success that Durham was in the early days.[43] Embattled farmers were unable to repay state loans, loans Mead insisted in his strict supervisory style must be repaid. When in 1923 he went to Australia and Palestine on irrigation consultancies, the farmers at home protested against their financial woes under Mead's administration. Mead returned to a devastating political reversal when conservative California Governor Friend W. Richardson appointed an arch critic, the private real-estate developer C. M. Wooster, as chair of the State Land Settlement Board. Mead resigned in protest. Shortly afterward, the state wound down its involvement in the colonies.[44] But Mead's personal career did not suffer. His long experience in irrigation was soon rewarded with his federal appointment in Washington, where he remained until his death in 1936.

In assessing Mead's failure in California, it is important to remember just how difficult it was to effect the garden ideal anywhere. The closer-settlement initiatives in Victoria and New South Wales were limited successes too. Irrigation did not pay its way at the time Mead left Australia, and criticism of the financial impost on the state may have been a factor in his decision to depart before his ambitions had been fully realized. The *Age* (Melbourne) pointed out in 1913 that Victoria was "still losing about £1100 a week on its irrigation expenditure," with an aggregate revenue deficit of £57,983. This was a "very serious load for any responsible man to carry."[45] Royal Commissions into Closer Settlement held in 1913 and 1915 presented further evidence that "the expense of irrigation development and closer settlement was not warranted by results."[46] In the 1920s irrigated farms in Australia still faced severe difficulties in finding markets for their produce. Nevertheless, it is significant that these schemes survived in Victoria rather than in California, and this survival stemmed from the greater role of government and the degree of state intervention tolerated in the market.[47]

While the Victorian programs did not become examples successfully emulated in California, the underlying message persisted in Mead's advocacy of comprehensive watershed development through large-scale irrigation projects financed by government and backed by rural credits. Mead never renounced the powerful and positive role of government, and as reclamation commissioner in Washington he continued to trot out the example of intervention that had made such a strong impact on him in Australia. As early as 1916, Mead became involved in the long saga of the Colorado River dam proposals. Pressure from Imperial Valley farmers to build a new canal that would provide them with more assured and larger water supplies entirely within U.S. territory conflicted with Reclamation Service ambitions to add storage capacity upstream, benefit a larger number of potential users, and spread costs through a unified Colorado scheme. Mead acted, in effect, as an intermediary between the Washington bureaucracy and Imperial Valley interests concerned with flooding and dissatisfied with both private land developers and aspects of the Imperial Irrigation District's management. His views largely agreed with those of Bureau of Reclamation chief Arthur P. Davis; both resented, too, the windfall profits of developers and proceeded from a desire to tax unearned land-value increments in Georgian style.[48]

Mead was an especially vigorous voice in California for the ambitious scheme under the control of the Reclamation Service. He lobbied Interior Secretary Franklin Lane and promoted, through congressional allies in 1918, "a bill providing for a vast reclamation and farm-making program in the whole of the Colorado River basin, along lines not before attempted in this country." In a reference to the successful 1915 interstate compact over the Murray, Mead argued that "the plan is now in successful operation in Australia" and would overcome failures of the previous Bureau of Reclamation schemes "to provide for this economic phase of the problem."[49] The role envisaged for technical help, government financial aid for farmers, and close bureaucratic scrutiny of projects closely followed his experience in Victoria. So too did his knowledge of Australian innovations prompt his attempt to give preferential treatment to returned soldiers, a provision added, through his lobbying, to a later bill of 1919. These dreams did not, however, capture majority support in Congress. Getting agreement from eastern politicians on a measure to support the West was difficult enough, without the added complications of Mead's visionary plans.[50] But an interstate compact was signed in 1922, and the watershed project eventually won congressional approval in 1928.

Mead saw very early the need for irrigation to be linked to the development of hydroelectric power, and in this advocacy he was more persuasive. In his draft of the "Colorado River Unified Development" bill of 1918, Mead advocated "Government ownership of all the hydroelectric power plants on the Colorado and leasing the power development to interests that desire to use it."[51] Whereas "formerly the factory had to go to the stream, now the ability to transmit electrical power along distances at low cost and with small loss is enabling cities to harness the distant water fall and is opening up new possibilities in mining, railway transportation and agriculture."[52] Mead did not forget the benefits of power development for farmers. In 1928 he pointed out that hydroelectric power could aid them immensely: "Cheap power enables farmers to light their homes and operate small farm machinery and home appliances" and so make the farm modern. But hydroelectricity did more than that. It made vast and expensive works like the Colorado economically viable because "on some projects the income from hydro-electric power is nearly equal to the payments from irrigation."[53] In this way, dams required for irrigation projects could be justified in terms of a multiple-use policy.

By the 1920s, irrigation policy had undergone a subtle transformation. The emphasis now rested not only on large-scale schemes but also implicitly on the need for irrigation to be harnessed to the creation of urban conglomerations, and to industrial power uses. Mead still believed in the garden ideal and linked the new strategy to its clichés. He still stressed the concerns for rural credits and the need for close supervision and selection of suitable farmers. But he now tried to promote the interests of the family farm in a tacit alliance with urban and industrial interests that were bound to subvert the ideal. The Salt River Project in Arizona might not pay in terms of farming, he conceded in 1929, but it had "transformed a hideous desert into a region of opulent vegetation, with alfalfa fields, palm-bordered roads and citrus groves, and this background has done more than anything else to create the city of Phoenix." The project gave to Arizona's miners "a cheap food supply and to the city the kind of background needed to make it an attractive Winter resort."[54] Mead parried the claims of those who said that irrigation merely increased the national agricultural surplus and so compounded farmers' problems. On the contrary, western irrigation products served, he argued, the growing industrial markets of the western region, and furnished "a steadily increasing market for the products of Eastern manufacture."[55] Irrigation was now being promoted as a complement to urban-industrial civilization, not as an antidote for its ills.

This policy shift presaged the real success of irrigation. Far from securing the garden paradise, irrigation promoted by the federal government now operated to consolidate agricultural holdings. A host of studies has pointed to the gap between stated intention and implementation in irrigation policy. Historians agree that agribusiness has come to dominate California's agriculture. One might expect this in private-enterprise America, but the consolidation of agricultural holdings occurred under federal administration and with the aid of government money through cheap, subsidized water.[56]

Similar agricultural patterns of land concentration appeared in Australia. The Murray and Murrumbidgee schemes were successful in supporting small-scale farming within their particular programs—more so than in the United States—but had little effect on overall land consolidation. In both Australia and California, landholdings tended to become more concentrated over time: in Victoria from 1925 to 1965, the increase was steady from 8.1 to 12.7 percent of the total in the 1,000–4,999-acre group of large farms. The other main gainer was the 100–499-acre group, where the growth was from 36 to 39.7 percent of the total acreage. In contrast, the smaller acreage farms (1 to 49 acres), associated closely with horticulture and the irrigated blocks, lost over the long haul in their proportional share, dropping from 27.9 to 21 percent.[57] These changes were similar in degree and direction to those noted for California.[58]

This does not mean that irrigation was completely ineffective in promoting the social objective of closer settlement in Australia. It would be more accurate to look at the effect of irrigated properties separately, because the importance of grazing and dry farming affected the statistics. Within the closer-settlement-scheme areas in Victoria, some success was achieved by 1936. The area of irrigated land had increased fivefold since 1900, and the size of irrigated farms in the closer-settlement schemes was 59 acres compared to 247 acres for dry farming, although the closer-settlement schemes occupied only 171,256 of the total irrigated area of 495,520 acres.[59] All in all, as the trenchant critic of irrigation Bruce Davidson has pointed out, Australian horticultural holdings remained smaller than in California, with negative consequences for economies of scale and efficiency in Australia. Australian fruit farms in the post–World War II period still tended to be 100 acres or fewer in area, in strong contrast "with the 200- to 500-acre irrigated holdings used for the same purpose in California."[60]

THE FAILURE IN COMPARATIVE PERSPECTIVE

Some American authors believe that the failure of irrigation to establish the agrarian yeoman lay in the National Reclamation Act and its interpretation. As the basis of federal involvement, the 1902 Act was certainly of some importance. Lip service was paid to the yeoman farmer idea by restricting parcels of irrigated land sold to 80 acres, and no farm family was to be allowed water for more than 160 acres. But loopholes remained, at least in administrative and judicial interpretation. The Act was construed in 1916 as meaning 80 acres for each family member, while many owners fraudulently defied the original purpose and remained noncompliant. In 1933, the Hoover administration blatantly undermined the Act's intention by ruling that it could not apply to the farmers of the Imperial Valley who were drawing water from the

Colorado before 1902. These supplies were defined as "old" water and the Act could only apply to "new" water, even though the water delivered would be from the new Hoover Dam not operational until 1935.[61]

Small-scale irrigation of the type horticulturalists pushed was, however, a failure in *both* countries insofar as the long-term trend of land consolidation could not be avoided. For this reason alone, the technicalities of the American 1902 Act and its interpretation will hardly suffice as explanation. Far more important was the drop in fruit prices in the first decade of the twentieth century and again in the 1920s, which rendered smaller properties uneconomical. The agricultural depression of the early 1920s affected both sides of the Pacific; this produced a shift in the 1930s toward other farm produce such as fodder crops and, in California, cotton.[62] Such products were highly amenable to large-scale production. After the 1920s no closer-settlement schemes were sponsored by the state of Victoria and, in the words of J. Rutherford, "some leases of unsuccessful farmers in older settlements were cancelled and their lands were divided and added to neighbouring blocks to bring them up to larger living areas."[63] Significant alterations in land use lay behind these changes. Salinization made some smaller holdings untenable, and settlements concentrated increasingly on areas of partial irrigation using larger quantities of land to produce the perennial summer-growing pastures of clover and soft grasses. These were the areas of irrigation that expanded after 1930 in Australia as in the United States.[64] This was not yet the agribusiness-government alliance that today grips so much of American agriculture, but the ground was being set.

For the fruit growers themselves, the drift toward large-scale business organization was reflected in the rise of advertising in the fruit industry. The surplus of fruit brought about by the expansion of irrigation necessitated improved marketing techniques. In California, the crisis hit earlier than in Australia, and between 1900 and 1904 already took up much time in the fruit growers' conventions. The growers heatedly and nervously debated this shift from the moral economy of nineteenth-century horticulture to twentieth-century business methods as dreams of a bucolic garden paradise faded. H. P. Stabler of Yuba City, a prominent grower and county horticultural commissioner, hailed "the age of advertising" and denounced the many growers who failed to "adopt the methods of all progressive businessmen."[65] On the other hand, a minority of growers resisted these demands for high-powered marketing because they believed that quality needed to be regulated first through cooperative production and packing. Sending low-quality fruit east would undermine the power of advertising, they argued. These growers were concerned with the implication that "a poor article well advertised will sell." Some likened the promotion campaign to those for "patent medicines" in which "half the cost is for advertising."[66]

At the same time, within the State Board of Horticulture itself there occurred a shift from the practical problems of fruit growing to examination of the economic problems of fruit selling.[67] Gone too was the emphasis upon the broader social and moral responsibilities of horticulture and the need for a careful balance between crops and between fruit growing and other forms of vegetation. Ellwood Cooper's solution to the marketing problems had been to back cooperative exchanges and new refrigeration experiments that would improve the ability of fruit to make it to eastern markets in good condition. In this way Cooper hoped that "the product will dictate the terms" of sale.[68] But under Cooper's successors, the emphasis shifted decisively after 1907 to recognizably modern consumer promotion.

The growers had attempted to forge unity of production in a series of cooperative associations after 1892, but this was not successful until the formation in 1905 of the California Fruit Growers Exchange.[69] A visiting advertising expert, E. W. Hazen of Philadelphia, was employed to report on the problems of marketing, and he told the growers they must have a distinctive trademark, as well as a centralized business organization with power to plan a definite selling campaign and to control methods of packing.[70] The Fruit Growers' Convention endorsed the new strategy despite some opposition, and the Fruit Growers Exchange began to promote citrus in the east using images of California sunshine. Taking up Hazen's suggestion that fruit be marketed like soap or any other product, the Exchange developed the trademark Sunkist, promoted fruit eating and juice drinking as part of a healthy lifestyle, and used the reputation of southern California as a health resort in order to stimulate the demand for fruit. Although the Fruit Growers Exchange was a cooperative, it operated as if it were an agribusiness, and was extremely successful in marketing California products in the east with these sophisticated advertising campaigns.

Australian horticulture faced a more severe marketing problem still, posed by the extreme distance of the fledgling fruit industry from the great world markets. However, the crisis in Australia's markets came later, and the industry was more successful in anticipating and overcoming, by astute organization and cooperation, fluctuations in the supply of and demand for fruit. The Mildura and Renmark Fruit Growers' Associations held their first combined meeting in 1904, and three years later amalgamated to form the Australian Dried Fruits Association (ADFA). New methods of production and new areas of concentration developed. The tray system of drying gave way to the more effective use of racks built in the vineyards, and sultana grapes suitable for Australian growing and marketing conditions found increasing favor. By 1914 ADFA had overtaken Australian domestic consumption and was starting to export, when the world war increased demand quite dramatically.[71]

Because of the war, it was not until the 1920s that a severe marketing crisis emerged in Australia. In the postwar agricultural slump, fruit growers faced a glut in the market locally, and prices dropped internationally after 1922 and again in the Great Depression. A conference had been held at Adelaide in 1919, presided over by Ben Chaffey, at which the likely problems of marketing in the postwar conditions were aired. Clement John (Jack) De Garis, a colorful irrigator and horticulturalist, suggested that a publicity campaign, financed by a levy on the tonnage of fruit similar to that enacted by the California Fruit Growers Exchange, be used "to awaken Australians to the vitamin value of Murray River products."[72] Just as California fruit growers had their highly successful Sunkist label, ADFA adopted under the leadership of De Garis the "Sun-Raysed" trademark. His clever marketing included recipe books, posters, cartoons, promotional films, and songs like the "Sun-Raysed Waltz" that extolled the virtues of the sun-drenched land of Mildura. Even the Spanish influenza epidemic was put to use in the slogan "I fear no more the dreaded flu, / For Sun-raysed [sic] fruits will pull me through." Although De Garis himself became involved in financial trouble, and took his own life in 1926, the reputation of Mildura and Renmark grew to a position in the Australian media and popular consciousness very similar to that occupied by the fruit lands of southern California in the United States.[73]

Despite these similarities, the Australian growers diverged from the Californians in important respects. After 1900, rail allowed Californian growers to concentrate on fresh fruit for eastern markets, but slow sea transport from Australia dictated reliance more upon dried fruit, particularly raisins, and upon preserved and canned fruits. Citrus thus did not dominate the Australian fruit landscape as in California, though oranges were important for the (smaller) domestic market.[74] Organizational divergence was apparent too. The California Fruit Growers Exchange was but one of a number of exchanges specializing in different types of fruit, and even though it controlled most of California's citrus marketing, it faced stiff competition from citrus interests elsewhere in the United States. The Exchange never so totally controlled the national market as the Australian Dried Fruits Association did by the 1920s, when it organized virtually all of the dried fruit industry in Australia.[75] Not only was ADFA nationally dominant, it also forged a close alliance with government. The California Fruit Growers and other cooperative fruit exchanges developed under government-sponsored marketing arrangements too,[76] though the process of government-business alliance went farther in Australia. As a complement to the schemes for closer settlement of repatriated soldiers, ADFA demanded of the state and federal governments an agreement for statutory quotas for home consumption and an export control board that would regulate the quantity of fruit to be sent overseas, secure Empire preference, and regulate prices.[77] The Dried Fruits Export Control Act was passed in 1924 and embodied these features, but ADFA's power was enhanced by the fact that, of the eight members on the control board, five were members of ADFA. As Ernestine Hill put it, "A.D.F.A. became a legal organisation of growers, packers, agents and merchants, the ward of State and Federal Governments, eliminating speculation and exploitation."[78] So successful was it that the marketing of canned fruit was modeled on the dried fruit example in a Commonwealth act passed in 1926. Later, in 1938, fresh apple and pear exports came under similar marketing arrangements.[79]

ADFA's quasi-governmental status was a response to the distance from world markets, the slump in fruit prices in the 1920s, and the successful lobbying of the fruit industry. The latter process was made easier by the rise of the Country Party as a force for farmers that could influence politics in conservative government circles in Australia in the 1920s, but the impetus cementing ADFA's power came from the fruit industry itself, and could probably not have been indefinitely ignored by any government.[80] These forces in turn perpetuated an attitude toward direct government intervention that was more favorable in Australia than in the United States, where proximity to markets—provided by fast rail service after 1900—continued to undermine the cohesiveness of growers of many different types of fruit. Rutherford has argued that Australia developed "irrigation under a highly centralized control of resource allocation" that differed from the American case, where centralized control was kept to a minimum. Yet this difference was not an immutable fact of political economy but always a matter of degree, and was subject to continual shifts in emphasis. The California legislation passed in 1917 to encourage grower cooperatives emphasizes this fact.[81]

Another critical difference between Australia and California in the 1920s was the degree to which irrigation policy was harnessed to urban development. California grew phenomenally after 1920, and in 1940 drew level with the whole of Australia in terms of population, for the first time, with around 7 million people. Within California, the tentacles of the "hydraulic society" spread, as a variety of authors have shown.[82] The engineering skills developed in the irrigation and horticultural projects could be applied more broadly through the activities of the Bureau of Reclamation as well as important state schemes. Vital to urban development in the interwar period was artificially harnessed water tapped by the city of Los Angeles at the expense of local users in the Owens River Valley; similarly, the damming of the Hetch Hetchy Valley underpinned urban development in San Francisco. Federal action also helped, though less directly at first. Hydroelectric power from the great dam projects built on the Colorado during the New Deal period spurred the growth of urban California still further after 1935. Relatively little water flowed from the Colorado to Los Angeles before the 1980s, but, as Norris Hundley points out, "the availability of Colorado River water beginning in the 1940s nonetheless had a profound psychological effect on city leaders" and "obliterated any sense of restraint about Los Angeles's capacity to absorb ever more people and industries."[83]

Australia was not so fortunate—if "fortunate" is the correct word. Australians had long dreamed of opening up the interior to farming by harnessing water supplies that flowed "wastefully" into the sea. Irrigable areas tended to lie farther from the major population centers than those in California, a fact that blocked a lock-step relationship from developing between horticulture and industrialization. The comparative advantage of pastoral production in Australia, with its little need for labor in open-range conditions, was a more fundamental inhibiting influence, however. The development of irrigation remained limited by availability of other arable land suitable for wheat and cattle that did not require irrigation, and by the fragmentation of effort that resulted from the distribution of powers between state and federal governments under the Australian constitution. Just as Mead had become frustrated by state control of water, land, and forests down under, Australian irrigation promoters in the 1930s envied the New Deal's exploitation of federal power.

Australia did not experience similar large-scale federal intervention before the ascension of the Labor Party to power in the wartime crisis of 1941 paved the way. Not until World War II ended could resources be spared for a massive campaign of economic intervention in conservation and power. In 1949, the Snowy Mountains hydroelectric scheme, the largest dam and power scheme undertaken in the Southern Hemisphere, was begun, aided by federal funds and the labor of migrants from war-torn Europe. This scheme, along with later efforts to develop national power and irrigation projects in Australia's north, was greatly influenced by the American examples.[84]

In the late 1930s, in the wake of the New Deal, the popular Australian writers Ion Idriess and Ernestine Hill had rekindled the idea of the development of the inland. Idriess argued that a garden paradise could still be created as the foundation of national greatness by turning the waters of the tropical north into the interior. When he summarized his arguments in *The Great Boomerang* and in *Onward Australia: Developing a Continent,* he demonstrated the American pull: "America has used her water in the building of numerous cities. Power generated through water criss-crosses the country and runs the wheels of many a great industry. By the conservation of water, America, years ago, made deserts bloom like the rose. Again and again her engineers have thus brought prosperity to desolate places. Mountain ranges have not stopped them, nor has anything else."[85] These arguments appeared again among politicians interested in "northern development" in the 1950s and 1960s, and demonstrated the resilience of the ideal of turning a desert into a garden. As the success of Idriess's publications indicated, the garden ideal lived on in popular imagination long after the dream of using it to build a democracy of small-scale farmers and a landscape of gardens, farms, and forests had been severely compromised.

Bug versus Bug

California's Struggle for
Biological Control

Biological control may seem a highly specialized and newfangled branch of environmental science in this era of pesticide abuse. Yet biological control predated Rachel Carson's indictment of DDT in *Silent Spring* by eighty years. Under the name "bug versus bug," or the "natural method," entomologists and amateur horticulturalists sought to introduce "beneficial insects" to control pests. Biological control was in the 1880s already a source of great controversy in California, and it became linked with the development of the distinctive regional approach to environmental transformation championed by Ellwood Cooper and fellow horticulturalists. Indeed, some called biological control the "California method" of fighting insect pests. It was intimately tied to the attempted creation of a garden paradise in California that would further the economic and social interests of horticulturalists. Though it was identified as the "natural" method, Californian horticulturalists did not envision a return to the primitive wilds. Rather they sought, as they did in eucalyptus introduction and in their irrigation efforts, an "improvement" of the environment that would create a balanced, sustainable garden landscape. Their failure has left us still in the grip of pesticides one hundred years later.

ECOLOGICAL IMPERIALISM

Biological control developed in response to humanmade changes that Alfred Crosby calls ecological imperialism. In the European invasion of the globe that followed the discovery of the Americas, many species were imported intentionally and many also unintentionally into Australia and the North American colonies. Most of these importations came directly from Europe or were European in origin. When contact developed between Australia and the American West Coast during the gold rushes, plants and animals were exchanged, and some of these were native to the Pacific region. Radiata pine and blue gum are the most obvious examples—but there were others, and some became pests. In 1907, the Victorian government proclaimed "Californian stinkweed," *Gilia squarrosa,* as a "troublesome and aggressive but non-poisonous" weed grass. According to a recent estimate, the incidence of such weed transfers across the Pacific "is still increasing."[1] Trans-Pacific weed exchanges comprised only a small number of plants and animals imported into each area, however. The most influential imports were Eurasian herd animals like sheep that were extremely destructive to the environment.[2]

The exchange of insect and plant pests between Australia and the United States in the nineteenth century was overshadowed by the volume of European introduced species, and sometimes by other introductions, such as South American lantana, a pest plant in many parts of the Pacific including Hawaii and east coast Australia. This connection reflected the similarity of climate between the tropical and subtropical zones of Latin America and those of Australia. Plant importations from Japan and China into California, such as cherry, plum, and prune trees and roses and other ornamentals, were also more numerous than from Australia. Australian plants, in contrast, came mostly in the form of seed, a form of import difficult to compare in volume with the North Pacific introductions. In theory, this meant that many of the introduced insect pests of plants ought to have come from East Asia.[3] But despite the smaller volume of plant trade with Australia, a key pest introduced into California was of Australian origin. The cottony cushion scale, *Icerya purchasi,* arrived in California around 1868–69. Development of a biological control for the scale represented a significant agricultural and horticultural innovation based on another Californian-Australian exchange.

THE VIEW FROM WASHINGTON

In 1894, far away from California's citrus groves, a vital figure in the new science of economic entomology reflected on the spectacular growth of his discipline. Leland O. Howard, then deputy to Charles Valentine Riley, chief of the Division of Entomology in the U.S. Department of

Agriculture (reorganized in 1904 as the Bureau of Entomology), gave his presidential address to the Association of Economic Entomologists in Washington, D.C. Poised to take over the top job in the division later that year, Howard reviewed the progress of his science since the 1850s, when Europeans had dominated it. American achievements since that time aroused "an exhibition of national pride" in Howard's breast that he hoped would be pardoned by his non-American colleagues. "All of the great advances in our science have come from America," he bluntly told the assemblage, "and it may justly be said that, aside from the one department of forestry insects, the whole world looks to America for instruction in economic entomology."[4] Howard ignored the important early case of Bordeaux, the remedy for mildew accidentally discovered in 1882 by farmers in the vineyards of France. He was similarly dismissive of American farmers' own pest remedies, and asserted American global dominance of the field because of the activities of the division's trained entomologists.[5] Under Howard's influence, American entomology after 1894 solidified this leading role and assumed international importance. There were by the 1920s more entomologists in the United States than in any other country, and their publication record was more substantial than that of entomologists in all the European countries combined. This reflected the rise of economic entomology in the United States and the role of commercial agriculture in demanding relief from injurious insects.[6]

Blunt though this speech was in 1894, Howard was essentially correct. When he reviewed the extent to which American expertise outstripped European, Howard predicted some of the reasons that would underline American superiority in the field over the years of his leadership. In Europe a "denser population and the resulting vastly smaller holdings in farms, the necessarily greatly diversified crops, the frequent rotation in crops, together with the clean and close cultivation necessitated by the small size of the holdings," had meant far fewer "injurious species" and far less "damage which may be done by injurious insects." The rise of economic entomology in American was, Howard indirectly but still candidly admitted, a response to broad-acre agriculture and to the interest-group pressure that farmers placed on the agriculture department in Washington to devise measures that would quickly achieve in newly disturbed environments the same results that in Europe had required intensive cultivation over long centuries. Economic entomology's connection to the market economy Howard spelled out with equal candor: "We have accomplished results which have added greatly to the productive wealth of the world. We have justified our existence as a class."[7]

Howard nonetheless noted that some other countries faced problems similar to those of the United States and could potentially help in the war against insects to a much greater extent than Europeans could. Howard praised, in particular, the Australian colonies for their interest in economic entomology, and he gave their achievements considerable space, along with those of South Africa and New Zealand. "With an energy and receptivity to new ideas akin to our own, their agricultural societies and departments of agriculture have not been content to allow injurious insects full sway," he rejoiced.[8]

Despite this recognition of achievements in the Southern Hemisphere, Howard and his predecessor, Riley, gave relatively little attention in practice to Australian entomological problems and precedents during the course of their administrations. Only when Californian interests pressured Washington did Howard and Riley discover the importance of this Pacific connection for economic entomology, and for the horticultural interests. Riley in particular was preoccupied with the plant louse *Phylloxera vitifoliae* and its effects on the European and Californian wine industry, and Howard's tenure was dominated by the concern over the boll weevil, hog cholera, the gypsy moth in the eastern states, and a host of other insects affecting the major American crops of cotton, wheat, and corn. In this his priorities reflected those of American agriculture at large. Because of the need to find quick remedies for threats to broad-acre crops, Howard and Riley typically responded to insect problems by recommending chemical control in the form of kerosene emulsions or the various popular chemical concoctions known commercially as "Paris green" or "London purple." Sprays were the easiest control available that could compensate for the absence of the intensive labor at cheap rates that could produce adequate cultural controls of insect problems. As the historians Thomas Dunlap and James Whorton have shown, the panacea of spraying was increasingly adopted after 1890 in the absence of the time, money, and willpower to achieve cultural or biological controls. After 1920, with cheaper chemicals and motorized and aerial spraying, the pattern already partly fixed in high-priced crops became widespread in American agriculture.[9]

Exceptions to this pattern did exist, and the most important of these involved California and Australia. It was not the Washington bureaucracy that proved most receptive to biological control strategies at the turn of the century. Rather, it was on the periphery of the dominant capitalist agricultural economy and among groups that aspired to a more holistic and balanced approach to agriculture that biological control was tried out seriously. To these groups, the Pacific connection loomed larger than it did to Riley and Howard, and regional interests in California had to impress the importance of trans-Pacific contacts upon a reluctant and skeptical national administration in Washington.

BIOLOGICAL CONTROL IN CALIFORNIA: THE STORY OF THE VEDALIA

The early development of fruit interests in California reads like a copy-book success story. During the 1880s, California's fruit interest boomed, attracting enthusiastic attention from foreign correspondents.[10] Californians did not wait for the congratulations of others, however. They praised themselves for having found substitute crops for wheat. Production of a variety of fruits increased dramatically in the 1880s on a base laid in the 1870s by pioneer irrigation colonies. Fresh fruit shipments by rail to the East multiplied by seventeen times from 1880 to 1888. The increases in dried fruit and raisin production were also spectacular, with dried fruit increasing nearly 5,000 percent.[11]

With relief, fruit growers noted that they had avoided serious pest insects that plagued their competitors in the eastern states. "Some mysterious quality in our climate" they rejoiced, was "detrimental to . . . diseases."[12] But the self-congratulation was short-lived; at the same time that the new markets and the new boom emerged in the 1880s, pests suddenly appeared. *Phylloxera* threatened the northern California wine industry as it did the Australian vineyards. Californians soon found that native American rootstock resisted its attack, and thus the *Phylloxera,* a North American native, did proportionately greater damage in France, Australia, and South Africa than it did in the United States.[13] But for other insect pests that appeared in the citrus areas farther to the south no such remedy could be found. When "the bugs came," as Alexander Craw put it retrospectively, "all that the glorious climate of California did for them was to furnish superior opportunities for their increase."[14]

Californians found that their garden paradise of orchards and eucalypts was not immune to pests. The insect threat became a matter of public concern in the early 1880s and was partly responsible for the establishment of the independent State Board of Horticulture in 1883. (Previously, an advisory board had been set up by the state viticultural board, itself established only in 1880 and charged with dealing with the menace of the *Phylloxera*.)[15] According to Samuel F. Chapin, inspector of fruit pests, *Icerya* was a "most serious danger" that threatened the very survival of the fledgling industry.[16]

The plague of insect problems had several origins. Importations of pests from the eastern states accelerated with improved rail transport links. At the same time, close and continuous cropping encouraged the spread of insects. Californian horticulture was becoming highly specialized, and pests were more likely to flourish in this environment than in mixed plantings. California responded by establishing state quarantine regulations progressively from 1881 onward, administered by the State Board of Horticulture, that were both pioneering and superior to those adopted elsewhere in the United States. In the 1890s California also lobbied Washington for a national quarantine law—finally enacted in 1912 but never purely relied upon—precisely because of the danger from contamination through interstate commerce.[17]

Irrigation also encouraged pests. Some said that water could be used to flush out insects, but the moist conditions allowed others to thrive. The orchardist Alvah Eaton put the point nicely when he said, "Water brings ten species to one it kills."[18] Eaton and others claimed to have found the *Eucalyptus globulus* helpful in dealing with the consequences of irrigation, and some fruit growers, according to *Insect Life*, proclaimed the gum "a panacea for all ills and insects," not just malaria.[19] Unfortunately for the purveyors of this remedy, Australian trees were a further source of trouble for the fruit interests. Many of the acacias and gum trees became infested with scale insects thought to have been imported along with the trees from Australia.

It is ironic, given the prominence of the Australian trees in the creation of California's garden landscape, that these very introductions threatened that lush environment. No one can be entirely sure how the introduction happened, but the cottony cushion scale appeared in northern California in the late 1860s.[20] Contemporaries blamed an importation of *Acacia latifolia*, though Mueller disputed this. The baron informed the Division of Entomology that all acacia had been imported by seed, and it is almost certain that he was correct. A stronger possibility canvassed later by the state board linked the scale with infected Australian lemon stock imported into San Mateo County in 1868.[21] The scale, originally derived from Australian natives, would not have been noticeable on the imported Australian citrus until introduced into the Californian environment, where it prospered. From there, the scale likely spread to the preferred acacias. Whatever the means of transmittal, it was discovered quickly that the scale thrived on the Australian ever-greens in California, and the acacias' presence in the citrus groves for ornamentation and shelter made them potent hosts.

From northern California the scale swept south to become a severe citrus pest by the early 1880s. When Charles V. Riley visited the fruit lands in 1887, the results were everywhere to be witnessed in "the attending evils of blighted and withering growth."[22] The impact upon the growers was not merely economic. Like Riley, they expressed revulsion at the aesthetic effect on their ideal landscape. Cooper reported that in Santa Barbara in 1884, "the two largest orchards in the county present a horrible and most disgusting appearance."[23] Faced with a crisis of nature, growers responded with cultural controls, severely pruning their orchard trees and embarking on a wholesale crusade against acacias. In 1888, the quarantine officer Waldemar G. Klee reported "thousands of acacia trees cut down"; Cooper himself uprooted all of the acacias on his Santa Barbara property and burned a large number of infected fruit trees as well.[24] Citrus growers stood to lose both their economic livelihood and their green landscape.

The immediate response of many growers was to spray, a measure that, along with cutting and burning, was also routinely undertaken by the Board of Horticulture. President Cooper himself used a nicotine-based spray and grew tobacco for this purpose at Ellwood. Californians not only employed insecticides used by other American farmers but also experimented in this area as they did in other aspects of agriculture. Indeed, the labor shortage meant that California was in the early 1880s already a leading national and international center in the search by amateurs for ways of fumigating citrus with hydrocyanic gas (HCN). But these methods were not effective against the *Icerya* scale.[25] Consequently, growers sought other methods, and they turned to Washington for help at the very moment that the struggle against scale intensified.

As early as 1880 the state board pressed Washington with petitions seeking relief.[26] By 1886 it was no longer possible to ignore these requests, and the federal Division of Entomology became involved. A research worker, Daniel W. Coquillett, was sent to Los Angeles, and Riley himself initiated inquiries in many countries to find the home of the scale. Riley soon suspected Australia as the source of the trouble, and said so in his annual report to the U.S. commissioner of agriculture, written late in 1886. Through an acquaintance, the English entomologist Eleanor Omerod, Riley began a correspondence with Mueller; William Miles Maskell, the registrar of the University of New Zealand (later University of Canterbury);[27] and Frazer Crawford of Adelaide. Crawford, an amateur entomologist active in the colony's Royal Horticultural Society, advised Riley in February of 1887 about parasites of the scale, and a sketch of one reached Riley through Omerod. Later, specimens of two parasites were sent to the federal entomology division's California representatives.[28] Evidence concerning one of these parasites, *Cryptochaetum iceryae,* convinced Riley that a mission to Australia must be undertaken.[29]

RILEY SENDS KOEBELE: THE 1888 VISIT

The next part of the story is familiar enough in the history of entomology.[30] In 1888, the occasion of the centennial exhibition in Melbourne, which was to have American State Department representation, gave Riley the opportunity to send an agent to Australia under the guise of representing the department. This pretext would get around a recently imposed congressional ban on overseas business travel by officials of the Division of Entomology. Albert Koebele, a German-American with the division based in Alameda, California, was chosen to accompany Frank McCoppin of San Francisco, the official U.S. Commissioner to the Exhibition, but with a quid pro quo. Koebele had instructions to report directly to the Department of State, and to study eucalypts and their economic properties as well.[31] On Riley's advice, he first met Mueller in Melbourne and then proceeded to Adelaide. In South Australia, he found the parasite recommended by Crawford on citrus in a North Adelaide garden, but found other promising insects too, including a predator ladybird.[32] At first the latter attracted little attention. Several shipments of parasites and predators were sent back to California, and not all survived the crossing of the tropics and the quarantine clumsiness in San Francisco. But one shipment of the beetle, known at the time as *Vedalia* (later *Rodolia*) *cardinalis* survived and was bred in isolation by Coquillett in Los Angeles. So successful was it on host trees that within a few months Riley approved a general release. The result was nothing short of miraculous. Soon the *Icerya* scale had been reduced to an insignificant pest. Modern biological control had been born.[33]

But the story did not end there. Almost immediately, the allies in Washington and California fell out. Their objectives were very different. They squabbled intensely over the significance of the vedalia triumph and over who should take credit for it. Riley was quick to censure inferiors, and his correspondence over many issues was frequently marked by suspicion and a cantankerous disposition. Riley often discovered "a petty rankling feeling" in opponents, although he circumspectly admitted that he did "not pretend to be free of foibles" himself.[34] One of those foibles was a desire to take greater credit for the vedalia's success than was his due.[35]

Riley based his claim on the evidence in his 1886 report. There he stated that "we know of no way in which the Department could more advantageously spend a thousand dollars than by sending an expert to Australia to study the parasites of the species there and secure the safe transport of the same to the Pacific coast."[36] Riley also appeared, late in 1887, to engineer the idea of the visit to Australia in connection with the 1888 exhibition. To Howard he confided that "I hope to arrange something in connection with the exhibition next year" and vowed to send Coquillett on an "Australian trip."[37]

Riley advocated the search for parasites in Australia, but this did not make him the first to do so. Nor did it mean that he placed the same stress upon parasite control as others did. Riley and his research workers were curiously reluctant to push the Pacific connection themselves, preferring instead to leave it up to the Californians. If Riley's surviving letters of the period are any guide, he spent much of his time discussing the planning of his visit to the Paris Exposition of 1889, other trips to Europe, and even speculation in southern California real estate.[38] Riley believed, as he reported to Coquillett, that the Californians could afford to spend the money themselves and should not wait for Washington to act. The two entomology division officials' principal interests, both scientific and economic, lay elsewhere.[39]

Even Riley admitted tacitly that whatever the inspiration for the trip to Australia, the political pressure came from California. He noted with some irritation "a tendency on the part of the California people to push things forward in this matter as much as possible" and feared that Californians would wish to claim the credit.[40] More detached Department of Agriculture officials conceded quite freely to Californians in 1889 that persistent pressure in the form of "numerous petitions from your State" in 1886 and 1887 had led to the investigation of the *Icerya* problem and the sending of Koebele to Australia.[41]

Such political pressure as this forced Riley to attend a special meeting of the State Fruit Growers' Convention at Riverside in April 1887. Toward the end of his very long address, Riley announced that he would like to send an agent to Australia to investigate the scale but did not have the money allocated. Any such effort, he claimed, would produce "laughter and ridicule on the part of the average committee in Congress."[42]

Since Riley was already under fire for use of departmental funds to make trips to Europe to attend meetings of entomologists, he made no effort to get these extra funds.[43] Instead, Riley argued that there were other equally efficacious and more immediate remedies. He told angry growers that he was skeptical of possible natural controls. Instead, he put his "faith" in "a remedy which gives satisfactory results without waiting." Growers had, he argued, "in the kerosene emulsion a satisfactory remedy."[44] Riley claimed to be the author of biological control, but this recourse to chemicals was no isolated incident. His typical response to problems of insect control was to recommend kerosene emulsion, coupled with the use of the spray nozzle device that he himself had invented.[45]

Apart from advising fruit growers to spray, Riley urged forbearance upon them. California's "insect troubles" were "connected with" its "unprecedented growth and prosperity." Singling out real estate speculation for special mention, he told the growers that conversion of orange orchards into town lots had allowed scale insects to spread. "No sooner does the owner of a grove subdivide and sell it than the different new owners allow it to 'run to grass,' so to speak; and for miles around all your thriving and growing centers of population may be found neglected orchards, upon which the insects are revelling."[46] Riley went on to suggest that the presence of the insects was something that the growers might turn to their ultimate benefit. "With your lovely climate, rich and varied soil, and the many other advantages which your beautiful country possesses for the cultivation of the oranges and the other fruits, the business would soon come to be overdone and rendered unprofitable." Under these circumstances, it seemed to Riley "that even the dreaded scale insects, by driving the thriftless to the wall, and giving the careful and intelligent man who persists in destroying and defeating them, better prices for his product, may, after all, prove a blessing in disguise."[47]

The growers had not invited Riley from Washington to tell them this. Many influential growers were hostile to chemical controls, suspicious about their effects, and concerned about their high costs. The alternatives were cultural controls such as pruning and weeding, or biological control. Californian officials and growers were already much more likely than Washington to emphasize biological control. At the April 1887 convention Waldemar Klee raised the possibility of using parasites, and argued that "in some of the countries of its nativity" the scale "is harmless." He concluded that "there must be an insect there which controls it,"[48] and he corresponded with Crawford to get him "to send parasites."[49] The Danish-born Klee had served as chief gardener at the experimental ground of the University of California's College of Agriculture, where he had been responsible for implementing the mass planting of eucalypts. There he had come under the influence of Professor Ezra Carr, who sought to transform California into a garden. In his new job, Klee became even more firmly aligned with the utopian ambitions of Cooper, Carr, and like-minded horticulturalists.[50]

Klee was not alone in feeling pique at Riley's claim. Alexander Craw, later inspector of quarantine at the port of San Francisco for the State Board of Horticulture and a major figure in the board's quarantine program, also sought credit.[51] He had suggested the antipodean example even earlier than Klee did.[52] Other figures in California also espoused natural controls and received equally pessimistic responses from Riley. Dr. Edwin Kimball of Hayward, the commissioner at large for the state board, announced that he had no faith in chemicals, arguing that "the great restorer of all things is nature, and it is our duty to make every effort that we can to find out her way, for that is the true way."[53]

Also prominent as an advocate of biological control was Cooper. As early as 1881, he discovered *Icerya purchasi* in his own groves and, he later recalled, "traced it satisfactorily to my mind from Australia." Cooper communicated with the United States Consul at Melbourne, Thomas Adamson, whom Cooper knew through previous correspondence about the eucalypts; Cooper also "corresponded with Baron Ferd. Von Mueller and others on the subject." In 1883 a Quaker friend, Amos Little, who was on his way around the world, visited Cooper, who asked him to search in Australia for the scale. Little reported that he could not find it. This satisfied Cooper "that there was a parasite keeping it in check."[54] The detail of the story is consistent with Cooper's long-term interest in Australia and with his recommendations for the treatment of another scale. Californian interest in biological control received an early stimulus from Cooper's 1882 work, *A Treatise on Olive Culture,* and Cooper extended this influence after he became president of the state board. Because Cooper's ranch specialized in fruits other than citrus, he was at first personally concerned less with the *Icerya* scale than with the black scale affecting his olive trees.[55]

He discussed in *A Treatise on Olive Culture* the possibility of using sprays but set strict conditions for their use.[56] Existing sprays were unreliable and quality control was poor, he argued, echoing points commonly made at the fruit growers' conventions and by other Board of Horticulture officials. Cooper claimed that the best remedy was pruning and regular inspection of the trees to remove insects manually. "Constant watching and constant fighting is the only sure plan to prevent the spread of insect pests. . . ."[57] The scheme implicitly required close supervision by the owner, the careful use of labor, and the concentration on products that had enough value to sustain the high costs involved.

Cooper's *Treatise* already contained a hint of the maverick stance on biological control that he was soon to adopt. This reflected his awareness of Pacific contacts. "I differ," he wrote, "from the conclusions of scientists as to the natural home of some of these insects. They do not, or can not exist where there are many degrees of frost." Nor could they come from Mediterranean countries, as the entomological authorities in Washington claimed, since the olive had thrived there for centuries. "The natural home is in a climate similar to Australia and that of California."[58] Cooper was already considering natural remedies before Klee, Craw, or Riley and exhibiting his strong commitment to Californian control of pest programs. Cooper hoped that, through biological methods and his style of agriculture based on intensive cultivation, California would become "the greatest fruit garden the world has ever seen."[59]

Riley was not greatly influenced by these arguments. In fact, he used the distinctive character of Californian problems to distance himself from responsibility. But an additional pressure obstructed the path to biological control. Conflicting evidence about the scale's origins distracted Riley. He was on the verge of concluding that Australia was indeed the necessary field for future research when Mueller temporarily led him astray by stating that the Australian natives had not been imported as live plants but rather as seeds. Backed up also by testimony from New Zealand's chief expert in entomological matters, L. M. Kirk, stating that acacia were "rarely or never introduced as live plants," Riley concluded that the scale must be the same as that previously identified by the French authority M. Signoret as originating in Mauritius (*I. sacchari*).[60] Riley was also staggered to learn that New Zealand's William Maskell, the first to identify the cottony cushion scale as a distinct species, had never seen a live specimen. Riley therefore discounted all of Maskell's testimony and theorized that the scale might have been simultaneously imported into Australia, New Zealand, and California on stray pieces of cane that accompanied sugar hogsheads from Mauritius. Riley switched his investigation to that island and decided to await a Parisian trip to consult European authorities on the scale's identity.[61] This delayed sending an agent to Australia. Only after his European trip in the fall of 1887 and his examination of specimens of *I. sacchari* did Riley conclude that the scale was a separate species that must come from Australia, as Cooper, Craw, and others had long insisted.[62]

The twists and turns of entomological research illustrate the complicated links between Australian and American investigations of insect pests. Californian authorities assumed, because of the presence of large numbers of Australian trees in their orchards and because of their contacts with a wide range of Australian botanists and entomologists, that the pest was Australian, while the Washington authorities were more inclined to seek the answer through European contacts. These conflicting perspectives reflected peculiar conditions that encouraged the earlier development of biological control in California.

THE SOURCES OF CALIFORNIA'S POLICIES

Commentators noted that Californian agriculture was marked by entrepreneurial energy. California's farmers were more innovative than others back East because they needed low production costs to compensate for isolation from eastern markets. In the California method of growing prunes, for example, "the saving of labor is manifest," commented the *American Garden* in 1891. "The yield of prunes per acre is said to be larger here than in France, and the crop is handled, on the whole, more cheaply."[63] The isolation of California encouraged changes in production associated with mechanization, preservation technologies, transport innovations, and the careful selection of crops and varieties. Ellwood Cooper was an instructive example of what one commentator called the "enterprising class" in California agriculture.[64] Cooper's experimentation with natural remedies was only part of a broader plan to market his fruit more effectively and develop new products, seen in his pioneering of olive and walnut cultivation and processing. These crops could be produced and brought to distant markets without spoiling. Because of the high cost of labor, he was constantly looking for effective but cheap remedies for insect damage as well.

Added to the entrepreneurial ethos was regionalism. The experience with biological control in California was conditioned by the state's role in the Pacific exchange of plants and environmental ideas concerning forests and irrigation technology. Tied to this was the knowledge Cooper and others had acquired in importing Australian native trees in the 1870s. The practical experience with Australian forestry made people like Cooper acutely aware of the risks in the acclimatization program.

Obviously helpful too were the new transport links of the 1870s with Australia and New Zealand. These allowed the growers to communicate regularly and easily with amateur entomologists like Frazer Crawford, and to read the Australian journals and newspapers that carried reports of innovations in colonial agriculture.[65]

As part of his campaign for biological control, Cooper and his assistants carried to an extreme the argument that California was distinct from other regions of the United States. The idea gained plausibility from scientific reports noting differences in California's soils, climate, and geology from those back East.[66] Cooper embraced these ideas and used them to emphasize the need to break with tradition. He spoke proudly of "our California method of fighting insect pests with their natural enemies."[67] In his 1899–1900 Board of Horticulture report, Cooper declared that California was "destined to become the greatest State the world ever saw. . . . The new conditions, our new possessions, the impetus given by the destiny of affairs," would bring to San Francisco "a trade with all the Pacific Islands and with the Orient not dreamed of by the most sanguine." This was a persistent theme, although exaggerated by the Pacific turn in American foreign policy after 1898.

Cooper's Californian chauvinism was conditioned also by competition with Florida, the other major citrus producing region. Because of the rivalry between the two, Cooper was reluctant to contribute to a national entomological program. He did not have a sense of national responsibility to share information with California's competitors. Cooper told Governor George C. Pardee in 1907 that the parasites brought in as part of the biological control program should not, under any circumstance, be shared with other states. If the program were ended, the parasites would be dumped in San Francisco Bay to prevent Florida from getting "the benefit of California's work."[68] This regionalism was shared by some other prominent Californians. In 1891, Democratic Congressman Anthony Caminetti praised the State Board of Horticulture and argued for a separate Pacific Coast Department of Agriculture based in San Francisco to deal with farm problems that were "entirely different and distinct from any other section."[69]

An abundant supply of sedentary labor would have made alternative cultural controls possible, but the relative shortage of workers in California made cultural controls impractical, compared to the South, which still had its reservoir of former slaves. Chinese workers could be used, but after 1880 this group was subject to increasingly racist attacks. It made sense to seek alternative pest control strategies. This desire to

minimize labor costs worked in favor of the use of sprays, but sprays were
not dependable in the 1880s and 1890s, and growers often complained
about a lack of quality control in available chemicals. The litany of com-
plaints about unreliable and deceptively advertised spray products was
summed up by the state board official John Isaac when he stated in 1904
that washes, dips and fumigation "are cumbersome, costly and inefficient." In contrast, Isaac stated, "nature has provided a better way."[70]

The reference to the "better way" of "nature" flagged the key consideration in determining the direction of Californian policy in the
1880s. Influential horticulturalists were trying to create a paradise that
they identified with a state of environmental "equilibrium" in nature.
Since this natural harmony had been lost, humans would have to restore
it by judicious acclimatizing policies. This interest in biological control
as an agent of the balance of nature stemmed from the afforestation
experience. In justifying the search for biological control, Cooper
returned to the themes of the "tree famine." He explained the rise and
fall of civilizations in terms of human disturbance of natural stability.
Until "invaded by man," all trees, shrubs, and flowers "flourish in their
beauty and grandeur," he declared. The moral message for insect control exemplified in the wholesale destruction of forests was clear. "If
we wish to succeed, we must follow nature."[71] The moral lesson of
forest destruction Cooper made plain. "Barbarians" did not destroy
the civilizations of the ancient Middle East, Cooper argued. "It was
wrong doing, wrong living." The floods and droughts that had devastated past societies came about "by man's destroying the equilibriums."
Insect damage fell into the same category. "The pests are among us,
and if we do not live rightly our destruction will surely come," he
warned.[72]

The mixed character of horticultural development in California in the
1880s encouraged these ideas of a natural balance. Sometimes the mixture aided biological controls in an ad hoc way, when growers tried, for
example, to use farm animals and birds such as turkeys in the fields to
eat the grubs on vegetable and vine crops at certain seasons.[73] But more
fundamentally, the garden ideal of horticulture itself shared cultural
landscape preferences with the ethic of biological control. Both were
expressions of preference for a harmony of forces, an equilibrium that
"restored" the California landscape to the normality of European perception.

Despite all these influences, it was the spectacular and singular success of the vedalia that enabled Cooper to sustain a program for bio-

logical control for nearly twenty years, in spite of opposition from some disgruntled growers and from Washington. None of Cooper's subsequent imports worked as effectively as the vedalia, yet every time the biological control program came under threat, Cooper had only to invoke the original success to secure further political support and funding. While the State Boards of Viticulture and Forestry were abolished in an attempt to save money during the depression of the 1890s, the Board of Horticulture survived because of the vedalia episode.

WASHINGTON STRIKES BACK

All the while the biological control program faced opposition from Washington. The opposition originated in the 1880s, undoubtedly exacerbated by Riley's own splenetic nature, but the bickering continued for twenty years. Riley's successor, Howard, followed up many leads and searched for a variety of biological controls. Yet, in contrast to Cooper, who depicted insects as an equal part of god's creation, Howard and the Washington establishment increasingly saw insects as the enemy. One of Howard's main claims to fame was his campaign against the common housefly as a bearer of disease. In this he later encouraged popular perception of a "war" against the insects.[74]

Scientific rivalry was also potent. The new university-trained entomologists defended their expertise. As Howard represented it, the Californians had embarked on a blind search for parasites "in an unscientific way and with the help of men of insufficient scientific training."[75] Washington experts, familiar with politics in the nation's capital, were quick to denounce the popular influence on entomology in California. "When applied entomology becomes coupled with politics," Riley complained of California's program in 1890, "there is always the danger that it will fall into the hands of incompetents."[76] The biological control program also raised hostility in Washington because it conflicted with accepted scientific theories about how insect pests adapted.[77] Howard believed that "there was little chance of success" in the idea of importing parasites from Australia, because the latter was in "an entirely different life zone, as well as in the other hemisphere."[78] Not only was Australia in a different "life zone"; it was also an island continent, and Howard observed that it was easier to obtain success in biological control on islands where imports could be more easily controlled.[79]

This is not to say that Howard and Riley avoided biological control entirely. Spurred partly by Californian pressure, they accepted it as one possible long-term solution to pest problems, but they stressed that short-term priorities had forced them to focus more on other measures that could give farmers immediate relief. Cooper's repeated offers to help Massachusetts fight the gypsy moth threat to the state's trees, beginning in 1893, stimulated New England demands for biological control, and the Bureau of Entomology countered persistent Californian meddling by initiating in 1905 a joint program with the state authorities in Boston to search for moth parasites. But Howard's enthusiasm for biological control did not increase as a result of this experience with the gypsy moth; rather, his interest waned. The attempt to find a biological control for the gypsy moth pest ended in failure before World War I. Alternative spraying methods were adopted by the state government there during the war with much greater success, though the long-term ecological damage these sprays could cause was not understood at the time.[80]

Howard was more interested in cultural controls than biological ones, but his ability to push the former methods was limited. In the resistance to cultural controls, the larger political economy was fundamentally important. Entomological policy was influenced by economic pressures on the bureau, and these came from industries that were politically powerful on the national level. The most important of the pressures on the bureau derived from the boll weevil's threat to the South's cotton industry.[81] Although the Department of Agriculture developed effective controls based on the life cycle of this pest, these were ignored by many farmers, and the pest continued to spread. Cultural controls depended on the farmers taking a long-term view of their prospects; in some cases the agricultural experts recommended that part of one year's crop be sacrificed by early planting, picking, and burning to interrupt the life cycle of the weevil.[82] But southern cotton was heavily farmed under the inefficient and inequitable systems of sharecropping and tenant farming, and the croppers lacked economic incentive to practice the laborious cultural control methods.[83] Nor did other cotton farmers always follow official recommendations on plant hygiene. Burning off, said the farmers, deprived the land of the natural fertilization of the rotting crop.[84] Instead, they demanded sprays like those proving effective in controlling the gypsy moth and already used for other crops under Bureau of Entomology direction. By 1920, new and more effective spraying devices and new poisons, particularly arsenate of lead, offered simpler and more convenient controls of the weevil. The Department of Agriculture relented,

and by the 1920s it pushed sprays as a practical solution to the immediate needs of the farmer.[85]

These pressures on Washington entomologists differed from those at
work in California. The antagonistic policies pursued by the two bureaucracies reflected different readings of the environment and different political and economic priorities. It is not surprising, therefore, that Washington entomologists attempted to discredit California's program. This
strategy was reflected in Howard's prejudices, which included a belief
that California's position and climate encouraged zany schemes of all
kinds. Claiming "a tendency for many years for persons with strange
beliefs to migrate to California, largely on account of its climate,"
Howard implied that Cooper was another product of the state's "het-
erodoxies."[86]

Despite a truce after the first squabble over the vedalia, the federal/
state struggle in California had resumed when Cooper sought to extend
his victory and undertook a more comprehensive program in the 1890s.[87]
After the California legislature gave $5000 for a second trip to Australia,
the Division of Entomology agreed in 1891 to allow Koebele to go again,
provided he report directly to Washington to prevent the possibility of
importing "any injurious species."[88] In Koebele's report, *Studies of Parasitic and Predaceous Insects in New Zealand, Australia, and Adjacent
Islands,* the German-born agent did not mention Riley and Howard at
all, but instead thanked the state board for its help, and "especially . . . Ellwood Cooper, who never failed to write with every outgo-
ing mail, keeping me informed of the doings of insects received by him."
This enraged Riley, who questioned Koebele's loyalty. Shortly after-
wards, the German left the division and went to work for the newly established Board of Agriculture and Forestry of Hawaii where he pioneered
biological control.[89]

A large part of the controversy now concerned the menace of the black
scale on olive trees. Cooper claimed to have found new parasites whose
success would exceed that of the vedalia, and Koebele agreed.[90] In the
black Australian ladybird, *Rhizobius ventralis,* the most promising of
these new parasites, Koebele envisaged an enemy of the black scale
greater than the vedalia was of the cottony cushion scale. As a result of
Cooper's "deep interest" and "the fidelity" with which Koebele's instructions were followed, Koebele claimed that four of the "most effective enemies of the Black Scale were already found breeding in large numbers"
in Santa Barbara in the summer of 1892. Riley's in-house publication,

Insect Life, also reported that the new predator was successful in the Santa Barbara area, but voiced criticism from the Pomological Society at Pasadena that elsewhere "the ladybird was not showing up in orchards in which colonies had been placed."[91]

This criticism did not deter Cooper, who became more shrill in his stance on biological control. In 1892, he boldly announced that "all noxious insects have parasites" that "prevent them from becoming a bar to successful fruit growing." Was it not wiser, therefore, "to search for these parasites, to prevent the spread of our dangerous foes, than to endeavor to take this matter out of the hands of the Creator to manage in our own way?" By "no other means" than biological control could "success be complete."[92] What had for some growers in the 1880s been one possible weapon in the struggle against insect pests became in the 1890s a crusade to create a harmonious balance in nature. Some enthusiasts carried matters even farther than Cooper did. One fruit grower, T. N. Snow, claimed that Australia was "the home and birthplace of insect life" and that "injurious insects" had been unknown in America prior to European exploration.[93]

The sudden death of Charles Valentine Riley ought to have helped heal the wounds between California and Washington. In September 1895, soon after a premature retirement that many linked to the vitriolic controversies with the California state board, Riley was tragically killed in a Washington bicycle accident. Gone was the man who had most fiercely contested the Californian program. The new chief, Howard, had already moved to improve relations with California immediately after his appointment late in 1894. For a few years, the bug controversy languished without Riley's contribution, but the truce did not last.

To the heat of the black scale debate was joined colorful human conflict introduced by George Compere's arrival on the scene as a special agent of the California state board in 1899. Although Compere had experience in the 1880s with the fumigation method, he was by the 1890s a staunch defender of "the California method" of the state board. Moreover, he was not professionally trained and had never been part of the Division of Entomology. Like Cooper, he was an enthusiastic as well as knowledgeable amateur. Cooper quickly dispatched his new agent to Australia in 1899 under the authority of the now much better endowed state board to do work independently of the federal government. Compere wrote from Sydney on 6 June 1900 in his first major communication, "The climate here will compare favorably with that of Southern California, and the country is a perfect paradise for insects, both beneficial and otherwise."[94] Buoyed by his work in Australia, Compere wrote in 1902 that "it is only a matter of time before all our pests will be taken care of by their natural enemies." Compere conducted fieldwork throughout the Pacific region and visited China and Japan. He was especially impressed, however, by the opportunities and parallels present in Australia. Despite an abundance of Coccidae unequaled anywhere, "not a single native form" was a pest there.[95]

Under Cooper's and Compere's advocacy, the state board now proclaimed a transnational crusade for biological control. This activity was based on the Australian work, though Cooper's ambitions had become global. The first step involved the appointment of Compere in 1901 as entomologist for the Western Australian government. Compere probably won this appointment because the head of the Department of Agriculture in Western Australia, Lancelot Lindley-Cowen, was an American familiar with the Californian program. Compere's work was Western Australia's first venture into biological control, since unlike most other states it had not established its own entomological section. Instead, the government called in American help.[96] Then, in 1904, Compere entered into an arrangement in which he served as joint agent of the Californian board and his Australian employer. Spurred by this endorsement, Cooper wrote to all of the Australasian governments requesting that they join California, Hawaii, and Western Australia in developing a Pacific, and ultimately a global, plan for biological control. He envisioned "a union of all intelligent nations" and promised "to call a world's convention" in Sacramento "to form a union to carry on this work." Cooper offered to contract with any government to share the results of the Californian–Western Australian research.[97]

The "union" was never achieved. Some Australian states parried Cooper's request and contacted the Bureau of Entomology in Washington for advice. Nonetheless, the "international" strategy raised hackles once more in Washington. Officials feared that Compere would, in all of his scurrying back and forth across the Pacific, introduce new and dangerous pests to the American mainland.[98] Howard constantly tried to discredit Compere, just as the latter tried to undermine Howard by claiming that the Washington program was inferior to California's. Yet Howard could not have succeeded ultimately without support in California. It was there that Cooper's policies were checked.

As it turned out, Compere and Cooper had their deadliest enemies in their own state. This opposition centered on the Southern California Pomological Society and included C. M. Heintz and H. W. Kruckeberg, respectively owner and editor of the *Rural Californian,* representing Southern California citrus interests.[99] These two had long concluded that the success of the vedalia was entirely due to the Division of Entomology in Washington. They denounced in the 1890s "political horticulturalists" and "corner grocery viticulturalists" in the state boards who "are given responsible positions requiring practical and scientific attainments." As an alternative, the *Rural Californian* argued that entomological work should be taken over by the University of California. Most important of all, Heintz and Kruckeberg proclaimed the "dismal failure" of the efforts of the horticultural board "to import parasitical and predaceous insects from Australia to feed upon the red and black scale."[100]

Kruckeberg's attacks were partly political in inspiration. When he advocated the wholesale retrenchment of the state bureaucracy, this involved supporting Democratic Governor James Budd in his campaign in 1895 against Cooper and his Republican allies in the state legislature.[101] These attacks were also entomologically inspired, as they had the covert backing of the Division of Entomology in Washington, which sought to use Kruckeberg to undermine Cooper. The *Oakland Tribune* noted the dissatisfaction in the south of the state over the black scale issue and called "the Australian lady bug a *casus belli* of a very irritating sort." But the controversy over the scale itself could not explain the *Rural Californian*'s opposition to Cooper, since that paper campaigned against him as early as 1891, before the black scale controversy began and while the vedalia was at the height of its prestige.[102]

The political campaign had also harnessed economic and sectional discontent among the southern Californian citrus growers, who felt that the board favored northern Californian interests and was headed by a man whose interests in walnuts and olives differed from their own. Disaffected citrus growers no longer saw the benefits of biological methods, and they deplored Compere's overseas jaunts. They sought a complete and quick control of all pests. To these growers, spraying appeared the most likely panacea. Though he supported the state board until 1904, Los Angeles Horticultural Commissioner J. W. Jeffrey defected in 1907 to the citrus camp, enlisted the aid of the federal Bureau of Entomology, and got Howard to lobby the governor of California to replace Cooper with himself. Jeffrey offered Howard complete loyalty and promised "staunch" cooperation in a national program of insect control. He linked his efforts to unseat Cooper to disquiet in Washington over Compere's globe-trotting and promised that underlings would no longer be permitted to "go on secret missions to discover 'the' parasite for an insect pest."[103]

THE DEMISE OF COOPER'S BIOLOGICAL CONTROL POLICIES

The tenure of the "natural method" was always shaky, since innovative farmers experimented with pesticides and natural controls simultaneously. For the citrus grower, the aim became, increasingly after the early 1890s, profits and efficiency rather than environmental harmony. The process of crop specialization triumphed in the citrus industry as markets developed back East with better rail links and refrigeration. As a result, growers began to place less emphasis on self-sufficiency. Though the moralists of the garden landscape still influenced horticultural politics and practice, reformers such as Cooper and Bidwell were subtly undermined over time by the very success of the fruit industry. William Ellsworth Smythe complained in 1905 that California citrus growers had themselves become, despite their ostensible challenge to wheat monoculture, far too dependent on their own version of single-crop agriculture: "As with the miner and wheat-farmer, so with the fruit-grower the aim was to get rich quickly, and the method speculation. Certain districts were devoted exclusively to prunes, others to wine grapes, others to raisins, and yet others to oranges."[104] Specialized fruit meant more pests, and so a rising chorus of growers called for a quick end to the problem of insects. With competition increasing, growers became more concerned with survival and profit than with an ecological utopia. Political economy and the intensive development of markets defeated dreams of a natural balance.

These arguments suggest that the circumstances favoring Cooper's schemes were temporary. He was likely to fall into disfavor the moment he could not deliver successful biological control. The signs seem clear in retrospect. The vedalia beetle's success itself owed much to an unusual combination of circumstances. *Novius cardinalis* reproduced twice a year, whereas the scale it combated reproduced only once. The preferred source of food for *Novius* was the *Icerya purchasi* scale; entomologists had introduced *Novius* into the Californian environment free from its own parasites that might have controlled it; it was difficult for insecticides to penetrate *Icerya,* a fluted scale, or destroy all the eggs; and finally, the vedalia was an active insect flying from tree to tree, while *Icerya* was fixed to a plant.[105] The element of luck had aided Cooper here, but now it deserted him.

Dissatisfaction with Cooper came to a head in 1907. Already under attack for failing to use hydrocyanic gas on other pest scales of oranges, Cooper's approach to the control of the citrus white fly would seal his political fate.[106] Despite California's state quarantine, this destructive pest had been introduced from Florida's groves around 1905. Cooper had ordered the removal of all infested trees, which were then to be burned, since, he claimed, "there was no known effective remedy in the form of sprays or fumigation."[107] Cooper used his time-honored methods of quarantine and cultural control. Soon he faced an attack from Professor C. W. Woodworth of Berkeley for his handling of the first serious fly outbreak, at Marysville, early in 1907.[108] Woodworth was a card-carrying advocate of spraying. A longtime professor at the University of California, he became chief entomologist for the California Spray Chemical Company after his retirement.[109] His first California publication, in 1890, was entitled "Spray and Band Treatment for Codling Moth," and his subsequent publishing career was heavily weighted toward advocating sprays and fumigation. A publicizer of hydrocyanic gas in the 1890s, he called this "the most effective insecticide known."[110] Woodworth actively encouraged greater business-university cooperation in the discovery and implementation of insecticide remedies and influenced the first state insecticide law regulating Paris green arsenates in 1901.[111]

Woodworth demanded that university-based scientists at Berkeley dominate the California program. He charged that the county horticultural commissioners under Cooper were essentially amateurs ignorant of the latest developments in pest control. In developing this case, Woodworth slammed the influence of regionalism: "Some have been so impressed with the fact that California is different from any other part of the country, and fear to fill their minds with things that will not apply under our conditions." Yet, Woodworth argued, "there is no excuse for remaining ignorant of the best knowledge."[112] In the case of the white fly, Woodworth felt Cooper had delayed too much in giving owners time to comply with control measures, and the professor also disagreed with the use of defoliation; he preferred sprays. An important bone of contention was Woodworth's wish to follow the procedures used in Florida to control this pest. But as one county commissioner of horticulture, R. P. Cundiff of Riverside, objected, what applied to Florida might "be very different in California."[113]

Woodworth's use of the authority of university science was not decisive, however. Many growers still distrusted universities, and some distrusted Woodworth for his one-sided attacks. Political influence was far more successful. J. W. Jeffrey plotted against Cooper effectively, exploiting his position as agricultural editor of the *Los Angles Times,* where he had access to sixty-five thousand subscribers.[114] He claimed to Howard that he was now supported "unanimously by the fruit growers of the Southern part of the state" and "by every fruit journal all over the State."[115] Jeffrey linked his campaign to the white fly issue and Cooper's failure to pursue its destruction by chemical means. There were, said Jeffrey, "now pending some investigations in which I am directly concerned . . . that will be of great benefit to the fruit interests."[116] These plans would be jeopardized if Cooper continued in office. Jeffrey claimed that Cooper "goes so far as to advocate the entire cessation of the use of insecticides."[117] In reference to the joint federal-state experiments with "fumigation" to control the fly, Jeffrey called "the use of cyanide [HCN gas] one of the most important investigations the State has undertaken for many years."[118] In contrast, Cooper backed Compere's extravagant claim that revelation of a parasite to control the white fly was imminent.[119]

Already Cooper had served as chairman of the State Board of Horticulture for twenty years, from 1883 to 1903. Past seventy, he had thought of retiring in 1900, but fruit growers and friends had persuaded him to continue. When the state legislature reorganized the bureaucracy in 1903 and created a commission in place of the board, with more centralized powers to streamline operations, Cooper still had sufficient influence to be the first State Commissioner of Horticulture. He was appointed by the conservation-minded governor George C. Pardee, and served from 1903 to 1907.[120] Then Cooper was removed by Pardee's successor—another Republican governor—James Gillett, and replaced by Jeffrey.

Though Cooper tried to interfere in the work of the state commission during Jeffrey's term, his influence quickly faded.[121] Nevertheless, it was not until Jeffrey's own demise in 1911 that Howard was happy. Jeffrey was, like Cooper, a practical horticulturalist, but his successor was a man of science, as defined by Howard. In 1911 the reformist Progressive governor Hiram Johnson appointed A. J. Cook as commissioner. Upon his appointment Cook began a large defoliating program with power sprays, and he advocated fumigation.[122] A professor of biology at Pomona College from 1894 to 1911, Cook "at once became active

among the fruit growers of California as a recognized leader." He
assisted in the "scientific study of orchard problems" and was active in
getting HCN investigations revived with Bureau of Entomology help.[123]
The Johnson administration came to power stressing the role of the
expert, economic efficiency, rationalization of government bureaucracies, and the sweeping away of special interests. Cook was true to this
rhetoric, and in 1911 reorganized the office of the State Commissioner
of Horticulture on professional lines.[124] Already elderly, Cooper retired
from political and industry life, sold his ranch in 1912 and died, aged
eighty-nine, on 30 December 1918.[125]

Biological control did not end in California as a result of this political upheaval; it continued as a research program under Professor Harry
Smith at the University of California, based at the Agricultural Experiment Station at Riverside founded in 1907. The citrus industry and
Woodworth had lobbied hard for these changes. Smith's associates continued to search widely for biological controls, and they even made trips
to Australia and other Pacific destinations in the 1920s in pursuit of new
pest controls. Historians of science and scientific agriculture have given
Smith credit for keeping the biological control initiatives alive in California during the years of pesticide dominance. But the role of the Board
of Horticulture in establishing California's tradition of biological control in the first place has been alternately forgotten or denigrated as the
work of amateurs.[126] So often is history remembered by the victors, and
in this case victory went to the research-oriented scientists allied with the
federal government's Bureau of Entomology. Yet this victory also
entailed the demise of Cooper's wider vision of a garden landscape of
small-scale farmers, and the diminution of his vision of decentralized
responsibility and grassroots initiative in techniques of environmental
management. Biological control was now closely supervised by the U.S.
Department of Agriculture, whose priorities lay in spraying and the
development of major industries like cotton, wheat, and corn. Not until
the post-DDT era did biological control reemerge as a serious competitor for chemical methods.[127]

Ironically, biological control did not, in the longer term, work as well
in agriculturally dominated political economies as it did in some devoted
to pastoral activities. After 1910, it was in the Australian outback, with
its labor-land ratios even lower than in California, that alternative strategies of pesticides and cultural control failed dismally and biological control registered new and spectacular successes. With products cultivated
more intensively, such as citrus, farmers could now afford to use pesti-

cides, especially when new poisons and new methods of application emerged as serious alternatives in the 1910s and 1920s. In contrast, the use of sprays over thousands of square miles in the Australian outback continued to lack economic justification. Ironically, in this way, biological control, first inspired by the ideal of natural harmony in the garden of the world, achieved its greatest success through the needs of a political and economic interest antagonistic to the garden ideal, the pastoral industry. Nonetheless, the transmission of biological control to Australia was greatly influenced by the California program in the 1880s and 1890s, and by the ideology of the garden landscape that had informed the dreams of Cooper.

CHAPTER 10

Blasting the Cactus

Biological Control in Australia

Thousands of miles from California's citrus groves, entomological enthusiasts in Australia and New Zealand had joined in the long and successful battle to combat the cottony cushion scale. Through these contacts, Australians and New Zealanders had an effect on California's development of biological control. New Zealand entomologist William Maskell had been the first to describe the cottony cushion scale, which entered New Zealand as well as California from Australia.[1] Almost immediately after the successful vedalia crusade in California, entomologists, farmers, and government officials back in Australia became intrigued about the possibility of biological controls for the pests that plagued their own food crops and trees. Impressed by California's success, agricultural officials reimported the vedalia from California into some colonies where it had been rare, and introduced it to New Zealand, where it had never existed naturally.[2]

This was the start of biological control in Australasia. Heavily dependent at first on Californian inspiration, by the 1920s an independent and path-breaking campaign emerged to eclipse California's initiatives. Just as the vedalia would symbolize the Californian campaign, a new insect, *Cactoblastis cactorum,* would soon attack a major pest in Australia, the prickly pear. Ironically, however, biological control would not help implement the horticultural paradise in Australia. Its greatest successes would occur far from the garden landscape—in the pastoral industry.

Australian visitors in the 1880s who marveled at Californian irrigation also noted the innovative application of biological control techniques, from the vedalia to the use of turkeys set loose in the vineyards to gobble up grubs.[3] As George Riddoch put it in 1903, "As soon as pests are discovered their enemies are sought for, and the authorities have searched the world to obtain insects to destroy them." Riddoch, a politician with interests in the Renmark irrigation settlement, took particular pride in "the ladybird, which had been obtained from Australia, being cultivated at San Francisco in a most scientific manner."[4] Similarly, the nurseryman and journalist John West, on his irrigation tour for the Victorian government in 1890, made one of his most striking observations upon the success of the vedalia in fighting the scale insect with "nature's weapons." This "illustrate[d] in a remarkable manner the splendid enterprise of the American people when they have difficulties to overcome." But like Riddoch, he was proud of the Australian contribution, noting that it was Frazer Crawford who alerted Californian authorities to the availability of "natural enemies of the scale" in Adelaide.[5]

Later visitors also praised "rapid advances" in American biological control and took this work as an inspiration for similar efforts in Australia. These views influenced official policy through the Advisory Council of the Commonwealth Institute of Science and Industry, founded under federal government auspices in 1916.[6] This in reorganized form became the basis for the Council on Scientific and Industrial Research (CSIR; after 1949 CSIRO) in 1926. Though influenced by the presence of British-trained scientists and the example of similar British initiatives to develop science-industry links, the Advisory Council also reflected the nature of Australian agricultural and pastoral development. Because of the links with California already forged in irrigation policy and entomology, scientists affiliated with the council looked to the United States for inspiration in biological control. Professor R. D. Watt, who was to be prominent in the control of prickly pear, was a member of the Advisory Council in 1920 and reported to it on American research.[7] As another scientist explained, "The United States, whether because of the magnitude and importance of their primary industries, or because of a quicker and clearer appreciation of the discoveries of biological science, have been more active in the application of 'natural' methods of pest control than any other country."[8] In *Science and Industry*, the council's journal, Ewen MacKinnon singled out biological control efforts in California and wondered when Australia would "profit by the lessons so plainly given."[9]

Despite Commonwealth participation in the 1920s, later developments should not be read back into the origins of biological control. The
pressure for biological methods was most clearly felt at the state, not the
federal, level, and the efforts of Queensland were especially important
prior to 1920. Biological control first developed through state departments of agriculture that had strong links with their American counterparts, rather than through the federal government. The new policy developments occurred not in spite of the fact that these organizations were
geared toward the small farmer, but precisely because the agricultural
departments were geared toward closer settlement. The later importance
of pastoralism as opposed to smaller scale agriculture should not obscure
the fact that the origins of biological control in Australia lay in the same
garden-landscape mentality that motivated its California partisans.[10]

The vedalia campaign in California involved important trans-Pacific
links in biological control between 1888 and 1901, prior to federation.
Most important was the stimulus provided by the earlier visits of Koebele in 1888 and 1891, and by the news of the success of the vedalia.
The New South Wales entomologist Walter Froggatt recalled in his presidential address before the Linnaean Society of New South Wales in 1912
that the visit of Koebele "aroused marked interest in entomology" in
Australia and led to the appointment of official entomologists in "prac-
tically all of the colonies" soon after, beginning with Victoria in 1891
and Tasmania in 1892.[11]

The Californian impact was especially important in Queensland,
where the groundwork for Australia's subsequent experiments in biological control was laid by 1891. Koebele twice visited Queensland
searching for enemies of the various citrus scales, and there he became
friends with Henry S. Tryon, who was entomologist at the Queensland
Museum. Spurred on by Koebele, Tryon began investigating biological
controls, arguing as early as 1889 that when parasites were found, the
entomologist "may advantageously forego the use of insecticides . . . and
rather trust to Nature's remedy."[12] Tryon's first goal was to seek parasites and predators for the pests that plagued the nascent sugar industry
in Queensland, particularly the gray-backed cane beetle. As a result of
his visits to the sugar districts of northern New South Wales, Koebele had
already conducted a study of the pests of sugarcane that was published
in *Insect Life* in 1892.[13] Three years later, Tryon wrote about the natural
enemies and control measures of the "grub pests of sugar cane."[14]

Like Victoria, the Queensland government desired closer settlement.
Bailey Brown had advocated the use of irrigation in development of

the "tropical and semi-tropical fruits" in the 1880s, claiming that there was "scarcely a limit" to "the number of the population and extent of the employment" that closer settlement could provide in Queensland.[15] But in the tropical North, the lack of potential white farmers meant that sugarcane rather than fruit seemed, with the aid of black labor imported from the Pacific Islands, more likely to introduce by its spin-off effects a more intensive form of economic development. The Queensland government pushed for the expansion of this industry, drawing on the Hawaiian model to establish a Bureau of Sugar Experiment Stations in 1900, and began investigating irrigation projects for sugar growing.[16]

In biological control, sugar was the unrecognized but crucial link between California and the later prickly pear campaign. Not only had Koebele and Tryon worked on sugarcane pests in the 1890s, but Queensland entomologists were also aware of efforts to control various pests of the cane in Hawaii, where Koebele had gone after his resignation from the Bureau of Entomology. From this background experience Tryon first pressed the issue of biological control of Queensland's preeminent pest plant, the prickly pear, in 1899.[17]

The link between the Queensland program and biological control in the United States was further promoted by the presence of a number of Americans in the Queensland agricultural bureaucracy. When the government sought to establish a department of agriculture, it asked the commissioner of agriculture in the United States to suggest a suitable person to appoint as "instructor of agriculture" to take charge of the spread of technical information and education. In February 1890, E. M. Shelton arrived. He was a graduate of Michigan Agricultural College and had taught at Kansas Agricultural College. In his first published report, Shelton argued the need for an agricultural college in Queensland, and one was established in 1896. The college bore the influence and inspiration of the American model of agricultural colleges with their practical bent.[18] Other American-trained scientists, Dr. Walter Maxwell, J. F. Illingworth, and A. A. Girault, worked in the Bureau of Sugar Experiment Stations.[19] Informed by his experience in the United States, Illingworth became one of the leaders in the campaign to find a natural control of the cane beetle in the form of a parasite or predator. He noted in his 1921 publication, *Natural Enemies of the Sugar Cane Beetle in Queensland,* that "undoubtedly man in his clearing of the forests has upset the balance of nature," and he demonstrated the need for alternative biological controls.[20]

The principle had won acceptance among Queensland entomologists and in elements of the bureaucracy, but how to apply biological control to the prickly pear remained unknown. Both the vedalia and sugarcane experiments had involved the search for an insect predator of an insect pest, in the classic bug vs. bug formula. But the prickly pear was a plant. Did the same or a similar principle apply? Again it was Koebele who was the pioneer. Tryon's interest in possible biological controls of the pear was further stimulated by Koebele's Hawaiian work, particularly the introduction of parasites from Mexico to control lantana in Hawaii in 1902. "In certain cases," Tryon later reported, "plant-eating insects may be advantageously introduced for weed destruction without detriment in any way to other vegetation."[21]

A final link was Alan Dodd, the man who eventually led the successful campaign against the prickly pear. Dodd was a Queensland scientist who had worked for six years on natural controls for the cane beetle as part of Illingworth's team at the Bureau of Sugar Experiment Stations, before moving on to the prickly pear in the early 1920s.[22] Ultimately the sugar research was to have a disastrous ecological impact as a result of introduction of the cane toad, *Bufo marinus*, from Hawaii in the mid-1930s. In the meantime, scientists were struggling with a much more severe pest than the cane beetle, one that threatened not just one industry in the northern state of Queensland but wholesale agricultural activity over vast areas of both Queensland and New South Wales.

The presence of the prickly pear *Opuntia inermis* and related prickly pear species in the eastern states was the product of thoughtless nineteenth-century introductions that fully justify Crosby's terminology of "ecological imperialism." Certain varieties of the pear had been brought to Australia in 1788 with the First Fleet, but the most serious pest forms of the pear were introduced later. The most aggressive of the pests, *inermis*, was introduced—probably in the late 1830s—as an ornamental hedge to surround homesteads, and it appealed to farmers and homemakers because of its attractive flowers. The plant, a native of the western Gulf Coast of the United States, spread easily because the climate in northern New South Wales and southern Queensland particularly suited it. Summers were wetter, rainfall more uniform, and winters warmer than in its native environment. These proved to be ideal conditions for the pear's reproduction. The destructive impact of *inermis* was complemented by that of *O. stricta* from Florida and of a number of lesser pears such as *O. monacantha* (a tree pear) from northern Mexico.

"In world history," says the historian W. Ross Johnston, "there has not been a plant pest so persistent and so dominating."[23] Though noted in the colonial press as a danger in the 1880s, the pear was not declared a noxious weed until 1893 in Queensland. It had covered ten thousand acres by 1900, but its major period of advance followed 1902, after the great drought of the turn of the century. By 1920 the pear covered 58 million acres and was expanding at the rate of 2.5 million acres a year. Four-fifths of the affected area was in southern Queensland, where over large areas "the infestation was almost continuous, with no large intervals of pear-free country."[24] In New South Wales, the minister for lands W. E. Wearne admitted that "the increased growth and spread of the pear" surpassed "even the ravages of the rabbit, inasmuch as the pear has no commercial value, and is unaffected by drought, flood, poorness of soil, or climatic conditions."[25]

The spread of the pear was not purely "natural," but, like so many cases of "ecological imperialism," was a product of human intervention. Pastoral activity encouraged the spread of the pest. As one observer noted, "The weed gained its hold when land holdings were large and population sparse."[26] The pest thrived in partially cleared and disturbed areas of eucalyptus, acacia, and casuarina forest and scrub in which cattle had been grazed. Clearing of the land and especially trampling of native seedlings exposed the ground to more sunlight and allowed the pear to develop; cattle and sheep carried seeds and pieces of pear cuttings in their coats, hooves, and manure droppings. This helped the pear to spread.

Of even greater importance, the labor-land ratio differed from that existing in California's fruit industry, where biological control had first won fame.[27] Labor was in even shorter supply than in California, where cheap Asian workers could be hired, and pastoral runs were immensely large in comparison with horticultural blocks. Nor did the pastoralists have the time to undertake manual controls. Moreover, cattlemen were divided about *Opuntia*'s value. As in the western states of America, many saw the possibility of using the pear—which had a moisture content of about 90 percent—to feed to stock in times of drought; in fact this use was widely adopted. The spread of the pear had been held back by the use of it for emergency fodder during the droughts of the 1890s, and that was why the greatest incursions did not come until after that drought had broken in 1902.

The pear began to be targeted as a pest as part of the same drive toward closer settlement that prompted development of irrigation in

Victoria and spurred interest in the same subject in New South Wales and Queensland. The Queensland government's Prickly Pear Selection Act of 1901 encouraged pear destruction on heavily infested land by offering low terms of lease to those prepared to redeem the land for farming. The state government expected landholders to clear the land, and more than seventy-seven hundred selections were made during the following twenty years, but in no more than four thousand of these cases did the farmers persist. Those who needed to clear their land for crops found that the amount of labor involved was beyond their resources. One Helidon, Queensland, farmer raised pigs and grew citrus, but spent his time "chippin, choppin, chappin and cussin."[28] Whereas pastoralists had learned to live with the pest, pear land was unsuitable for subdivision, and this is why the government sought to remove it. It conflicted with the aspirations of the small-scale agriculturalist and horticulturalist that were connected intricately with the idea of the garden landscape.

EARLY SOLUTIONS

Mechanical forms of clearing were quickly devised. In the early 1890s, Dr. A. Bruce-Suttor tried to clear land in the Scone district in New South Wales of its "exuberant growth" with a patented crushing roller that halved the cost of clearing. The cost was over five pounds an acre compared to the ten to fifteen pounds for previous mechanical methods, but still far too great to make its use economical. More important, such mechanical aids were ineffective or even impossible to use on timbered land, yet the pear often flourished in scrub settings and lightly timbered country rather than in open pastures.[29]

Farmers also tried chemical controls. Spraying with arsenic proved effective in tests during World War I at Dulacca in Queensland, but the cost of up to ten pounds per acre "exceeded the value of most average quality grazing land."[30] The "possibility of long-term environmental consequences" resulting from spraying was not explored, but the labor-intensive nature of the work was well understood. The chemical was frequently injected manually into the pear and was therefore both costly and dangerous to workers who suffered from poisoning. Around Gayndah, according to one farm boy who observed the increasing danger, the men working on the job were poorly protected and began to itch after using arsenic pentoxide.[31]

At the turn of the century, the only alternative to spraying seemed to be to make use of the pear by cultivating it for newsprint, fruit, or stock feed.[32] At Sydney's Botanic Gardens, Joseph Maiden devoted years to this research after 1900.[33] Though cattlemen remained positive about the fodder value, the cattle themselves were resistant. Professor R. D. Watt noted that "Southern Texas carries twice as many cattle as if the pear were not there. Cattle eat most of the species without treatment of the prickles."[34] But in Australia, stock disliked the larger number of sharp spines that the pears most numerous in Australia carried. For sheep and cattle use, pears had to be boiled, which again increased labor costs. With the pear's domestication in mind, Australians attempted several times to produce a spineless type. This brought to the notice of the Departments of Agriculture in Queensland and New South Wales the work of the hybridist Luther Burbank of Santa Rosa, California.

The contact that followed reveals the operation of the concept of the garden in the prickly pear episode. Farmers, journalists, and government officials sought to breed a hybrid pear that might, they surmised, displace the pears causing so much trouble.[35] Burbank attracted much publicity in Australia in the first decade of the twentieth century because he claimed to do just that. Australians ought to welcome the work of Burbank, said the Australasian edition of *Review of Reviews:* "The man could cover our arid regions with vigorous and useful plant life" in place of the existing pear and "useless" native scrub. Burbank boasted that he would reclaim "millions of acres of arid land" through the aid of the spineless cactus which would "convert the desert into a garden." Irrigators claimed they would do this too, but Burbank's method promised to be cheaper and more effective because he achieved his aim not with expensive engineering works, but "by means of the desert itself." Burbank, said the *Review,* bred "this pariah among plants, until it has become the producer of a delightful, nutritious food for man and beast."[36]

This expected miracle cactus was, however, only a hybrid of a Central American prickly pear variety and an Arizona cactus. Neither Burbank's nor any other hybrid ever displayed the aggressive behavior of *Opuntia inermis.* Moreover, the hybrid did not seed true to type, and thus the spreading of the beneficial plant would depend upon a gigantic labor input in planting and propagating, if the pear were ever to displace its more aggressive relative. The exaggerated interest within Australian horticultural circles in Burbank's plans tells more about the attempts to turn Australia into a diversely productive and heavily vegetated landscape than it does about the practical fight against the pear.[37]

The ineffective and expensive nature of the existing remedies led first to a Queensland Government Travelling Commission, which investigated internationally from 1913 to 1914 the pear's enemies. The commission returned without success, but at the end of World War I a combined Queensland–New South Wales effort was organized, under Commonwealth auspices and with the support of the Advisory Council on Science and Industry, to find a biological control. A Commonwealth Prickly Pear Board was established, and it held its first meeting in April 1920. It had joint representation from the Queensland and New South Wales governments and the CSIR, with a scientific controller as a non-voting member. Professor T. Harvey Johnston held the latter post until 1923; Alan Dodd became officer-in-charge in late 1925. The board established a permanent base at Uvalde, Texas. As Dodd reasoned, "The United States was the obvious choice" as a source of insects. The prior association of that country with biological control influenced this decision, as did the fact that some of the leading pest pears flourished in the southwestern United States. During the first four years of operation, from 1920, the investigation continued to focus on the United States but spread increasingly to all of the Americas; from Uvalde, board officers made several visits to collect parasites in northern Mexico, Argentina, and elsewhere.[38]

Although the home of *inermis* was not California, the experience with biological control there shaped the search for a solution. The 1913–14 traveling commission of the Queensland Government had headed immediately for the United States, and the Commonwealth Prickly Pear Board had done the same.[39] There, the board's officials were fortunate enough to find a Department of Agriculture pamphlet on cactus insects by W. D. Hunter, who had led the investigation of pests of the pear in the American Southwest. Hunter's volume, *The Principal Cactus Insects of the United States,* remained the standard work the board relied upon for its basic scientific information.[40] Alan Dodd recalled that "the valuable information in this bulletin has been the basis upon which the Board's entomologists have built their knowledge of the insect enemies of prickly-pears and other cacti."[41]

THE FALSE LEAD

Unfortunately, the enemies of prickly pear described by Hunter proved in most cases to be useless in the control of the Australian pest pears. Moreover, the whole emphasis in the American program was on the control of predators and parasites that might destroy the pear, rather than a search for new ones that could attack the pear. David Griffith, a U.S.

Department of Agriculture officer stationed at the agency's Chico Experiment Station in California, said in 1921, "In our arid regions we welcome the spread of prickly pear, while you are afraid of it."[42] The reason for this was the vastly different ecology of the pear in Australia as opposed to the western United States. California simply did not have a pest problem with the pears that grew there (for example, O. lindheimeri).[43] None of the pears mentioned as pests in Australia came from California, although one species introduced into California from central and northern Mexico, O. monacantha, was a weed in Australia. But this species, said Griffiths, was "much dwarfed wherever grown in this country" and did "not seem to increase its spines or spicules" under the conditions prevalent in the southwestern United States.[44] Only in the case of O. littoralis, which infested Santa Cruz Island off the coast of California, did similar conditions of infestation occur, and its eradication was not attempted until 1951, long after the pioneering Australian work.[45] Even though the pears of the American Southwest were less rampant than those growing in Australia, Australian scientists and agricultural officials were repeatedly drawn, as in other aspects of environmental policy, to investigate precedents in California. But in the case of the pear, the American scientific investigations were particularly unhelpful because Griffith's research program differed so markedly from the Australian program.[46]

Despite these different objectives, the insects introduced in the 1920s were mostly North American. This strategy the Commonwealth Prickly Pear Board adopted even though the parasites and predators from the Northern Hemisphere were often more difficult to introduce than those from South America because of the differences of the seasons. But with the cochineal insect species Dactylopius, little trouble was encountered, since, Alan Dodd reported, "these insects possess a short life history and have several generations annually."[47] This circumstance allowed the first important introduction to come from the American West as part of the strategy to explore the pests of the pear in the American arid regions. The board introduced Dactylopius opuntiae, the common cochineal of southwestern United States and Mexico, "where it infests many kinds of shrubs and tree pears." The first introduction to Australia was made by the Queensland Department of Lands in 1920 with material obtained from the experiment station at Chico, later termed "Chico cochineal." (Soon Texan and Arizonan strains entered the field to work on pears that did not respond to the Californian insect.) Released on inermis at Dulacca, Queensland, in July 1921, the Chico strain quickly became

established. Between 1924 and 1926, the Queensland government "conducted an energetic distribution campaign." The insect "wrought excellent destruction to both O. *inermis* and *stricta* in the early years after its
establishment," but it was more effective in thick, native brigalow (*Acacia harpophylla*) scrub areas than in open pasture. This preference
apparently reflected the fact that "the prickly pear of the scrubs was of
a much more succulent nature," but in the scrub microclimate the insect
also had weather protection that enabled it to multiply and do its work.
On the other hand, in open country its work "was restricted to the
destruction of fruit, individual segments and seedlings," and did not
cause the death of established plants or "reduce the density of the
pest."[48]

Partly because the cochineal was uneven in its impact, the local agricultural community became extremely sceptical of biological control.
Critics poured scorn upon the prickly pear work as a "grand circus tour"
and "menagerie."[49] "A storm of adverse criticism of biological control
had broken out," one newspaper later commented, criticism led by elements in the pastoral industry, but feeding also off anti-intellectualism
and antiscience feeling in the less educated rural population. Opponents
called the work "experimental" and "uneconomic," and some cattlemen
still argued that "the pear ought to be left for use as fodder in times of
drought."[50]

Government officials remained extremely sensitive to pressure from
pastoral interests. In 1923 the Queensland government had held a Royal
Commission into the Prickly Pear, which did not abandon the search for
biological control but did urge government intervention to maximize the
use of other methods such as poisoning and manual clearing. In
response, the government established a Prickly Pear Lands Commission
in 1924 to oversee efforts to find a control in Queensland (a similar commission was established in New South Wales). Charged with reclaiming
infested pastoral properties for agricultural settlement, the commission
began under the vigorous leadership of William Labatte Payne to attack
the pest by every means possible. The commission subsidized the cost of
poisons and released what Payne called "cheap and effective" arsenic
compounds. The Brisbane *Daily Mail* noted approvingly in April 1924
that the Prickly Pear Lands Commission under Payne "considers that the
chemical pear-destroyers at present operate more satisfactorily than the
cochineal and other insects."[51]

In 1924, the forces of biological control and those favoring chemicals
were finely balanced: the battle could have gone either way. But then, a

lucky discovery favored biological control decisively. Two officers of the Commonwealth Board found specimens of the moth *Cactoblastis cactorum* in Uruguay and northern Argentina late in 1924. Henry Tryon had encountered this insect in the Botanic Gardens in La Plata, Argentina, in 1912, and had tried to send a shipment back to Queensland, but the larvae had died. When the board's officers subsequently visited the gardens in 1920, they found them permanently closed, and the matter was dropped until 1924–25. As Dodd recalled, "There was no particular reason in 1925 to believe that *Cactoblastis* might be more successful in Australia" than the "North American cactus insects."[52] The chance Uruguay encounter produced a collection of specimens shipped to Brisbane in March 1925, where they thrived in field stations when supplied with *O. inermis*. After being successfully reared to adult moths, a trial consignment was released in heavily invested territory in nineteen locations in Queensland and New South Wales. By the end of 1927, more than 10 million eggs had been released, but the mass assault occurred from 1928 to 1933, by which time 1.6 billion eggs had been distributed.[53]

RESULTS

The dramatic effects of the moth campaign fully justified the name *Cactoblastis cactorum*. The moth grubs won a decisive victory in the field, eating the flesh of the pear and causing its rapid collapse. Millions of acres were liberated within a matter of months. When significant pear regrowth appeared likely to occur in 1931, the Commonwealth Board simply released more insects, and the final victory was won by 1935. Only the case of the vedalia rivaled the decisive nature of the triumph in the history of biological control.

The easiest way of documenting the moth's success is to cite the reclamation of the land. By 1932, more than 1 million acres had already been opened up for closer settlement, taken on by 1,165 settlers with an average of eight hundred to nine hundred acres per farmer. Three-quarters of a million additional acres had been reopened for grazing. Eventually, 25 million acres became available for dairying, mixed farming, or grazing.[54]

As in the case of the vedalia beetle, biological control had been spurred by a vision of social and economic renovation. Prickly pear control served to implement popular visions of land use that had won backing from scientists and government in Queensland under the Labor Party administration of E. G. Theodore in the early 1920s. The land was not reclaimed for its "natural" purpose. The pressure behind the development was the perceived need for closer settlement. The environmental dream of expanding agriculture, first planned after the depression of the 1890s and then extended in the wake of World War I with the idea of soldier settlement, now came to partial fruition. The creation of a closely settled garden landscape was an appealing part of the pear eradication policies. The *Courier* (Brisbane) commented in 1929 that "one has but to look at photographs, showing luxuriant orchards where formerly there was luxuriant useless pear, to be convinced that the ultimate great profit will be on the side of those who regard pear as a pest and are treating it accordingly."[55]

In the war against the pear, Queensland authorities declared a simultaneous offensive against the wildlife that allegedly spread the pest, and native vegetation that harbored it to rampant growth. Scientists had long suspected that "emu droppings frequently contain the seed" and were "an efficient means of disposal," as these birds ranged widely and quickly across the outback.[56] Other "seed-carrying birds came under fire" in the 1920s: "crows and scrub magpies" were, along with the emus, destined for destruction funded by a Prickly Pear Lands Commission subsidy.[57] But once the pear had been decisively defeated by *Cactoblastis*, the government lifted the bounty on native birds; in this sense, biological control did ease the immediate pressure on native species. The overall effect of the campaign was not to spur the restoration of a landscape, however. The program encouraged, rather, the construction of new landscapes that involved even greater environmental transformation than any that had gone before.

The Prickly Pear Lands Commission in Queensland still advocated arsenic poisons as a supplement to stop reinfestations,[58] but more important in its environmental impact was the devastation of the native scrub. Because the pear had coexisted with native brigalow,[59] the trees had to be removed to open up ample tracts of Queensland and New South Wales for agricultural activities. The areas liberated of pear were viewed as "unproductive," covered with stands of timber that "merely clutter the land." Reclamation, according to government publications, "required the destruction of the trees by ringbarking or by felling and burning."[60] Wire fences had to be constructed to keep out the native dingoes and the introduced rabbits that infested the land. The 1930s witnessed, in the wake of *Cactoblastis*, a veritable war on the brigalow that in turn meant removal of the cover essential for native wildlife.

The aim was to renovate the natural environment and turn it to the purposes of settled agriculture. At one penny an acre, the disposal cost of the prickly pear by *Cactoblastis* was cheap beyond expectation, but heavier costs were incurred in preparing the land for yeoman farms. By far the greater part of this expenditure financed the destruction of tree cover. One hundred and fifty thousand pounds was spent in the Roma district of central Queensland alone clearing scrub for dairying, alfalfa, citrus, and other farm pursuits. So extensive was the attack that the Prickly Pear Lands Commission had to warn farmers to retain 10 percent of the native vegetation as cover for stock in storms and extreme heat. "Ring barking, like other good things, can be over-done," the commission cautioned.[61]

Government officials and scientists naturally tried to stress the advance of agriculture as the net result. Dodd rejoiced that "there are many hundreds of new settlers, with their new homes, dairy and wool sheds, and other improvements, dotted over the re-won country."[62] Sturdy farmers occupied formerly "useless" pastoral properties, having surrounded themselves with neat homesteads and farm improvements, while the government built new roads, bridges, and schools. Yet the reality was not to be closer settlement, and the garden dream was soon defeated once more.

The triumph of pastoral uses in the wake of the pear's destruction was the most striking, as well as ironic, outcome. The reclamation of prickly pear lands coincided with the onset of the Great Depression and the fall of agricultural prices internationally. Closer settlement was still a popular aspiration, but the depression-conscious Queensland government now looked for the cheapest and swiftest redevelopment. The costly clearing of the brigalow necessary for small-scale farming had limited financial appeal in the straightened circumstances of the 1930s. Consequently, Queensland's Prickly Pear Lands Commission now opted pragmatically to emphasize grazing and discourage yeoman farmer aspirations, and New South Wales did the same.[63] While some land in the southeast of Queensland was turned to small-scale dairying and fruit orchards, the commission earmarked the bulk of the lands for the very pastoral activity that had contributed to the spread of the pear in the first place.[64]

THE EFFECT ON BIOLOGICAL CONTROL

One final result of the prickly pear campaign was to strengthen international interest in biological control, but not in the United States. Under Dodd's now prestigious leadership, poisoning of pear in Queensland was soon abandoned in the 1930s, and *C. cactorum* was exported to other countries experiencing infestations. (Poisoning continued to be used for some pears at higher elevations in central eastern New South Wales, where the moth had proved less adaptable to the climate.)[65] Internationally the chief targets for export were Ceylon and South Africa rather than the United States, where the pears did not pose a threat. The effects of this spectacular campaign in biological control remained little known in the United States. At the end of his career, Howard called this work "most original" and acknowledged that it was "almost novel in the history of economic entomology."[66] But it was not until the 1940s that another major assault on insects and other pests through biological control was attempted in the United States, and even then the use of biological control was outweighed by the vastly greater exploitation of new synthesized insecticides like DDT in the 1950s and 1960s to control pests dangerous to commercial agriculture. Integrated pest management, spurred by the biological control program still operating at the University of California at Riverside would not come into its own until the era of *Silent Spring*.

Rachel Carson, author of *Silent Spring*, lauded the prickly pear case as an "extraordinarily successful and economical example of weed control," achieved at a tiny fraction of the cost of the chemical alternative.[67] But Carson was not part of the U.S. Department of Agriculture fraternity, and in the 1950s was intensely critical of the impact of USDA use of toxic chemicals. Even exponents of biological control gave relatively little publicity to the prickly pear eradication program in comparison to the vedalia. American commentators have rarely discussed the case of *Cactoblastis*, or have underrated the significance of the achievement. One Californian authority, Professor Richard Doutt, called the vedalia "the outstanding project in biological control" without mentioning the parallel claims of the prickly pear project.[68] Perhaps the campaign against prickly pear was neglected because it concerned a weed, while much biological control has been devoted to the destruction of pest insects. More likely, the case sank into obscurity because it occurred far away from American shores and concerned a plant that Americans did not fear.

Australian authorities, too, have emphasized the exceptionalism of the Australian project. According to Boris Schedvin, we must understand the "unique circumstances of prickly pear control." The search for a natural enemy was helped in Schedvin's view by the fact that potential "predators were comparatively abundant" in the pear's home environment. The absence, too, of a "similarity between the plant and the native flora in Australia" removed "the possibility of an indiscriminate attack" upon economically valuable crops or the native vegetation.[69]

As with the vedalia, the early success was not quickly duplicated, and many disappointments in biological control occurred, such as that experienced in the attempt to find a solution to the sheep blowfly problem. Attention to the American connection also waned when the Australian program became tied in the 1930s to imperial interests through the Empire Marketing Board; British scientists would do the basic research and the field trials would be held in Australia. This "ideal of imperial scientific collaboration" contained no recognition of the prior importance of the Pacific connection.[70] Success would occur in a number of projects in the years beyond the scope of this book, but most would follow the pattern already set in the focus on cattle and sheep, Australia's major rural industries of those years. These projects would also center on the CSIRO and the national level. The role of the garden landscape in the creation of biological control would soon be as forgotten as the contribution of the Pacific exchange in its early development.[71]

Epilogue

The Death of the Garden?

Ellwood Cooper's career ended in bitter circumstances. He had hoped that economic development could be harmonized with nature, and preached the gospel of biological control, afforestation by eucalyptus, and the garden landscape. Toward the end of his life, Cooper began to despair of the possibility of reform that would create the sustainable environment he had dreamed of for so long. He saw, in particular, the effects of the Great War, with its tragic deaths, as evidence that the internationalism he preached in science and horticulture had failed. Nationalism seemed to hold sway.[1] California had no autonomy in such a system. Its horticultural policies would be determined in Washington, D.C., and links with other countries would subsequently be mediated through the federal government.

Cooper's plans for biological control for California had failed, and his work and that of the horticultural board would be largely forgotten in the years that followed, or dismissed as the antics of amateur entomologists.[2] Yet a greater sense of failure beset Cooper in his attempts to preserve in his own farm a model of his ideals. Ellwood Ranch had become an exemplar of the mixed garden environment Cooper wished to see flourish in California, but when he offered to transfer the farm to state control on the proviso that it be used to provide practical agricultural training in association with the University of California, the state refused. Instead, California chose a demonstration farm in the interior, and Governor George Pardee pointed out that coastal and atypical Santa

Barbara could never be suitable. Old and disappointed, the Coopers sold out in 1912, and in 1928 one of the most profitable oil fields on the Californian coast was discovered at the site.[3]

The fate of the other characters in this story was as diverse as life itself, yet a number seemed to suffer inordinate disappointment. Some devotees of the garden landscape died with their vision in tatters. The acclimatizers brought problems in the form of rampant exotic vegetation and have been forever linked to the ill-fated introductions of such animals as the European wild rabbit. Even Mueller could not entirely escape criticism on this score. Abbot Kinney's crusade to make afforestation the basis of California's forest policy in the 1880s proved impractical, and the State Board of Forestry was abolished in the cutbacks of the 1890s. His real estate development of Venice, it may be recalled, had proved unmarketable, his elaborate plans for providing culture to the masses were ignored, his canals had to be filled in, and his suburban subdivisions across the Los Angeles region lost their uniformity of plantings. Theodore Lukens, Jack London, Grant Wallace, and others who spearheaded investments in eucalyptus plantations saw their investors' money, and in some cases their own, go up in smoke, often quite literally. Jeanne Carr's beloved Carmelita had been burdened with debt in the 1890s property downturn. It would be whittled away in the years after her death in 1903, and the rest would become part of Pasadena's park system.[4] George Chaffey remained in California after the failure of his Imperial Valley scheme, and he concentrated more profitably on real estate development and banking with his son, Andrew. But his reputation never recovered from the Salton Sink flooding and the financial problems experienced at Mildura. The rest of his life was marked, as made clear in J. A. Alexander's sympathetic biography, by a search for vindication. The gritty Elwood Mead, on the other hand, rose to the top of the federal bureaucracy, although he had never succeeded in implementing his closer-settlement schemes on the national level. Indeed, the prototypes of these had come apart back in California in the mid-1920s.

Others met gloomier fates. Albert Koebele returned to Germany, where he died in obscurity and poverty after World War I; and Clement De Garis, one of Australia's own ideologues of the irrigated garden landscape, committed suicide when his overly ambitious plans for the Sunraysed concept faltered in 1925. His demise serves, along with that of the disparaged engineering wizard Chaffey, as a metaphor for the wider failures of irrigation-driven environmental transformation in Australia. When John Bidwell of Rancho Chico, the friend of Frances Willard, died in April 1900, the land he had developed as a model of sustainable agriculture was under grave financial threat. Several years later, most of the land would be sold and the rest offered by his beloved Annie Bidwell to the city of Chico as a park.[5] Bidwell mansion would remain as a monument, with its rambling garden where the Bidwells had entertained both Frances Willard and John Muir. Muir himself died bitterly disappointed in 1913, shortly after the decision to dam the Hetch Hetchy Valley, which Muir believed was second only to the Yosemite in natural beauty. From this event many authorities date the divergence of rational economic conservation measures and the wilderness movement in the United States. The date can also be considered a point of termination for the American branch of nineteenth-century environmental reform, which had sought to encompass both economic use and preservation of natural beauty in an aesthetic of balance.

Not only had the leaders in the story of the Pacific exchange departed; the lands of which they had dreamed changed under the impact of larger, more impersonal forces than they had sought to wield. California itself had changed. Oil rigs, automobiles, and movies began to replace horticulture by the 1920s as the new leading sectors of the economy. Interest in irrigation persisted, but in California the damming of rivers became more closely linked to urban than rural development. In southern California, real estate developers laid the foundations of today's conurbation, though the transformation of much of the fruit lands would not occur until the 1950s. Australians were still enticed to participate in California's natural wonders, but now movie studios and the remnants of redwood forests beckoned, and tourism rather than the search for scientific information drew antipodean visitors.

The Pacific exchange itself came under threat. Australia's links with Britain, always strong, were reaffirmed in the interwar period. World War I had been a terrible experience for Australians, but one that drew them closer to Britain. The enhanced power of Japan in the Pacific made Australia seem strategically and racially more vulnerable to "Asian" invasion, while economically the war had exposed Britain's weakness and America's strength. Both British and Australian interests focused anew on building imperial connections in economic and strategic terms. In addition, gluts worldwide for Australian primary produce, including fruit, led to successful efforts in the 1920s to find tied markets in Britain.

These arrangements became even more important after the 1929 crash and resulted in development of the comprehensive Imperial Preference Scheme under the Ottawa Agreement of 1932. Imperial loans and migration initiatives in the 1920s also drew Australia closer to the empire in afforestation policy, and science in fruit- and other export-oriented primary industries became closely linked during the Depression to British programs of research. The Pacific exchange receded in importance, though the wider American influence grew in popular culture despite the lamentations of social conservatives.[6]

The rise of national science bureaucracies and universities also changed the Pacific relationship. The "professionalization of nature" took place as the amateur, "vernacular" links of the 1870s to 1890s gradually gave way to those of trained experts. Usually, the scientists who conversed in the 1920s met in formal international entomological or irrigation conferences and communicated through national bureaucracies. Leland Howard keenly advocated such exchanges as promotive of international understanding, but only on a nation-to-nation basis and among experts.[7] Although the prickly pear episode had its origins in Californian cooperation with colonial and state authorities, by 1914 Commonwealth experts began to look only to Washington for advice, and after 1926 the national CSIR took over much, though not all, Australian research on biological control. In irrigation, too, the role of the expert had been enhanced. Amateur irrigation entrepreneurs like George Chaffey flourished in the 1880s, but after the passing of the National Reclamation Act in the United States, federal bureaucracy became crucial, and a national conservation elite influenced irrigation more. Mead survived this process better than anybody else, precisely because he was a trained expert who could move the garden landscape concept into a new urban and industrial era.

The importance of the garden concept in farming also diminished by 1930. In agriculture, sprays had replaced the search for biological control in the very industry—horticulture—that had first experimented in natural methods. Australian farmers and scientists proved as easily seduced as Americans by the prospects of chemical control.[8] They did so because markets encouraged them to seek cheaper and more uniform quality fruit, while labor could be replaced with machinery and chemicals. After World War II, Australians joined in the vogue for organochlorines, which were to have quite severe ecological consequences for both countries. Nor would the early successes with the vedalia and cactoblastis be easily duplicated. Biological control required the time and financial investment that neither governments nor farmers were willing to give in the 1930s. Biological control remained marginalized in the United States, limited to a University of California program rather than becoming central to political power in Washington and to the agricultural bureaucracy; and in Australia it became marginalized in a different way by the focus on the study of severe problems affecting the pastoral interests. The prickly pear episode, stunning success that it was, nevertheless marked the end of a long period of cross-national influences between Californians and Australians in environmental matters relating to the garden landscape.

Irrigation to produce the garden landscape presented a similar case of faded dreams. The hopes for small-scale settlement had been dashed in California by the 1920s, though Mead continued to peddle his ethic of closer settlement, which at the same time actually served to foster development of an urban-industrial civilization. Planned, small-scale settlement was slightly more successful in Australia but became dogged by the problems of salinization that affected California's agriculture. Also, landed property concentration proceeded despite the efforts of Deakin, Mead, and their successors in Victoria and New South Wales. In both countries, irrigation came by the 1940s to be linked less to dreams of closer settlement that remained unfulfilled than to the development of large-scale engineering—in the Australian case through hydroelectric power in the Snowy Mountains. Much later, the Ord River scheme of the 1960s and the Namoi Valley cotton irrigation of the 1980s paralleled the move toward agricultural consolidation in United States irrigation history.

In neither California nor Australia did the introduction of exotic trees from the other side of the Pacific prove successful in aiding the transformation of the timber industries to a basis of sustainable forestry, but in both cases the introductions of exotics provided important precedents. In Australia, and especially New Zealand, the introduced softwood *Pinus radiata* served marginal aesthetic purposes but became more important as a key source of softwoods by the 1950s. Australians generally neglected the development of eucalyptus plantations, however. This failure reflected the largesse of Australian native forests and their capacity for regeneration rather than the example of California itself, where the eucalyptus proved "successful" in the long run as an aesthetic statement, not as an economic resource. In both cases the wider demands of the national forestry industries for low-cost, low-labor regeneration meant, together with climate restrictions, that the impact of exotics would remain limited in an economic sense. Though Mueller's eucalyptus genus would continue to be planted in dry, subtropical countries for utilitarian purposes, the role of the Australian trees in California would be largely ornamental.

✿

The complicated tale of Californian-Australian environmental contacts does not present simple contrasts, such as might be derived from inherited ideology. The greater role for the state in irrigation development and other environmental policies in Australia should not lead to ahistorical conclusions that contrast a laissez-faire and ideologically "liberal" America with a "socialist" Australia. That might suit a George Chaffey or a historian like Louis Hartz, but reality was always more complicated. One of the most striking features of the exchanges studied in this book was the degree of cooperation and experimentation undertaken, the cross-fertilization, the interest in solutions derived from each other's experience. Greater Australian resort to state involvement in horticulture and irrigation, especially after 1900, reflected the failure of earlier, more hesitant strategies and private initiatives. Dictating the shift was a harsher environment, the lack of available capital, and the need for more cohesive and collective action to combat the advantages competitors in other countries had in market access.[9]

Differences in state intervention were matters of degree, and the sharpest difference was one that did not easily fit into any rigid polarization. In California, the influence of the federal government over land and other resource policies was vast, and it interfered with state environmental management before 1900. After the rise of the Progressive movement, national conservation policies took precedence, and Californian environmental dreams became more dependent on (positive) federal action that was, as early as 1902, potentially larger in extent than any possible at the time in Australia. In Australia, land and hence resource policy remained with the states after federation in 1901. The result was fragmentation of the considerable intervention at state level and greater difficulty in developing massive federal environmental initiatives such as occurred in the United States in the 1930s. Not until the 1980s was federal supremacy over environmental law enhanced through High Court rulings, as in the Franklin Dam and other cases that utilized the external treaties power of Canberra.[10]

There is another, broader message in the eclipse of the Pacific exchange. Long before the current environmental controversies over growth, some people realized the dangers of unbalanced economic development and sought to correct the imbalance that this development produced. It is both comforting and disturbing to know that before this generation others dreamed of creating an environmental balance—comforting because we can find inspiration in the past for modern movements yet disturbing because the ideas failed to convince others and dropped for a time from intellectual circulation. That regression in environmental thinking may occur again.

Why Ellwood Cooper and his allies failed is a complex question. Fundamentally, however, local and regional structures and sentiments succumbed to national ones in which political-economic questions of board-acre agriculture dominated; we have seen how this happened in the eclipse of biological control, and a similar pattern affected the limits to afforestation projects involving the exchange of exotics from each country. Forces within the horticultural movement also undermined biological control and the larger project of a sustainable society. The fruit growers' vision of the future landscape had been determined by the need to produce staple goods for export, and by the geographic position of both California and Australia as peripheral areas in the world capitalist economy in the second half of the nineteenth century. But the position of California vis-à-vis Australia changed radically after 1900. California ceased to be peripheral, while Australia remained doggedly so. The explanation for this critical shift lies in the problem of isolation.

A major force behind the incorporation of California horticulture in the national political economy after 1900 was the changing nature of transport links. Sea transport had fundamentally shaped California's agriculture, especially its wheat exports, and the vagaries of communications shaped the early development of horticulture as well. Dried, preserved, and canned fruit industries flourished by the 1880s because they were unaffected by the long transit times of sea freight, and Ellwood Cooper had successfully encouraged the olive and walnut industries, neither of which relied upon quick access to markets.[11] The transcontinental rail link of 1869 had done little to alter California's peripheral position, partly because the Central Pacific's single line to

Oakland constituted a monopoly, partly because rail was then inadequate and uneconomical for the carrying of bulk commodities that
shaped California's outlook on the world.

The beginnings of the crucial shift in outlook came in 1886–87, not
1869. For the first time railroad rate competition came to southern California with the arrival of the Santa Fe, and in that same period the railroads began trial shipments of fruit by refrigerated cars to the Midwest
and East.[12] (These began just four years after similar experiments with
ship-based refrigeration of meat and dairy products in Australia and
New Zealand, a development reported in California's agricultural press.)
Even though the rate war did not last and the early fruit shipments were
unsatisfactory, experimentation in linking the horticultural industry to
urban and eastern markets began in earnest. The development of the
fruit industry from that point became predicated upon the marketing of
fresh produce by means of faster and more efficient rail services. Horticulturalists still fought the railroads and resented their discriminatory
rate policies, but increasingly the industry recognized that it must work
with the railroads and not against them. Though isolationism died hard
because of the obstacles railroad rates placed in the way of effective marketing, the industry gradually accepted greater incorporation in the
national economy.[13] This development became decisive in the period
1902–07, precisely the period of Cooper's demise and the shift in horticultural policy from problems of production to those of consumption
and advertising. Australians, in contrast, remained dependent upon the
sea lanes and markets in Europe, though the use of cooperatives, influenced by the American example, became important in Australia by the
1920s as growers there also faced problems of oversupply.

The railroad's promise of a quicker land route to the eastern states
encouraged greater fruit production and fueled the speculative boom in
citrus that began in the mid-1880s. A deeper and deeper involvement in
this market system undermined the balance and harmony that Cooper
projected. Fruit production increasingly became specialized, with new
areas in the Central Valley achieving greater economies of scale in the
production of particular fruits that had previously been more widely
grown.[14] In place of garden communities of diverse produce, regions specialized in particular crops just as wheat farmers had done. Lower costs
of production remained crucial because labor shortages impinged upon
the ability to compete against growers in the east and south. This economic question repeatedly surfaced in the arguments of dissenters
against Cooper's program of biological control. Many horticulturalists

lacked an ideological commitment to Cooper's position. When he failed, they abandoned him in favor of quick if short-term remedies like fumigation that could save market shares.

Cultivation practices and orchard management also reflected the shift toward questions of economic efficiency. As citrus grew in importance, this change became noticeable. Citrus growers in Riverside as early as the 1890s, for example, were perfectly prepared to manipulate the farm environment in a mechanistic way foreign to Cooper's ethic. This tendency appeared revealingly in attempts to control the weather. Key problems were winter winds and the frosts that could damage citrus buds. Rather than try other, less vulnerable crops or rely on carefully placed trees that could serve as windbreaks, innovative growers sought greater certainty. They raised the temperature in their orchards by placing in the citrus rows large bins of coal, and later oil, that could be burned at night during freezing periods.[15] Such practices became quite common after 1902, when they were widely discussed in the fruit growers' conventions and manuals. The shift betrayed a manipulative attitude toward environmental change that presaged the fertilizers and sprays that would dominate the industry's approach to fruit-growing in the twentieth century.

The failure to continue afforestation as a complement to farms also illustrates the corrosive effects of national market integration. Farmers often abandoned the idea of tree planting because windbreaks could reduce the profitability of agriculture. In California this decision occurred gradually and unevenly, part of the periodic concern that eucalyptus trees would rob the soil of nutrients and reduce agricultural yields. In Australia, instead of planting the windbreaks commonly recommended in the period before World War I, farmers shifted their attention, particularly after World War II, to manufactured fertilizer as the magic bullet that would solve problems of declining agricultural yields. The 1950s ushered in a "golden age" for agriculture in Australia, but prosperity was powered not by concepts of sustainability but rather by foreign markets and the superphosphate revolution. Moreover, the expansion of crop cultivation, especially of wheat over pastoral activities while prices were high in the 1950s, led to the destruction of large amounts of native bush that could coexist with cattle; the planting of trees even for aesthetic and ornamental purposes diminished on farms.[16]

As far as forests were concerned, the conservation movement itself also hindered an ethic of sustainability. After 1900, the idea that forests should be developed as a renewable economic resource became influential in Washington, D.C., through the work of Gifford Pinchot, but the stress on rational conservation for economic purposes led to an increasing polarization of wilderness and conservation ideas. The concept of sustainability here did not involve environmental but rather economic concepts, and the diverse interests of agriculture and horticulture were no longer integral to the thinking of those who directed the forest service. Afforestation took second place to reforestation, and preservation became the special aim of the wilderness movement. Neither preserved the idea that trees should be cultivated as part of a patchwork of diverse landscapes, and by the 1920s forests in Australia as in the United States came to be considered as "farms," distinguished only by the nature of the crop they produced. Wilderness and conservation now became mirror images of each other.

Was the story of the Pacific exchange unremittingly negative? Environmental historians may be condemned by the lay public and professional colleagues for taking a view of environmental transformations that rates all change as declension from some pristine state and signals a worldview hostile to progress. The contest of change versus preservation, however, is not the point of the story I have been telling. Rather, the Pacific exchange shows how humans struggled to come to grips with lands already transformed by early European settlement. The environmental reformers I discuss in this book achieved some success in redressing imbalances. Ironically, however, the garden blueprint that would supposedly restore balance was itself capable of creating environmental transformations whose effects could be equal in severity to—though different from—those which garden ideologues sought to overcome. The conflict was never a case of environmental change versus no change, or good versus bad, but rather a question about which environmental vision should be implemented. In this sense, all environments were "cultural landscapes" constructed by humans, and they reflected the racial, class, and gender aspirations of the groups that contended for power in California and Australia.

Within their own terms, the garden ideologues did not fail so completely as the metaphors of death and dashed hopes convey. Throughout, this study has sought to acknowledge the meanings that promoters and apologists of change assigned to their own work. J. A. Alexander's biography of George Chaffey is a pertinent example. The title to the final chapter is "Dreams That Came True." No emphasis here on fossil fuels misspent, nor mention of salinization of soils as the result of excessive use of irrigated water; rather, the failure of his engineering efforts in the Imperial Valley scheme left Chaffey in the fifty-fifth year of his life with the chance to dream up just one more project. He received a "long-delayed" reward for his pioneering efforts in irrigation by participating in the further development of southern California. His last project was the development of "the beautiful East Whittier–La Habra Valley," which had laid "dormant" before Chaffey's water arrived. By 1929, East Whittier and La Habra were "famed for producing citrus fruits of the highest class." But it was not just horticulture that benefited; these towns were "twin districts filled with beautiful homes, set amid orange and lemon groves, palms and flowers" largely owing "their present-day prosperity to George Chaffey's enterprise and foresight."[17] The cultural landscapes of the garden ideal survived in these statements.

Despite shortcomings of the pioneering efforts of garden advocates, the cultural landscape had been changed by their partially implemented vision. Towns like Mildura and Ontario were built, farms were carved out of deserts, cities grew with the essential ingredient of water for industry and people, and trees aplenty flourished in forests, gardens, farms, streets, and parks. Beauty defined in terms of greenery had been added to arid landscapes. While failures had been prominent in acclimatization, irrigation, and the panacea of biological control, victories had been won and examples for the future laid down. The changes had not been entirely negative, since the original landscape had already undergone such extensive alteration. Restoration was not possible; renovation was all that could realistically be achieved.

Much of southern California lost its important horticultural presence in the 1950s as fruit lands gave way to suburbia, but in this development the final twist emerged. Chaffey's dream of the garden ideal could better serve to invigorate suburban than rural development. While Jeanne Carr denounced the forces of "evil" that, in her opinion, as early as the 1890s threatened to undermine the southern Californian landscape in the interests of real estate development, towns that sprang up with their tree-lined streets and wide boulevards left the imprint of the late-nineteenth-century reformers. The garden itself survived in modified form in the suburban plot, though stripped of any chance of sustainability, dependent now upon the automobile to make the promise of the garden landscape available to all. The democratic instrument of the internal combustion engine preserved the garden ideal as an important part of the aesthetic of the middle-class property owner in towns like Pasadena, where the Carrs had lived.

This class development was not entirely unprecedented. After all, class was always an important dimension in the thinking of the garden

ideologues. They had sought in part to escape from the city and its atten-
dant social problems. They had dreamed of constructing an Anglo paradise that excluded other visions of gardens derived from the experience
of Native Americans and Japanese and Chinese immigrants. Hobos,
Chinese market-gardeners, and unionists had never been a part of their
radicalism. The untidy and multipurpose garden of the Chinese settlers
as much as the "wastelands" of the Mexican vaqueros gave way to manicured strips of lawn and carefully tended garden beds in the garden ideal
of modern Pasadena and surrounding city-suburbs; this pleasant strip of
suburbia, tended, ironically, so often by Mexican-American gardeners,
was not so very far away from the ideal that William Ellsworth Smythe
had promoted in his *Conquest of Arid America* at the century's turning.

How much of this denouement applies to the other side of the Pacific
equation? The garden ideal never flourished in Australia as it did in California. The attempt to turn scrub into gardens was particularly quixotic
in a country where the economies of scale and distance clearly favored
pastoral industries, and where arable land not needing irrigation was still
available for the dry-farming wheat technology that developed after the
1890s. In the light of such realities, the determination with which the
state pursued ideals of small-scale horticultural settlement into the 1920s
highlighted how far politicians, and the people they represented, were
prepared to reconstruct the already altered natural environment in line
with their vision of the cultural landscape. Government intervention
proved to be more extensive in the Australian case, and more vital to the
survival of the dream against the odds, but even government aid on the
scale pioneered by Mead in Victoria could not stop the drift to the cities.
Visions of diverse farming notwithstanding, pastoral and broad-acre
agricultural activity continued to dominate the Australian economy into
the post–World War II period, and in this sense the impact of the garden
was more marginal than in the Californian case.

Nonetheless, the suburban form of the garden paradise flourished
down under. So evident in the way Mildura, Renmark, and Mulgoa near
Sydney were promoted by Chaffey, the idea struck an enduring chord of
sympathy in the city rather than the bush. Mulgoa failed as a "colony"
in the early 1890s as part of the collapse of Chaffey's Australian ventures, but the ideas contained in the Mulgoa prospectus resurfaced in the
garden suburb. Chaffey had spoken of a "home in one's own garden"
lined with vegetables, trees, shrubs, and lawn, an arrangement he considered "superior to renting a section of somebody else's terrace" where
space was restricted and scope for children playing in a pleasant envi-

ronment rare.[18] In the Sydney "federation" housing development of Haberfield, promoted before World War I by Richard Stanton—and in similar ventures in other major Australian cities—the same ideas recurred. Thereby, the garden landscape persisted as the ideal of the middle class in a society much more urbanized than the American. This concept of the garden suburb did not draw so much on the carefully designed and socially complex communities promoted by the Englishman Ebenezer Howard in his Garden City idea, as develop along the lines of Pasadena and other Californian towns, where, in market-driven real estate subdivisions, developers sought to cater to the middle-class desire for isolation from the social pressures and problems of urban life. They planned parklike and purely residential suburbs with spacious tree-lined streets, and developed an informal and ample type of bungalow housing that drew loosely upon Californian architectural styles of the same period. Australia's bungalows incorporated English and British imperial elements, but also American features such as the shingles that graced the landmark Gamble House of 1908 in Pasadena, and the Spanish-revival style of California that rose to prominence in the 1920s and 1930s.[19] In pastiche form, in the suburb of Rosebery in Sydney (founded 1917), the garden suburb ideal would be extended down the social scale, and with a direct link to the California ideal of emergent suburbia. For the first time, houses marketed as "Californian bungalows" would provide an escape route from city tenements and outback drudgery alike, just as Chaffey had promised in his earlier promotions. Relatively few Australians could afford the comfort of even this modest style in the 1920s, but democratization was on its way in the form of the explosion of suburbia in the 1950s. In the 1920s and beyond, the garden did indeed still live, and dreams did come true, for some.

Today, the high energy usage of sprawling suburban development based on segregation of social classes and the extension of private transportation is being severely questioned. Historians and other social critics have drawn attention to the environmental consequences of what Kenneth Jackson calls the "crabgrass frontier" and its "automobile-based circulation system."[20] Common to most North American and Australian cities, suburban development of this type was especially prominent in California, though the ideal has become national and even international in scope. But effective criticism, both cultural and ecological, of the suburban ideal lay well in the future at the time of the Pacific environmental exchange. The vision of the suburban garden quite successfully drew legitimacy from the campaigns of late-nineteenth-century social critics like Henry George and a welter of conservationists, but stripped those campaigns of their wider hopes for social reform and environmental balance. To be fair, this suburban landscape was only one possible outcome of the schemes that the ideologues of the garden offered. The larger vision of the sustainable society must be recognized. So too must the critique of the inequalities of land distribution that allowed George's ideas to flourish. The Californians and Australians who embraced the garden ideal failed to implement the vision of beauty, balance, and harmony. Yet the recovered and remembered history of their efforts may be a more enduring legacy of the hopes and ideals of Ellwood Cooper and his allies than any dam, forest, farm, or suburb that owes its original being to the Pacific exchange.

Notes

INTRODUCTION

This introductory section incorporates some material first published in Ian Tyrrell, "Peripheral Visions: Californian-Australian Environmental Contacts, c. 1850s–1910," *Journal of World History* 8 (fall 1997): 275–302.

1. National Woman's Christian Temperance Union, *Annual Report for 1883* (Evanston, Ill.: WCTU, 1883), p. 66.

2. Bruce A. Woodard, *The Garden of the Gods Story* (Colorado Springs, Colo.: Democrat Publishing, 1955), pp. 6–7; *Under the Turquoise Sky in Colorado* (N.p.: Passenger Dept., Rock Island System, 1905), pp. 1, 37.

3. On this concept, see Donald W. Meinig, ed., *The Interpretation of Ordinary Landscapes: Geographical Essays* (New York: Oxford University Press, 1979), esp. pp. 1–7, 169–71; and Denis Cosgrove, *Social Formation and Symbolic Landscape* (Totowa, N.J.: Barnes and Noble, 1985). According to Stephen Dovers, ed., *Australian Environmental History: Essays and Cases* (Melbourne: Oxford University Press, 1994), p. 10, landscape can be defined "as everything that can be seen of and on the land but also everything that might be deduced from that view, its history and component influences. . . . It is common to talk of natural or human landscapes . . . [but in] environmental history, a better notion is that of *cultural landscapes*. This recognises the interdependencies of humans and environment, and the fact that purely natural or purely human landscapes are rare."

4. Cosgrove, *Social Formation and Symbolic Landscape,* pp. 174–80; Henry Nash Smith, *Virgin Land: The American West as Symbol and Myth* (Cambridge: Harvard University Press, 1950).

5. *Pacific Ensign,* 20 April 1893, p. 3; *California White Ribbon Signal,* March 1914, p. 2. On John Bidwell, see Will S. Green, "John Bidwell: A Character

Study," *Out West* 19 (December 1903): 625–34; *Dictionary of American Biography,* s.v. "Bidwell, John"; on Annie Bidwell, see Valerie S. Mathes, "Annie E. K. Bidwell: Chico's Benefactress," *California History* 57 (spring-summer 1989): 14–25.

6. T. K. Dow, *A Tour in America* (Melbourne: Australasian Office, 1884), p. 17; on Dow and his brother John, see Hume Dow, "John Lamont Dow," *Australian Dictionary of Biography,* vol. 4 (1851–90), pp. 93–95.

7. Dow's descriptions are confirmed in Bidwell's papers. See, for example, William Proud to John Bidwell, 26 November 1888, Box 1, John and Annie Bidwell Papers, Bancroft Library; John to Annie K. Bidwell, 20 June 1874, 10 January 1875, Box 127, John Bidwell Papers, California State Library.

8. Even then, it took, for example, a full three weeks just to get up the West Coast from Panama. James P. Delgado, *To California by Sea: A Maritime History of the California Gold Rushes* (Columbia: University of South Carolina Press, 1990), pp. 54–55, illustrates just how difficult the passage still was; Geoffrey Blainey, *The Tyranny of Distance: How Distance Shaped Australia's History* (Melbourne: Sun Books, 1966); Morton Rothstein, "West Coast Farmers and the Tyranny of Distance: Agriculture on the Fringes of the World Market," *Agricultural History* 49 (January 1975): 272–80.

9. See the address of Ellwood Cooper, *Official Report of the Twenty-eighth Fruit-Growers' Convention of the State of California . . . Los Angeles . . . 1903* (Sacramento: W. W. Shannon, 1903), p. 16. Excellent on the problem of the railroad are William Deverell, *Railroad Crossing: Californians and the Railroad, 1850–1910* (Berkeley and Los Angeles: University of California Press, 1994), and R. Hal Williams, *The Democratic Party and California Politics, 1880–1896* (Stanford: Stanford University Press, 1973), esp. pp. 13, 88, 92, 103, 135.

10. See, for example, "Our Australian Competitors," *California Fruit Grower and Fruit Trade Review,* 16 July 1892, p. 45. For an exploratory framework that anticipates my own interest in staple theory, see Morris W. Wills, "Sequential Frontiers: The Californian and Australian Experience," *Western Historical Quarterly* 9 (October 1978): 483–94.

11. Ian McLean, "No Flash in the Pan: Resource Abundance and Economic Growth in California, 1848–1910" (manuscript, Department of Economics seminar, University of New South Wales, 1992); Jay Monaghan, *Australians and the Gold Rush: California and Down Under, 1849–1854* (Berkeley and Los Angeles: University of California Press, 1966); E. Daniel and Annette Potts, *Young America and Australian Gold: Americans and the Gold Rush of the 1850s* (St. Lucia: University of Queensland Press, 1974); Geoffrey Serle, *The Golden Age: A History of the Colony of Victoria, 1851–1861* (Melbourne: Melbourne University Press, 1963); Weston Bate, *Victorian Gold Rushes* (Fitzroy, Vic.: McPhee Gribble, 1988).

12. Andrew Markus, *Fear and Hatred: Purifying California and Australia, 1850–1901* (Sydney: Hale and Iremonger, 1979), addresses the issue only in a skimpy way. See also, Charles Price, *The Great White Walls Are Built: Restrictive Immigration to North America and Australia, 1836–1888* (Canberra: Australian National University Press, 1974), pp. 268–69; and Alexander Saxton,

The Indispensable Enemy: Labor and the Anti-Chinese Movement in California (Berkeley and Los Angeles: University of California Press, 1971).

13. Potts, *Young America and Australian Gold,* pp. 52–62; J. M. Powell, *Environmental Management in Australia, 1788–1914* (Melbourne: Oxford University Press, 1976), pp. 37–39.

14. Weston Bate, *Lucky City: The First Generation at Ballarat, 1851–1901* (Melbourne: Melbourne University Press, 1978), p. 122.

15. T. A. Rickard, "The Bendigo Gold-Field," *Transactions of the American Institute of Mining Engineers* 20 (June-October 1891): 472; J. Blackburne, "Natural and Artificial Reproduction of Native Hardwoods," *Journal of the Department of Agriculture* (Victoria) 3 (December 1905): 697; Neil Barr and John Cary, *Greening a Brown Land: The Australian Search for Sustainable Land Use* (Melbourne: Macmillan, 1992), pp. 54–55.

16. David Goodman, "Gold Fields/Golden Fields: The Language of Agrarianism and the Victorian Gold Rush," *Australian Historical Studies* 23 (April 1988): 21–41; and *Gold Seeking: Victoria and California in the 1850s* (Sydney: Allen and Unwin, 1994), analyzes the disturbing environmental consequences of gold for popular thought but restricts his analysis to the 1850s. The adjustments accelerated after 1860, became more complicated, and in many ways more comparable in the two societies than a study of the 1850s suggests.

17. Donald Denoon, *Settler Capitalism: The Dynamics of Dependent Development in the Southern Hemisphere* (Oxford: Clarendon Press, 1983), raised an important debate in Australia about the settlement society idea. However, Denoon only tangentially considered the United States (pp. 229–30). An important contribution to the environmental history of settler societies appeared after this book was completed. See Tom Griffiths and Libby Robin, eds., *Ecology and Empire: Environmental History of Settler Societies* (Melbourne: Melbourne University Press, 1997).

18. The role of export staples in Australian history is conveniently and positively reviewed in W. A. Sinclair, *The Process of Economic Development in Australia* (Melbourne: Longman Cheshire, 1976), pp. 16–18; for California, see Ronald Tobey and Charles Wetherell, "The Citrus Industry and the Revolution of Corporate Capitalism in Southern California, 1887–1944," *California History* 74 (spring 1995): 6–19.

19. For the citrus industry as part of that complex, see the special issue on "Citroculture," *California History* 74 (spring 1995), edited with an introduction by Hal S. Barron. This work emphasizes the period of the development of agribusiness and corporate capitalism, particularly after 1900. Other important explorations of the entrepreneurial model are Steven Stoll, "The Fruits of Natural Advantage: Horticulture and the Industrial Countryside in California" (Ph.D. diss., Yale University, 1995); and H. Vincent Moses, "The Flying Wedge of Cooperation: G. Harold Powell, California Orange Growers, and the Corporate Reconstruction of American Agriculture, 1904–1992" (Ph.D. diss., University of California at Riverside, 1994).

20. Paul Rhode, "Learning, Capital Accumulation, and the Transformation of California Agriculture," *Journal of Economic History* 55 (December 1995): 773–800.

21. Carey McWilliams, *Factories in the Field* (1939; reprint, Santa Barbara: Peregrine Smith, 1971).

22. *An Official Guide to the National Park of New South Wales* (Sydney: Charles Potter, 1893); John Muir Diaries, 16 December 1903 to 7 January 1904, microfilm, Bancroft Library, University of California at Berkeley.

23. On the contemporary debate over wilderness as a theme, see especially, William Cronon, "The Trouble with Wilderness; or, Getting Back to the Wrong Nature," *Environmental History* 1 (January 1996): 7–28, and the critiques of this article, which follow in the same issue.

24. Colin M. Hall, *Wasteland to World Heritage: Preserving Australia's Wilderness* (Carlton, Vic.: Melbourne University Press, 1992), pp. 91–102. A good contemporary survey is W. H. Selway, "The National Parks and Forest Reserves of Australia," *Transactions and Proceedings and Reports of the Royal Society of South Australia* 34 (1910): 275–305.

25. Charles Dudley Warner, *Our Italy* (New York: Harper and Bros., 1891), pp. 120, 123; Moses, "Flying Wedge of Cooperation," p. 74; Department of Agriculture, New South Wales, *Farmers' Bulletin,* no. 90 (Sydney: W. A. Gullick, 1916), pp. 23–24.

26. W. O. Campbell, "Luther Burbank: An Interview," *Agricultural Gazette of New South Wales* 16 (2 November 1905): 1090–94. Other plant exchanges include those with Francesco Franceschi. See J. H. Maiden to Francheschi, 9 March 1905, Box 17, Franceso Francheschi Correspondence and Papers, Bancroft Library; F. Franceschi, "Evergreen Trees about Santa Barbara," *Rural Californian* 18 (April 1895): 175.

27. For the fruit industry and capitalism, see Tobey and Wetherell, "The Citrus Industry and the Revolution of Corporate Capitalism"; the critical comment by Grace Larsen, "The Economics and Structure of the Citrus Industry," ibid., pp. 38–45, and other contributions to Barron, ed., "Citroculture." On the concept of the market, see Karl Polanyi, *The Great Transformation* (Boston: Beacon Press, 1944); and on its application to American circumstances, see Charles Sellers, *The Market Revolution: Jacksonian America, 1815–1846* (New York: Oxford University Press, 1991).

28. For an outline of the concept, see Ann R. M. Young, *Environmental Change in Australia since 1788* (Melbourne: Oxford University Press, 1995), pp. 201–05.

29. Richard Gird, in Department of Agriculture, Victoria, *Report by Mr. James W. Sinclair on the Sugar-Beet Industry and Tobacco Culture of the United States* (Melbourne: Robert S. Brain, Govt. Printer, 1895), p. 11. Reclamation terminology became the specific property of irrigators, discussed below in chapter 5.

30. Alan Gilbert, "The State and Nature in Australia," *Australian Cultural History* 1 (1982): 9–28.

31. Alfred Crosby, *Ecological Imperialism: The Biological Expansion of Europe* (New York: Cambridge University Press, 1989); Richard Grove, *Green Imperialism: Colonial Expansion, Tropical Island Edens, and the Origins of Environmentalism, 1600–1860* (Cambridge: Cambridge University Press, 1995).

32. See, for example, John West, reported in *Mildura Cultivator* 1, no. 10 (1891): 232.

33. *California Horticulturalist and Floral Magazine* 6 (Sept. 1876): 267–69. *Pacific Rural Press*, 11 April 1896, p. 236. Americans were interested in Australian methods of poisoning and/or utilizing the vast rabbit populations of the outback.

34. Richard White, *Inventing Australia: Images and Identity, 1688–1980* (Sydney: George Allen and Unwin, 1981), esp. pp. 50–52 (quote at p. 50).

35. See William Lines, *Taming the Great South Land: A History of the Conquest of Nature in Australia* (Sydney: Allen and Unwin, 1991), esp. chap. 7.

36. Kevin Starr, *Material Dreams: Southern California through the 1920s* (New York: Oxford University Press, 1990), p. 69; Donald Worster, *Rivers of Empire: Water, Aridity, and the Growth of the American West* (New York: Pantheon, 1985).

CHAPTER 1

1. Richard Grove, *Green Imperialism: Colonial Expansion, Tropical Island Edens and the Origins of Environmentalism, 1600–1860* (Cambridge: Cambridge University Press, 1995), pp. 2, 25.

2. David Lowenthal, *George Perkins Marsh: Versatile Vermonter* (New York: Columbia University Press, 1958), p. 269.

3. Michel F. Girard, "Conservation and the Gospel of Efficiency: Un modèle de gestion de l'environnement venu d'Europe?" *Histoire Sociale / Social History* 23 (May 1990): 63–80.

4. Hays, *Conservation and the Gospel of Efficiency* (Cambridge: Harvard University Press, 1959), pp. 27–28. Hays is not alone in this interpretation. A similar point is made by Stephen Fox in *John Muir and His Legacy: The American Conservation Movement, 1890–1975* (Boston: Houghton Mifflin, 1981). In an influential Australian study, historical geographer J. M. Powell has argued that the "organized forestry movement" in the United States at the turn of the century made "much the same decision" as (later) in Australia "to shift the emphasis from the objective of saving trees from destruction to the promotion of planned, long-range or sustained-yield management." Powell, *Environmental Management in Australia, 1788–1914* (Melbourne: Oxford University Press, 1976), p. 119.

5. Donald J. Pisani, "Forests and Conservation, 1865–1890," *Journal of American History* 72 (September 1985): 358.

6. Sargent wound up this publication in 1897 because of an apparent decline of interest in the subject (ibid., p. 355). "There are not persons enough in the United States interested in the subjects which have been presented . . . to make a journal of its class and character self-supporting." See *Garden and Forest,* 29 December 1897, p. 518. But the problem was not lack of interest. Sargent refused horticultural advertising so that the subject could be kept free of commercial overtones often present in similar journals. Without this advertising, all such rural publications would have collapsed.

7. Marsh, *Man and Nature: Or, Physical Geography as Modified by Human Action* (1864; reprint, Cambridge: Harvard University Press, 1965), p. 203. Also see the subsequent editions of this book, under the titles *The Earth as Modified by Human Action: A New Edition of Man and Nature* (New York: Scribner, Armstrong and Co., 1874) cited hereafter as Marsh, 1874 ed.; and *The Earth as Modified by Human Action: A Last Revision of Man and Nature* (New York: C. Scribner's Sons, 1885), cited hereafter as Marsh, 1885 ed.

8. Marsh, *Man and Nature*, p. 280. See also Marsh, 1874 ed., pp. 304–5.

9. *Man and Nature*, pp. 327–29.

10. Jules Clavé, *Études sur l'économie forestière* (Paris: Guillâumin, 1862), pp. 124–25, quoted in ibid., p. 261.

11. *Man and Nature*, p. 260.

12. Ibid., p. 279; 1874 ed., pp. 394–96; and 1885 ed., p. 383 n.

13. Reported by David Lowenthal, *Man and Nature*, p. 279 n.

14. Linden Gillbank, "The Origins of the Acclimatisation Society of Victoria: Practical Science in the Wake of the Gold Rush," *Historical Records of Australian Science* 6 (December 1986): 359–64; Powell, *Environmental Management in Australia*, pp. 31, 33, 45, 48, 71–72; M. E. Hoare, "Learned Societies in Australia: The Foundation Years in Victoria, 1850–1860," *Records of the Australian Academy of Science* 1 (December 1967): 7–29. See, for the French society's work, Michael A. Osborne, *Nature, the Exotic, and the Science of French Colonialism* (Bloomington: Indiana University Press, 1994).

15. Thomas Dunlap, "Remaking the Land: The Acclimatization Movement and Anglo Ideas of Nature," *Journal of World History* 8 (fall 1997): 303–19.

16. "A Memorandum (Service to My Country)," in Thomas Jefferson, *Writings,* comp. Merrill Peterson (New York: Library Classics of the United States, 1984), p. 703.

17. Hugh M. Smith, *A Review of the History and Results of the Attempts to Acclimatize Fish and Other Water Animals in the Pacific States,* Bulletin of the U.S. Fish Commission for 1895 (Washington: Government Printing Office, 1896), p. 379.

18. Lowenthal, *Marsh,* p. 309; Marsh to Sargent, 23 January 1879 in *Nation* 35 (17 August 1882): 136.

19. Marsh, *Man and Nature*, p. 61.

20. Ibid., p. 75; Marsh, "The Camel," in *Ninth Annual Report of the Board of Regents of the Smithsonian Institution* (Washington: Beverley Tucker, 1855), pp. 98–122; see also Marsh, *The Camel: His Organization, Habits, and Uses, Considered with Reference to His Introduction into the United States* (Boston: n.p., 1856), pp. 28, 170–76.

21. George Perkins Marsh, *Report Made under Authority of the Legislature of Vermont, on the Artificial Propagation of Fish* (Burlington, Vt.: Free Press Printing, 1857), pp. 18 (quote), 19–20.

22. *Man and Nature*, p. 117; Marsh, 1885 ed., p. 149.

23. Marsh, 1885 ed., pp. 106–7.

24. Marsh, *Man and Nature*, p. 267, also pp. 263–67 generally.

25. *Garden and Forest*, 28 May 1890, p. 266.

26. Ibid., 11 July 1888, p. 61.

27. Marsh to Sargent, 20 July 1882, in *Nation*, 17 August 1882, p. 136.

28. Marsh, 1885 ed., pp. 384–85; 1874 ed., pp. 394–96; 1885 ed., p. 383.

29. Franklin Hough, "Experimental Plantation of the Eucalyptus, near Rome," *American Journal of Forestry* 1 (1882–83): 412.

30. Marsh, 1885 ed., p. 325.

31. Ibid., p. 383.

32. Ibid., p. 325.

33. Mueller, "Forest Culture in Its Relation to Industrial Pursuits," in Mueller, *Forest Culture and Eucalyptus Trees,* comp. Ellwood Cooper (San Francisco: Cubery, 1876), p. 16 (subsequently cited as Mueller ed.).

34. Deidre Morris, "Baron Sir Ferdinand Jakob Heinrich von Mueller," *Australian Dictionary of Biography,* vol. 5 (1851–90), p. 308.

35. Edward Kynaston, *A Man on Edge: A Life of Baron Sir Ferdinand von Mueller* (London: Allen Lane, 1981), p. 164.

36. Ellwood Cooper, *Forest Culture and Eucalyptus Trees* (San Francisco: Cubery, 1876), p. 117 (subsequently cited as Cooper ed.).

37. Acclimatisation Society of Victoria, *The Third Annual Report of the Acclimatisation Society of Victoria* (Melbourne: Wilson and Mackinnon, 1864), pp. 34–35.

38. Gillbank, "Origins of the Acclimatisation Society," p. 359.

39. Acclimatisation Society of Victoria, *Third Annual Report of the Acclimatisation Society of Victoria,* pp. 34–35.

40. The European salmon had already failed, except in New Zealand. *Proceedings of the Zoological and Acclimatisation Society of Victoria, and Report of the Annual Meeting of the Society . . . 1878* (Melbourne: Sands and McDougall, 1878), pp. 43–163 ff; George Bennett, *Acclimatisation: Its Eminent Adaptation to Australia. A Lecture* (Melbourne: Goodhugh and Co., 1862), p. 37; Eric C. Rolls, *They All Ran Wild: The Animals and Plants That Plague Australia,* rev. ed. (Sydney: Angus and Robertson, 1984), p. 332.

41. Lucille Brockway, *Science and Colonial Expansion: The Role of the British Royal Botanic Gardens* (New York: Academic Press, 1979). On the earlier history of colonial plant exchanges involving Kew, see also Grove, *Green Imperialism,* esp. pp. 331, 336, 414.

42. Kynaston, *A Man on Edge,* pp. 167–68.

43. Mueller, in Cooper ed., 1876, pp. 109, 119.

44. Mueller ed., pp. 89, 91; see also Frank R. Moulds, "Tall Stories and Tall Trees," in John Dargavel and Sue Feary, eds., *Australia's Ever-Changing Forests II: Proceedings of the Second National Conference on Australian Forest History* (Canberra: Centre for Resource and Environmental Studies, 1993), pp. 15–16.

45. Cooper ed., p. 119.

46. Mueller ed., p. 89.

47. Ibid., p. 91.

48. Ibid., pp. 114–15, 116, 76.

49. Cooper ed., p. 204.

50. Ibid.

51. The aboriginal peoples have inhabited Australia for at least forty thousand years. Their hunter-gatherer cultures were considered by many white

colonials in the nineteenth century to be "inferior" and destined for extinction. For an accessible introduction to the pre-European history of Australia, see Geoffrey Blainey, *Triumph of the Nomads: A History of Ancient Australia* (Melbourne: Sun Books, 1975).

52. Cooper ed., p. 204.

53. Ibid., pp. 203–4; Henry Nash Smith, *Virgin Land: The American West as Symbol and Myth* (Cambridge: Harvard University Press, 1950).

54. F. R. Chapman, ed., *Acclimatization Laws. A Handbook of Laws Relating to Acclimatization, Fish, Fisheries, and the Protection of Animals and Birds* (Otago: Otago Acclimatization Society, 1892), esp. pp. 6–8.

55. Barbara J. Best, *George William Francis, First Director of the Adelaide Botanic Garden* (Adelaide: Hyde Park Press, 1986), pp. 131, 133.

56. Rolls, *They All Ran Wild*, p. 328.

57. Colin M. Hall, *Wasteland to World Heritage: Preserving Australia's Wilderness* (Carlton, Vic.: Melbourne University Press, 1992), p. 95; *The National Park of South Australia* (Adelaide: Commissioners of the Park, n.d.); *An Official Guide to the National Park of New South Wales* (Sydney: Charles Potter, 1893), p. 53.

58. *Transactions of the Queensland Acclimatisation Society for the Quarter Ended December 31, 1893* (Brisbane: Pole, Outridge, and Co., 1894); Chapman, ed., *Acclimatization Laws*.

59. Mueller's interest in the pines of America was consolidated by his successor as director of the Botanic Gardens after 1873, William Guilfoyle. See R. T. M. Pescott, *W. R. Guilfoyle, 1840–1912: The Master of Landscaping* (Melbourne: Oxford University Press, 1974), pp. 9, 64, 83, 85.

60. Royal Commission on Vegetable Products, *First Progress Report, Together with Minutes of Evidence . . .* (Melbourne: Robert S. Brain, 1886), esp. pp. 42–53.

61. Donald W. Meinig, *On the Margins of the Good Earth: The South Australian Wheat Frontier, 1869–1884* (1962; reprint, Adelaide: Rigby, 1970).

62. Lloyd G. Churchward, "American Enterprise and the Foundation of the Pacific Mail Service," *Historical Studies* 3 (November 1947): 224.

63. Cooper ed., p. 114.

64. Ibid., p. 115; W. W. Campbell to R. E. C. Stearns, 16 February 1877, Regents Files, University of California Archives, Bancroft Library; C. Hartley Grattan, *The United States and the Southwest Pacific* (Cambridge: Harvard University Press, 1961), p. 110.

CHAPTER 2

1. David Lowenthal, *George Perkins Marsh: Versatile Vermonter* (New York: Columbia University Press, 1958), p. 259.

2. Quoted in Donald Worster, ed., *The Ends of the Earth: Perspectives on Modern Environmental History* (Cambridge: Cambridge University Press, 1988), p. 12.

3. The issue of land fraud has long been debated, but the fact of large land accumulation under the Land Law of 1850, the Swamp Land Act of 1851, and

subsequent acts is indisputable. See Leonard Pitt, *The Decline of the Californios: A Social History of the Spanish-Speaking Californians, 1846–1890* (Berkeley and Los Angeles: University of California Press, 1970), chap. 5, esp. p. 89. See also Paul W. Gates, *History of Public Land Law Development* (Washington, D.C.: Govt. Printing Office, 1968), p. 327; Gates, "Public Land Disposal in California," *Agricultural History* 49 (January 1975): 161–64. On one prominent example of land aggrandizement, that of Henry Miller, see M. Catherine Miller, *Flooding the Courtrooms: Law and Water in the Far West* (Lincoln: University of Nebraska Press, 1993), pp. 2, 11, 187 n. 6.

4. George, *Our Land and Land Policy* (1871) p. 70, in *The Writings of Henry George*, vol. 9 (New York: Doubleday and McClure, 1901).

5. Alexander Saxton, *The Indispensable Enemy: Labor and the Anti-Chinese Movement in California* (Berkeley and Los Angeles: University of California Press, 1971), pp. 92–99.

6. George, *Our Land and Land Policy*, pp. 36–74. While George's Californian environmentalism is almost entirely neglected in historical literature, my theme is hinted at in Charles Barker, "Henry George and the California Background of *Progress and Poverty*," *California Historical Quarterly* 24 (June 1945): 97–115.

7. George, *Our Land and Land Policy*, p. 70.

8. Ibid., pp. 68, 69.

9. George, *Social Problems*, quoted in John L. Thomas, *Alternative America: Edward Bellamy, Henry George, Henry Demarest Lloyd, and the Adversary Tradition* (Cambridge: Harvard University Press, Belknap Press, 1987), p. 193. Thomas has seen the significance of George astutely. George "had begun his career in California" with a vision of "a freely operating decentralized economy organized on a regional scale . . . dominated by small productive units." (pp. 123, 114).

10. George, *Progress and Poverty*, quoted in Thomas, *Alternative America*, p. 114.

11. Quoted in Thomas, *Alternative America*, p. 190.

12. George, *Our Land and Land Policy*, p. 74.

13. Ezra Carr, *The Patrons of Husbandry on the Pacific Coast* (San Francisco: A. L. Bancroft, 1875), pp. 103, 299.

14. Ibid., pp. 426, 430, 444.

15. *Transactions of the California State Agricultural Society during the Year 1879* (Sacramento: J. D. Young, 1880), pp. 451–66; *Transactions of the California State Agricultural Society during the Year 1881* (Sacramento: J. D. Young, 1882), pp. 38–39. For a brief sketch hostile to the board and its objectives, see Gerald Nash, *State Government and Economic Development: A History of Administrative Policies in California, 1849–1933* (Berkeley: Institute of Governmental Studies, University of California, 1964), pp. 148, 232–33.

16. For internal workings of the board, see Minutes of the State Board of Horticulture, 1883–1902, Manuscript volume, California State Archives, Sacramento; E. O. Essig, *A History of Entomology* (1931; reprint, New York: Hafner Publ., 1965), pp. 505–11.

17. Charles Shinn, "The Spirit of the California Fruit-Growers," *Garden and Forest*, 28 December 1892, p. 621.

18. Quoted ibid.

19. Ibid., p. 622.

20. *Rural Californian* 18 (August 1895): 385.

21. U.S. Department of Agriculture, Bureau of Animal Industry, *Special Report on the Present Condition of the Sheep Industry of the United States* (Washington: Government Printing Office, 1892), pp. 970, 974; Thomas Senior Berry, *Early California: Gold, Prices, Trade* (Richmond, Va.: Bostwick Press, 1984), pp. 218–20.

22. Commissioner of Horticulture, *First Biennial Report of the Commissioner of Horticulture of the State of California for 1903–1904* (Sacramento: W. W. Shannon, 1905), p. 276.

23. Hiram A. Reid, *History of Pasadena* (Pasadena: Pasadena History Company, 1895), p. 301.

24. Works Progress Association, *Los Angeles: A Guide to the City and Its Environs* (Los Angeles: Federal Writers' Project of the WPA, 1941), p. 354.

25. California State Board of Horticulture, *Annual Report of the State Board of Horticulture of the State of California, for 1889* (Sacramento: J. D. Young, 1890), p. 313 (hereafter *Rept. St. Bd. Hort., 1889*).

26. *Biographical Directory of the United States Congress, 1774–1984*, Bicentennial edition (Washington, D.C.: Govt. Printing Office, 1989), pp. 773–74. Chipman was also a prominent supporter of irrigation laws for the Sacramento and San Joaquin Valleys; *Out West* 16 (February 1902): 214.

27. Carr, *Patrons of Husbandry*, pp. 301–302; John S. Hittell, *The Resources of California* (San Francisco: A. Roman and Co., 1863); Hittell, *Commerce and Industries of the Pacific Coast* (San Francisco: A. L. Bancroft, 1882).

28. Reid, *History of Pasadena*, p. 120.

29. John Hammond Moore, ed., *Australians in America, 1876–1976* (St. Lucia: University of Queensland Press, 1977), p. 28. See also William Ellsworth Smythe, *The Conquest of Arid America* (1905; reprint, Seattle: University of Washington Press, 1969), pp. 148, 100, 101.

30. On landholding in California, see Carey McWilliams, *Factories in the Field* (1939; reprint, Santa Barbara: Peregrine Smith, 1971); W. W. Robinson, *Land in California: The Story of Mission Lands, Ranchos, Squatters, Mining Claims, Railroad Grants, Land Scrip, Homesteads* (Berkeley and Los Angeles: University of California Press, 1948), pp. 88–90; Donald J. Pisani, "Land Monopoly in Nineteenth-Century California," *Agricultural History* 65 (fall 1991): 15–37; Paul W. Gates, *Land and Law in California* (Ames: University of Iowa Press, 1991). The role of the smaller scale proprietors has, however, not received the attention it deserves. See David Vaught, "'An Orchardist's Point of View': Harvest Labor Relations on a California Almond Ranch, 1892–1921," *Agricultural History* 69 (fall 1995): 563–91, esp. p. 567.

31. California Olive Industry, *Proceedings of the Second State Olive Growers' Convention, Held under the Auspices of the State Board of Horticulture, at San Francisco, July 21, 1892* (Sacramento: A. J. Johnston, 1892), p. 50.

32. Cooper, in California State Board of Horticulture, *Annual Report of the State Board of Horticulture of the State of California, for 1891* (Sacramento: A. J. Johnson, 1892), p. 16; Norton P. Chipman to C. C. van Lieu, 28 April 1900, Box 3, John and Annie K. Bidwell Papers, Bancroft Library; George Hussmann, in *Pacific Rural Press,* 31 January 1891, p. 91. On the increase of raisin and sultana grapes as opposed to wine grapes, see *Garden and Forest,* 25 February 1891, p. 94. Prohibition movements in Riverside were supported by the editor of *Pacific Rural Press,* 8 July 1893, p. 23; in Pasadena, another leading horticultural community, temperance movements had a long and powerful influence. See Reid, *History of Pasadena,* pp. 240–77.

33. California State Board of Viticulture, *Second Annual Report of the Chief Executive Viticultural Officer to the State Board of Viticultural Officers, for the Years 1882–3 and 1883–4* (Sacramento: James J. Ayers, 1884), pp. 44–48, esp. p. 48; California State Board of Viticulture, *Annual Report of the Board of State Viticultural Commissioners for 1887* (Sacramento: J. D. Young, 1888), pp. 7–12, for a history of the early years of the board, and p. 119, on the difficulties of marketing wines domestically; Royal Commission on Water Supply, *First Progress Report,* by Alfred Deakin, *Irrigation in Western America* (Melbourne: John Ferres, Govt. Printer, 1885), p. 87; Commissioner of Horticulture, *Second Biennial Report of the Commissioner of Horticulture of the State of California, for 1905–1906* (Sacramento: W. W. Shannon, 1907), pp. 358–67.

34. *Rept. St. Bd. Hort., 1889,* p. 332.

35. Ibid., p. 427, 428. Other state conventions similarly witnessed enthusiastic discussions of the moral benefits of floral culture. California State Board of Horticulture, *Annual Report of the State Board of Horticulture of the State of California, for 1891* (Sacramento: A. J. Johnston, 1892), pp. 324, 460–62 (hereafter *Rept. St. Bd. Hort., 1891*).

36. California State Board of Horticulture, *Fourth Biennial Report of the State Board of Horticulture of the State of California, for 1893–94* (Sacramento: A. J. Johnston, 1894), p. 118; Commissioner of Horticulture, *First Biennial Report of the Commissioner of Horticulture of the State of California for 1903–1904* (Sacramento: W. W. Shannon, 1905), p. 192.

37. *Rept. St. Bd. Hort., 1891,* p. 16.

38. Charlotte Perkins Gilman, *Herland* (1915; reprint, New York: Pantheon Books, 1979), pp. 59, 68, 77, 80.

39. Mary Hill, *Charlotte Perkins Gilman: The Making of a Radical Feminist, 1860–1896* (Philadelphia: Temple University Press, 1980), pp. 132–33, 156–57; *American Garden* 6 (June 1890): 375.

40. Rodman W. Paul, "Harriet Williams Russell Strong," *Notable American Women,* 3: 405–6; Sandra Myres, *Westering Women and the Frontier Experience, 1800–1915* (Albuquerque: University of New Mexico Press, 1982), p. 262.

41. *Rept. St. Bd. Hort., 1891,* p. 463.

42. On the gendering of Nature in America, see Mario Klarer, "Woman and Arcadia: The Impact of Ancient Utopian Thought on the Early Image of America," *Journal of American Studies* 27, no. 1 (1993): 1–17; on women and "civilization" more generally, see Sylvana Tomaselli, "The Enlightenment Debate on Women," *History Workshop,* no. 20 (autumn 1985): 101–24.

43. California State Board of Horticulture, *Official Report of the Twenty-sixth Fruit-Growers' Convention of the State of California . . . 1901* (Sacramento: A. J. Johnston, 1902), pp. 78–80; Mrs. John S. Dore, "Rancho Del Fuerte, and Its Lessons," ibid., pp. 80–82.

44. Kinney campaigned with Helen Hunt Jackson, author of *Century of Dishonor.* See Robert F. Heizer and Alan J. Almquist, *The Other Californians: Prejudice and Discrimination under Spain, Mexico, and the United States to 1920* (Berkeley and Los Angeles: University of California Press, 1971), pp. 82, 91; Robert Johnson, ed., *The Twentieth Century Biographical Dictionary of Notable Americans,* s.v. "Kinney, Abbot"; Will S. Green, "John Bidwell: A Character Study," *Out West* 19 (December 1903): 625–34; *Dictionary of American Biography,* s.v. "Bidwell, John"; on Annie Bidwell, see Valerie S. Mathes, "Indian Philanthropy in California: Annie Bidwell and the Mechoopda Indians," *Arizona and the West* 25, no. 2 (1983): 153–66.

45. Flora Kimball, "Address of Welcome," *Rept. St. Bd. Hort., 1889,* p. 332; also Richard Gird, quoted in Department of Agriculture, Victoria, *Report by Mr. James W. Sinclair on the Sugar-Beet Industry and Tobacco Culture of the United States* (Melbourne: Robert S. Brain, Govt. Printer, 1895), p. 11.

46. In "Disorientation and Reorientation: The American Landscape Discovered from the West," *Journal of American History* 79 (December 1992): 1048, Patricia Nelson Limerick speaks of "the encounter with landscape" that "was also a complex and often conflict-ridden encounter with other groups of people."

47. Robert Kelley, *Gold vs. Grain: The Hydraulic Mining Controversy in California's Sacramento Valley* (Glendale, Calif.: Arthur H. Clark, 1959), esp. pp. 229–42.

48. John Bidwell, "California's Productive Interests," in *Transactions . . . California State Agricultural Society . . . 1881,* pp. 28–29.

49. John Bidwell to Annie K. Bidwell, 17 December 1874, Box 127, Folder 19, John Bidwell Papers, California State Library.

50. Bidwell, "California's Productive Interests," p. 32.

51. *Rept. St. Bd. Hort., 1889,* pp. 306, 310; see also *Transactions of the California State Agricultural Society during the Year 1886* (Sacramento: P. L. Shoaff, 1887), p. 190.

52. California State Board of Horticulture, *Annual Report of the State Board of Horticulture of the State of California, for 1892* (Sacramento: A. J. Johnston, 1892), p. 37. Lelong (1858–1901) was secretary of the board 1887–1901. See Essig, *History of Entomology,* pp. 685–87.

53. Charles Shinn, "Land, Gold, and Journalism," *American Garden* 12 (January 1891): 6.

54. Charles Shinn, "Garden Art in California," *American Garden* 11 (January 1890): 23.

55. George, *Our Land and Land Policy,* pp. 66–67, 68.

56. California State Board of Horticulture, *Annual Report of the State Board of Horticulture of the State of California, for 1890* (Sacramento: J. D. Young, Govt. Printer, 1890), p. 141.

57. Ibid., p. 142. This would, he added, "destroy the farming interest."

58. J. M. Powell, *Mirrors of the New World: Images and Image-Makers in the Settlement Process* (Canberra: Australian National University Press, 1978), p. 107.

59. John Muir, in Carolyn Merchant, *Major Problems in American Environmental History* (Lexington, Mass.: D. C. Heath, 1993), pp. 392–93.

60. *Rept. St. Bd. Hort., 1890*, p. 149. On the other hand, securing wood for packing cases for the fruit industry did not emerge as an issue until after the mass expansion of citrus marketing under the California Fruit Growers Exchange after 1907.

61. In California, too, as Samuel Hays has observed, "steep slopes and torrential rainfall created acute flood and erosion problems." These problems meshed with the concerns of irrigators and urban populations in San Francisco to secure water for city and farm use. Hays, *Conservation and the Gospel of Efficiency* (Cambridge: Harvard University Press, 1959), pp. 24, 36. Michael Williams, *Americans and Their Forests: A Historical Geography* (Cambridge: Cambridge University Press, 1989) notes that the linking of irrigation and forests was a stock argument in turn-of-the-century conservation thought (p. 420).

62. *Garden and Forest*, 28 May 1890, p. 266; reprinted in *Pacific Rural Press*, 14 March 1891, p. 245.

63. Sarah Cooper, "Floral Culture," in Twelfth State Fruit Growers' Convention, in *Rept. St. Bd. Hort., 1889*, pp. 425–26.

64. Mr. White, at Tenth State Fruit Growers' Convention, in ibid., p. 327; Lucy E. Weister, "California Wild Flowers," in *Twenty-sixth State Fruit Growers' Convention*, pp. 83–84.

65. *Rept. St. Bd. Hort., 1890*, p. 122.

66. *Rept. St. Bd. Hort., 1889*, p. 327; *Garden and Forest*, 28 May 1890, p. 266; Edward J. Wickson, *The California Fruits and How to Grow Them* (San Francisco: Dewey and Co., 1891), p. 583.

67. "Forestry; Redwoods," *Rept. St. Bd. Hort., 1891*, pp. 324–29, at 328–29.

68. Fifteenth State Fruit Growers' Convention, in *Rept. St. Bd. Hort. 1891*, p. 402. Fowler and Clark also urged redwoods and sequoias to be regrown rather than simply preserved; thus they were advocates of reforestation as much as preservation.

69. It was admitted that this latter measure concerned only a small part of the forest lands. California State Board of Horticulture, *Third Biennial Report of the State Board of Horticulture of the State of California, for the Thirty-eighth and Thirty-ninth Fiscal Years* (Sacramento: J. D. Young, 1888), p. 127. See also Memorial [to Congress], in California State Board of Forestry, *Third Biennial Report of California State Board of Forestry, for the Years 1889–90* (Sacramento: J. D. Young, Govt. Printer, 1890), pp. 67–68.

70. The agitation over the San Bernardino Mountains began as early as 1885. See California State Board of Forestry, *First Biennial Report of the California State Board of Forestry, for the Years 1885–86* (Sacramento: James J. Ayers, 1886), pp. 3–4; California State Board of Forestry, *Fourth Biennial Report of the California State Board of Forestry, for the Years 1891–92* (Sacramento: A. J.

Johnston, 1892), pp. 5–10, esp. pp. 6, 20–22; Hays, *Conservation and the Gospel of Efficiency,* p. 24; Abbot Kinney to Stephen M. White, 22 January 1893, Box 2, Stephen M. White Papers, Stanford University; Ronald F. Lockmann, "Improving Nature in Southern California: Early Attempts to Ameliorate the Forest Resource in the Transverse Ranges," *Southern California Quarterly* 58 (winter 1976): 485.

71. Muir to Carr, 12 January 1877, 12 August 1877, in *Letters to a Friend: Written to Mrs. Ezra S. Carr, 1866–1879* (1915; reprint, Dunwoody, Ga.: Norman S. Berg, 1973), pp. 182, 185; Harlean James, *Romance of the National Parks* (1939; reprint, New York: Macmillan, 1972), p. 42.

72. Merchant, *Major Problems,* pp. 391–94. On Muir's Protestant background, particularly helpful is Donald Worster, "John Muir and the Roots of American Environmentalism," in Worster, *The Wealth of Nature: Environmental History and the Ecological Imagination* (New York: Oxford University Press, 1993), pp. 184–202.

73. Calculated from the list of addresses and names in *List of Members of the Sierra Club, May 1900* (n.p., 1900).

74. *Garden and Forest,* 2 November 1892, p. 526; ibid., 1 April 1896, pp. 131–32; F. H. Clark, "Forestry; Redwoods," *Rept. St. Bd. Hort., 1891,* pp. 328–29.

75. John Muir to Jeanne Carr, 29 May 1870, in *Letters to a Friend,* pp. 81–82; Jeanne Carr, "A Sabbath in the Yo semite [*sic*]," in Jeanne Smith Carr Papers, Box 2, Huntington Library; John Muir to John Bidwell, 15 April 1896, Box 2, Bidwell Papers, Bancroft Library; Green, "John Bidwell," pp. 626–28. I owe this idea to Professor Richard Searles, Department of Biological Sciences, Duke University, whose forebears grew up in the Central Valley and experienced relief from summer heat in the mountains.

76. On the Sierra as a region that especially appealed to Californians, see Kevin Starr, *Americans and the California Dream, 1850–1915* (New York: Oxford University Press, 1973), esp. pp. 176–83, quote at 183.

77. Muir to Carr, 9 April 1879, *Letters to a Friend,* p. 193.

78. Muir to Carr, 29 May 1870, ibid., pp. 83–84.

79. Muir to Carr, 12 August 1877, ibid., p.186; see also Muir to Carr, 23 June 1877, ibid., p. 184.

80. *Rept. St. Bd. Hort., 1889,* p. 426; *Rept. St. Bd. Hort., 1890,* p. 122.

81. California State Board of Forestry, *First Biennial Report of the California State Board of Forestry, for the Years 1885–86* (hereafter called *St. Bd. For. Rept., 1885–86*), pp. 8–9.

82. *Garden and Forest,* 2 November 1892, p. 526; also ibid., 1 April 1896, pp. 131–32; "Report of the Executive Officer," in *St. Bd. For. Rept., 1891–92,* p. 22. The conservation, as opposed to preservation, ethic in the Sierra Club, 1892–1905, is briefly discussed in Michael Cohen, *The History of the Sierra Club, 1892–1970* (San Francisco: Sierra Club Books, 1988), p. 18.

83. "Report of the Executive Officer," in *St. Bd. For. Rept., 1891–92,* p. 21.

84. Shinn, "California Forests and Irrigation," in *Garden and Forest,* 3 September 1890, p. 427.

CHAPTER 3

1. *Garden and Forest,* 10 September 1890, pp. 445.

2. Charles Dudley Warner, *Our Italy* (New York: Harper and Bros., 1891), pp. 120, 123; H. Vincent Moses, "The Flying Wedge of Cooperation: G. Harold Powell, California Orange Growers, and the Corporate Reconstruction of American Agriculture, 1904–1992" (Ph.D. diss., Univ. of Calif./Riverside, 1994), p. 74; *California Fruit Grower and Fruit Trade Review,* 26 May 1894, p. 416.

3. Kevin Starr, *Material Dreams: Southern California through the 1920s* (New York: Oxford University Press, 1990), p. 184.

4. Viola Lockhart Warren, "The Eucalyptus Crusade," *Southern California Quarterly* 44 (March 1962): 31.

5. Robert F. Zacharin, *Emigrant Eucalypts: Gum Trees as Exotics* (Melbourne: Melbourne University Press, 1978), pp. 76, 117; National Conservation Commission, *Report of the National Conservation Commission* (Washington: Govt. Printing Office, 1909), 3:218.

6. Alfred J. McClatchie, *Eucalypts Cultivated in the United States,* U.S. Department of Agriculture, Bureau of Forestry, bulletin no. 35 (Washington: Government Printing Office, 1902), p. 2. McClatchie pointed out that red box (*E. polyanthemos*) was "one of the few species tested at the Experiment Station farm near Phoenix that has been entirely uninjured by either the frosts of winter or the heat of summer" (p. 73).

7. Margaret Willis, *By Their Fruits: A Life of Ferdinand von Mueller, Botanist and Explorer* (Sydney: Angus and Robertson, 1949), p. 181; Robert Zacharin, *Emigrant Eucalypts,* pp. 32, 57; Edward Kynaston, *A Man on Edge: A Life of Baron Sir Ferdinand von Mueller* (London: Allen Lane, 1981); Kenneth Thompson, "The Australian Fever Tree in California: Eucalypts and Malaria Prophylaxis," *Annals of the Association of American Geographers* 60 (June 1970): 236.

8. Franklin Hough, "Experimental Plantation of the Eucalyptus, Near Rome," *American Journal of Forestry* 1 (1882–83): 404.

9. Norman Hall, *Botanists of the Eucalypts* (Melbourne: CSIRO, 1978), p. 16; Viola Warren, "Eucalyptus Crusade," p. 31; F. Gutzkow, George Chismore, and Alice Eastwood, *Doctor Hans Hermann Behr . . .* (San Francisco: California Academy of Science, 1905), p. 2; Robert T. Legge, "Hans Herman [*sic*] Behr: German Doctor, California Professor and Academician, and 'Bohemian,'" *California Historical Society Quarterly* 32 (September 1953): 243–62, esp. pp. 244–48.

10. E. W. Hilgard, H. H. Behr, and W. G. Klee, "Report to the State Horticultural Society on Baron von Mueller's 'Select Extra-Tropical Plants,'" pp. 141–52, in E. W. Hilgard, T. C. Jones, and R. W. Furnas, *Report on the Climatic and Agricultural Features and the Agricultural Practices and Needs of the Arid Regions of the Pacific Slope . . .* (Washington, D.C.: Government Printing Office, 1882), p. 151.

11. *Pacific Rural Press,* 31 July 1880, p. 71; Gutzkow, Chismore, and Eastwood, *Doctor Hans Hermann Behr,* p. 2; E. O. Essig, *A History of Entomology* (1931; New York: Hafner Pub., 1965), pp. 553–56.

12. Catalogues for Walker's and Nolan's nurseries, and *Transactions of the*

California State Agricultural Society, 1858, p. 266, cited in H. M. Butterfield, "The Introduction of Eucalyptus into California," *Madrono: A West American Journal of Botany* 3 (October 1935): 150, 152.

13. Merritt B. Pratt, *Shade and Ornamental Trees of California* (Sacramento: California State Board of Forestry, 1922), p. 69.

14. Charles Nordoff, "California. II: What to See There, and How to See It," *Harper's New Monthly Magazine* 45 (August 1872): 65–81.

15. California State Board of Horticulture, *Annual Report of the State Board of Horticulture of the State of California, for 1890* (Sacramento: J. D. Young, Govt. Printer, 1890), pp. 140, 123.

16. Thompson, "Australian Fever Tree," p. 230.

17. Biographical sources for Cooper include: [Ellwood Cooper], *The Life of Ellwood Cooper* ([Santa Barbara]: privately printed, c. 1913); *National Cyclopaedia of American Biography* (New York: James T. White, 1943), 30:530–31; Essig, *History of Entomology*, pp. 585–87; Hall, *Botanists*, pp. 40–41.

18. Ellwood Cooper, *Forest Culture and Eucalyptus Trees* (San Francisco: Cubery, 1876), hereafter referred to as Cooper ed. The other edition of this work, with the same bibliographical details, is referred to here as Mueller ed.

19. E. E. Pescott, "Notes on Mueller's Literary Work," *Victorian Naturalist* 38 (January 1922): 101, accused Cooper of "one of the most disgraceful cases of plagiarism on record." I thank Sara Maroske of the Ferdinand Mueller Project in the Department of History and Philosophy of Science, University of Melbourne, for this reference.

20. Cooper ed., p. 24.

21. Ibid., p. 14.

22. Ibid., pp. 29–30.

23. Ibid., pp. 15, 16.

24. Ibid., p. 16; Robert Kelley, *Gold vs. Grain: The Hydraulic Mining Controversy in California's Sacramento Valley* (Glendale, Calif.: Arthur H. Clark, 1959), esp. pp. 229–42.

25. Cooper ed., pp. 44, 100.

26. Ferdinand von Mueller, *Forest Culture and Eucalyptus Trees,* comp. Ellwood Cooper (San Francisco: Cubery, 1876), p. 64 (Mueller ed.).

27. I am indebted for this insight to Professor Richard Searles, chair of the Department of Biological Sciences at Duke University. See also Royal Commission of Inquiry on Forestry, *Final Report of the Commissioners, Part II, Minutes of Proceedings, Minutes of Evidence, and Appendix* (Sydney: Govt. Printer, 1908), p. 460.

28. Cooper ed., pp. 28–29.

29. Cf. Richard Grove, *Green Imperialism: Colonial Expansion, Tropical Island Edens and the Origins of Environmentalism, 1600–1860* (Cambridge: Cambridge University Press, 1995).

30. Cooper ed., p. 30.

31. Ibid.

32. Ibid., pp. 213, 214, 29; cf. Donald Worster, *The Wealth of Nature: Envi-*

ronmental History and the Ecological Imagination (New York: Oxford University Press, 1993), pp. 9–12.

33. Cooper ed., pp. 215, 236, 237.

34. Ibid., p. 29.

35. Hall, *Botanists*, p. 40.

36. Essig, *History of Entomology*, p. 585; also Hall, *Botanists*, p. 40; *National Cyclopaedia of American Biography*, 30:530–31.

37. Starr, *Material Dreams*, p. 246.

38. *Garden and Forest*, 26 March 1890, p. 319.

39. John L. Dow, quoted John Hammond Moore, ed., *Australians in America, 1876–1976* (St. Lucia: University of Queensland Press, 1977), p. 28; J. L. Dow, *The Australian in America* (Melbourne: *Leader* Office, 1884), pp. 145–47; T. K. Dow, *A Tour in America* (Melbourne: *Australasian* Office, 1884), p. 49.

40. Theodore P. Lukens to Abbot Kinney, 29 November 1901; Kinney to Lukens, 1 September 1900; J. W. Jeffrey to Lukens, 1 February 1904; Lukens to Frances Cuttle, 12 November 1906, Box 1, Theodore Parker Lukens Papers, Huntington Library.

41. Department of Agriculture, Victoria, *Report by Mr. James M. Sinclair on the Sugar-Beet Industry and Tobacco Culture of the United States* (Melbourne: Robert S. Brain, 1895), p. 11; Muir, quoted by Donald Worster, in Ian Tyrrell: "Environmental History: The Contribution of Donald Worster," *Australasian Journal of American Studies* 13 (July 1994): 66.

42. *Santa Barbara Daily Press*, 7 December 1880, p. 143, in Scrapbook 1, Charles F. McGlashan Scrapbooks, Bancroft Library; *Life of Ellwood Cooper*, p. 20.

43. Richard Gird, quoted in Department of Agriculture, Victoria, *Report by Mr. James M. Sinclair*, p. 11.

44. Warren, "Eucalyptus Crusade," p. 37; Works Progress Association, *Los Angeles: A Guide to the City and Its Environs* (Los Angeles: Federal Writers' Project of the WPA, 1941), p. 354. See also James D. Hart, *A Companion to California*, new ed., rev. and expanded (Berkeley and Los Angeles: University of California Press, 1987), p. 262; "Abbot Kinney," in J. M. Guinn, ed., *A History of California and an Extended History of Its Southern Coast Counties and Containing Biographies of Well-Known Citizens of the Past and Present* (Los Angeles: Historical Record Co., 1907), pp. 608–10, is the most detailed source and lists 1880 as the date of his permanent settlement in California, though Hart gives 1873 as the date, which is too early.

45. Hall, *Botanists*, p. 79; see also *Who Was Who in America*, vol. 1; Rossiter Johnston, ed., *The Twentieth Century Biographical Dictionary of Notable Americans*, s.v. "Kinney, Abbot."

46. Warren, "Eucalyptus Crusade," pp. 37–38.

47. Abbot Kinney, *Eucalyptus* (Los Angeles: B. R. Baumgardt, 1895), pp. 65–66.

48. Kinney pointed out, ibid., p. 51, that "real estate men putting tracts on the market will often plant trees on their new streets. As a rule they select cheap ones that require little care."

49. "Tree Culture Experiments," in California State Board of Forestry, *First Biennial Report of the California State Board of Forestry, for the Year 1885–86* (Sacramento: James J. Ayers, 1886), p. 228.

50. Alfred J. McClatchie, "The Eucalypts of the Southwest," *Out West* 20 (April 1904): 336.

51. Kinney, *Eucalyptus,* p. 71.

52. "Committee on Grounds and Buildings Biennial Report," Box 1, Regents' Files, University of California Archives, Bancroft Library.

53. *California Horticulturalist and Floral Magazine* 6 (May 1876): 139; *The Development of Golden Gate Park and Particularly the Management and Thinning of Its Forest Tree Plantations. A Statement from the Board of Park Commissioners* . . . (San Francisco: Bacon and Co., 1886), p. 27.

54. Ellis to Gilman, 17 March 1873, Box 1, Regents' Files, University of California Archives, Bancroft Library.

55. Charles Shinn, "The California University Gardens," *Garden and Forest,* 12 March 1890, p. 123. The planting was supervised by Robert E. C. Stearns, secretary of the board of regents, but also influential was Ezra Carr, professor of agriculture. Carr's stormy career ended in 1875 with his sacking by the board of regents. See Verne A. Stadtman, *The University of California, 1868–1968* (New York: McGraw-Hill, 1970), pp. 143–44, 150.

56. *The Argonaut,* 22 April 1877, p. 4, quoted Thompson, "Australian Fever Tree," p. 243.

57. *Pacific Rural Press,* 3 July 1880, p. 3.

58. Ibid., 16 July 1881, p. 33. The tree was portrayed by some orchardists as a monster, with "an enormous appetite" whose "thirst is never quenched." *California Fruit Grower,* 13 April 1889, p. 4.

59. *Pacific Rural Press,* 21 February 1880, p. 120; 27 March 1880, p. 199.

60. Ibid., 24 August 1889, p. 153; 23 January 1892, p. 71.

61. Edward J. Wickson, *The California Fruits and How to Grow Them,* 2d rev. ed. (San Francisco, Dewey and Co., 1891), p. 582. The *Pacific Rural Press* agreed that "we [still] have immense areas of hillside and hilltop which might . . . be planted with the blue gum for timber and to tangle up the winds in their courses." *Pacific Rural Press,* 16 July 1881, p. 33; 24 August 1889, p. 153.

62. Cooper cited Mueller as saying that in Valencia, Spain, the eucalyptus was "vulgarly called the fever-tree, on account of its properties for preventing malarial fevers." Cooper ed., p. 44.

63. *Pacific Rural Press,* 14 May 1881, p. 349; see also, "Does Eucalyptus Prevent Fever?" in *Pacific Rural Press,* 31 July 1880, p. 71.

64. Cooper ed., p. 22.

65. A. C. Sullivan, "Where the Eucalyptus Grows Outdoors," *American Garden* 12 (November 1891): 687.

66. Zacharin, *Emigrant Eucalypts,* pp. 34–35.

67. Kenneth Thompson, "Irrigation as a Menace to Health in California: A Nineteenth Century View," *Geographical Review* 59 (April 1969): 195–214; Thompson, "Australian Fever Tree," pp. 230–44.

68. Cooper ed., p. 44.

69. Kinney, *Eucalyptus,* pp. 144–45.

70. Gerald D. Nash, "The California State Board of Forestry, 1883–1960," *Southern California Quarterly* 47 (September 1965): 291–301.

71. E.g., Kinney to Adolph Sutro, 14 September 1886, Adolph Sutro Papers, S 17, Huntington Library; Warren, "Eucalyptus Crusade," p. 37; see also Kinney to Lukens, 24 June 1899, 28 June 1899, Box 1, Lukens Papers, Huntington Library; *Rept. St. Bd. For., 1885–86*, p. 3.

72. California State Board of Forestry, *Third Biennial Report of the California State Board of Forestry, for the Years 1889–90* (Sacramento: J. D. Young, 1890), pp. 10–11; William S. Lyon, "Some Notes on the Genus Eucalyptus," in ibid., pp. 25–31; California State Board of Forestry, *Fourth Biennial Report of the California State Board of Forestry, for the Years 1891–92* (Sacramento: A. J. Johnston, 1892), p. 32.

73. California State Board of Forestry, *Second Biennial Report of the California State Board of Forestry, for the Years 1887–88* (Sacramento: J. D. Young, 1888), pp. 8, 10.

74. *Rept. St. Bd. For., 1889–90*, pp. 20–23.

75. Hilgard, Behr, and Klee, "Report to the State Horticultural Society on Baron von Mueller's 'Select Extra-Tropical Plants,'" p. 151; Hilgard to Mueller, 16 July 1886, Hilgard Letterbooks, Vol. 12, Eugene W. Hilgard Papers, Bancroft Library; California State Board of Horticulture, *Fourth Biennial Report of the State Board of Horticulture of the State of California, for 1893–94* (Sacramento: A. J. Johnston, 1894), pp. 328–29.

76. Hilgard to Mueller, 20 April 1895, 3 December 1895, Vol. 20 (quote); Hilgard, *Arid Regions*, p. 151.

77. William S. Lyon, "Trees Suitable for Alkali Lands," in *Rept. St. Bd. For., 1891–92*, p. 34. Casuarinas could also be justified for ornamental reasons. The noted Pasadena gardening authority Mira Saunders wrote enthusiastically about the way the she-oak "enlivens a background of conifers" planted in the Berkeley Hills. Charles F. Saunders Papers, Box 10, Folder 5, Huntington Library.

78. *Rept. St. Bd. For., 1891–92*, p. 47; Pratt, *Shade and Ornamental Trees of California*, p. 102.

79. Quarantine records reveal that these importations were significant, e.g., California State Board of Horticulture, *Fifth Biennial Report of the California State Board of Horticulture, for the Years 1895–96* (Sacramento: A. J. Johnston, 1896), pp. 28–29, 31.

80. *Rept. St. Bd. For., 1889–90*, pp. 36–38.

81. Ibid., p. 39; *Rept. St. Bd. For., 1891–92*, pp. 46, 47; Pratt, *Shade and Ornamental Trees of California*, p. 46.

82. Hilgard, *Arid Regions*, p. 149.

83. Luther Burbank, *How Plants Are Trained to Work for Man*, 8 vols. (New York: P. F. Collier and Son., 1914), 8:144.

84. California State Board of Horticulture, *Third Biennial Report of the State Board of Horticulture of the State of California, for the Thirty-eighth and Thirty-ninth Fiscal Years* (Sacramento: J. D. Young, 1888), pp. 89, 90; *Rept. St. Bd. For., 1889–90*, pp. 42, 44. More than sixty species of acacias were planted out on the state university grounds alone, in 1873. *Rept. St. Bd. Hort., 1890*, p. 123; Kinney, *Eucalyptus*, p. 119.

85. Kinney, *Eucalyptus,* pp. 107, 120–24; Kinney, "Forests of Los Angeles, San Bernardino, and San Diego Counties, California," *Rept. St. Bd. For., 1885–86,* p. 29; *Pacific Rural Press,* 2 May 1896, p. 284.

86. *Rept. St. Bd. For., 1885–86,* p. 34. For Kinney's work with the State Board of Horticulture, see "Forest Culture," *Rept. St. Bd. Hort., 1890,* pp. 141–49; Mueller quoted by Cooper, *Rept. St. Bd. Hort., 1893–94,* pp. 117, 240–41. For Kinney's use of eucalyptus trees, particularly *E. globulus,* see *Rept. St. Bd. Hort., 1893–94,* pp. 326–28.

87. By the abolition, ranching interests gained a political victory against the Board of Forestry, which had started to direct its efforts against the sheepherders and lumber interests that were damaging the state's watersheds. See "Forest Legislation in California," in California State Board of Forestry, *Fifth Biennial Report of the State Forester of California* (Sacramento: State Printing Office, 1914), p. 11.

88. In 1900, Kinney served as president of the Southern California Forest and Water Association. Johnson, *The Twentieth Century Biographical Dictionary of Notable Americans; Pacific Rural Press,* 14 March 1891, p. 239; Kinney, *Forest and Water* (Los Angeles: Post Publishing, 1900).

89. Warren, "Eucalyptus Crusade," p. 38.

90. Richard T. Baker, *The Hardwoods of Australia and Their Economics* (Sydney: William Applegate Gullick, Govt. Printer, 1919), pp. 456–57.

91. Royal Commission of Inquiry on Forestry, *Final Report, Part II,* p. 459; "Tree Planting by Santa Fe Railroad," *Arboriculture* 6 (January 1907): 329.

92. G. Lull, *A Handbook for Eucalyptus Planters* (Sacramento: State Printer, 1908), p. 43; Warren, "Eucalyptus Crusade," p. 39.

93. *Monrovia* (Calif.) *News,* 26 November 1907, cited in Royal Commission of Inquiry on Forestry, *Final Report, Part II,* p. 460.

94. A. V. Galbraith, *Mountain Ash (Eucalyptus regnans) —F. von Mueller: A General Treatise on Its Silviculture, Management, and Utilization* (Melbourne: H. G. Green, Govt. Printer, 1937), pp. 27, 45–48; William S. Lyon, "Forestry Bulletin, No. 6," in *Rept. St. Bd. For., 1889–90,* p. 65.

95. *California Horticulturalist and Floral Magazine* 3 (February 1873): 52.

96. Dwight Whiting to Richard T. Baker, 29 May 1905, and 14 January 1907, in Royal Commission of Inquiry on Forestry, *Final Report, Part II,* pp. 392, 393.

97. Hall, *Botanists,* p. 12.

98. Richard T. Baker and Henry G. Smith, *A Research on the Eucalypts, Especially in Regard to Their Essential Oils* (Sydney: Government Printer, 1902).

99. Whiting to Baker, 14 January 1907, in Royal Commission of Inquiry on Forestry, *Final Report, Part II,* p. 393.

100. McClatchie, *Eucalypts Cultivated in the United States,* p. 2; Royal Commission of Inquiry on Forestry, *Final Report, Part II,* p. 393; Hall, *Botanists,* p. 88.

101. National Conservation Commission, *Report of the National Conservation Commission,* 2:212.

102. Ibid., p. 680.

103. Louis Margolin, *Yield from Eucalyptus Plantations in California,* Cali-

fornia State Board of Forestry, bulletin no. 1 (Sacramento: W. W. Shannon, 1910).

104. Don C. Miller, "A Eucalyptus Patriarch," *Westways* 52 (March 1960): 18–19; Warren, "Eucalyptus Crusade," pp. 39–41; Starr, *Material Dreams,* p. 184.

105. This timber was known in the United States as Douglas fir (*Pseudotsuga menziesii*) but popularly called "Oregon" in Australia. Oregon was cheaper and lighter and hence easier to handle in such important components as roofing timbers, where it began to replace eucalyptus in the 1890s. *Daily Telegraph* (Sydney), 12 December 1924, p. 6; Royal Commission of Inquiry on Forestry, *Final Report, Part II,* pp. 89, 240.

106. Baker, *Hardwoods of Australia,* pp. 399, 403.

107. *Rept. St. Bd. Hort., 1893–94.* pp. 328, 329–30.

108. Royal Commission of Inquiry on Forestry, *Final Report, Part II,* p. 460.

109. Australian Forestry Conference, *Report of Proceedings of the Australian Forestry Conference, Brisbane, April, 1922* (Brisbane: James J. Wrigley, 1922), p. 133.

110. Royal Commission of Inquiry on Forestry, *Final Report, Part II,* p. 460; *American Lumberman,* 20 March 1909, cited in *The Harman Timber Company* (Los Angeles: n.p., 1910), n.p.

111. Cf. Miller, "Eucalyptus Patriarch," pp. 18–19; Warren, "Eucalyptus Crusade," pp. 39–40; Starr, *Material Dreams,* p. 184.

112. The 1910 study had been far from definitive, and the same author, Louis Margolin, was simultaneously advocating eucalyptus plantings for Hawaii and boosting the eucalyptus in 1911 as "some of the most valuable timber in the world." Margolin, *Eucalyptus Culture in Hawaii,* Terr. of Hawaii, Board of (Commissioners of) Agriculture and Forestry, Division of Forestry, bulletin no. 1 (Honolulu: Hawaiian Gazette Co., 1911), p. 9.

113. *Lumber World Review,* 10 May 1913, p. 42; "Our Plantation," in Grant Wallace, *The Most Valuable Tree in the World: Mahogany Eucalyptus: A Rapid, Certain and Perpetual Source of Income* (Chicago: American Eucalyptus Timber Corp., 1913), p. 2.

114. Wallace, *Most Valuable Tree,* p. 2.

115. Ibid., p. 40.

116. Ibid., p. 5; Warren, "Eucalyptus Crusade," p. 39; Miller, "Eucalyptus Patriarch," p. 19. See also Grant Wallace to Jack London, 25 September 1909, Box 184, Folder 51, Jack London Collection, Huntington Library; William E. Graves, *Studies in Eucalyptus* (St. Louis: Eucalyptus Timber Corp., 1910).

117. John B. Anderson (Office of the Chief of the USDA Forest Service) to Theodore Parker Lukens, 3 September 1904, 18 October 1905, and 25 July 1905, Box 1; Lukens to F. S. Churchill, 11 June 1909, Book 2, Lukens Letterbooks, Lukens Papers, Huntington Library.

118. See the *Harman Timber Company* prospectus, n.p. Lukens's efforts for reforestation of native forests—but not his love of eucalyptus—have received attention. See Ronald F. Lockmann, "Improving Nature in Southern California: Early Attempts to Ameliorate the Forest Resource in the Transverse Ranges," *Southern California Quarterly* 58 (winter 1976): 490–94.

119. *Sunset Magazine,* January 1914, p. 195, in Box 6, Lukens Papers, Huntington Library; also Letterbook, Lukens to A. E. Pomeroy, 2 April 1917; Lukens to O. M. Grizzle, 13 November 1915; and envelope of clippings, "Clippings from various sources in regard to forestry," Box 6, Lukens Papers.

120. Cf. Michael Williams, *Americans and Their Forests: A Historical Geography* (Cambridge: Cambridge University Press, 1989), p. 488; *The Statistical History of the United States from Colonial Times to the Present* (New York: Basic Books, 1976), pp. 540–41.

121. *Lumber World Review,* 10 February 1912, p. 36.

122. Peter Shergold, "American Spectator Sport: A Technological Perspective," in Richard Cashman and Michael McKernan, eds., *Sport in History: The Making of Modern Sporting History* (St. Lucia: University of Queensland Press, 1979), p. 23.

123. Donald J. Pisani, "Forests and Conservation, 1865–1890," *Journal of American History* 72 (September 1985): 356.

124. *Lumber World Review,* 25 September 1912, p. 30.

125. Williams, *Americans and Their Forests,* chap. 14.

126. Hilgard, *Arid Regions,* p. 21.

127. Wallace, *Most Valuable Tree,* p. 50; Lukens to O. M. Grizzle, 4 Dec. 1914, Letterbook, Lukens Papers, Huntington Library.

128. Pratt, *Shade and Ornamental Trees of California,* pp. 69–72; John McLaren, *Gardening in California: Landscape and Flowers* (San Francisco: A. M. Robertson, 1907), pp. 100, 101; Charles F. Saunders, *Trees and Shrubs of California Gardens* (New York: Robert M. McBride, 1926), p. 26.

129. Eric Walther, "A Key to the Species of Eucalyptus Grown in California," *Proceedings of the California Academy of Sciences,* 4th ser., 27 (June 1928): 67.

130. Butterfield, "Introduction of Eucalyptus into California," p. 152.

131. Miller, "Eucalyptus Patriarch," p. 18; Food and Agricultural Organization of the United Nations, *Eucalypts for Planting* (Rome: Food and Agricultural Organization of the United Nations, 1979), pp. 137–39; Wallace, *Most Valuable Tree,* p. 42; California State Board of Forestry, *Third Biennial Report of the State Forester of the State of California* (Sacramento: W. W. Shannon, 1910), pp. 133–35.

132. Fire potential was not an issue in the period before 1914, when eucalyptus plantations were established; since that time people have built houses in the forested hill areas of Californian cities. U.S. Senate, Committee on Banking, Housing, and Urban Affairs, *Predisaster Assistance for Eucalyptus Trees in California: Hearing before the Subcommittee on Small Business,* 93d Cong., 1st sess., 1973 (Washington, D.C.: Government Printing Office, 1973), pp. 14–15, n. 130.

133. Ibid., pp. 23, 77, and passim.

134. Hilgard, *Arid Regions,* p. 21. See also on the failure of the eucalyptus to seed in California, *Garden and Forest,* 25 December 1889, p. 61: They do not germinate "on the hill-sides," but only in the "moist valleys" do they grow "from self-sown seed" (p. 615). G. Lull also reported in his *Handbook,* p. 9 that there could be no reliance on self-seeding.

135. Food and Agricultural Organization of the United Nations, *Eucalypts*

for Planting (Rome: Food and Agricultural Organization of the United Nations, 1955), p. 48; also Food and Agricultural Organization of the United Nations, *Eucalypts for Planting*, 1979 ed., pp. 137–39.

136. Royal Commission of Inquiry on Forestry, *Final Report, Part II*, p. 393.

137. Ibid., p. 204. Another who was impressed with the Californian eucalyptus plantings was Russell Grimwade, an up-and-coming Australian industrialist and philanthropist. Grimwade published in 1920 a reverential catalogue illustrating the beauty of the genus, but his interest was not merely aesthetic. The family's chemical business included medicines derived from the eucalypts, and Grimwade had already urged in 1912 their wider use in Australia in perfumes, medicinal preparations, and the like. Grimwade wondered, like MacMahon, whether the genus would become better known abroad than at home. Though Grimwade's plans for eucalyptus plantations did not prosper, he became the chief backer of the Australian Forest League, which sought to make Australians more aware of the value of their hardwood forests. Grimwade, *An Anthography of the Eucalypts* (Sydney: Angus and Robertson, 1920); J. R. Poynter, *Russell Grimwade* (Melbourne: Melbourne University Press, 1967), pp. 107–8, 209–10.

138. Royal Commission of Inquiry on Forestry, *Final Report, Part II*, p. 460.

139. Ibid., pp. 282–83, 240.

140. W. H. Selway, "The National Parks and Forest Reserves of Australia," *Transactions and Proceedings and Reports of the Royal Society of South Australia* 34 (1910): 279–305.

141. Poynter, *Grimwade*, pp. 107–8, 209–10.

142. Royal Commission of Inquiry on Forestry, *Final Report, Part II*, p. 394.

CHAPTER 4

1. Sir Arthur P. Douglas, *The Dominion of New Zealand* (London: Isaac Pitman, 1910), p. 114.

2. Nineteenth-century botanists drew a distinction between *insignis* and *radiata*. *Radiata* was said to be "the large-coned form." The leaves of *insignis* were much longer, while the cones of the *radiata* had scales much more elevated. Quoted in California State Board of Forestry, *Second Biennial Report of the California State Board of Forestry, for the Years 1887–88* (Sacramento: W. W. Shannon, 1888), p. 114.

3. Edward J. Wickson, *The California Fruits and How to Grow Them*, 2d rev. ed. (San Francisco: Dewey and Co., 1891), p. 583. The state forester Merritt Pratt noted in 1922 that Monterey pine was effective as an ornamental because it has "a very symmetrical, narrow and rounded topped crown, and rich green leaves beautifully arranged in clumps on the branches." Merritt B. Pratt, *Shade and Ornamental Trees of California* (Sacramento: California State Board of Forestry, 1922), p. 37.

4. Pratt, *Shade and Ornamental Trees of California*, p. 37; Shinn, *Pacific Rural Handbook* (San Francisco: Dewey and Co., 1879), p. 28.

5. Theodore Lukens to D. E. Hutchins, 28 July 1902, Box 1, Theodore Parker Lukens Papers, Huntington Library; A. D. Lindsay, *Report on Monterey Pine*

(Pinus Radiata D. Don) in Its Native Habitat, Commonwealth Forestry Bureau, bulletin no. 10 (Canberra: Govt. Printer, [1937, orig. prepared 1931–32]), p. 5.

6. Lukens to D. E. Hutchins, 28 July 1902, Box 1, Lukens Papers, Huntington Library; California State Board of Forestry, *Third Biennial Report of the State Forester of the State of California* (Sacramento: W. W. Shannon, Govt. Printer, 1910), p. 103.

7. M. H. Field, "Under the Pines at Monterey," *Rept. St. Bd. For., 1887–88,* pp. 115–16. The state forestry botanist called them "beautiful trees of medium size, extremely local, with headquarters at Point Pinos. Readily yielding to cultivation and very fast-growing." J. G. Lemon, "Pines of the Pacific Slope," ibid., p. 76. Charles Sprague Sargent called them "beautiful representatives of their class." *Garden and Forest,* 11 July 1888, p. 61.

8. Alexander Rule, *Forests of Australia* (Sydney: Angus and Robertson, 1967), p. 117.

9. Winsome Shepherd and Walter Cook, *The Botanic Garden [of] Wellington: A New Zealand History, 1840–1987* (Wellington, N.Z.: Millwood Press, 1988), pp. 95–111.

10. "Report on the Advisability of Establishing State Forests," *Victorian Parliamentary Papers, 1864–65,* no. 77, cited in Powell, *Environmental Management in Australia, 1788–1914* (Melbourne: Oxford University Press, 1976), p. 66.

11. Cooper, *Forest Culture and Eucalyptus Trees* (San Francisco: Cubery, 1876), p. 116; Neil Barr and John Cary, *Greening a Brown Land: The Australian Search for Sustainable Land Use* (Melbourne: Macmillan, 1992), pp. 55, 84.

12. Ferdinand von Mueller, *Forest Culture and Eucalyptus Trees,* comp. Ellwood Cooper (San Francisco: Cubery, 1876), p. 42.

13. Among pines recommended were the Norwegian spruce, "Douglas pine" [*sic*] "or any of the Pitch-pines of North America," ibid., p. 35.

14. See map, in appendix to E. Julius and A. L. Pinches, *South Australia: Empire Forestry Conference, 1928: Forestry Handbook* (Adelaide: Govt. Printer, 1928). An excellent overview of forestry policy in Australia on a statewide basis is L. T. Carron, "A History of Forestry and Forest Product Research in Australia," *Historical Records of Australian Science* 5 (November 1980): 7–57.

15. Julius and Pinches, *South Australia . . . Forestry Handbook,* p. 19; N. B. Lewis, *Silviculture of Exotic Plantation Species in South Australia,* (Adelaide: Govt. Printer, 1957), p. 6.

16. Donald Worster, *Rivers of Empire: Water, Aridity, and the Growth of the American West* (New York: Pantheon, 1985), p. 133.

17. Donald W. Meinig, *On the Margins of the Good Earth: The South Australian Wheat Frontier, 1869–1884* (1962; reprint, Adelaide: Rigby, 1970), pp. 59–60.

18. Meinig, *Margins of the Good Earth,* pp. 59–60; Samuel Aughey, *Sketches of the Physical Geography and Geology of Nebraska* (Omaha: Daily Rep. Book and Job Co., 1880), cited in C. W. Thornthwaite, "Modification of Rural Microclimates," in William L. Thomas, ed., *Man's Role in Changing the Face of the Earth* (Chicago: University of Chicago Press, 1956), p. 569.

19. Meinig, *Margins of the Good Earth,* p. 52.

20. *Educator* (Adelaide, South Australia), July 1893, pp. 83–85.

21. Mueller ed., p. 47.

22. Richard Refshauge, "John Ednie Brown," *Australian Dictionary of Biography*, vol. 3 (1851–1900), p. 261.

23. Meinig, *Margins of the Good Earth*, p. 71.

24. Brown, *A Practical Treatise on Tree Culture* (Adelaide: E. Spiller, Govt. Printer, 1881), p. 94.

25. Ibid., pp. 36–37.

26. Cooper ed., p. 16.

27. Brown, *Practical Treatise*, pp. vii; see also, *Educator* (Adelaide, South Australia), July 1893, p. 85, for a similar view.

28. George S. Perrin, *Woods and Forests of Tasmania. Annual Report, 1886–7* (Hobart: William Thomas Strutt, Govt. Printer, 1887), p. 16.

29. Brown, *Practical Treatise*, p. 93.

30. Julius and Pinches, *South Australia . . . Forestry Handbook*, p. 41.

31. W. S. Logan, "The Changing Landscape Significance of the Victoria–South Australia Boundary," in J. M. Powell, ed., *The Making of Rural Australia: Environment, Society and Economy: Geographical Readings* (Melbourne: Sorrett Publishing, 1974), p. 95.

32. Perrin, *Woods and Forests of Tasmania. Annual Report, 1886–7*, pp. 4, 13.

33. Lewis, *Silviculture of Exotic Plantation Species*, p. 6.

34. W. S. Gill's testimony, Royal Commission of Inquiry on Forestry, *Final Report, Part II. Minutes of Proceedings, Minutes of Evidence, and Appendix* (Sydney: W. A. Gullick, 1908), p. 561; see also Julius and Pinches, *South Australia. . . Forestry Handbook*, p. 23; Hugh Corbin, *The Necessity of Adequate Forests in South Australia; Being a Lecture Delivered to the Australian Natives' Association, Adelaide, September 3rd, 1917* . . . (Adelaide: Govt. Printer, 1917), p. 7.

35. Lewis, *Silviculture of Exotic Plantation Species*, pp. 6, 15.

36. For the spread of plantation pine agriculture on a state basis, consult also Carron, "History of Forestry and Forest Product Research," pp. 11, 13, 25, 35, 36, 38, 39; and John Dargavel, "Constructing Australia's Forests in the Image of Capital," in Stephen Dovers, ed., *Australian Environmental History: Essays and Cases* (Melbourne: Oxford University Press, 1994), p. 95.

37. Harry Tieamann, "Remarkable Pine Growth," *Journal of Forestry* 20 (April 1922): 431–32.

38. This is an observation I have made from a study of the landscape between the Blue Mountains and Bathurst in New South Wales, but see also Barr and Cary, *Greening a Brown Land*, pp. 84–85.

39. Royal Commission on Afforestation, *Report of the Royal Commission on Afforestation, Together with Appendices and Map (Minutes of Evidence Not Printed)*, South Australian Parliamentary Papers, no. 56 (Adelaide: Frank Trigg, Govt. Printer, 1936), pp. 27, 120, copy in E. H. F. Swain Papers, Mitchell Library, A3126; *Year Book of the Commonwealth of Australia. No. 48. 1962*, p. 1018; *The Australian Encyclopedia* (Sydney: Grollier Society of Australia, 1963), 2:256.

40. Dargavel, "Constructing Australia's Forests," pp. 95–96.

41. Field observations made by the author in July 1994 and July 1995 in New South Wales; Marilyn D. Fox, "Mediterranean Weeds: Exchanges of Invasive Plants between the Five Mediterranean Regions of the World," in F. di Castri, A. J. Hansen, and M. Debussche, eds., *Biological Invasions in Europe and the Mediterranean Basin* (Dordrecht, Neth.: Kluwer Academic Publications, 1990), p. 194; Julius and Pinches, *South Australia . . . Forestry Handbook,* p. 41.

42. Royal Commission of Inquiry on Forestry, *Final Report, Part I* (Sydney: W. A. Gullick, 1909), p. xxx.

43. R. M. Black, "The History of the Pinus Plantations in New South Wales," *New South Wales Forestry Recorder* 1 (January 1948): 30–37; Rule, *Forests of Australia,* p. 122.

44. Royal Commission of Inquiry on Forestry, *Final Report, Part II,* p. 558.

45. Ibid., p. 254; see also Corbin, *The Necessity of Adequate Forests in South Australia,* p. 7.

46. Australian Forestry Conference, *Report of Proceedings of the Australian Forestry Conference, Brisbane, April, 1922* (Brisbane: James Wrigley, Govt. Printer, 1922), p. 34.

47. D. E. Hutchins, *A Discussion of Australian Forestry* (Perth: Govt. Printer, 1916).

48. Pratt, *Shade and Ornamental Trees of California,* p. 37.

49. Royal Commission of Inquiry on Forestry, *Final Report, Part II,* p. 566.

50. Royal Commission of Inquiry on Forestry, *Final Report, Part I,* p. xxx.

51. *Science and Industry* 1 (December 1919): 459.

52. See also W. G. Pickering, chair of the Royal Commission on Forestry of Western Australia, in Australian Forestry Conference, *Australian Forestry Conference . . . 1922,* p. 29.

53. The sawmill that the state had established to utilize the pine had turned out more than 1 million fruit cases by 1922. Ibid., p. 28, 34.

54. Jane Lennon, "Victorian School of Forestry: Demonstration Forest," in John Dargavel and Sue Feary, eds., *Australia's Ever-Changing Forests II: Proceedings of the Second National Conference on Australian Forest History* (Canberra: Centre for Resource and Environmental Studies, 1993), p. 137.

55. Australian Forestry Conference, *Australian Forestry Conference . . . 1922,* p. 29.

56. Lewis, *Silviculture of Exotic Plantation Species,* p. 6; Lewis, *A Hundred Years of State Forestry. South Australia: 1875–1975* (Adelaide: Govt. Printer, 1975), pp. 15, 56.

57. Rule, *Forests of Australia,* p. 120; Julius and Pinches, *South Australia . . . Forestry Handbook,* pp. 35, 37.

58. Norman Hall, *Botanists of the Eucalypts,* (Melbourne: CSIRO, 1978), p. 60. Hall incorrectly states that Gill made the first plantings.

59. N. W. Jolly, *The Thinning of Pinus Radiata Plantations in the South-East of South Australia,* South Australian Woods and Forests Department, bulletin no. 4 (Adelaide: K. M. Stevens, Govt. Printer, 1950), p. 6.

60. Brian H. Bednall, *The Problem of Lower Volumes Associated with Second Rotations in Pinus Radiata Plantations in South Australia,* South Australian

Woods and Forests Department, bulletin no. 12 (Adelaide: Govt. Printer, 1968), pp. 4, 11.

61. *Australian Encyclopedia*, 8:503.

62. Andrew Clark, *The Invasion of New Zealand by People, Plants, and Animals: The South Island* (New Brunswick, N.J.: Rutgers University Press, 1949), p. 374.

63. Royal Commission on Afforestation, *Report*, pp. 55, 129.

64. T. A. Foley, *Radiata Pine Is a Proven Building and Utility Timber* (N.p.: [New Zealand Timber Trade Commissioner], [1956]), pp. 2, 11–12, typescript copy in Mitchell Library, Sydney.

65. An example of softwood specialization is reported in Michael Roche, John Dargavel, and Jenny Mills, "Tracking the KTC from Kauri to Karri to Chatlee," in Dargavel and Feary, eds., *Australia's Ever-Changing Forests II*, pp. 187–95, 200.

66. Clark, *Invasion of New Zealand*, p. 372; J. S. Yeates, "Sap-Stain in Timber of Pinus Radiata (Insignis)," *New Zealand Journal of Science and Technology* 8 (November 1924): 248; Shepherd and Cook, *The Botanic Garden Wellington*, pp. 95–111. See also Tom Brooking, "Economic Transformation," in W. H. Oliver with B. R. Williams, ed., *The Oxford History of New Zealand* (Wellington and Oxford: Oxford University Press and the Clarendon Press, 1981), p. 230.

67. *The Forestry Question in New South Wales with Special Reference to the Present and Future Timber Supply* (Sydney: W. A. Pepperday, and Co., 1915), pp. 6, 9.

68. Jones, in Australian Forestry Conference, *Australian Forestry Conference . . . 1922*, p. 61.

69. Colin M. Hall, *Wasteland to World Heritage: Preserving Australia's Wilderness* (Carlton, Vic.: Melbourne University Press, 1992).

70. Richard T. Baker, *The Hardwoods of Australia and Their Economics* (Sydney: W. A. Gullick, Govt. Printer, 1919), p. 413, 421. Edward Swain also reflected this aesthetic. He was a champion of the sustained yield of Queensland rain forests in the 1920s primarily for their value as cabinet timber. L. T. Carron, "Edward Harold Fulcher Swain," *Australian Dictionary of Biography*, vol. 12 (1891–1939), p. 146.

71. *Forestry Question in New South Wales*, pp. 1, 6. Appreciation of the timber value for high quality woodwork was an important part of the aesthetic appreciation of eucalyptus for Russell Grimwade, a key figure in the Australian Forest League of Victoria. See his *An Anthography of the Eucalypts* (Sydney: Angus and Robertson, 1920); and J. R. Poynter, *Russell Grimwade* (Melbourne: Melbourne University Press, 1967).

72. Quoted in I. L. Irby, "The Redistribution and Readjustment of Tree Life as It Affects Australian and Tasmanian Forestry," in Australian Forestry Conference, *Australian Forestry Conference . . . 1922*, p. 58.

73. Royal Commission on Afforestation, *Report*, p. 27.

74. E. H. F. Swain, *An Australian Study of American Forestry* (Brisbane: Anthony J. Cummings, 1918), p. 69. For an endorsement, but one possibly written anonymously by Swain himself, see [Agricola], "Afforestation," *Forum* (Sydney), 9 April 1924, p. 4.

75. Australian Forestry Conference, *Australian Forestry Conference...* *1922*, pp. 34, 61; Ivan Holliday and Ron Hill, *A Field Guide to Australian Trees* (Adelaide: Rigby, 1969), p. 58.

76. Swain, *An Australian Study of American Forestry*, pp. 68, 69; Australian Forestry Conference, *Australian Forestry Conference... 1922*, p. 31. Where Swain did introduce pines, he showed an American influence and made extensive and economically valuable plantings of southern yellow pine in the region north of Brisbane. Edward Harold Fulcher Swain Papers, Envelope 1, p. 47, Oxley Memorial Library.

77. Swain Papers, Envelope 1, p. 47.

78. However a good deal of attention was given to such matters as thinning for regrowth, aerial seeding, and other regenerative measures. On the history of Australian forestry policy, see Carron, "History of Forestry and Forest Product Research," esp. pp. 12, 21, 32.

79. Poynter, *Grimwade*, pp. 107–8, 209–10.

80. Lennon, "Victorian School of Forestry," p. 138; Australian Forestry Conference, *Australian Forestry Conference... 1922*, p. 61; Royal Commission of Inquiry on Forestry, *Final Report, Part II*, p. 394. Today, South Australia's *radiata* plantations are rotated, on average, at thirty-seven years. See *Sydney Morning Herald*, 26 September 1994, p. 22.

81. Sue Feary, "Penders Perpetual Forest Plantation," in Dargavel and Feary, *Australia's Ever-Changing Forests II*, p. 78. See also the early example in J. Blackburne, "Natural and Artificial Reproduction of Native Hardwoods," *Journal of the Department of Agriculture* (Victoria) 3 (December 1905): 696–99.

82. *Daily Telegraph* (Sydney), 12 December 1924, p. 6; Ivan M. Elchibegoff, *United States International Timber Trade in the Pacific Area* (Stanford, Calif.: Stanford University Press, 1949), pp. 103, 106.

CHAPTER 5

1. David Lowenthal, *George Perkins Marsh: Versatile Vermonter* (New York: Columbia University Press, 1958), pp. 307–8.

2. Donald J. Pisani, *From the Family Farm to Agribusiness: The Irrigation Crusade in California and the West, 1850–1931* (Berkeley and Los Angeles: University of California Press, 1984), pp. 8, 156.

3. *Irrigation: The Mulgoa Irrigation Settlement* (N.p., [c. 1891]), p. 15; E. W. Hilgard, T. C. Jones, and R. W. Furnas, *Report on the Climatic and Agricultural Features and the Agricultural Practice and Needs of the Arid Regions of the Pacific Slope...* (Washington: Govt. Printing Office, 1882), p. 28.

4. Paul Rhode, "Learning, Capital Accumulation, and the Transformation of California Agriculture," *Journal of Economic History* 55 (Dec. 1995): 787.

5. Henry A. Brainard, "Irrigation for the Development of Fruit," California State Board of Horticulture, *Fourth Biennial Report of the State Board of Horticulture of the State of California, for 1893–94* (Sacramento: A. J. Johnston, 1894), pp. 216–20; California State Board of Horticulture, *Annual Report of the State Board of Horticulture of the State of California, for 1892* (Sacramento: A. J. Johnston, 1892), p. 40.

6. Hilgard, *Arid Regions*, p. 130.

7. Ibid.

8. *Rept. St. Bd. Hort., 1893–94*, p. 302; J. L. Thompson, "Olive Culture," *Agricultural Gazette of New South Wales* 2 (August 1891): 473.

9. Brainard, "Irrigation for the Development of Fruit," p. 220; California State Board of Horticulture, *Third Biennial Report of the State Board of Horticulture of the State of California, for the Thirty-eighth and Thirty-ninth Fiscal Years* (Sacramento: J. D. Young, 1888), p. 272.

10. Kenneth Thompson, "Irrigation as a Menace to Health in California: A Nineteenth Century View," *Geographical Review* 59 (April 1969): 195–214.

11. Hilgard, *Arid Regions*, p. 58.

12. Thomas Bard to James De Barth Shorb, 10 August 1886, and 27 May 1886, Box 8, James De Barth Shorb Collection, Huntington Library.

13. Ellwood Cooper, "Address," in California State Board of Horticulture, *Biennial Report of the State Board of Horticulture of the State of California, for 1885 and 1886. Also Appendix for 1887* (Sacramento: P. L. Shoaff, 1887), p. 33.

14. Charles R. Kutzleb, "Can Forests Bring Rain to the Plains?" *Forest History* 15 (October 1971): 21; David M. Emmons, "Theories of Increased Rainfall and the Timber Culture Act of 1873," ibid., pp. 6–14.

15. Lawrence B. Lee, "William Ellsworth Smythe and the Irrigation Movement: A Reconsideration," *Pacific Historical Review* 41 (August 1972): 304–5.

16. *California Fruit Grower and Fruit Trade Review*, 28 April 1894, p. 327.

17. *Rural Californian* 18 (January 1895): 12. See also Hiram A. Reid, *History of Pasadena . . .* (Pasadena: Pasadena History Company, 1895), p. 412.

18. California State Board of Horticulture, *Seventh Biennial Report of the State Board of Horticulture of the State of California, for 1899–1900* (Sacramento: A. J. Johnston, 1901), pp. 81, 78.

19. Brainard, "Irrigation for the Development of Fruit," p. 216.

20. *California Fruit Grower and Fruit Trade Review*, 7 October 1893, p. 287.

21. See William Cronon, "Landscapes of Abundance and Scarcity," in Clyde A. Milner II, Carol A. O'Connor, and Martha A. Sandweiss, eds., *The Oxford History of the American West* (New York: Oxford University Press, 1994), pp. 616–17.

22. International Irrigation Congress, *Official Report of the International Irrigation Congress Held at Los Angeles, California, October, 1893* (Los Angeles: Chamber of Commerce, 1893), p. 8. B. M. Lelong spoke of the "science of irrigation," *California Fruit Grower and Fruit Trade Review*, 12 November 1892, p. 412.

23. See, for example, *California Fruit Grower and Fruit Trade Review*, 7 October 1893, pp. 287, 290, 21 October 1893, p. 330; *Rural Californian* 18 (September 1895): 448–49, 451.

24. James Boyd, "Irrigation," in California State Board of Horticulture, *Fourth Biennial Report of the State Board of Horticulture of the State of California, for 1893–94* (Sacramento: A. J. Johnston, 1894), p. 324.

25. William E. Smythe, "Forest and Irrigation," in *Rept. St. Bd. Hort., 1899–1900*, pp. 137–43.

26. Ibid. Still, the focus was on California's peculiar problems. The 1902 convention asked for the secretary of agriculture to implement Elwood Mead's work on irrigation and drainage in California for the Department of Agriculture's Office of Irrigation. See California State Board of Horticulture, *Eighth Biennial Report of the State Board of Horticulture of the State of California, for 1901–1902* (Sacramento: A. J. Johnston, 1902), pp. 250, 377, 423.

27. Twelfth State Fruit Growers' Convention, in California State Board of Horticulture, *Annual Report of the State Board of Horticulture of the State of California, for 1889* (Sacramento: J. D. Young, 1890), p. 462.

28. The Memorial of the Fruit Growers of California to the Congress, passed at the 1889 convention also demonstrated the priorities of fruit growers. *Rept. St. Bd. Hort., 1893–94*, p. 328.

29. Kinney, *Forest and Water* (Los Angeles: Post Publishing, 1900), p. 74.

30. People like Shorb, as Donald J. Pisani notes, were not disinterested observers. Pisani, *Family Farm to Agribusiness*, p. 218; Donald Worster, *Rivers of Empire: Water, Aridity and the Growth of the American West* (New York: Pantheon, 1985), pp. 100–101, also emphasizes the speculation behind the garden concept. For a good brief discussion, see Norris Hundley, *The Great Thirst: Californians and Water, 1770s–1990s* (Berkeley and Los Angeles: University of California Press, 1992), pp. 89–90.

31. *Transactions of the California State Agricultural Society, during the Year 1874* (Sacramento: G. H. Springer, 1874), p. 437; Arthur Maass and Raymond L. Anderson, *. . . and the Desert Shall Rejoice: Conflict, Growth, and Justice in Arid Environments* (Cambridge: MIT Press, 1978), pp. 157–70.

32. M. Catherine Miller, *Flooding the Courtrooms: Law and Water in the Far West* (Lincoln: University of Nebraska Press, 1993), p. 13.

33. William Ellsworth Smythe, *The Conquest of Arid America*, rev. ed. (1905; reprint, Seattle: University of Washington Press, 1969), pp. 100, 101–2, 104.

34. Quoted in Charles Shinn, "An Old-Fashioned Countryside," *American Garden* 11 (August 1890): 452. See more generally, Glenn S. Dumke, *The Boom of the Eighties in Southern California* (San Marino, Calif.: Huntington Library, 1944), esp. pp. 212–13.

35. Benedict to Shorb, 28 March 1890, Box 10, Shorb Collection, Huntington Library.

36. Jeanne Carr to Frank Chauncey Patten, 13 May 1896, Box 5, Jeanne C. Carr Papers, Huntington Library. Smythe lamented the way the Riverside cooperative venture was overtaken by "the speculative instinct." Smythe, *Conquest of Arid America*, p. 101.

37. Alexander Craw, "Foreign Pests and Diseases," in *Rept. St. Bd. Hort., 1893–94*, p. 142.

38. *Garden and Forest*, 23 November 1892, p. 561; Shinn, "Old-Fashioned Countryside," p. 452.

39. Smythe, *Conquest of Arid America*, p. 94; Kevin Starr, *Americans and the California Dream, 1850–1915* (New York: Oxford University Press, 1973), esp. pp. 200–202; see also Spencer J. Olin Jr., "Bible Communism and the Origins of Orange County," *California History* 58 (fall 1979): 230; *Mulgoa Irrigation*, p. 15.

40. Smythe, *Conquest of Arid America,* pp. 42, 121–22.

41. Abbot Kinney, *Eucalyptus* (Los Angeles: B. R. Baumgardt, 1895), pp. 65–66.

42. Charles Dudley Warner, *Our Italy* (New York: Harper and Bros., 1891).

43. Smythe, *Conquest of Arid America,* pp. 41–42.

44. Ibid.; Robert V. Hine, *California's Utopian Colonies* (San Marino, Calif.: Huntington Library, 1953).

45. On this, see Rhys Isaac, *The Transformation of Virginia, 1740–1790* (Chapel Hill: University of North Carolina Press, 1983), pp. 12–13; Erwin Panofsky, *Meaning in the Visual Arts* (Garden City, N.J.: Anchor Books, 1955), pp. 295–320; and Simon Schama, *Landscape and Memory* (London: Fontana Press, 1995).

46. Warner, *Our Italy,* p. 15. Warner's aesthetic appreciation was exuberant. He spoke of "a land of perpetual sun and ever-flowing breeze, looked down on by purple mountain ranges tipped here and there with enduring snow."

47. Smythe, *Conquest of Arid America,* p. 151; Hilgard, *Arid Regions,* p. 29.

48. Shorb, quoted in Cooper, "Address," p. 33; Smythe, *Conquest of Arid America,* p. 38.

49. Hilgard, *Arid Regions,* p. 58.

50. Smythe, *Conquest of Arid America,* p. 149.

51. Ibid., p. 128.

52. Elwood Mead, *Report of Irrigation Investigations in California . . . ,* U.S. Department of Agriculture, Office of Experiment Stations, bulletin no. 100 (Washington, D.C.: Government Printing Office, 1901), p. 29.

53. Ibid., p. 28.

54. *Rept. St. Bd. Hort., 1893–94,* p. 325.

55. Smythe, *Conquest of Arid America,* p. 44. By "industrial" he did not mean the creation of large-scale industrial production, however logical or inevitable this may seem in retrospect.

56. T. Rooke, "Irrigation Work in California, and Its Relation to the Transmission of Electricity," *Journals and Proceedings of the Royal Society of New South Wales* 40 (1906): lxxii–c.

57. *California Fruit Grower and Fruit Trade Review,* 7 October 1893, p. 290.

58. Quoted in John L. Thomas, *Alternative America: Edward Bellamy, Henry George, Henry Demarest Lloyd, and the Adversary Tradition* (Cambridge: Harvard University Press, Belknap Press, 1987), p. 193.

59. Ebenezer Howard, *Tomorrow: A Peaceful Path to Real Reform* (London: n.p., 1898) republished as *Garden Cities of Tomorrow,* ed. Lewis Mumford (London: Faber and Faber, 1946); Thomas, *Alternative America,* p. 192.

60. Lewis Mumford, "The Garden City Idea and Modern Planning," in *Garden Cities of Tomorrow,* pp. 29–40, quote at 29. The first British garden city, Letchworth, was commenced in 1903.

61. There was even a settlement based on artesian irrigation in Kansas called "Garden City," and Smythe reported on this. Smythe, *Conquest of Arid America,* p. 110.

62. Ibid., p. 102.

63. Ibid., p. 46.

64. *California Horticulturalist and Floral Magazine* 3 (March 1873): 72. See also, ibid., 3 (February 1873): 40.

65. *California Fruit Grower and Fruit Trade Review*, 7 January 1893, p. 4. The same publication spoke of irrigation as a "a civilized method of producing crops" in comparison with the "barbarous mode of cattle-grazing" common in the American West.

66. *Rept. St. Bd. Hort., 1893–94*, pp. 324–25.

67. Elwood Mead, "Relation of Land Settlement to Irrigation Development," in *Proceedings of the Pan-Pacific Science Congress, Australia, 1923*, 2 vols. (Melbourne: H. J. Green, Govt. Printer, 1923), 1:61.

68. *Rept. St. Bd. Hort., 1893–94*, pp. 324–25.

69. Cited by Hilgard, *Arid Regions*, p. 74.

70. Ibid., p. 77; *Rept. St. Bd. Hort., 1893–94*, pp. 324–25.

71. Smythe, *Conquest of Arid America*, pp. 104, 45.

72. On women and nature, see Mario Klarer, "Woman and Arcadia: The Impact of Ancient Utopian Thought on the Early Image of America," *Journal of American Studies* 27, no. 1 (1993): 1–17, esp. p. 17; on women and "civilization," see Sylvana Tomaselli, "The Enlightenment Debate on Women," *History Workshop*, no. 20 (autumn 1985): 101–24. See also, more generally, Carolyn Merchant, *The Death of Nature: Women, Ecology, and the Scientific Revolution* (San Francisco: Harper and Row, 1980).

73. Smythe's chosen illustration, a four-month-old ranch in northern Yakima, Washington, is a picture of isolation and shows both husband and wife tending cows. *Conquest of Arid America*, pp. xx, xxi, 46.

74. *California Fruit Grower and Fruit Trade Review*, 1 June 1895, p. 438; H. P. Stabler, "The California Fruit-Grower, and the Labor Supply," in *Rept. St. Bd. Hort., 1901–1902*, pp. 268–72, and discussion, pp. 272–81.

75. McBride, "A Woman's Orchard," *Rept. St. Bd. Hort., 1893–94*, p. 194.

76. "Report of San Joaquin Horticultural Commission," *Rept. St. Bd. Hort., 1887–88*, p. 272.

77. California State Board of Horticulture, *Biennial Report of the State Board of Horticulture, 1884* (Sacramento: James J. Ayers, 1884), p. 55.

78. *California Fruit Grower*, 9 November 1889, p. 5; Smythe, *Conquest of Arid America*, p. 149. See California Employment Committee of the Fruit Growers Convention, in *Rept. St. Bd. Hort., 1901–1902*, pp. 271, 273; and California State Board of Horticulture, *First Biennial Report of the Commissioner of Horticulture of the State of California, for 1903–1904* (Sacramento: W. W. Shannon, 1905), p. 387.

79. Donald J. Pisani, *To Reclaim a Divided West: Water, Law, and Public Policy, 1848–1902* (Albuquerque: University of New Mexico Press, 1992), p. 251.

80. Hundley, *Great Thirst*, p. 98.

81. Donald J. Pisani, "Reclamation and Social Engineering in the Progressive Era," *Agricultural History* 57 (1983): 46–63.

82. Mead to John D. Works, 24 December 1912, Box 4, John D. Works Papers, Bancroft Library.

83. Mead to Franklin K. Lane, 26 July 1915, in Box 4, Works Papers, Ban-

croft Library; A. P. Davis to Elwood Mead, [26? July 1915], and Mead to Davis, 22 July 1915, Box 1, Elwood Mead Papers, Water Resources Center Library.

CHAPTER 6

1. Rev. James Ballantyne, *Our Colony in 1880: Pictorial and Descriptive* (Melbourne: M. L. Hutchinson, Glasgow Book Warehouse, 1880), p. 116.

2. Sir Colin Campbell Scott-Moncrieff to Alfred Deakin, 19 February 1888, Box 29, Folder 1, Series 10, Alfred Deakin Papers, National Library.

3. Beverley Kingston, *1860–1900: Glad Confident Morning,* vol. 3 of The Oxford History of Australia, ed. Geoffrey Bolton (Melbourne: Oxford University Press, 1988), 258–70; on the comparative position, see Gary Cross, "Comparative Exceptionalism: Rethinking the Hartz Thesis in the Settler Societies of Nineteenth-Century United States and Australia," *Australasian Journal of American Studies* 14 (July 1995): 15–43.

4. William Hammond Hall to Hugh McColl, 24 October 1884, and 10 April 1885, Box 3, Letterbook 1, William Hammond Hall Papers, Bancroft Library; J. M. Powell, *Watering the Garden State: Water, Land, and Community in Victoria, 1834–1988* (Sydney: Allen and Unwin, 1989), pp. 89–90, 99–100; Valerie Yule, "Hugh McColl," *Australian Dictionary of Biography,* vol. 5 (1851–1890), pp. 131–32; *Victorian Parliamentary Debates,* 29 November 1881, pp. 917–20 (hereafter *VPD*).

5. Donald S. Garden, "George Gordon," *Australian Dictionary of Biography,* vol. 4 (1851–1890), p. 270.

6. See Royal Commission on Water Supply, *First Progress Report,* by Alfred Deakin, *Irrigation in Western America* (Melbourne: John Ferres, Govt. Printer, 1885), pp. 120–30, where the bill is reproduced; *VPD,* 24 June 1886, pp. 424–25; Powell, *Watering the Garden State,* p. 101; Donald J. Pisani, *From the Family Farm to Agribusiness: The Irrigation Crusade in California and the West, 1850–1931* (Berkeley and Los Angeles: University of California Press, 1984), chap. 9.

7. Deakin, *Irrigation in Western America,* p. 52.

8. Cf. Donald Worster, *Rivers of Empire: Water, Aridity, and the Growth of the American West* (New York: Pantheon, 1985), p. 146; see Deakin, *Irrigation in Western America,* pp. 94, 12, 36–38.

9. *VPD,* 14 September 1886, p. 1454.

10. Ibid., 24 June 1886, p. 428.

11. Royal Commission on Water Supply, *Fourth Progress Report. Irrigation in Egypt and Italy. A Memorandum for the Members of the Royal Commission on Water Supply* (Melbourne: Robert S. Brain, 1887), pp. 21, 41.

12. Deakin, *Irrigation in Western America,* p. 87.

13. Victoria Water Supply Department, *Proceedings of the First Conference of Irrigationists, Held in Melbourne on 25th, 26th, and 28th March, 1890* (Melbourne: Robert S. Brain, 1890), p. 15.

14. *VPD,* 24 June 1886, p. 429.

15. Hall to Deakin, 16 August 1885, and 26 December 1885, Box 3, Letterbook 1, William Hammond Hall Papers, Bancroft Library.

16. *VPD*, 24 June 1886, p. 427.

17. Ibid., p. 430; Lionel Frost, "Government and Economic Development: The Case of Irrigation in Victoria," *Australian Economic History Review* 32 (March 1992): 52–53.

18. *VPD*, 24 June 1886, pp. 427–28, 430.

19. J. M. Powell, *Plains of Promise, Rivers of Destiny: Water Management and the Development of Queensland, 1824–1990* (Bowen Hills, Qld.: Boolarong Publications, 1991), pp. 66–67; Deakin, *Irrigation in Western America*, pp. 32–33, 49.

20. Alfred Deakin, "Irrigation in Australia," *The Year-Book of Australia for 1892* (London: E. A. Petherick and Co., 1893), p. 84.

21. *Agricultural Gazette of New South Wales* 14 (February 1903): 110; [William Rowan Brown], "Artesian Water," *Australian Encyclopedia* (1963 ed.), 1:262–69, esp. p. 265.

22. George Gordon, "American and Australian Irrigation," in *Transactions and Proceedings of the Victorian Engineers' Association, 1883–85* (Melbourne: Haase, Duffus, and Co., 1886), 1:109–10, 128. Gordon's work was reprinted in the *Australian Irrigationist* and circulated in the United States. See William Hammond Hall to Deakin, [1886], Box 1, Folder 1, Ms. 913, William Hammond Hall Papers, California Historical Society.

23. *VPD*, 14 September 1886, p. 1461, 30 September 1886, p. 1697.

24. Ibid., 30 September 1886, p. 1690 (Mr. G. D. Carter, West Melbourne).

25. Ibid., 24 June 1886, pp. 427, 445–47.

26. Margaret Steven, "John Edward West," *Australian Dictionary of Biography*, vol. 12 (1891–1939), p. 446; West, "Dried Fruits," in Department of Agriculture, Victoria, *Course of Lectures Delivered by Officers of the Department of Agriculture, during the Year 1891, in the Working Men's College, Melbourne* (Melbourne: Robert S. Brain, Govt. Printer, [c. 1891]), pp. 51–56.

27. Alexander Bruce, "The Live Stock and Meat Trade of the United States of America," *Agricultural Gazette of New South Wales* 5 (November 1894): 782–83.

28. *California Fruit Grower and Fruit Trade Review*, 22 April 1893, p. 335; 28 January 1893, p. 71. Other Australian visitors were P. P. Fraser, "Universal Irrigation," *New Zealand Country Journal* 15 (September 1891): 390–94; and W. A. Hutchinson, reported in *Irrigation: The Mulgoa Irrigation Settlement* (N.p., [c. 1891]), p. 22.

29. George Riddoch, *Dairying and Irrigation in Great Britain and America. Report by the Hon. Geo. Riddoch, M.L.C. upon the Dairying Industry and Irrigation Schemes of Great Britain and the United States of America* (Adelaide: n.p., 1903); Riddoch, *Irrigation and Other Matters in Egypt, America, and India. Reports Furnished by Hon. Geo. Riddoch, M.L.C. as Honorary Commissioner to the Government of South Australia* (Adelaide: Vardon and Pritchard, 1905), esp. pp. 18–19; Leith MacGillivray, "John Riddoch and George Riddoch," *Australian Dictionary of Biography*, vol. 11 (1891–1939), pp. 390–91; A. J. Hill, "Sir Henry Somer Gullett," *Australian Dictionary of Biography*, vol. 9 (1891–1939), pp. 137–39; Frank Clarke, *Californian Notes. Report*

Made to the Hon. F. Hagelthorn on Immigration, Irrigation, Fruit-Growing, and Trade (Melbourne: Albert J. Mullett, Govt. Printer, 1915).

30. See, for example, Alfred J. McClatchie, "Crops under Irrigation," *Journal of the Department of Agriculture* (Victoria) 2 (May 1903): 15–17; "Means to Ameliorate the Conditions of Arid Regions," *Agricultural Gazette of New South Wales* 14 (February 1903): 97–110. Not all such information was positively received. See H. G. McKinney, "Irrigation," *Agricultural Gazette of New South Wales* 2 (December 1891): 269.

31. Bailey Brown, *Second Chapter of Revelations: Practical and Practicable Suggestions on Land Settlement, Irrigation, Crops, and Industries Which Will Build Up the Colony* (Brisbane: Muir and Morcom, 1891).

32. John West, "Irrigation Development in Western America," in *Lectures Delivered by Officers of the Department of Agriculture, during the Year 1891*, p. 5. See also John L. Dow in Lloyd G. Churchward, *Australia and America, 1788–1972: An Alternative History* (Sydney: APCOL, 1979), p. 79; *Mulgoa Irrigation*, p. 13.

33. Deakin letter, November 1885, in *Transactions and Proceedings of the Victorian Engineers' Association* 1 (1883–85): 139.

34. West, "Irrigation Development," p. 10.

35. Quoted in *Mulgoa Irrigation*, pp. 12–13.

36. West, "Irrigation Development," p. 10; *Mildura Cultivator* 1 (January 1891): 75.

37. John L. Dow, *The Australian in America* (Melbourne: *Leader* Office, 1884), pp. 42, 59–63; T. K. Dow, *A Tour in America* (Melbourne: *Australasian* Office, 1884), p. 133.

38. Harold U. Faulkner, *The Decline of Laissez Faire, 1897–1917*, vol. 7 of *The Economic History of the United States* (New York: Holt, Rinehart, and Winston, 1951), 132, 346, 348; Irvin M. May Jr., "Research in Land-Grant Universities: The Agricultural Experiment Station," in Trudy H. Peterson, ed., *Farmers, Bureaucrats, and Middlemen: Historical Perspectives on American Agriculture* (Washington, D.C.: Howard University Press, 1980), pp. 177–99.

39. Alan W. Black, "The Genesis of Australian Agricultural Colleges in the Nineteenth Century," *Australian Journal of Politics and History* 21 (April 1975): 42–55; Churchward, *Australia & America*, pp. 79–80.

40. See, for example, Queensland Department of Agriculture, *Annual Report of the Department of Agriculture, for the Year 1890–91* (Brisbane: James C. Beal, 1891), esp. pp. 37–38; E. M. Shelton, *Canning and Otherwise Preserving Fruits for the Home and Market*, Department of Agriculture, bulletin no. 5 (Brisbane: James C. Beal, 1890); on the influence of American personnel in Western Australia, see *Journal of the Department of Agriculture of Western Australia* 7 (January-June 1903): 170–73.

41. Dow, *The Australian in America*, p. 42.

42. Quoted in John Hammond Moore, ed., *Australians in America, 1876–1976* (St. Lucia: University of Queensland Press, 1977), p. 30.

43. *Sydney Mail*, 27 December 1890. See also *Irrigation in New South Wales: The Mulgoa-Chaffey Irrigation Colony . . .* (Sydney: S. E. Lees, 1891), p. 6.

44. On the role of the state in Australian economic and environmental development, see especially Alan Gilbert, "The State and Nature in Australia," *Australian Cultural History* 1 (1982): 9–28; Cross, "Comparative Exceptionalism," passim.

45. *California Fruit Grower and Fruit Trade Review,* 22 April 1893, p. 335, 22 January 1893, p. 71.

46. Ibid., 1 April 1893, p. 274.

47. Ibid., 3 June 1893, p. 451; 8 July 1893, p. 37.

48. Ibid., 9 March 1895, p. 187. Smith stressed that "Messrs. Chaffey Brothers' methods of packing in neat, handy packets were superior to those of California," that "the quality and appearance of their goods were even better than those of the Pacific slope," and that "the Murray Irrigation Colonies have the chance of doing as successfully as in California" because "their natural opportunities are equal to anything I saw in any part of California."

49. Evidence of George Ward, Royal Commission on Vegetable Products, *Fourth Progress Report, and Continuation of the Minutes of Evidence . . .* (Melbourne: Robert S. Brain, 1887), pp. 52–61.

50. George Geiger, *The Philosophy of Henry George* (New York: Macmillan, 1933), p. 71.

51. Dow, *The Australian in America,* p. 38; West, "Irrigation Development," p. 7.

52. Dow, *Our Land Acts and a Land Tax: Or, the Land Question and How to Deal with It* (Melbourne: Dunn and Collins, 1877), pp. 10, 12.

53. Ibid. Cf. Geiger, *Philosophy of Henry George,* pp. 386, 392; J. M. Powell, *Environmental Management in Australia, 1788–1914* (Melbourne: Oxford University Press, 1976), pp. 95, 149, 202.

54. Powell, *Watering the Garden State,* p. 149.

55. Kingston, *Glad Confident Morning,* pp. 268–69. By the 1880s and 1890s, the Single Tax became linked with the rise of the labor movement and socialist doctrines in Australasia. Robin Gollan, *Radical and Working Class Politics: A Study of Eastern Australia, 1850–1910* (Melbourne: Melbourne University Press, 1960), pp. 119–21.

56. Bruce Scates, "Millennium or Pandemonium?: Radicalism in the Labour Movement, Sydney, 1889–1899," *Labour History,* no. 50 (May 1986): 74, 80, demonstrates the moral dimensions of the Single Tax crusade and its lower-middle-class constituency in New South Wales.

57. *Land of Sunshine* 15 (December 1901): 487–500. Two recent volumes that focus on the Progressive reform movement, William Deverell and Tom Sitton, eds., *California Progressivism Revisited* (Berkeley and Los Angeles: University of California Press, 1994); and, more indirectly, William Deverell, *Railroad Crossing: Californians and the Railroad, 1850–1910* (Berkeley and Los Angeles: University of California Press, 1994), provide a good frame of reference for my study, but these books do not deal with the pre-Progressive politics of the farmers and horticulturalists.

58. Ballantyne, *Our Colony in 1880,* pp. 116–17.

59. *Mulgoa Irrigation,* p. 4.

60. Deakin Diary, Letters to Catherine Deakin transcribed, 29 January 1885,

Box 9, Series 2, Deakin Papers, National Library; George Seddon and Mari Davis, eds., *Man and Landscape in Australia Towards an Ecological Vision* (Canberra: Aust. Govt. Pub. Service, 1976), p. 42.

61. Bernard Smith, ed., *Documents in Art and Taste in Australia: The Colonial Period, 1770–1914* (Melbourne: Oxford University Press, 1975), pp. 135–36; Geoffrey Serle, *From Deserts the Prophets Come: The Creative Spirit in Australia, 1788–1972* (Melbourne: Heinemann, 1973), p. 17.

62. Rod Ritchie, *Seeing the Rainforests in Nineteenth-Century Australia* (Sydney: Rainforest Publishing, 1989); Deakin Diary, Letters to Catherine Deakin transcribed, 31 March, 4 April 1885, Box 9, Series 2, Deakin Papers, National Library.

63. Quoted in Frederick D. Kershner Jr., "George Chaffey and the Irrigation Frontier," *Agricultural History* 27 (October 1953): 117–118 n.; A. S. Kenyon, "The Story of the Mallee," *Victorian Historical Magazine* 4 (June 1915): 175–98; James McColl, "Hugh McColl and the Water Question in Victoria," *Victorian Historical Magazine* 5 (June 1917): 145–63.

64. A. R. E. Burton, *Mildura, the True Australia Felix, How to Get Rich in Victoria* (Melbourne: Spectator Publishing, 1892), pp. 4, 5. For biographical information and details of Burton's career as Organizing Secretary of the Australian Scripture Education League, see Australian Scripture Education League Scrapbook, 1889–1894, p. 51, David Scott Mitchell Library.

65. *Mulgoa Irrigation*, p. 4.

66. Burton, *Mildura*, p. 14; Deakin also noted this point in his *Irrigation in Western America*, pp. 60–61.

67. *Mulgoa Irrigation*, p. 20. Nature was to be transformed by technology, as in California. In their "accidental natural conditions," trees were "obviously impoverished," but under "human intelligence" a tree "becomes a machine with a regular output."

68. West, "Irrigation Development," p. 6.

69. Henry S. Gullett, *Irrigation and Intense Culture in Other Countries: A Series of Articles Dealing with Agriculture in Italy and America . . .* (Melbourne: J. Kemp, Govt. Printer, [c. 1910]), p. 13.

70. *Argus* (Melbourne), 15 April 1885, p. 7; Moore, *Australians in America*, pp. 27–28.

71. Denis Cosgrove, "An Elemental Division: Water Control and Engineered Landscape," in Cosgrove and Geoff Petts, eds., *Water, Engineering, and Landscape: Water Control and Landscape Transformation in the Modern Period* (London: Belhaven Press, 1990), pp. 1–11; Deakin, *Irrigation in Western America*, pp. 34–37.

72. Dow, *Our Land Acts and a Land Tax*, p. 10; Burton, *Mildura*, p. 4.

73. Burton, *Mildura*, pp. 22–23.

74. Lionel Frost, *The New Urban Frontier: Urbanisation and City-Building in Australasia and the American West* (Kensington, N.S.W.: University of New South Wales Press, 1991), p. 38.

75. *Mulgoa Irrigation*, p. 11.

76. Ibid., pp. 11–12.

77. Brown, *Second Chapter of Revelations*, p. 8. The *Sydney Mail* hoped

irrigation would combat the failure to develop in the cities "avenues for employ-ment" for "young men and women." These were forced to "work for wages that shrink in consequences to a starvation limit." *Sydney Mail,* 27 December 1890.

78. Rev. Horace Tucker, *The New Arcadia: An Australian Story* (London: George Robertson, 1894), pp. 176–77; J. M. Powell, "Arcadia and Back: 'Vil-lage Settlement' in Victoria, 1894–1913," *Australian Geographical Studies* 11 (April 1973): 134–49; Kingston, *Glad Confident Morning,* p. 267; Colin S. Mar-tin, *Irrigation and Closer Settlement in the Shepparton District, 1836–1906* (Melbourne: Melbourne University Press, 1955), pp. 74–75.

79. West, "Irrigation Development," pp. 6–7; *Mildura Cultivator* 1, no. 7 (1891): 166.

80. Deakin Diary, 1885, Letters to Catherine Deakin transcribed, 29 Janu-ary, 11 February 1885, Deakin Papers, National Library.

81. Andrew Markus, "The Anti-Chinese Movement in Eastern Australia and California, 1850–1888: A Comparative Study," in Norman Harper and Elaine Barry, eds., *American Studies Down Under* (La Trobe University: ANZASA, [1978]), pp. 144–45; on California, Sucheng Chan, *This Bitter-Sweet Soil: The Chinese in California Agriculture, 1860–1910* (Berkeley and Los Angeles: Uni-versity of California Press, 1986), chap. 8, plays down the role of Chinese cheap labor and emphasizes Chinese tenancy in breaking up the big estates.

82. *VPD,* 30 November 1881, p. 931.

83. West, "Woman's Opportunity in Australia," *Australia To-Day,* 1 Decem-ber 1911, p. 113; see also, John West, "Dried Fruits," pp. 56–57: T. K. Dow, "Irrigation in California," *New Zealand Country Journal* 8 (May 1884): 186.

84. *Australia To-Day,* 15 December 1905, p. 3.

85. Julian Thomas [pseud.], *The Australian Irrigation Colonies* (Melbourne: Leader Office, 1894).

86. Quoted in Burton, *Mildura,* p. 23.

87. Deakin, quoted in Powell, *Watering the Garden State,* p. 111. See Deakin, *Irrigation in Western America,* pp. 98, 99.

88. John West, "Woman's Opportunity in Australia," p. 117.

89. Ibid.

90. Ibid.

91. Thomas, *Australian Irrigation Colonies,* p. 19.

92. Ibid.

93. Jessie Ackermann, *What Women Have Done with the Vote* (New York: William B. Feakins, 1913), p. 58; *Australia: From a Woman's Point of View* (London: Cassell, 1913), pp. 78–79; for the broader historiographical literature on this subject, see the summary in Raymond Evans, "A Gun in the Oven: Mas-culinism and Gendered Violence," in Raymond Evans and Kay Saunders, eds., *Gender Relations in Australia: Domination and Negotiation* (Sydney: Harcourt, Brace, Jovanovich, 1992), pp. 203–5.

94. West, "Woman's Opportunity in Australia," p. 117; Thomas, *Australian Irrigation Colonies,* p. 19; see also *Mulgoa Irrigation,* p. 10, which explains the "monotonous and uninteresting labour" and the "deprivation of social life" associated with typical settlement patterns on broad-acre farms in Australia.

95. William Lines, *Taming the Great South Land: A History of the Conquest*

of Nature in Australia (Sydney: Allen and Unwin, 1991), pp. 212–13; Ion Idriess, *The Great Boomerang* (Sydney: Angus and Robertson, 1943); Ernestine Hill, *Water into Gold* (Melbourne: Robertson and Mullins, 1937); Bruce Davidson, *The Northern Myth* (Melbourne: Melbourne University Press, 1965); Davidson, *Australia Wet or Dry? The Physical and Economic Limits to the Expansion of Irrigation* (Melbourne: Melbourne University Press, 1969); obituary for Bruce Davidson, *Australian*, 6 April 1994, p. 13; Powell, *Plains of Promise, Rivers of Destiny*, pp. 154–62; CSIRO and Department of National Development, P. M. Fleming et al., *Burdekin Project Ecological Study* (Canberra: Australian Govt. Publishing Service, 1981), pp. xiv–xv, xxv, and passim.

CHAPTER 7

1. J. A. La Nauze, *Alfred Deakin: A Biography* (Melbourne: Melbourne University Press, 1965), 1:88. He added that time showed that "water conservation on a larger scale than was then contemplated, was an essential factor in successful irrigation."

2. See, for example, Bruce Davidson, *Australia Wet or Dry? The Physical and Economic Limits to the Expansion of Irrigation* (Melbourne: Melbourne University Press, 1969).

3. J. M. Powell, *Watering the Garden State: Water, Land and Community in Victoria, 1834–1988* (Sydney: Allen and Unwin, 1989), p. 113. As Powell says, the well-cited "nationalization" clause concerning control of water rights was preceded by the Spanish Law of Waters of 1866; but according to Powell and others, the "revolutionary character" of the Victorian law "lies in the fact that it was the 'first statute of a purely common law jurisdiction' to declare State ownership of water use rights and to abolish previously recognised riparian rights in order to establish State management." Initially under the Water Conservation Act of 1883, the Trusts were allowed to borrow independently on the bond market, but without any government funding. Because only one Trust was actually established under this law, an 1885 act gave government financial aid in the form of state loans. See also Deakin, "Irrigation in Australia," *The Year-Book of Australia for 1892* (London: E. A. Petherick and Co., 1893), p. 90; La Nauze, *Alfred Deakin*, p. 86.

4. Report of the Royal Commission on Water Supply, *Victorian Parliamentary Papers*, 1896, Vol. 3, No. 20.

5. Mead, "Irrigation in Victoria," in *Victoria, The Garden State of Australia: A Handbook. . .* (Melbourne: By Direction of the Minister for Agriculture, the Proprietors of *Australia To-Day*, 1909), pp. 169–83.

6. Ibid.; Henry Brieu Jr. et al. to Deakin, 7 February 1897, Box 29, Folder 1, Series 10, Deakin Papers, National Library; Colin S. Martin, *Irrigation and Closer Settlement in the Shepparton District, 1836–1906* (Melbourne: Melbourne University Press, 1955), pp. 57–58; Lionel Frost, "Government and Economic Development: The Case of Irrigation in Victoria," *Australian Economic History Review* 32 (March 1992): 59–63.

7. John West, "Victoria, The Garden State," in *Australia To-Day*, 15 December 1905, p. 40; J. Rutherford, "Interplay of American and Australian Ideas for

Development of Water Projects in Northern Victoria," in J. M. Powell, ed., *The Making of Rural Australia: Environment, Society and Economy: Geographical Readings* (Melbourne: Sorrett Publishing, 1974), pp. 123–24.

8. Elwood Mead, "Relation of Land Settlement to Irrigation Development," in *Proceedings of the Pan-Pacific Science Congress, Australia, 1923*, 2 vols. (Melbourne: H. J. Green, Govt. Printer, 1923), 1:58; Mead, "Irrigation in Victoria," pp. 169–83; West, "Victoria, the Garden State," p. 40.

9. Martin, *Irrigation and Closer Settlement*, p. 38.

10. Quoted in J. A. Alexander, *The Life of George Chaffey: A Story of Irrigation Beginnings in California and Australia* (Melbourne: Macmillan, 1928), p. 94.

11. Emma H. Jolliffe, "Ontario," *Rural Californian* 7 (November 1884): 214.

12. Starr, *Material Dreams: Southern California through the 1920s* (New York: Oxford University Press, 1990), p. 16; *Argus* (Melbourne), 15 April 1885, p. 7; Deakin Diary, Letters to Catherine Deakin transcribed, 11 February 1885, Box 9, Series 2, Deakin Papers, National Library.

13. Frederick D. Kershner Jr., "George Chaffey and the Irrigation Frontier," *Agricultural History* 27 (October 1953): 115–22 (quote at p. 115).

14. Peter Westcott, "Chaffey, George, and Chaffey, William Benjamin," *Australian Dictionary of Biography*, vol. 7 (1891–1939), pp. 599–601.

15. Alexander, *Life of George Chaffey*, p. 148. For the details, see the text of the agreement, ibid., pp. 156–58; see also Powell, *Watering the Garden State*, p. 122; and the illustration in Alexander, *Life of George Chaffey*, p. 149.

16. A. R. E. Burton, *Mildura, the True Australia Felix, How to Get Rich in Victoria* (Melbourne: Spectator Publishing, 1892), p. 12.

17. Morris Wills, "The California-Victoria Irrigation Frontier," in William W. Savage Jr. and Stephen I. Thompson, eds., *The Frontier: Comparative Studies* (Norman: University of Oklahoma Press, 1979), 2:243; on the mutual water company as an innovation, see Norris Hundley Jr., *The Great Thirst: Californians and Water, 1770s–1990s* (Berkeley and Los Angeles: University of California Press, 1992), pp. 102–5.

18. Alexander, *Life of George Chaffey*, pp. 38–40; Kershner, "Chaffey and the Irrigation Frontier," p. 116.

19. Burton, *Mildura*, p. 15; Royal Commission on Vegetable Products, *Eighth Progress Report, and Continuation of the Minutes of Evidence. . .* (Melbourne: Robert S. Brain, 1890), pp. v–vi, 109–14. Chaffey's work also received the engineering endorsement of William Davidson, inspector-general of Public Works, ibid., pp. 114–18.

20. *Irrigation: The Mulgoa Irrigation Settlement* (N.p., [c. 1891]), p. 9.

21. Alexander, *Life of George Chaffey*, p. 159; Burton, *Mildura*, pp. 10–11.

22. Royal Commission on Vegetable Products, *Eighth Progress Report*, pp. 118–19, 124.

23. Chaffey indenture agreements, in Box 29, Folder 3, Series 10, Deakin Papers, National Library.

24. Burton, *Mildura*, pp. 4, 5; Australian Scripture Education League Scrapbook, 1889–1894, p. 51, David Scott Mitchell Library, Sydney; A. S. Kenyon,

"The Story of the Mallee," *Victorian Historical Magazine* 4 (June 1915): 183; James H. McColl, "Hugh McColl and the Water Question in Victoria," *Victorian Historical Magazine* 5 (June 1917): 145–63.

25. Burton, *Mildura*, pp. 10–11. See also Burton, "An Oasis in the Mallee," *Banker's Magazine of Australasia* 5 (June 1892): 695–708.

26. Burton, *Mildura*, p. 15; *Mildura Cultivator* 1 (November 1891): 50.

27. Burton, *Mildura*, pp. 12, 20.

28. Julian Thomas [pseud.], *The Australian Irrigation Colonies* (Melbourne: Leader Office, 1894), p. 7.

29. Mildura Royal Commission, *Mildura Settlement, Report of the Mildura Royal Commission, Victorian Parliamentary Papers, 1896*, vol. 3, no. 19, repr. as *Mildura. 1896 Royal Commission on the Mildura Settlement* (N.p.: Australian Dried Fruits Industry, n.d., facsimile), pp. xxiii–xxiv, 234; R. Norris, "Alfred Deakin," *Australian Dictionary of Biography*, vol. 8 (1891–1939), pp. 249–50.

30. Starr, *Material Dreams*, p. 17.

31. Kershner, "Chaffey and the Irrigation Frontier," p. 118; J. M. Powell, *Plains of Promise, Rivers of Destiny: Water Management and the Development of Queensland, 1824–1990* (Bowen Hills, Qld: Boolarong Publications, 1991), pp. 58–59.

32. Royal Commission, *Mildura*, pp. ix–x.

33. Ernestine Hill, *Water into Gold* (Melbourne: Robertson and Mullins, 1937), p. 205.

34. Some of the other American settlers remained and prospered too. See Hill, *Water into Gold*, p. 308. Westcott, "Chaffey," p. 600; Kershner, "Chaffey and the Irrigation Frontier," p. 119.

35. In the judgment of the historian J. A. La Nauze, by "their genius they transformed a wilderness into the thriving Mildura settlement we know today." *Alfred Deakin*, 1:87.

36. Deakin to Chaffey, 2 October 1907, reprinted in Alexander, *Life of George Chaffey*, p. 363; Stuart Murray to Deakin, 1 October 1907, Box 29, Folder 1, Deakin Papers, National Library.

37. Alexander, *Life of George Chaffey*, p. viii.

38. Ibid., p. 306; Donald Worster, *Rivers of Empire: Water, Aridity, and the Growth of the American West* (New York: Pantheon, 1985), p. 203.

39. H. T. Cory, *Imperial Valley and Salton Sink* (San Francisco: John J. Newbegin, 1915), quoted in Alexander, *Life of George Chaffey*, p. 41.

40. Worster, *Rivers of Empire*, p. 196.

41. The story is well told in Starr, *Material Dreams*, esp. pp. 30–41.

42. U.S. House of Representatives, Committee on the Public Lands, January 18, 1907, *Salton Sea, California, Imperial Valley, and Lower Colorado River*, 59th Cong., 2d sess., 1907 (Washington: Govt. Printer, 1907), pp. 48–49.

43. Hall to Deakin, [1886], Box 1, Folder 1, Ms. 913, William Hammond Hall Papers, California Historical Society.

44. William Hammond Hall, *Report on Irrigation Legislation and Enterprise in the American States, Australian Colonies and Several Countries of Europe as Applicable to Cape Colony* (Cape Town: W. A. Richards and Sons, Govt. Printers, 1898), pp. 39, 41.

45. Ibid., pp. 64, 65, for Hall's policy recommendations; see also for a similar view, Hall to Deakin, [1886], and Hall to Henry C. Schneider, 3 March 1896, Box 1, Folder 1, Ms. 913, Hall Papers, California Historical Society.

46. George Chaffey to Deakin, 23 March 1907, Box 29, Folder 1, Series 10, Deakin Papers, National Library; Alexander, *Life of George Chaffey,* pp. 358–59.

47. Richard J. Hinton, *Progress Report on Irrigation in the United States, Part 1 . . .* (Washington: Government Printing Office, 1891), pp. 237–61; C. L. Ingersoll to Alfred Deakin, 19 April 1892, F. H. Newell to Alfred Deakin, 22 March 1894, 21 December 1894, Box 29, Folder 1, Deakin Papers, National Library.

48. International Irrigation Congress, *Official Report of the International Irrigation Congress Held at Los Angeles, California, October 1893* (Los Angeles: Chamber of Commerce, 1893), pp. 46–47; "Australia's Exhibit at Chicago," *California Fruit Grower,* 16 July 1892, p. 38.

49. National Irrigation Congress, *Official Proceedings of the Third National Irrigation Congress, Held at Denver, Colorado, Sept. 3rd to 8th, 1894* (Denver, Colo.: Committee of Arrangements, 1894), p. 29.

50. Mead, *Report of Irrigation Investigations in California . . .* U.S. Department of Agriculture, Office of Experiment Stations, bulletin no. 100 (Washington: Govt. Printing Office, 1901), p. 69.

51. See, for example, International Irrigation Congress, *Proceedings of the International Irrigation Congress Held in Salt Lake City, Utah, October, 1912* (Washington, D.C.: n.p., 1913), pp. 4, 5.

52. McColl, "McColl and the Water Question," p. 161.

53. George Swinburne circular letter, 28 February 1905; and Swinburne to Deakin, 14 November 1905, Box 29, Folder 1, Deakin Papers, National Library; Powell, *Watering the Garden State,* pp. 113, 147.

CHAPTER 8

1. *VPD,* Water Acts Consolidation and Amendment Bill, 18 July 1905, p. 363. The 1905 Water Act was designed in part to achieve this result. J. M. Powell, *Watering the Garden State: Water, Land, and Community in Victoria, 1834–1988* (Sydney: Allen and Unwin, 1989), pp. 144–45. On Swinburne, see, especially, E. H. Sugden and F. W. Eggleston, *George Swinburne: A Biography* (Sydney: Angus and Robertson, 1931), pp. 242–44.

2. On Mead, see James L. Kluger, *Turning on Water with a Shovel: The Career of Elwood Mead* (Albuquerque: University of New Mexico Press, 1992); Paul Conkin, "The Vision of Elwood Mead," *Agricultural History* 34 (April 1960): 88–97; Donald J. Pisani, "Reclamation and Social Engineering in the Progressive Era," *Agricultural History* 57 (January 1983): 46–63; J. Rutherford, "Interplay of American and Australian Ideas for Development of Water Projects in Northern Victoria," in J. M. Powell, ed., *The Making of Rural Australia: Environment, Society and Economy: Geographical Readings* (Melbourne: Sorrett Publishing, 1974), pp. 126–28.

3. For Mead's disagreements with this act, see Mead to Hilgard, 20 December 1902, Box 16, Eugene W. Hilgard Papers, Bancroft Library; Mead, *Irrigation Institutions* (New York: Macmillan and Co., 1903), pp. 344–83; Kluger,

Water with a Shovel, pp. 24, 38; Donald J. Pisani, *To Reclaim a Divided West, Water, Law, and Public Policy, 1848–1902* (Albuquerque: University of New Mexico Press, 1992), pp. 308–10.

4. Mead, *Forest Conservation: A National Duty* (Melbourne: Victorian Branch of the Australian Forest League, 1913), pp. 1–2.

5. Mead, *Report of Irrigation Investigations in California . . .* U.S. Department of Agriculture, Office of Experiment Stations, bulletin no. 100 (Washington, D.C.: Govt. Printing Office, 1901), p. 53.

6. Ibid., pp. 26, 17.

7. See John West, "Victoria, the Garden State," *Australia To-Day,* 15 December 1905, pp. 40–41.

8. See the illustration from the frontispiece of Elwood Mead, *Helping Men Own Farms: A Practical Discussion of Government Aid in Land Settlement* (New York: Macmillan, 1920).

9. Elwood Mead, Introduction to Henry S. Gullett, *Irrigation and Intense Culture in Other Countries. A Series of Articles Dealing with Agriculture in Italy and America . . .* (Melbourne: J. Kemp, Govt. Printer, [c. 1910]).

10. T. K. Dow, "The World's Christmas Climate: How Australia Corners the Summer," *Life* 1 January 1909, p. 34.

11. See Mead, *Helping Men Own Farms,* pp. 33–35, quote at p. 34.

12. George Swinburne to Deakin, 14 November 1905, Box 29, Folder 1, Series 10, Deakin Papers, National Library; Alison Patrick, "George Swinburne," *Australian Dictionary of Biography,* vol. 12 (1891–1939), pp. 150–52.

13. A. S. Kenyon, "Unauthorized Diversions from the Murray River within the State of Victoria," 7 September 1904, Murray River. Papers Relating to Irrigation Systems for the Murray River Basin, 1898–1931, National Library, Canberra.

14. George Swinburne circular letter, 28 February 1905; and Swinburne to Deakin, 14 November 1905, Box 29, Folder 1, Series 10, Deakin Papers, National Library.

15. J. M. Powell, *Environmental Management in Australia, 1788–1914* (Melbourne: Oxford University Press, 1976), p. 136.

16. Elwood Mead, "Address by the President: Ellwood [*sic*] Mead." Section H. Engineering and Architecture. *Report of the Thirteenth Meeting of the Australasian Association for the Advancement of Science, Held at Sydney, 1911* (Sydney: W. E. Smith, 1912), pp. 619–20.

17. Mead, *Forest Conservation: A National Duty,* p. 4. On the interstate rivalries, see David J. Gordon, *The "Nile" of Australia. Nature's Gateway to the Interior. A Plea for the Greater Utilization of the Murray and Its Tributaries* (Adelaide: W. K. Thomas and Co., 1906); Robert T. McKay, *The Murray River. Irrigation and Navigation (A Lecture Delivered before the [Sydney University Engineering] Society on August 19th, 1903)* (Sydney: The Society, 1903).

18. Mead, "Address," p. 620.

19. Ernestine Hill, *Water into Gold* (Melbourne: Robertson and Mullins, 1937), p. 263; Powell, *Watering the Garden State,* p. 143.

20. A. F. Partridge to Mead, 17 February 1923, Carton 4, Folder 2, uncataloged Mead Papers, Bancroft Library.

21. J. M. Powell, *Plains of Promise, Rivers of Destiny: Water Management and the Development of Queensland, 1824–1990* (Bowen Hills, Qld: Boolarong Publications, 1991), pp. 109–11.

22. A Murrumbidgee Canals Construction Act had been passed in 1906; the MIA was placed under a trust in 1910 and then became a responsibility of the Water Conservation and Irrigation Commission formed in 1912. "Extract from the Report of Elwood Mead, Chairman of the State Rivers' Commission, Victoria, Australia, to the Government of New South Wales, Australia, on the Development and Administration of the Murrumbidgee Irrigation Scheme, May 1911," Box 2, Folder 14, Elwood Mead Papers, Water Resources Center Library; Powell, *Watering the Garden State,* p. 166.

23. The wartime situation, particularly for South Australia, is described in Samuel McIntosh (commissioner of irrigation, South Australia) to Mead, 23 June 1923, Carton 4, Folder 2, uncataloged Mead Papers, Bancroft Library.

24. *Daily Telegraph* (Sydney), 5 January 1923, in Folder 12, and F. L. Kempster to Mead, 16 June 1923, Carton 4, Folder 2, uncataloged Mead Papers; *Daily Telegraph* (Sydney), 12 October 1920.

25. *Wanted: Men, Money, Markets* (Leeton: Murrumbidgee Irrigator Press, 1922), p. 4.

26. "Notes, Confidential," Carton 4, Folder 4, uncataloged Mead Papers.

27. Elwood Mead, *Report on the Murrumbidgee Irrigation Scheme* (Sydney: Alfred James Kent, Govt. Printer, 1923), p. 7.

28. The political conflict between Mead and some influential members of the New South Wales government, notably Sir Joseph Carruthers, is copiously documented in Carton 4, uncataloged Mead Papers; Rutherford, "Interplay of American and Australian Ideas for Development of Water Projects," p. 126.

29. *Wanted: Men, Money, Markets,* p. 2.

30. A. F. Partridge to Mead, 17 February 1923, Carton 4, Folder 2, uncataloged Mead Papers; Powell, *Plains of Promise, Rivers of Destiny,* pp. 113, 120, 122.

31. Mead to John D. Works, 24 December 1912, Box 4, John D. Works Papers, Bancroft Library.

32. Mead told California Senator John D. Works that the United States was "too far behind the England of Lloyd George or the Australia of Andrew Fisher in social and industrial laws." Mead to Works, 24 December 1912, Works Papers, Bancroft Library; Pisani, "Reclamation and Social Engineering in the Progressive Era," p. 59.

33. Mead, *Helping Men Own Farms,* p. 206.

34. Ibid., pp. 205–6.

35. Reported in Mead to Works, 7 April 1916, Works Papers, Bancroft Library.

36. Speech by Elwood Mead, reclamation commissioner, before Irrigation Conference held at Cheyenne, Wyoming, 22 June 1925, Box 2, Folder 15, Mead Papers, Water Resources Center Library; Kluger, *Water with a Shovel,* pp. 89, 126, 130. (Kreutzer was head of Reclamation Economics in Washington until his death in 1929.) See also Mead to Works, 17 July 1916, Works Papers, Bancroft Library.

37. Mead, *Forest Conservation: A National Duty,* pp. 3–4.

38. "Plan for the Creation of Organized Rural Communities in the South" [c. 1926], Box 2, Folder 13, Mead Papers, Water Resources Center Library; "The Rural Credit Scheme Needed to Develop the West," pp. 4–5, Box 2, Folder 13, Mead Papers, Water Resources Center Library.

39. Mead, *Helping Men Own Farms,* p. 5; Mead, "Making the American Desert Bloom," *Current History* 31 (October 1929): 129. Mead's figures come to 105 percent, however.

40. See Mead, "The Japanese Land Problem of California," *Annals of the American Academy* 93 (January 1921): 51–55.

41. Mead, *Helping Men Own Farms,* p. 131.

42. Ibid., pp. 132, 133, 68–69.

43. Thomas H. Means, comment on "Present Policies of the United States Bureau of Reclamation Regarding Land Settlement," American Society of Civil Engineers, *Transactions,* paper no. 1609, Summer Meeting, Salt Lake City, Utah, 8 July 1925, in Box 2, Folder 13, Mead Papers, Water Resources Center Library.

44. The story of the California colonies is best told in J. M. Powell, "Elwood Mead and California's State Colonies: An Episode in Australasian-American Contacts, 1915–31," *Journal of the Royal Australian Historical Society* 67 (March 1982): 328–53.

45. Edward F. Adams to H. M. Grunsky, 5 October 1913, Box 2, Folder 14, Mead Papers, Water Resources Center Library; *Age* (Melbourne), 28 August 1913.

46. Neil Barr and John Cary, *Greening a Brown Land: The Australian Search for Sustainable Land Use* (Melbourne: Macmillan, 1992), pp. 215–16.

47. Rutherford, "Interplay of American and Australian Ideas for Development of Water Projects," pp. 130, 132.

48. Norris Hundley, "The Politics of Reclamation: California, the Federal Government, and the Origins of the Boulder Canyon Act—a Second Look," *California Historical Quarterly* 52 (winter 1973): 292–325, esp. p. 316; M. S. Cook to Benjamin Ide Wheeler, 2 October 1916, Mead to Will R. King, 13 December 1915, Mead to Davis, 29 August 1916, Mead to Franklin K. Lane, 9 August 1916, Mead to LeRoy Holt, 14 December 1916, Mead to Thomas F. Hunt, 28 November 1917, Box 1, Mead Papers, Water Resources Center Library.

49. Enclosure of Mead press release in Ralph W. Crossman (*Christian Science Monitor*) to Mead, 2 February 1918, Box 1, Mead Papers, Water Resources Center Library.

50. Hundley, "Politics of Reclamation," p. 316; Kluger, *Water with a Shovel,* p. 138.

51. Mead to Thomas F. Hunt, 10 January 1918, Box 1, Mead Papers, Water Resources Center Library.

52. Mead, "Titles to Water," c. 1920, Box 2, Folder 10, Mead Papers, Water Resources Center Library.

53. "Federal Reclamation as a National Policy," Box 2, Folder 16, Mead Papers, Water Resources Center Library. Some of this material duplicates that in Mead, "Making the American Desert Bloom," pp. 123–32.

54. Mead, "Making the American Desert Bloom," p. 126.

55. Ibid., pp. 130–31.

56. Donald Worster, *Rivers of Empire: Water, Aridity, and the Growth of the American West* (New York: Pantheon, 1985); Norris Hundley Jr., *The Great Thirst: Californians and Water, 1770s-1990s* (Berkeley and Los Angeles: University of California Press, 1992), esp. chap. 4; Kevin Starr, *Material Dreams: Southern California through the 1920s* (New York: Oxford University Press, 1990), pp. 59–61; Marc Reisner, *Cadillac Desert: The American West and Its Disappearing Water* (New York: Viking, 1986).

57. Powell, *Watering the Garden State*, pp. 229–30.

58. Donald J. Pisani, *From the Family Farm to Agribusiness: The Irrigation Crusade in California and the West, 1850–1931* (Berkeley and Los Angeles: University of California Press, 1984), p. 451. In California "the number and size of farms" in excess of one thousand acres increased "dramatically" between 1920 and 1945. Though the statistics are not strictly comparable, the rate of increase in the total acreage of the larger properties appears to have been not much more dramatic than in Victoria (a 41 percent increase in Victoria, and 46 percent in California).

59. *Victorian Year-Book, 1935–36,* pp. 385, 388. This figure includes the "agricultural labourers' allotments" and all other irrigable areas under the closer-settlement scheme. For farms alone, the figure was 129,516 acres. Of the total irrigated land in the state, only 13.6 percent in 1935 was utilized for vineyards and orchards. Pasture accounted for 50.8 percent.

60. Bruce Davidson, *Australia Wet or Dry?: The Physical and Economic Limits to the Expansion of Irrigation* (Melbourne: Melbourne University Press, 1969), p. 99.

61. Worster, *Rivers of Empire*, p. 212.

62. Ibid., pp. 222, 278.

63. Rutherford, "Interplay of American and Australian Ideas for Development of Water Projects," p. 131.

64. Ibid., p. 129 (see Figure 4); Worster, *Rivers of Empire*, p. 278.

65. California Commissioner of Horticulture, *First Biennial Report of the Commissioner of Horticulture of the State of California, for 1903–1904* (Sacramento: W. W. Shannon, 1905), pp. 387, 402.

66. Ibid., pp. 412–13.

67. California Commissioner of Horticulture, *Third Biennial Report of the Commissioner of Horticulture of the State of California, for 1907–1908* (Sacramento: W. W. Shannon, 1909), pp. 38–39.

68. Ellwood Cooper to George C. Pardee, 1 November 1905, Box 49, George C. Pardee Papers, Bancroft Library.

69. H. Vincent Moses, "'The Orange-Grower Is Not a Farmer': G. Harold Powell, Riverside Orchardists, and the Coming of Industrial Agriculture, 1893–1930," *California History* 74 (spring 1995): 31–32. The exchange was an umbrella organization encompassing fifteen thousand individual citrus growers, in 201 local packing associations, which reported in turn to twenty-five district exchanges under the control of the governing board of the central exchange. Kevin Starr, *Inventing the Dream: California through the Progressive Era* (New York: Oxford University Press, 1985), p. 162.

70. California Commissioner of Horticulture, *First Biennial Report of the Commissioner of Horticulture of the State of California, for 1903–1904*, pp. 394–95; Starr, *Inventing the Dream*, pp. 162–63.

71. Hill, *Water into Gold*, pp. 177, 178, 180.

72. Ibid., p. 208.

73. Janet McCalman, "Clement John De Garis," *Australian Dictionary of Biography*, vol. 8 (1891–1939), p. 269; *Triad*, 10 March 1920, p. 32; C. J. De Garis, *The Victories of Failure: A Business Romance of Fiction, Blended with, and Based on, Fact* (Melbourne: Modern Printing, 1925), pp. 274–75; ADFA, *Sun-Raysed Dried Fruit and Raisin Recipes* (Melbourne: ADFA, 1922), pp. 1–2; H. S. Taylor, *The Australian Dried Fruits Association: Its Maintenance Essential to the Dried Fruits Industry and the Irrigation Areas* ([Mildura: ADFA, 1923]), pp. 5–6; F. Fox Benton, "A Miracle of Irrigation," *Ladies' Sphere*, 15 January 1920, pp. 16, 20; "Mildura," *National Magazine of Health*, February 1929, p. 7; Hill, *Water into Gold*, pp. 209–10.

74. *Official Year Book of the Commonwealth of Australia*, no. 22, 1929, pp. 714–16.

75. H. S. Taylor favorably contrasted the orderly cooperation of ADFA with the example of the Californian raisin industry's own hesitant attempts at cooperative selling. See Taylor, *Australian Dried Fruits Association*, pp. 5–6.

76. Steven Stoll, "The Fruits of Natural Advantage: Horticulture and the Industrial Countryside in California" (Ph.D. diss., Yale University, 1995), pp. 145–61.

77. "Six Platform Planks for Any Party," *Triad*, 10 March 1920, p. 32; and Hill, *Water into Gold*, pp. 237–39.

78. Hill, *Water into Gold*, p. 243.

79. *Official Year Book of the Commonwealth of Australia*, no. 48, 1962, p. 944.

80. B. D. Graham, *The Formation of the Australian Country Parties* (Canberra: Australian National University Press, 1966), p. 228.

81. Stoll, "Fruits of Natural Advantage," p. 152. Rutherford himself notes that the Australian difference reflected "considerable social pressures for rapid development of an open economy, founded on nationalistic motives." Rutherford, "Interplay of American and Australian Ideas for Development of Water Projects," p. 132; "Six Platform Planks for Any Party," p. 32.

82. Hundley, *Great Thirst*; Reisner, *Cadillac Desert*; Worster, *Rivers of Empire*.

83. Hundley, *Great Thirst*, pp. 229–30. See also Starr, *Material Dreams*, pp. 59–61.

84. New South Wales Premier William McKell visited the United States in 1945 and paid "particular attention" to the development of reclamation schemes in the American West, as "was to be expected in view of his 'master plan' for rural industry, and his involvement in the Snowy controversy." See Lionel Wigmore, *Struggle for the Snowy: The Background of the Snowy Mountains Scheme* (Melbourne: Melbourne University Press, 1967), p. 122.

85. Ion Idriess, *Great Boomerang* and *Onward Australia: Developing a*

Continent (Sydney: Angus and Robertson, 1943 and 1944, respectively), pp. 61, 22–23 on the Ord River scheme and the models of TVA and the Colorado.

CHAPTER 9

1. *Journal of the Department of Agriculture,* (Victoria), 6 (October 1908): 592–93; "Common Introduced Plants," vol. 7, part 99 of *Australia's Wildlife Heritage* (Dee Why West, N.S.W.: Paul Hamlyn, n.d.), p. 3157. For a review of the exchange of pest plants in Mediterranean climatic zones, see Marilyn D. Fox, "Mediterranean Weeds: Exchanges of Invasive Plants between the Five Mediterranean Regions of the World," in F. di Castri, A. J. Hansen, and M. Debussche, eds., *Biological Invasions in Europe and the Mediterranean Basin* (Dordrecht, Neth.: Kluwer Academic Publications, 1990), pp. 179, 189, 193, 194.

2. *Report of the National Conservation Commission,* 3 vols. (Washington, D.C.: Govt. Printing Office, 1909), 2:339, 369.

3. Charles Shinn, "Garden Art in California," *American Garden* 11 (January 1890): 24. California State Board of Horticulture, *Seventh Biennial Report of the State Board of Horticulture of the State of California, for 1899–1900* (Sacramento: A. J. Johnston, 1901), p. 17, shows that Australian and New Zealand shipments carrying plants, trees, shrubs, and fruit between 2 October 1898 to 31 October 1900 concerned only 7.6 percent of the total number, but some may have come indirectly from Australasia via the Sandwich Islands (11.5 percent) or various South Sea islands (2 percent).

4. *Insect Life* 7, no. 2 (1894–95): 98.

5. On Bordeaux and its use in Australia, see Neil Barr and John Cary, *Greening a Brown Land: The Australian Search for Sustainable Land Use* (Melbourne: Macmillan, 1992), p. 185; on American applications, see James C. Whorton, *Before Silent Spring: Pesticides and Public Health in Pre-DDT America* (Princeton, N.J.: Princeton University Press, 1974), p. 65 n.; for Howard's history of economic entomology, see *Insect Life* 7, no. 2 (1894–95): 98–99.

6. L. O. Howard, *A History of Applied Entomology (Somewhat Anecdotal),* Smithsonian Miscellaneous Collections (Washington, D.C.: Smithsonian Institution, 1930), 84:173.

7. *Insect Life* 7, no. 2 (1894–95): 74, 99.

8. Ibid., p. 93.

9. Thomas Dunlap, *DDT: Scientists, Citizens, and Public Policy* (Princeton, N.J.: Princeton University Press, 1981), chap. 1; Whorton, *Before Silent Spring,* pp. 54–107; John Perkins, "Insects, Food, and Hunger: The Paradox of Plenty for U.S. Entomology, 1920–1970," *Environmental Review* 7 (spring 1983): 71–96; Thomas Dunlap, "The Triumph of Chemical Pesticides in Insect Control, 1890–1920," *Environmental Review,* no. 5 (1978): 38–47.

10. John West, "Dried Fruit," in Department of Agriculture, Victoria, *Course of Lectures Delivered by Officers of the Department of Agriculture, during the Year 1891...* (Melbourne: Robert Brain, [c. 1891]), pp. 51, 56–57; *Irrigation: The Mulgoa Irrigation Settlement* (N.p.: [c. 1891]), p. 14; John L. Dow, *The Australian in America* (Melbourne: Leader Office, 1884), p. 35; *California Fruit Grower and Fruit Trade Review,* 9 March 1895, p. 187.

11. Cited in *Mulgoa Irrigation,* p. 13.

12. Discussed in Alexander Craw, "Foreign Pests and Diseases," in California State Board of Horticulture, *Fourth Biennial Report of the State Board of Horticulture of the State of California, for 1893–94* (Sacramento: A. J. Johnston, 1894), p. 142; *California Horticulturalist and Floral Magazine* 6 (January 1876): 21.

13. E. O. Essig, *A History of Entomology* (1931; reprint, New York: Hafner Publ., 1965), pp. 110–17; *Agricultural Gazette of New South Wales* 4 (January 1893): 56–57.

14. Craw, "Foreign Pests and Diseases," pp. 142–43.

15. Essig, *History of Entomology,* pp. 505, 502, 508.

16. California State Board of Horticulture, *Biennial Report of the State Board of Horticulture. 1884* (Sacramento: James J. Ayers, 1884), p. 35; S. F. Chapin to James De Barth Shorb, 6 November 1884, Box 20, James De Barth Shorb Collection, Huntington Library.

17. *Official Report of the Twenty-fourth State Fruit-Growers' Convention of the State of California* . . . (Sacramento: A. J. Johnston, 1900), p. 97; Alexander Craw, "Suggestions on Horticultural Quarantine," *Rept. St. Bd. Hort., 1893–94,* pp. 290–94 and discussion following; Essig, *History of Entomology,* pp. 110–17, 505, 502, 506–8, and passim.

18. "On Irrigation and Its Effects on Insects," *Insect Life* 5, no. 4 (1892–93): 258.

19. Ibid., p. 269.

20. Riley said that the scale was introduced by a George Gordon of Menlo Park in about 1868. California State Board of Horticulture, *Biennial Report of the State Board of Horticulture of the State of California, for 1885 and 1886. Also, Appendix for 1887* (Sacramento: P. L. Shoaff, 1887), p. 450; see also Essig, *History of Entomology,* p. 119.

21. John Isaac, "Bug vs. Bug," in *Rept. St. Bd. Hort., 1899–1900,* p. 80; letters from Mueller and L. M. Kirk, in *Rept. St. Bd. Hort., 1885–86,* pp. 396–97.

22. *Rept. St. Bd. Hort., 1885–86,* p. 460.

23. *Rept. St. Bd. Hort., 1884,* p. 50; *Pacific Rural Press,* 24 August 1889, p. 153.

24. California State Board of Horticulture, *Third Biennial Report of the State Board of Horticulture of the State of California for the Thirty-eighth and Thirty-ninth Fiscal Years* (Sacramento: J. D. Young, 1888), p. 90; *Rept. St. Bd. Hort., 1893–94,* p. 244; *Pacific Rural Press,* 17 December 1887, p. 483.

25. Essig, *History of Entomology,* pp. 403–80; California State Board of Horticulture, *First Report of State Board of Horticultural Commissioners* (Sacramento: State Printer, 1882), pp. 20–21; Ellwood Cooper, *A Treatise on Olive Culture* (San Francisco: Cubery, 1882), pp. 17–19.

26. Howard Seftel, "Government Regulation and the Rise of the California Fruit Industry: The Entrepreneurial Attack on Fruit Pests, 1880–1920," *Business History Review* 59 (autumn 1985): 386.

27. On Maskell, see Clare F. Morales, "William Miles Maskell," *The Dictionary of New Zealand Biography,* vol. 2, 1870–1900 (Wellington, N.Z.: Bridget Williams Books, 1993), pp. 314–15.

28. Crawford at first sent the *Cryptochaetum iceryae* (Lestophonus) parasite to the California State Board, much to Riley's displeasure. Riley to Crawford, 20 July 1888, Box 10, Series E5, Record Group 7, Records of the Bureau of Entomology, National Archives.

29. Essig, *History of Entomology*, p. 123; Riley to E. Omerod, 16 June and 21 July 1887, Box 27, Charles Valentine Riley Papers, Smithsonian Institution; *Insect Life* 3, nos. 5–6 (1890–91): 354; Crawford to Riley, 21 February 1887, in *Rept. St. Bd. Hort., 1885–86*, pp. 395–96; Howard to Crawford, 28 March 1887, Box 8, E5; Riley to Crawford, 1 May 1888, Box 9, E5, Record Group 7, Records of the Bureau of Entomology; Riley's instructions to Koebele, in Riley to Koebele, 3 July 1888, Box 10, E5, Record Group 7.

30. Richard L. Doutt, "Vice, Virtue, and the Vedalia," *Bulletin of the Entomological Society of America* 4 (October 1958): 119–23.

31. Another official representing the commissioner of agriculture, Professor F. M. Webster, was to travel with the party, paid by the commission, to report on agricultural conditions and represent the State Department at the exhibition. See Webster's testimony to the Victorian government, Royal Commission on Vegetable Products, *Seventh Progress Report, and Continuation of the Minutes of Evidence . . .* (Melbourne: Robert S. Brain, 1889), pp. 69–78.

32. Essig, *History of Entomology*, p. 319; Riley to Crawford, 3 July 1888, and 3 December 1888, Box 10, E5, Record Group 7, Records of the Bureau of Entomology.

33. Riley to Koebele, 7 January 1889, Box 11, E5. Klee was the first to breed them. Howard to Coquillett, 10 July 1889, Box 11, E5, Record Group 7, Records of the Bureau of Entomology.

34. Riley to Charles Richmond Dodge, Box 27, [1888], Riley Papers.

35. *American Garden* 11 (July 1890), clipping in Scrapbook 82, Box 19, Riley Papers.

36. U.S. Commissioner of Agriculture, *Report of the Commissioner of Agriculture, 1886* (Washington, D.C.: Govt. Printing Office, 1887), p. 489; Riley reaffirmed this in Riley to Coquillett, 7 January 1890, Box 27, Riley Papers.

37. Riley to Howard, 13 November 1887, Box 27, Riley Papers.

38. Riley to Coquillett, 23 May 1887, and 7 January, 1890, Box 27, Riley Papers.

39. During the same period, Coquillett was involved in private schemes to develop a hydrocyanic gas fumigator for chemical control for the scale. *Insect Life* 1, no. 9 (1888–89): 266–67; Essig, *History of Entomology*, p. 590.

40. Riley to Koebele, 3 July 1888, in Letterbook, p. 269, Box 10, E5, Record Group 7, Records of the Bureau of Entomology.

41. Edwin Willetts to Ellwood Cooper, 10 June 1889, Box 11, E5, Record Group 7, Records of the Bureau of Entomology.

42. *Rept. St. Bd. Hort., 1885–86*, p. 461.

43. U.S. Commissioner of Agriculture, *Report of the Commissioner of Agriculture, 1886*, pp. 488–89.

44. *Rept. St. Bd. Hort., 1885–86*, p. 477.

45. E. M. Shelton to Riley, 8 June 1892, and Riley to Shelton, 14 July 1892, in *Insect Life* 5, no. 1 (1892–93): 45–46; Bureau of Sugar Experiment Stations,

Division of Entomology, *Australian Sugar-Cane Beetles and Their Allies,* bulletin no. 16 (Brisbane: Anthony J. Cummings, 1921), pp. 7–8.

46. *Rept. St. Bd. Hort., 1885–86,* p. 462.

47. Ibid.

48. Ibid., p. 476.

49. See Crawford to Klee, December 1887, *Rept. St. Bd. Hort., 1887–88,* p. 179.

50. W. G. Klee to Riley, 11 November 1888, Box 58, E2, Record Group 7, Records of the Bureau of Entomology. On Klee (1853–1891), see Essig, *History of Entomology,* pp. 672–73.

51. On Craw's claim, see Riley to Coquillett, 7 January 1890, Box 27, Riley Papers. Riley had already discussed this matter in U.S. Commissioner of Agriculture, *Report of the Commissioner of Agriculture, 1886,* p. 489.

52. Howard to Craw, 11 September 1885, Box 6, E5, Record Group 7, Records of the Bureau of Entomology. Essig confirms Craw's argument. *History of Entomology,* p. 593.

53. *Rept. St. Bd. Hort., 1885–86,* pp. 476, 477.

54. *Rept. St. Bd. Hort., 1893–94,* p. 244.

55. Cooper, *A Treatise on Olive Culture,* p. 14.

56. Ibid., p. 19.

57. Ibid., p. 17.

58. Ibid., p. 26.

59. California State Board of Horticulture, *Annual Report of the State Board of Horticulture of the State of California, for 1892* (Sacramento: A. J. Johnston, 1892), p. 454; Ellwood Cooper, *Forest Culture and Eucalyptus Trees* (San Francisco: Cubery, 1876), p. 30.

60. L. M. Kirk to Riley, 25 March 1887, in Box 58, E2, Record Group 7, Records of the Bureau of Entomology; *Pacific Rural Press,* 4 June 1887, reprinted in *Rept. St. Bd. Hort., 1885–86,* pp. 394–95.

61. Riley to Howard, 19 August 1887, Box 27, Riley Papers. Howard to Mueller, 28 March 1887, Box 8, E5; Mueller to Riley, 21 March 1887, Box 65, E2, Record Group 7, Records of the Bureau of Entomology. This letter is dated 21 May but is corrected in *Rept. St. Bd. Hort., 1885–86,* p. 396; and this fits with Howard's reply of 28 March. See also for a full explanation, Riley to President, Section 10, British Association for the Advancement of Science, 8 Sept. 1887, Box 27, Riley Papers; Morales, "Maskell," pp. 314–15.

62. Riley to Crawford, 17 January 1888, Box 9, E5, Riley Papers; cf. Howard to Crawford, 15 Aug. 1887, Box 11, E5, Record Group 7, Records of the Bureau of Entomology. Klee also appears to have been misled. See *Rept. St. Bd. Hort., 1885–86,* p. 397.

63. *American Garden* 12 (February 1891): 119.

64. California Commissioner of Horticulture, *First Biennial Report of the Commissioner of Horticulture of the State of California, for the Year 1903–1904* (Sacramento: W. W. Shannon, 1905), p. 276.

65. Howard acknowledged the work of Frazer Crawford. *Insect Life* 3, nos. 5–6 (1890–91): 354.

66. Michael Smith, *Pacific Visions* (New Haven: Yale University Press, 1988). Eugene Hilgard told the State Board of Horticulture in 1894 that the "arid regions" of the American West must be treated differently from "the humid regions" because of differences in climate, soil, and rural economy. *Rept. St. Bd. Hort., 1893–94*, pp. 303–4.

67. *Rept. Com. Hort., 1903–1904*, p. 194; Isaac, "Bug vs. Bug," in *Rept. St. Bd. Hort., 1899–1900*, p. 81.

68. J. W. Jeffrey to Howard, 19 December 1907, Box 63 E2, Record Group 7, Records of the Bureau of Entomology.

69. *Rept. St. Bd. Hort., 1891*, p. 448.

70. *Rept. Com. Hort., 1903–1904*, p. 83.

71. *Rept. St. Bd. Hort., 1891*, p. 291.

72. Ibid., pp. 291–92.

73. John Hammond Moore, ed., *Australians in America, 1876–1976* (St. Lucia: University of Queensland Press, 1977), p. 28.

74. Ellwood Cooper, *Intelligence of Plants and Animals* (Santa Barbara: n.p., 1916), pp. 13, 16; Leland O. Howard, *Fighting the Insects: The Story of an Entomologist* (New York: Macmillan, 1933).

75. Howard, *Applied Entomology*, p. 155.

76. Clipping from *American Garden* 11 (July 1890), Scrapbook 82, Box 27, Riley Papers.

77. Howard, *Fighting the Insects*, p. 93.

78. Ibid., p. 49.

79. "Some of the greatest successes . . . are much more easily reached in small and rather peculiarly situated countries, and especially in islands, where the climate is equable and where the native fauna and flora are simple." Ibid., p. 92; O. H. Swezey, "Benefits Derived in the Hawaiian Islands from the Control of Sugar Cane Insects by the Introduction of their Natural Enemies," *Proceedings of the Pan-Pacific Science Congress, Australia, 1923*, 2 vols. (Melbourne: H. J. Green, Govt. Printer, 1923), 1:398–99.

80. Dunlap, *DDT*, p. 34; Howard, *Applied Entomology*, p. 156; Ellwood Cooper, *Bug vs. Bug: Parasitology* (N.p.: [c. 1916]), pp. 16–19; George Compere to L. O. Howard, 30 November 1901, Box 24, E2, Record Group 7, Records of the Bureau of Entomology.

81. Howard, *Applied Entomology*, pp. 160, 163, 170.

82. U.S. House of Representatives, Committee on Agriculture, *Study and Investigation of Boll Weevil and Hog Cholera Plagues*, 63d Cong., 2d sess., doc. no. 463, esp. p. 16.

83. Dunlap, *DDT*, p. 28.

84. *Boll Weevil and Hog Cholera Plagues*, p. 16.

85. Arsenate of lead applied by a hand-held gun was advocated as early as 1913. Ibid., pp. 16–17; Howard, *Fighting the Insects*, pp. 73–74.

86. Howard, *Applied Entomology*, p. 152.

87. *Rept. St. Bd. Hort., 1891*, p. 16.

88. *Insect Life* 4, nos. 5–6 (1891–92): 163.

89. Albert Koebele, *Studies of Parasitic and Predaceous Insects in New*

Zealand, Australia, and Adjacent Islands (Washington, D.C.: Govt. Printing Office, 1893), p. 5; Essig, *History of Entomology*, p. 677.

90. Koebele, *Parasitic and Predaceous Insects*, p. 5.

91. Ibid.; *Insect Life* 7, no. 1 (1894–95): 48. Essig reported concerning the black ladybird in 1930 that it "now occurs throughout most of the state and is an effective predator of the black scale and other unarmored scales." Essig, *History of Entomology*, p. 677. Still, the insect never fulfilled the extravagant claims made by Cooper (pp. 295–96).

92. *Rept. St. Bd. Hort., 1892*, p. 454.

93. *Insect Life* 7, no. 1 (1894–95): 48; Howard to Cooper, 27 December 1894, Box 6, E3, Record Group 7, Records of the Bureau of Entomology; T. N. Snow, quoted in the *Pacific Rural Press*, 21 July 1894, from the *Santa Barbara Press*, on the progress of the black ladybird, *Rhizobius ventralis*, at Ellwood, California. Snow's was only an exaggerated version of the position Koebele also held. In *Parasitic and Predaceous Insects*, Koebele had said, "If once thoroughly known[,] the number of Coccidae and their enemies in Australia will be something astonishing, and it will be found that this country is the original home of many species that have spread over the greater part of the globe." Koebele, *Parasitic and Predaceous Insects*, p. 13.

94. *Rept. St. Bd. Hort., 1899–1900*, p. 160.

95. Compere to Howard, 22 April 1902, Box 24, E2, Record Group 7, Records of the Bureau of Entomology.

96. *Journal of the Department of Agriculture of Western Australia* 7 (January–June 1903): 170–73. In Western Australia, Lindley-Cowen, a native of Virginia, established his own vineyard and advised farmers in that newly self-governing colony on the establishment of "the vine and fruit-growing industry." See also Compere to Howard, 19 February 1902, Box 24, E2, Record Group 7, Records of the Bureau of Entomology.

97. Cooper to George C. Pardee, 14 June 1906; Cooper to R. W. Forster, 25 September 1905, Box 49, George C. Pardee Papers, Bancroft Library.

98. Charles Marlatt to J. W. Jeffrey, 7 July 1908, Box 63, E2, Record Group 7, Records of the Bureau of Entomology.

99. The *Rural Californian* was the official organ of the Southern California Horticulture Society and the Pomological Society of Southern California.

100. *Rural Californian* clipping, February 1893, in Scrapbook 1, Box 23, Riley Papers.

101. In March 1895, Kruckeberg published a vitriolic attack on the secretary of the State Board of Horticulture, Byron M. Lelong, and condemned the board's "devious methods" and excessive costs. Scrapbook 95, Box 23, Riley Papers. Riley himself urged the "abolishment" [*sic*] of the board. See also *Oakland Tribune*, 3 February 1895, Box 22, Riley Papers.

102. Kruckeberg to Riley, 17 July 1891, Box 58, E2, Record Group 7, Records of the Bureau of Entomology; California State Board of Horticulture, *Fifth Biennial Report of the State Board of Horticulture of the State of California, for 1895–96* (Sacramento: A. J. Johnston, 1896), p. 132.

103. Jeffrey to Howard, 1 April 1907 and 15 June 1908, Box 63, E2, Record Group 7, Records of the Bureau of Entomology.

104. William Ellsworth Smythe, *The Conquest of Arid America,* rev. ed. (1905; reprint, Seattle: University of Washington Press, 1969), p. 129; Carey McWilliams, *California: The Great Exception* (1949; reprint, Santa Barbara, Peregrine Smith, 1976), pp. 114, 124.

105. Ewen MacKinnon, "Beneficial *versus* Injurious Insects: I," *Science and Industry* 2 (August 1920): 480; Riley to Pres., BAAS, Box 27, Riley Papers.

106. I. W. Wolfe and others to Department of Agriculture, D.C., 2 June 1906, Box 63, E2.

107. Essig, *History of Entomology,* p. 157.

108. See "Ointment Now Has White Fly in It," *Riverside Enterprise,* 14 Aug. 1907, in Box 1, E69, Record Group 7, Records of the Bureau of Entomology. See also Essig, *History of Entomology,* p. 157; Steven Stoll, "Insects and Institutions: University Science and the Fruit Business in California," *Agricultural History* 69 (spring 1995): 216–40.

109. Essig, *History of Entomology,* pp. 801, 157.

110. Ibid., p. 480.

111. Ibid., pp. 522–23; Stoll, "Insects and Institutions," pp. 233–37.

112. C. W. Woodworth, "The Entomological Equipment of the Horticultural Commissioner," *Rept. Com. Hort., 1903–1904,* pp. 322–28, quote at p. 326.

113. See C. W. Woodworth, *White Fly in California,* California Agricultural Experimental Station Circ. 30, June 1907; *Riverside Enterprise,* 14 August 1907, in Box 1, E 69, Record Group 7, Records of the Bureau of Entomology.

114. Jeffrey to Howard, 20 June 1906, Box 63, E2, Record Group 7.

115. Jeffrey to Howard, 18 Sept. 1907, Box 63, E2, Record Group 7.

116. Jeffrey to Howard, 11 Dec. 1906, Box 63, E2, Record Group 7.

117. Jeffrey to Howard, 1 April 1907, Box 63, E2, Record Group 7.

118. Jeffrey to Howard, 2 December 1907, Box 63, E2, Record Group 7.

119. Jeffrey to Howard, 19 December 1907, Box 63, E2, Record Group 7.

120. Essig, *History of Entomology,* pp. 511–12.

121. Jeffrey to Howard, 30 June 1908, Box 63, E2, Record Group 7.

122. Essig, *History of Entomology,* pp. 159, 481; Whorton, *Before Silent Spring,* pp. 26–27.

123. Essig, *History of Entomology,* pp. 143, 579–80.

124. Ibid., pp. 514, 515; Spencer C. Olin Jr., *California's Prodigal Sons: Hiram Johnson and the Progressives* (Berkeley and Los Angeles: University of California Press, 1968), p. viii.

125. Norman Hall, *Botanists of the Eucalypts* (Melbourne: CSIRO, 1978), p. 40.

126. Gerald Nash, *State Government and Economic Development: A History of Administrative Policies in California, 1849–1933* (Berkeley: Institute of Governmental Studies, University of California, 1964), p. 148; Richard C. Sawyer, *To Make a Spotless Orange: Biological Control in California* (Ames, Iowa: Iowa State University Press, 1996).

127. Doutt, "Historical Development of Biological Control," pp. 40–41; Carolyn Merchant, *Radical Ecology: The Search for a Livable World* (New

York: Routledge, 1992), p. 216; Paul DeBach, *Biological Control by Natural Enemies* (Cambridge: Cambridge University Press, 1974), chap. 10.

CHAPTER 10

1. E. O. Essig, *A History of Entomology* (1931; reprint, New York: Hafner Publ., 1965), pp. 703–4.

2. R. J. Tillyard, "History of the Introduction of Beneficial Insects into New Zealand," in *Proceedings of the Pan-Pacific Conference, Australia, 1923*, 2 vols. (Melbourne: H. J. Green, Govt. Printer, 1923), 1:386.

3. John Hammond Moore, ed., *Australians in America, 1876–1976* (St. Lucia: University of Queensland Press, 1977), p. 28.

4. George Riddoch, *Dairying and Irrigation in Great Britain and America. Report by the Hon. Geo. Riddoch, M.L.C., upon the Dairying Industry and Irrigation Schemes of Great Britain and the United States of America* (Adelaide: n.p., 1903), p. 31.

5. John West, "Irrigation Development in Western America," in Department of Agriculture, Victoria, *Course of Lectures Delivered by Officers of the Department of Agriculture, during the Year 1891* . . . (Melbourne: Robert S. Brain, Govt. Printer, [c. 1891]), p. 8.

6. C. B. Schedvin, *Shaping Science and Industry: A History of Australia's Council for Scientific and Industrial Research, 1926–49* (Sydney: Allen and Unwin, 1987).

7. R. D. Watt, "Prickly Pear in U.S.A.," *Science and Industry* 2 (November 1920): 679–81.

8. E. N. R. "The Blow-Fly Pest: Scheme of Biological Experimentation," *Science and Industry* 2 (July 1920): 428.

9. Ewen MacKinnon, "The Relation of Insects to the Dissemination of Diseases," *Science and Industry* 2 (November 1920): 658.

10. Cf. Schedvin, *Shaping Science and Industry*, pp. 6–10.

11. *Insect Life* 7, no. 2 (1894–95): 93–95; L. O. Howard, *A History of Applied Entomology (Somewhat Anecdotal)*, Smithsonian Miscellaneous Collections (Washington, D.C.: Smithsonian Institution, 1930), 84:384; Walter Froggatt, "Australian Ladybird Beetles," *Agricultural Gazette of New South Wales* 13 (September 1902): 895–96.

12. Henry S. Tryon, *Report on Insect and Fungus Pests* (Brisbane: Dept. of Lands, 1889), p. 17. For biographical details on Tryon, see G. N. Logan, "Henry Tryon," *Australian Dictionary of Biography*, vol. 12 (1891–1939), pp. 272–73.

13. Albert Koebele, "Sugar Cane Insects in N.S.W.," *Insect Life* 4, nos. 11–12 (1891–92): 385–89.

14. Henry S. Tryon, *Grub Pests of Sugar Cane* (Brisbane: Govt. Printer, 1895).

15. Bailey Brown, *Second Chapter of Revelations: Practical and Practicable Suggestions on Land Settlement, Irrigation Crops, and Industries Which Will Build Up the Colony* (Brisbane: Muir and Morcom, 1891), p. 10.

16. J. M. Powell, *Plains of Promise, Rivers of Destiny: Water Management*

and the Development of Queensland, 1824–1990 (Bowen Hills, Qld.: Boolarong Publications, 1991), p. 145.

17. Schedvin, *Shaping Science and Industry*, p. 92; Alan P. Dodd, *The Biological Campaign against Prickly-Pear* (Brisbane: Govt. Printer, 1940), p. 27; Essig, *History of Entomology*, p. 678; Howard, *Applied Entomology*, p. 517; Leland O. Howard, *Fighting the Insects: The Story of an Entomologist* (New York: Macmillan, 1933), p. 212.

18. Alan W. Black, "The Genesis of Australian Agricultural Colleges in the Nineteenth Century," *Australian Journal of Politics and History* 21 (April 1975): 42–55.

19. Powell, *Plains of Promise*, p. 107.

20. J. F. Illingworth, *Natural Enemies of the Sugar Cane Beetle in Queensland* (Brisbane: Govt. Printer, 1921), pp. 8, 10.

21. Henry Tryon and T. Harvey Johnston, *Report of the Prickly-Pear Travelling Commission. 1st March, 1912–30th April, 1914* (Brisbane: Anthony J. Cummings, Govt. Printer, 1914), p. xiii.

22. On Dodd (1897–1981), see *Sydney Morning Herald*, 7 July 1981, p. 9.

23. W. Ross Johnston and P. Lloyd, "The Fight against Cacti Pests in Queensland," *Queensland Agricultural Journal* 58 (July–August 1982): 215.

24. Dodd, *Biological Campaign against Prickly-Pear*, p. 20.

25. *Report upon Land Settlement Submitted to Cabinet by the Hon. W. E. Wearne, Minister for Lands in New South Wales* (Sydney: John Spence, Govt. Printer, 1923), Box 4, Folder 15, uncataloged Mead Papers, Bancroft Library.

26. Dodd, *Biological Campaign against Prickly-Pear*, p. 25. See also, more generally, Johnston and Lloyd, "Fight against Cacti Pests," pp. 215–20.

27. Johnston and Lloyd, "Fight against Cacti Pests," p. 218.

28. Quoted ibid., p. 217.

29. A. Bruce-Suttor, "Clearing Prickly-Pear (*Opuntia vulgaris*, Mill.)," *Agricultural Gazette of New South Wales* 4 (November 1893): 878–80.

30. Schedvin, *Shaping Science and Industry*, p. 92.

31. Oral history interview, Dennis Loakes, 13 December 1992, Brisbane. Loakes had been a farm boy in the area during and just after World War I. See also Johnston and Lloyd, "Fight against Cacti Pests," p. 218.

32. Schedvin, *Shaping Science and Industry*, p. 91.

33. See the series, Maiden, "Chats about the Prickly Pear, Nos. 2–8," *Agricultural Gazette of New South Wales*, vols. 31–32 (1920–21).

34. Watt, "Prickly Pear in U.S.A.," p. 680.

35. Maiden had been experimenting with a view to improving the fruit to a type with "very few spines" that "really is good to eat." Royal Commission of Inquiry on Forestry, *Final Report of the Commissioners. Part II* (Sydney: Govt. Printer, 1908) p. 258.

36. "Australia's Opportunity: A Wonder-Worker of Science," *Review of Reviews* (Australasian edition), April 1905, pp. 351–53.

37. In W. O. Campbell, "Luther Burbank: An Interview," *Agricultural Gazette of New South Wales* 16 (2 November 1905): 1090–94, Burbank admitted the experimental nature of his plantings.

38. Dodd, *Biological Campaign against Prickly-Pear*, pp. 33–34.

39. Tryon and Johnston, *Prickly-Pear Travelling Commission,* p. ix.

40. W. D. Hunter, F. C. Pratt, and J. D. Mitchell, *The Principal Cactus Insects of the United States* (Washington, D.C.: Govt. Printer, 1912).

41. Dodd, *Biological Campaign against Prickly-Pear,* p. 36.

42. J. H. Maiden, "Chats about the Prickly Pear, No. 9," *Agricultural Gazette of New South Wales* 32 (February 1921): 97–104.

43. According to Dodd, this was "the common prickly pear of south-east Texas," but it also grew in California. Dodd, *Biological Campaign against Prickly-Pear,* p. 19; "The Cactus Plants of California," [c. 1900], clipping, Folder 3, George K. Cowlishaw Papers, National Library.

44. David Griffiths, *The "Spineless" Prickly Pears,* U.S. Department of Agriculture, Bureau of Plant Industry, bulletin no. 140 (Washington, D.C.: Govt. Printing Office, 1909), p. 10.

45. L. A. Andres and R .D. Goeden, "The Biological Control of Weeds by Introduced Natural Enemies," in C. B. Huffaker, ed., *Biological Control* (New York: Plenum Press, 1971), pp. 155–58.

46. Watt, "Prickly Pear in U.S.A.," p. 680.

47. Dodd, *Biological Campaign against Prickly-Pear,* p. 73.

48. Ibid., p. 101.

49. *Daily Guardian,* 6 June 1924, cited in Jason Keene, "The Triumph of Biological Control: The Eradication of Prickly-Pear in Australia" (B.A. honors thesis, University of New South Wales, 1991), pp. 38–39.

50. *Courier* (Brisbane), 5 November 1930, 24 October 1929.

51. *Daily Mail* (Brisbane), 24 April 1924, and 15 May 1924, in William Labatte Payne Scrapbook, Oxley Memorial Library. See M. French, "Sir William Labatte Ryall Payne," *Australian Dictionary of Biography,* vol. 11 (1891–1939), p. 171.

52. Dodd, *Biological Campaign against Prickly-Pear,* p. 109.

53. Ibid., p. 114.

54. Johnston and Lloyd, "Fight against Cacti Pests," p. 221.

55. *Courier* (Brisbane), 24 October 1929; see also *Report on Proposed Settlement of Prickly-Pear Lands* (Brisbane: Govt. Printer, 1931), p. 6.

56. J. Burton Cleland, "The Prickly Pear Pest," *Science and Industry* 1 (May 1919): 18.

57. Johnston and Lloyd, "Fight against Cacti Pests," p. 219.

58. *Rockhampton Morning Bulletin,* 17 February 1928, in Payne Scrapbook, Oxley Memorial Library.

59. Dodd, *Biological Campaign against Prickly-Pear,* pp. 12–13.

60. *Proposed Settlement of Prickly-Pear Lands,* p. 3; Dodd, *Biological Campaign against Prickly-Pear,* p. 11.

61. *Proposed Settlement of Prickly-Pear Lands,* p. 11.

62. Dodd, *Biological Campaign against Prickly-Pear,* p. 13.

63. *Proposed Settlement of Prickly-Pear Lands,* pp. 3–5.

64. In New South Wales, the pear had been less widespread and less dense than in Queensland, and the redevelopment less spectacular. Pastures replaced pear-infested timberland, but fewer new settlers arrived. Dodd, *Biological Campaign against Prickly-Pear,* p. 13.

65. Alan P. Dodd, "The Biological Control of Prickly Pear in Australia," in

A. Keast, R. l. Crocker, and C. S. Christian, eds., *Biogeography and Ecology in Australia* (The Hague: Uitgeverrij Dr. W. Junk, 1959), pp. 565–77.

66. Howard, *Applied Entomology*, p. 390.

67. Rachel Carson, *Silent Spring* (1962; reprint, Ringwood, Vic.: Penguin, 1965), pp. 85, 86.

68. Andres and Goeden, "Biological Control of Weeds," pp. 144, 155–58; Richard Doutt, "The Historical Development of Biological Control," in Paul DeBach, ed., *Biological Control of Insect Pests and Weeds* (London: Chapman and Hall, 1964), p. 38.

69. Boris Schedvin, "Environment, Economy, and Australian Biology, 1890–1939," *Historical Studies* 21 (April 1984): 25.

70. Ibid., p. 26.

71. Ibid., pp. 26, 27.

EPILOGUE

1. Ellwood Cooper, *Intelligence of Plants and Animals* (Santa Barbara: n.p., 1916), pp. 16, 18.

2. Gerald Nash, *State Government and Economic Development: A History of Administrative Policies in California, 1849–1933* (Berkeley: Institute of Governmental Studies, University of California, 1964), p. 148; L. O. Howard, *A History of Applied Entomology (Somewhat Anecdotal)*. Smithsonian Miscellaneous Collections (Washington, D.C.: Smithsonian Institution, 1930), 84:154.

3. Pardee minute to Cooper to Pardee, 19 March 1906, Box 49, Pardee Papers, Bancroft Library; Owen H. O'Neill, ed., *History of Santa Barbara County, State of California. Its People and Its Resources* (Santa Barbara: Union Printing, 1939), pp. 375–76.

4. Carr to Elizabeth Mills, 8 September 1896, Box 5, Jeanne C. Carr Papers, Huntington Library; Mira Saunders, "Carmelita, Pasadena's Park of Many Associations," Box 10, Folder 15, Charles F. Saunders Papers, Huntington Library.

5. Annie K. Bidwell to Franklin C. Lusk, 16 March 1904, and Bidwell to Mr. Crittenden, 7 February 1911, Box 5, John and Annie K. Bidwell Papers, Bancroft Library; *Dictionary of American Biography*, s.v. "Bidwell, John."

6. W. K. Hancock, *Survey of British Commonwealth Affairs*, vol. 2, *Problems of Economic Policy, 1918–1939, Part 1* (London: Oxford University Press, 1940), pp. 200–203; *Year Book of the Commonwealth of Australia*, no. 43, 1957, pp. 328–29.

7. Donald Worster, "World without Borders: The Internationalization of Environmental History," in Kendall E. Bailes, ed., *Environmental History: Critical Issues in Comparative Perspective* (Lanham, Md.: University Press of America, 1985), pp. 665–66; Leland O. Howard, *Fighting the Insects: The Story of an Entomologist* (New York: Macmillan, 1933), pp. 212–16.

8. Neil Barr and John Cary, *Greening a Brown Land: The Australian Search for Sustainable Land Use* (Melbourne: Macmillan, 1992), pp. 185–87.

9. Louis Hartz, *The Liberal Tradition in America* (New York: Harcourt, Brace, and World, 1955); Gary Cross, "Comparative Exceptionalism: Rethink-

ing the Hartz Thesis in the Settler Societies of Nineteenth-Century United States and Australia," *Australasian Journal of American Studies* 14 (July 1995): 15–43; Alan Gilbert, "The State and Nature in Australia," *Australian Cultural History* 1 (1982): 9–28.

10. The Commonwealth government has power to enact laws under treaties made with foreign countries; the treaties include United Nations conventions such as that on World Heritage and the protection of wilderness. The Franklin Dam controversy involved the damning of the Franklin River within a Tasmanian national park proposed for World Heritage status. The Commonwealth government blocked the building of the dam, and its stance was upheld by the High Court. Gilbert, "State and Nature in Australia"; David Farrier, *Environmental Law Handbook* (Sydney: Redfern Legal Centre Publishing, 1988), pp. 179–83.

11. See, for example, Ellwood Cooper, *Pure Olive Oil as a Food and Medicine* (Santa Barbara: privately printed, n.d.), pp. 1–15.

12. R. Hal Williams, *The Democratic Party and California Politics, 1880–1896* (Stanford: Stanford University Press, 1973), p. 92, correctly observes, "None of the experiments proved entirely successful, but they reduced dependence on local markets."

13. "Proceedings of the Thirty-second Fruit-Growers' Convention," in California Commissioner of Horticulture, *Second Biennial Report of the Commissioner of Horticulture of the State of California, for 1905–1906* (Sacramento: W. W. Shannon, 1907), pp. 494–98; California State Board of Horticulture, "President Cooper's Address," *Official Report of the Twenty-eighth Fruit-Growers' Convention of the State of California* (Sacramento: W. W. Shannon, 1903), p. 16; Royal Commission on Vegetable Products, *First Progress Report, Together with Minutes of Evidence . . .* (Melbourne: Robert S. Brain, 1886), p. 34. Valuable on complicated attitudes toward the Southern Pacific is William Deverell, *Railroad Crossing: Californians and the Railroad, 1850–1910* (Berkeley and Los Angeles: University of California Press, 1994).

14. On the specialization of later California agriculture, see Carey McWilliams, *California: The Great Exception* (1949; reprint, Santa Barbara: Peregrine Books, 1976), p. 114.

15. *Garden and Forest,* 23 November 1892, p. 561; gradually, artificial warming became more generally used, and was advocated by the state board as market realities dictated after 1902, though many growers still remained loyal to tree cover and better management of the groves as a solution. See A. J. Cook for the State Commission of Horticulture, *California Citrus Culture* (Sacramento: Friend W. Richardson, 1913), pp. 10–11, compared to the earliest edition of this state board publication, Byron M. Lelong, *A Treatise on Citrus Culture in California* (Sacramento: J. D. Young, 1888).

16. Barr and Cary, *Greening a Brown Land,* pp. 80–81, 85–86.

17. J. A. Alexander, *The Life of George Chaffey: A Story of Irrigation Beginnings in California and Australia* (Melbourne: Macmillan, 1928), p. 369.

18. *Irrigation: The Mulgoa Irrigation Settlement* (N.p.: [c. 1891]), p. 11.

19. Robin Boyd, *Australia's Home: Its Origins, Builders, and Occupiers* (1951; reprint, Melbourne: Melbourne University Press, 1961), pp. 71–79, 81–82, esp. pp. 71, 81.

20. Kenneth T. Jackson, *Crabgrass Frontier: The Suburbanization of the United States* (New York: Oxford University Press, 1985), pp. 117, 121–22, 176, 178–81, 265–66 (quote at p. 266); David Goodman, "Comparative Urban and Suburban History: An Interview with Kenneth Jackson," *Australasian Journal of American Studies* 12 (July 1993): 65–72.

Bibliography

In each chapter I have given the first reference to a book or article as a full reference. The references listed below refer only to the manuscript and other major primary sources used.

MANUSCRIPTS

Australian Scripture Education League Scrapbook, 1889–94, David Scott Mitchell Library, Sydney.

Bidwell: John Bidwell Papers, California State Library, Sacramento.

Bidwell: Papers of John and Annie K. Bidwell, Bancroft Library, University of California at Berkeley.

California State Board of Horticulture, Manuscript Minutes of the State Board of Horticulture, 1883–1902. Bound volume. California State Archives, Sacramento.

Carr: Jeanne Smith Carr Papers, Huntington Library, San Marino, California.

Cowlishaw: George Keith Cowlishaw Papers, National Library, Canberra.

Deakin: Alfred Deakin Papers, National Library, Canberra.

Franceschi: Francesco Franceschi Correspondence and Papers, Bancroft Library, University of California at Berkeley.

Hall: William Hammond Hall Papers, Bancroft Library, University of California at Berkeley.

Hall: William Hammond Hall Papers, California Historical Society, San Francisco.

Heintz: William Heintz Papers, Huntington Library, San Marino, California.

Hilgard: Eugene W. Hilgard Papers, Bancroft Library, University of California at Berkeley.

Lane-Poole: Charles Edward Lane-Poole Papers, National Library, Canberra.

Loakes: Oral History Interview, Dennis Loakes, 13 December 1992, Brisbane, author's collection.

London: Jack London Collection, Huntington Library, San Marino, California.

Lukens: Theodore Parker Lukens Papers, Huntington Library, San Marino, California.

McGlashan: Charles F. McGlashan Scrapbooks, Bancroft Library, University of California at Berkeley.

Mead: Elwood Mead Papers, Water Resources Center Library, University of California at Berkeley.

Mead: Uncataloged Elwood Mead Papers, Bancroft Library, University of California at Berkeley.

Muir: John Muir Diaries. Microfilm. Bancroft Library, University of California at Berkeley.

Murray River: Newspaper clippings, 1884–1902. Relating to Irrigation, 7 June–13 September, 1884 . . . and Relating to the Corowa Conference to Consider the Murray River Scheme, April 1902, MS 7995, La Trobe Library, Melbourne.

Murray River: Papers Relating to Irrigation Systems for the Murray River Basin, 1898–1931, National Library, Canberra.

Orcutt: Charles R. Orcutt Papers, Huntington Library, San Marino, California.

Pardee: George C. Pardee Papers, Bancroft Library, University of California at Berkeley.

Payne: William Labatte Payne Scrapbook, Oxley Memorial Library, Brisbane.

Record Group 7, Records of the Bureau of Entomology, National Archives, Washington, D.C.

Regents' Files, University of California Archives, Bancroft Library, University of California at Berkeley.

Riley: Charles Valentine Riley Papers, Smithsonian Institution, Washington, D.C.

Rust: Horatio Nelson Rust Papers, Huntington Library, San Marino, California.

Saunders: Charles F. Saunders Papers, Huntington Library, San Marino, California.

Shorb: James De Barth Shorb Collection, Huntington Library, San Marino, California.

Soldier Settlements: Material Relating to Soldier Settlements in Victoria, c. 1925–27, MS 11356, La Trobe Library, Melbourne.

Stanford University Archives, Records of the Arboretum, Department of Special Collections, Stanford University, Palo Alto, California.

Sutro: Adolph Sutro Papers, Huntington Library, San Marino, California.

Swain: E. H. F. Swain Papers, David Scott Mitchell Library, Sydney.

Swain: Edward Harold Fulcher Swain Papers, Oxley Memorial Library, Brisbane.

Welsh: Charles R. Welsh Papers, Bancroft Library, University of California at Berkeley.

White: Stephen M. White Papers, Department of Special Collections, Stanford University, Palo Alto, California.

Works: John D. Works Papers, Bancroft Library, University of California at Berkeley.

U.S. GOVERNMENT DOCUMENTS

Griffiths, David. *The "Spineless" Prickly Pears.* U.S. Department of Agriculture, Bureau of Plant Industry, bulletin no. 140. Washington, D.C.: Government Printing Office, 1909.

Hilgard, E. W., T. C. Jones, and R. W. Furnas. *Report on the Climatic and Agricultural Features and the Agricultural Practice and Needs of the Arid Regions of the Pacific Slope.* . . . Washington, D.C.: Government Printing Office, 1882.

Hinton, Richard J. *Progress Report on Irrigation in the United States, Part 1.* . . . Washington, D.C.: Government Printing Office, 1891.

Hunter, W. D., F. C. Pratt, and J. D. Mitchell. *The Principal Cactus Insects of the United States.* U.S. Department of Agriculture, Bureau of Entomology, bulletin no. 113. Washington, D.C.: Government Printer, 1912.

Koebele, Albert. *Studies of Parasitic and Predaceous Insects in New Zealand, Australia, and Adjacent Islands.* Washington, D.C.: Government Printing Office, 1893.

McClatchie, Alfred J. *Eucalypts Cultivated in the United States.* U.S. Department of Agriculture, Bureau of Forestry, bulletin no. 35. Washington, D.C.: Government Printing Office, 1902.

Mead, Elwood. *Report of Irrigation Investigations in California.* . . . U.S. Department of Agriculture, Office of Experiment Stations, bulletin no. 100. Washington, D.C.: Government Printing Office, 1901.

National Conservation Commission. *Report of the National Conservation Commission.* 3 vols. Washington, D.C.: Government Printing Office, 1909.

Smith, Hugh M. *A Review of the History and Results of the Attempts to Acclimatize Fish and Other Water Animals in the Pacific States.* Bulletin of the U.S. Fish Commission for 1895. Washington: Government Printing Office, 1896.

U.S. Commissioner of Agriculture. *Report of the Commissioner of Agriculture, for the Year 1871.* Washington, D.C.: Government Printing Office, 1872.

——— . *Report of the Commissioner of Agriculture, 1886.* Washington, D.C.: Government Printing Office, 1887.

U.S. Department of Agriculture. *Report of the Department of Agriculture, 1899.* Washington, D.C.: Government Printing Office, 1899.

——— . Bureau of Animal Industry. *Special Report on the Present Condition of the Sheep Industry of the United States.* Washington, D.C.: Government Printing Office, 1892.

U.S. House of Representatives. Committee on Agriculture. *Study and Investigation of Boll Weevil and Hog Cholera Plagues.* 63d Cong., 2d sess., doc. no. 463. Washington, D.C.: Government Printing Office, 1914.

U.S. House of Representatives. Committee on the Public Lands. *Salton Sea, California, Imperial Valley, and Lower Colorado River.* 59th Cong., 2d sess., January 18, 1907. Washington, D.C.: Government Printing Office, 1907.

U.S. Senate. Committee on Banking, Housing, and Urban Affairs. *Predisaster Assistance for Eucalyptus Trees in California: Hearing before the Subcommittee on Small Business.* 93d Cong., 1st sess., 1973. Washington, D.C.: Government Printing Office, 1973.

Works Progress Association. *Los Angeles: A Guide to the City and Its Environs.* Los Angeles: Federal Writers' Project of the WPA, 1941.

CALIFORNIA GOVERNMENT DOCUMENTS

STATE BOARDS AND COMMISSIONS

Commissioner of Horticulture, 1903–09

California Commissioner of Horticulture. *First Biennial Report of the Commissioner of Horticulture of the State of California for 1903–1904.* Sacramento: W. W. Shannon, 1905.

———. *Second Biennial Report of the Commissioner of Horticulture of the State of California for 1905–1906.* Sacramento: W. W. Shannon, 1907.

———. *Third Biennial Report of the Commissioner of Horticulture of the State of California for 1907–1908.* Sacramento: W. W. Shannon, 1909.

State Board of Forestry, 1885–92 and State Forester, 1905–22

California State Board of Forestry. *Fifth Biennial Report of the State Forester of California.* Sacramento: State Printing Office, 1914.

———. *First Biennial Report of the California State Board of Forestry, for the Years 1885–86.* Sacramento: James J. Ayers, 1886.

———. *Fourth Biennial Report of the California State Board of Forestry, for the Years 1891–92.* Sacramento: A. J. Johnston, 1892.

———. *Fourth Biennial Report of the State Forester of the State of California.* Sacramento: Friend W. Richardson, 1912.

———. *Report of the State Forester, for the Period July 12, 1905, to November 30, 1906, Being the First Public Report of the Office.* Sacramento: W. W. Shannon, 1906.

———. *Second Biennial Report of the California State Board of Forestry, for the Years 1887–88.* Sacramento: J. D. Young, 1888.

———. *Second Biennial Report of the State Forester of the State of California.* Sacramento: W. W. Shannon, 1908.

———. *Third Biennial Report of the California State Board of Forestry, for the Years 1889–90.* Sacramento: J. D. Young, 1890.

———. *Third Biennial Report of the State Forester of the State of California.* Sacramento: W. W. Shannon, 1910.

Margolin, Louis. *Yield from Eucalyptus Plantations in California.* California State Board of Forestry, bulletin no. 1. Sacramento: W. W. Shannon, 1910.

Morrison, Ben Y. *Street and Highway Planting.* California State Board of Forestry, bulletin no. 4. Sacramento: Friend W. Richardson, 1913.

Pratt, Merritt B. *Shade and Ornamental Trees of California.* Sacramento: California State Board of Forestry, 1922.

State Board of Horticultural Commissioners and State Board of Horticulture: 1882–1903

California Olive Industry. *Proceedings of the Olive Growers' Convention, Held* under the auspices of the State Board of Horticulture at San Francisco, July 8, 1891. Sacramento: A. J. Johnston, 1891.

——— . Proceedings of the Second State Olive Growers' Convention, Held under the Auspices of the State Board of Horticulture, at San Francisco, July 21, 1892. Sacramento: A. J. Johnston, 1892.

California State Board of Horticulture. Annual Report of the State Board of Horticulture of California . . . 1883. Sacramento: James J. Ayers, 1883.

——— . Annual Report of the State Board of Horticulture of the State of California, for 1889. Sacramento: J. D. Young, 1890.

——— . Annual Report of the State Board of Horticulture of the State of California, for 1890. Sacramento: J. D. Young, 1890.

——— . Annual Report of the State Board of Horticulture of the State of California, for 1891. Sacramento: A. J. Johnston, 1892.

——— . Annual Report of the State Board of Horticulture of the State of California, for 1892. Sacramento: A. J. Johnston, 1892.

——— . Biennial Report of the State Board of Horticulture. 1884. Sacramento: James J. Ayers, 1884.

——— . Biennial Report of the State Board of Horticulture of the State of California, for 1885 and 1886. Also, Appendix for 1887. Sacramento: P. L. Shoaff, 1887.

——— . Eighth Biennial Report of the State Board of Horticulture of the State of California, for 1901–1902. Sacramento: A. J. Johnston, 1902.

——— . Fifth Biennial Report of the State Board of Horticulture of the State of California, for 1895–96. Sacramento: A. J. Johnston, 1896.

——— . First Report of the State Board of Horticultural Commissioners. Sacramento: State Printer, 1882.

——— . Fourth Biennial Report of the State Board of Horticulture of the State of California, for 1893–94. Sacramento: A. J. Johnston, 1894.

——— . Seventh Biennial Report of the State Board of Horticulture of the State of California, for 1899–1900. Sacramento: A. J. Johnston, 1901.

——— . Third Biennial Report of the State Board of Horticulture of the State of California, for the Thirty-eighth and Thirty-ninth Fiscal Years. Sacramento: J. D. Young, 1888.

Official Report of the Twenty-eighth Fruit-Growers' Convention of the State of California . . . Los Angeles. . . 1903. Sacramento: W. W. Shannon, 1903.

Official Report of the Twenty-fourth State Fruit-Growers' Convention of the State of California. . . . Sacramento: A. J. Johnston, 1900.

Official Report of the Twenty-sixth Fruit-Growers' Convention of the State of California. . . . 1901. Sacramento: A. J. Johnston, 1902.

State Board of Viticulture, 1881–87

California State Board of Viticulture. Annual Report of the Board of State Viticultural Commissioners for 1887. Sacramento: J. D. Young, 1888.

——— . First Annual Report of the Chief Executive Viticultural Officer of the State Board of Viticultural Commissioners, for the Year 1881. Sacramento: J. D. Young, 1882.

———— . *Second Annual Report of the Chief Viticultural Officer to the Board of State Viticultural Commissioners, for the Years 1882–3 and 1883–4.* Sacramento: A. J. Ayers, 1884.

OTHER CALIFORNIA GOVERNMENT DOCUMENTS

Cook, A. J., for the State Commission of Horticulture. *California Citrus Culture.* Sacramento: Friend W. Richardson, 1913.
Hall, William Hammond, *Irrigation in [Southern] California.* Sacramento: J. D. Young, 1888.
Lull, G. *A Handbook for Eucalyptus Planters.* Sacramento: State Printer, 1908.

AUSTRALIAN AND STATE-COLONIAL
GOVERNMENT DOCUMENTS

YEAR BOOKS AND PARLIAMENTARY DEBATES

New South Wales Parliamentary Debates, 1889–1923.
New South Wales Year Books, 1884–1940.
Official Year Book of the Commonwealth of Australia, nos. 1–48, 1902–62.
Victorian Parliamentary Debates, 1880–1916.
Victorian Year Books, 1901–40.

ROYAL COMMISSIONS

Interstate Royal Commission on the River Murray, Representing the States of New South Wales, Victoria, and South Australia. *Report of the Commissioners; with Minutes of Evidence, Appendices and Plans.* Sydney: W. A. Gullick, 1902.
Mildura Settlement. Report of the Mildura Royal Commission. In *Victorian Parliamentary Papers, 1896.* Vol. 3, no. 19. Reprinted as *Mildura. 1896 Royal Commission on the Mildura Settlement.* N.p.: Australian Dried Fruits Industry, n.d. Facsimile.
Report of the Royal Commission on Water Supply. In *Victorian Parliamentary Papers, 1896,* Vol. 3, No. 20.
Royal Commission of Inquiry on Forestry. *Final Report. Part I.* Sydney: William Gullick, Government Printer, 1909.
Royal Commission of Inquiry on Forestry. *Part II. Minutes of Proceedings, Minutes of Evidence, and Appendix.* Sydney: William Gullick, Government Printer, 1908.
Royal Commission on Afforestation. *Report of the Royal Commission on Afforestation, Together with Appendices and Map (Minutes of Evidence Not Printed).* South Australia, Parliamentary Papers, no. 56. Adelaide: Frank Trigg, Government Printer, 1936.
Royal Commission on Vegetable Products. *Eighth Progress Report, and Continuation of the Minutes of Evidence . . . .* Melbourne: Robert S. Brain, 1890.
———— . *First Progress Report, Together with Minutes of Evidence . . . .* Melbourne: Robert S. Brain, 1886.

————. *Fourth Progress Report, and Continuation of the Minutes of Evidence.* . . . Melbourne: Robert S. Brain, 1887.

————. *Seventh Progress Report, and Continuation of the Minutes of Evidence.* . . . Melbourne: Robert S. Brain, 1889.

————. *Third Progress Report, and Continuation of the Minutes of Evidence.* Melbourne: Robert S. Brain, 1886.

Royal Commission on Water Supply. *First Progress Report,* by Alfred Deakin, *Irrigation in Western America.* Melbourne: John Ferres, Government Printer, 1885.

————. *Fourth Progress Report. Irrigation in Egypt and Italy. A Memorandum for the Members of the Royal Commission on Water Supply.* Melbourne: Robert S. Brain, 1887.

OTHER AUSTRALIAN GOVERNMENT DOCUMENTS

Australian Forestry Conference. *Report of Proceedings of the Australian Forestry Conference, Brisbane, April, 1922.* Brisbane: James J. Wrigley, Government Printer, 1922.

Bednall, Brian H. *The Problem of Lower Volumes Associated with Second Rotations in Pinus Radiata Plantations in South Australia.* South Australian Woods and Forests Department, bulletin no. 12. Adelaide: Government Printer, 1968.

Brown, John Ednie. *A Practical Treatise on Tree Culture.* Adelaide: E. Spiller, Government Printer, 1881.

Bureau of Sugar Experiment Stations, Division of Entomology. *Australian Sugar-Cane Beetles and Their Allies.* Bulletin no. 16. Brisbane: Anthony J. Cummings, 1921.

CSIRO and Department of National Development, P. M. Fleming, R. H. Gunn, A. M. Reece, and J. R. McAlpine. *Burdekin Project Ecological Study.* Canberra: Australian Government Publishing Service, 1981.

Department of Agriculture, New South Wales. *Farmers' Bulletin.* No. 90. Sydney: W. A. Gullick, 1916.

Department of Agriculture, Victoria. *Report by Mr. James W. Sinclair on the Sugar-Beet Industry and Tobacco Culture of the United States.* Melbourne: Robert S. Brain, Government Printer, 1895.

Department of Agriculture, Victoria; and A. E. V. Richardson. *Agricultural Education and Agricultural Development in America.* Melbourne: H. J. Green, Government Printer, 1918.

National Park of South Australia. Adelaide: Commissioners of the Park, n.d.

Perrin, George S. *Woods and Forests of Tasmania. Annual Report, 1886–7.* Hobart: William Thomas Strutt, Government Printer, 1887.

Queensland Department of Agriculture. *Annual Report of the Department of Agriculture, for the Year 1890–91.* Brisbane: James C. Beal, 1891.

————. *Annual Report of the Department of Agriculture, for the Year 1892–93.* Brisbane: Edmund Gregory, 1893.

————. *Bulletin No. 5.* Brisbane: James C. Beal, 1890.

————. *Tree-Planting for Shade and Ornament*. Bulletin no. 17. Brisbane: James C. Beal, 1892.

Report on Proposed Settlement of Prickly-Pear Lands. Brisbane: Government Printer, 1931.

Report upon Land Settlement Submitted to Cabinet by the Hon. W. E. Wearne, Minister for Lands in New South Wales. Sydney: John Spence, Government Printer, 1923.

Shelton, E. M. *Canning and Otherwise Preserving Fruits for the Home and Market*. Brisbane: James C. Beal, 1890.

Victoria Water Supply Department. *Proceedings of the First Conference of Irrigationists, Held in Melbourne on 25th, 26th, and 28th March, 1890*. Melbourne: Robert S. Brain, 1890.

OTHER GOVERNMENT DOCUMENTS

Food and Agricultural Organization of the United Nations. *Eucalypts for Planting*. Rome: Food and Agricultural Organization of the United Nations, 1955.

Food and Agricultural Organization of the United Nations. *Eucalypts for Planting*. Rome: Food and Agricultural Organization of the United Nations, 1979.

Hall, William Hammond. *Report on Irrigation Legislation and Enterprise in the American States, Australian Colonies, and Several Countries of Europe as Applicable to Cape Colony*. Cape Town: W. A. Richards and Sons, Government Printers, 1898.

REPORTS OF ORGANIZATIONS

Acclimatisation Society of Victoria (later Zoological and Acclimatisation Society). *Annual Reports*. Victoria: Acclimatisation Society of Victoria, 1862–99.

International Irrigation Congress. *Official Report of the International Irrigation Congress Held at Los Angeles, California, October, 1893*. Los Angeles: Chamber of Commerce, 1893.

————. *Proceedings of the International Irrigation Congress Held in Salt Lake City, Utah, October 1912*. Washington, D.C.: n.p., 1913.

National Irrigation Congress. *Official Proceedings of the Third National Irrigation Congress, Held at Denver, Colorado, Sept. 3rd to 8th, 1894*. Denver: Committee of Arrangements, 1894.

National Women's Christian Temperance Union. *Annual Report for 1883*. Evanston, Ill.: WCTU, 1883.

Proceedings of the Royal Agricultural and Horticultural Society of South Australia for the Year Ending 31st March, 1882. Adelaide: The Society, 1882.

Queensland Acclimatisation Society. *Transactions of the Queensland Acclimatisation Society*. Queensland: Queensland Acclimatisation Society, 1893–95.

Transactions of the California State Agricultural Society during the Year 1874. Sacramento: G. H. Springer, 1874.

Transactions of the California State Agricultural Society during the Year 1879. Sacramento: J. D. Young, 1880.

Transactions of the California State Agricultural Society during the Year 1881.
Sacramento: J. D. Young, 1882.
Transactions of the California State Agricultural Society during the Year 1886.
Sacramento: P. L. Shoaff, 1887.
Victorian Engineers' Association. *Transactions and Proceedings of the Victorian Engineers' Association.* Vol. 1. Victoria: Victorian Engineers' Association, 1883–85.

PERIODICALS AND NEWSPAPERS

Age (Melbourne), 1885, 1913.
Agricultural Gazette of New South Wales, 1891–1922.
American Garden, vols. 11–12; 1890–91.
Argus (Melbourne), 1885.
California Fruit Grower (later *California Fruit Grower and Fruit Trade Review*), 1888–96.
California Horticulturalist and Floral Magazine, 1870–79.
California White Ribbon Signal, 1914.
Courier (Brisbane), 1923–29.
Daily Telegraph (Sydney), 1904–05, 1920–24.
Garden and Forest, 1888–97.
Insect Life, vols. 1–7; 1888–95.
Irrigation Age, 1893–95.
Journal of Forestry.
Journal of the Department of Agriculture (Victoria), 1899–1914.
Journal of the Department of Agriculture of Western Australia, 1900–09.
Ladies Sphere, 1920–21.
Lone Hand, 1914–19.
Lumber World Review, 1912–14.
Nation, 1882.
National Magazine of Health (Melbourne), 1928–29.
Out West/Land of Sunshine, vols. 12–19; 1900–03.
Pacific Ensign, 1893.
Pacific Rural Press, 1879–96.
Rural Californian, 1884–95.
San Francisco Chronicle, 1901.
San Francisco Examiner, 1901.
Science and Industry, 1919–29.
Sydney Mail, 1890.
Sydney Morning Herald, 1862, 1878, 1882, 1885, 1890–91, 1927–37.
Triad, 1917–20.
Union Signal, 1886–87.
Vigneron (later *Australian Vigneron and Fruit-Growers' Journal*), 1886–90.

Index

Compositor: Braun-Brumfield, Inc.
Text: 10/13 Sabon
Display: Sabon